Of Eagles and Falcons

Of Eagles and Falcons

Revisions and Additional Material
By
Guy Falkenau

RENE PAUL FALKENAU

© Guy Falkenau 2011

Published by Falcon Press
2 Benton View, Forest Hall, Newcastle upon Tyne, NE12 7JJ
Telephone: 0191 2809144

ISBN 978-0-9568384-0-7

A catalogue record for this book is available from the British Library

Cover Design: Illustration taken from the souvenir wedding magagazine "Die Woche" published in 1911 to mark the wedding of Franz and Irma Falkenau, containing amongst other things, a series of fake advertisements based upon the use of family names.

Prepared and printed by:
York Publishing Services Ltd
64 Hallfield Road
Layerthorpe
York YO31 7ZQ
Tel: 01904 431213

Website: www.yps-publishing.co.uk

Foreword

Prior to his death in 1991, my father, Rene Paul Falkenau, had written two memoires. The first centred on the experience of his mother, a Belgian woman who had married a Czechoslovakian from Prague. As a result, on her marriage in 1911, she was deemed to be an Austrian citizen. When World War 1 broke out in 1914 she faced possible internment as an enemy alien in her country of birth. She initially moved to stay with relatives in neutral Holland, but circumstances eventually lead to her joining her husband in the Austrian Tyrol where she spent the next few years, as Rene Paul characterised it, 'amongst her enemies'. The second memoire is essentially my father's biography, culminating in the events of the Second World War and its immediate aftermath, in which his own part is arguably as dramatic as any. Evacuated at Dunkirk, he returned to France two days later, to continue the war and ensure the safety of his parents and sister. Following the armistice between Germany and France and the establishment of the Vichy regime, he was recruited into the underground movement which organised the escape route getting Allied troops back to Britain. Facing arrest by Vichy police in early 1942, Rene Paul was forced to make his own escape and a month later was in London where he rejoined the Belgian army. By the end of the war he had gone through the campaigns in northern France and Holland and played a role in the conviction of Nazi war criminals at the infamous Belsen concentration camp.

On reading the two manuscripts it was immediately apparent that they would benefit from some editing and redrafting. My father's use of English reflected both the benefits and shortcomings of being multilingual. At once charming and idiosyncratic, his grammar often inclined more to French construction, his native tongue, than English, thereby, occasionally obscuring his meaning. On discovering his manuscripts, some years after his death, my original intention was simply to tidy up his infelicitous use of English and I set to work, rather episodically, to edit each of them. As I did so and read and reread their contents I came to appreciate that together they represented a highly personal, but also panoramic view of the drama and tragedy of two of the major events of the twentieth century. I decided to merge the two manuscripts into a single narrative, which would not only tell the story of my father's remarkable family, but serve to present a view of events in Europe not always understood in Britain. At the same time I have taken the liberty of expanding his original narrative. There were a number of members of his family who appeared in his original text as mere bit part players. I considered that they deserved larger roles. They include his cousin Pierre Billotte, who served on General De Gaulle's staff during World War 2 and his uncle, Marcel Roost, who by the end of the war was heading up the Belgian secret service. Together with others they provide a clearer and stronger picture of the multi national nature of my father's family.

The story which emerges is one which would be familiar to many mainland European families, particularly those of Jewish origin, whose family members are often drawn from several different nationalities, often either bi-lingual or multi lingual, and in the case of Jewish families able to fall back on Hebrew or Yiddish – clearly the forerunner of the Esperantist ideal, in which a common language surmounts national frontiers. It is a story both typical and unique. Typical in the tragedy which two world wars gave rise to, unique in the way in which family members responded to these events.

In families such as these, events in one country can have profound effects for family members on the other side of national frontiers, – sometimes on the other side of the world. The result is that it is no longer possible to talk of a British experience, or a French experience or a German experience. It is a mixture of all these and more, that becomes the collective experience of family members.

The name Falkenau is German, literally translated, "falcon's nest", hence the Falcons of our title. It was also, throughout the history of the Austro-Hungarian Empire and beyond until 1945, when all Germanic names were expunged in Czechoslovakia, the name of a town in north west Bohemia from which my father's family derived. The Eagles of our title are the Adlers, also a literal translation from the German, who became my grandfather's in laws. Originally from Krakow in Poland, they settled in Antwerp, Belgium, in the late 1870s, contributing in their own small way to the dramatic build up of Antwerp's Jewish population in the first decade of the 20th century. From a population of 1,200 at the time of the Adler's arrival, shortly before 1880, it increased to over thirty thousand, making a sizable contribution to the city's economy and culture. Like most of those coming from central and eastern Europe they had migrated to escape anti-semitism and instead of continuing on to America, as tens of thousands of others had done, they stayed, drawn by the city's liberal and tolerant climate. For many years the city provided a congenial haven, but in time ant-semitism came to visit them again. This book is dedicated to all those members of my father's family who fell victim to Nazi persecution.

Guy Falkenau June 2010

Acknowledgements

Thanks are due to my brother, William Paul Falkenau and my sister, Francine Evans, who recovered and preserved my father's manuscripts after his death and were good enough and trusting enough to hand them over to me. I hope that the book which has emerged justifies their act of faith.

I am grateful for the encouragement I have received in this project from my cousin, Peter Elliott, who is a diligent family historian. Our dialogue over the years on matters associated with our respective family histories has certainly acted as a spur to the completion of this task. I have also received encouragement from his sister, Judith Nichols and my niece, Helen Whittington. The anticipatory noises they have occasionally made about the completion of the book has also stiffened my resolve at moments when I have needed it.

Following the death of my father's cousin, Cecile Daly-Nathan in 2005,various members of the family participated in the clearing of personal effects from the apartment she had inherited in Paris from her parents, Eddie and Helene Nathan. I am grateful to my cousins, Andrew Manasseh and Robert Osselaer, who acted as executors to Cecile's estate, who allowed me unfettered access to family papers, documents, artefacts and photos. These have greatly contributed to my knowledge of the lives of the Nathan family, both in Singapore and in France. It has enabled me to expand my father's original text to include details of this branch of the family and in particular their experience of World War 2. Simultaneously, it has added to my understanding of the inter–relationship between the Nathan and Manasseh families and allowed me to reflect their place in the story of the Adler family.

I should also acknowledge the role of the Singapore National Archives in enabling me to build a picture of the Manasseh and Nathan family holdings in the city, as well as other aspects of their life there.

I am grateful to Dr. Petra Matejovicova, Curator at the Museum of Decorative Arts and Crafts,(UPM) in Prague for her assistance in providing details of the career of Abraham, David, Falkenau and enabling me to access material concerning the jewellery manufacturing business of 'Bruders Falkenau' in that city. Thanks are also due to staff at the State and City Archives in Prague for information concerning the business premises of the family firm, as well as details of its assets, as demanded by the Protectorate of Bohemia.

I am grateful to my friend and fellow family historian, Robert De Bauw in Brussels, for the postcard of Adolphe Adler's workshop in Antwerp, which appears in a book he has produced which uses postcards exchanged between family and friends to exemplify family links. His work has also served as encouragement to me in my own endeavours. I must also express gratitude to another Belgian friend and family historian, Dr. Charles Mahler, in Antwerp, who provided me with an article published concerning the Adler family.

Various websites have also played an invaluable role in providing background information, as well as source material, which has enabled me to piece together relevant facts about the history of the Adler and Falkenau families. Chief amongst these are the various Jewishgen special interest group sites, which enabled me to access police registers of Jewish residents in Prague, the JRI-Poland website which enabled me to access birth, marriage and death records for members of the Adler family in Krakow and which also enabled me to pinpoint the date(s) of the family's migration to Antwerp. The website of the Brigade Piron, the Belgian Independent Brigade, which served in World War 2, enabled me to verify some of my father's references to the Brigade's actions during the conflict and I am grateful to the webmaster, Jean-Louis Marechal who helped me in accessing the military records of Rene Falkenau and Marcel Roost.

I must also express appreciation for the help of my dear friends Brenda Corcoran and John Charlton who read the proofs of the manuscript and didn't tell me to tear it up and stuff it in the wastebin, but actually seemed to think it might be worth getting into print. For their suggestions and corrections, I am duly grateful.

Finally, may I also express my deep appreciation and gratitude for the forebearance of my dear wife, Lucy Falkenau, who despite those occasional comments about what I might have been doing, stuck at a computer all day, now seems to think there may have been some point and purpose in it after all. Thank you my darling.

Prague August 1885

The morning of August 31, 1885 was a bright sunny one in Prague and Augusta the pretty young wife of Sigmund Falkenau, one of the city's most prosperous jewellery manufacturers, had every reason to feel cheerful as she swished along the heavily carpeted passage in the family's luxurious apartment overlooking the Moldau.

Already the mother of two lovely children, she was now preparing to bring her third into the world, and enjoying the pampering of her successful and handsome husband, and the clucking care of their old cook Mary, who, during Augusta's seven months of pregnancy, had shared with her every glow of coming motherhood.

The two children were a handful, but Frau Falkenau had the help of a pretty young nursemaid called Jane in coping with their normal, spirited, demands on her time. On this bright morning though, she was preparing to chide the girl for having overslept and failing to arouse and dress her two young charges.

Frau Falkenau knocked on the nursemaid's stout bedroom door, but received no response. She knocked twice more, more loudly than before. Turning the porcelain knob, she pushed the heavy door wide open. It was a small, but adequately furnished room and a quick sweep of her eyes took it all in, almost immediately. She gasped as she took in the scene. Around the bed were vases full of white flowers and candles, now flickering their last feeble glow, having obviously dripped their waxen lives away during the night. The first thing that caught her attention on the bed was the blue pallor of Jane's features, contrasting so vividly with the snowy pillow on which her head rested.

A crown of orange blossom sat like a halo on her light brown curls. Her hands rested on her bosom, clasping a rosary and crucifix. Two envelopes were propped up carefully on the bedside table, and beside these was a tell-tale bottle lying on its side, readily recognized by Augusta as her own prescribed sleeping draught. She did not have to take more than a single step into that room to grasp what had happened, and with the realization of the tragedy hitting her so quickly, so did the shock of her discovery. Her hands involuntarily shot to her mouth, as if to try and stifle the piercing wail which hit the quiet of the house like the death cries of a mortally injured animal.

She screamed twice more before the old cook reached her, as she slid to the floor, quivering and moaning for her beloved husband. Mary rushed to call their neighbours and with their help, carried Frau Falkenau to her room and put her to bed and sent for the doctor. Another neighbour located Herr Falkenau who arrived at the same time as the police. He rushed to his wife's room, and found that she was slowly recovering, the doctor having recommended complete rest.

The letters Jane had written were opened by the police and they confirmed her intention to take her own life, explaining that she had been orphaned in early childhood, and that her fiance had recently broken off their engagement and she now had no more reason to live. After writing the letters, she had put on her wedding dress, lain on the bed and swallowed all of the sleeping tablets. Jane's body was removed, but later that afternoon, the doctor was recalled as Frau Falkenau was now obviously in labour. One hour later she prematurely gave birth to a tiny baby boy.

The doctor told Herr Falkenau that the chances of survival of this seven month baby were very remote. In his opinion the baby would not live more than a few days, but he would do everything he could to try and prolong its life. Since incubators were unknown in 1885, the only way to protect the newborn baby was to wrap him in cotton wool. As he was so tiny, he hadn't the strength to draw milk from his mother's breast, so he was fed by means of a fountain pen filler.

The baby put up a tremendous fight for survival, and after a few weeks it was clear that he would survive. The baby had been named Franz. He was the third child of the family and his fight for survival became a great source of excitement for his parents, his brother Paul, and his sister Melanie.

In later years, Franz kept the imprint of his birth, as he always remained small and slim, contrasting immensely with his elder brother, whose size was above average. Franz took advantage of his small size and became a keen, sportsman, later excelling in acrobatic cycling, horse riding,and many athletic pursuits. He often joked about the doctor's forecast that he would only live for a few days, but he lived and grew to be a healthy adult with a love of adventure.

Was it for the sake of his wife or because he remembered the old saying that as long as there is life there is hope that Herr Falkenau kept to himself the prediction of the doctor? We will never know, but one thing is certain, Franz lived and grew healthy and strong.

When six years later a second sister, Margarette was born, her arrival overshadowed the undivided attention his mother had, up to now, bestowed upon him. This event coincided with his first visit to primary school. His parents had chosen the Piarist School on Prague's Herrengasse for their son. Run by an order of Catholic priests, it was popular with middle class Jewish families, like that from which Franz came, providing tuition in German, their preferred language. Several leading Czech, Jewish intellectuals, such as Max Brod and Egon Irwin Kisch were to receive their education at the school, during the time Franz attended. He was taken to school that morning by his brother Paul and the contrast in their sizes did not go unobserved. Franz who was now as healthy as any normal child, was full of gaiety and smiles and went on to gain awards in all forms of sport. He became the idol of his form, but this did not prevent him giving his full attention to academic subjects.

Having finished his six years at primary school he started at the German Gymnasium or grammar school on the Old Town Square, where he continued his friendship with the boy who was to become his army pal, Egon Irwin Kisch. In time Kisch, like another of the Gymnasium's pupils, Franz Kafka, would become one of Czechoslovakia's leading writers.

Of his teenage years, Franz would later remember the pleasant things; good teachers, close school friendships, the funny pranks of his friend Kisch and the weekly indigestion caused by the Sunday meals. "They were fantastically delicious," he would say, remembering with a watering mouth, the full plates of whipped sweet cream or the meringue cakes that his mother used to prepare and that he would help to make disappear in no time. He also spoke of weekly visits to his grandmother, when, with his cousin they would anxiously await the moment when the old lady produced a bundle of keys and would open with care one particular cupboard, containing some of their favourite sweets. He long remembered the hard lesson his grandmother gave him on one occasion.

This was a day when the old lady had omitted to replenish her supplies and, when opening the cupboard, discovered that all she had to offer the two boys was one dry fig. She cut it in two and offered the two cousins one half each. Franz declared, with disdain, that he never ate half figs. Grandmother understood his point and gave the two halves to his cousin. This unexpected outcome gave Franz a lesson which he never forgot.

An event which was to be a small milestone in the life of the young boy, was the day his father told him that if he brought home a good school report, he would take him on the following Saturday to see the trials of an electrically driven tramcar. Tramcars were just beginning to be introduced in Prague and to see one in motion was as big an adventure then for small boys, as to watch the progress of a rocket to the moon might be today. Having watched the tramcars on two Sundays, Herr Falkenau treated his family to a ride.

Franz's first ride in a motor car was also a big event in his life. At a time when very few motor cars existed and those which did were owned by the very rich, Franz liked to show off, and he was pleased to draw the envious attention of other boys of his age, watching him sitting down in the bucket seat of an open car belonging to one of his father's wealthy friends.

When he became twenty, Franz would have to do his national service in the army. If he finished his studies satisfactorily and passed his school exams, he would do one year's service and become a reserve officer, but if he failed, he would have to serve for three years, with very little hope of promotion.

Another six years elapsed and Franz, having completed his secondary education, was faced with the choice of a career. He wanted to join the army and become an officer, but his father did everything he could to discourage this ambition. Could one imagine the son of so important an industrialist becoming a small insignificant lieutenant? For Sigmund it was unthinkable, especially in an army in which Czechs were considered inferior. As a province of the Austro-Hungarian Empire, Czechs considered their country under the occupation of the Austrian invaders. They awaited that one propitious moment when they could chase the occupiers from their territory for ever, and repair the wrongs done to their Kingdom of Bohemia.

Although the Austrians had done everything possible to give the same rights to the Czechs and Slovaks as to the citizens of Vienna, the feuding between the two races was growing from day to day. It was therefore understandable, that independently of the plan Herr Falkenau had made for the future of his son, the idea of seeing him join the army, was looked upon with contempt. Being an industrialist, he wanted his son to become one, or to be as nearly connected with his own line of business as possible.

The firm of 'Bruders Falkenau' or 'Brothers Falkenau' had been founded in 1869 by the sons of Abraham David Falkenau, who had been born in Mnichovo Hradiste north west of Prague around 1798. He had trained in Prague under the tutelage of master goldsmith Prokop Cermak between 1821 and 1827, before returning to Mnichovo Hradiste and establishing his own workshop. In 1833 he had been admitted to the Jewish Goldsmiths' Guild and in 1840 produced the meisterstuck or masterpiece, a gold engraved gentleman's ring, which can still be seen in the Moravian Gallery in Brno, which gained him admission to the Master Goldsmiths' Guild. In 1857 he moved his workshop to the town of Jicin, 40 kilometres north of Prague. Here his sons Moritz and Wilhelm had been apprenticed to him, before establishing their own business. In turn their sons Emile and Sigmund had brought the business to the Bohemian capital of Prague, continuing a profession which it was said the Falkenaus had practiced at least since the reign of the Empress Marie Theresa, when they had been granted a licence to mint coin for the imperial treasury. Falkenau under Eger from which the family took its name, was a region of Bohemia known for its mineral deposits of coal, lead and silver.

It was impossible for Sigmund to employ Franz in the management of the family firm because, when in 1869 the company of 'Bruders Falkenau' had been founded, it had been agreed that only the eldest sons of each branch of the family would be able to join the management of the factory.

Antwerp, Belgium 1903

When Franz finished his education at the German Realschule at the age of 17, his father had devised a plan for his future. Knowing that on attaining the age of 20, Franz would face having to undertake his compulsory period of national service in the army, he had arranged that after leaving school, and before joining the army, to send him to receive training abroad on the conduct of the diamond trade. He had made arrangements with Adolphe Adler, a business friend, who was his main supplier of cut diamonds in Antwerp, to employ Franz in his office and diamond cutting factory. Monsieur Adler also traded in pearls imported from the far east and Sigmund considered knowledge of this trade would also benefit his son.

Franz travelled to Antwerp by train and as he was reaching his destination his first impressions were most depressing, – grey skies, rain coated streets and very austere looking houses. Franz said later that he felt like taking the first train back home. At the Central Station his future employer, Monsieur Adler, was waiting for him and took him by horse drawn carriage to a hotel, where a room had been booked for him.

Next day, being a Sunday, Franz was invited for lunch to Monsieur Adler's house. He was introduced to the very distinguished looking Madame Adler and their four daughters aged thirteen, twelve, eleven and two respectively, They were a noisy little crowd, with big inquisitive and sarcastic eyes, ready to make fun at any opportunity. No wonder that the seventeen-year old boy felt a bit out of place in this household where females were in a majority. Monsieur Adler also realised this and he soon decided to do something about it. The Adler family had some very good friends, Monsieur and Madame Hurbain, who had four sons and one daughter. The youngest of the boys was Franz's age and the others were eighteen, nineteen, and twenty-one. Monsieur Adler arranged to introduce the four boys to Franz during the week and it was then agreed that they would introduce Franz to their parents at lunch on the following Sunday.

The four boys, being practical jokers, had warned Franz that their mother was very old fashioned and very appreciative of good manners. They, therefore, suggested that Franz should learn off by heart a particular phrase in Flemish which should be used each time he was offered something by Madame Hurbain. He was told that the sentence in Flemish he was to use was, "Smool too madame," which in fact means, "Shut your trap, madame," but they made Franz believe it meant "Thank you, madame." One can imagine her shock, when after being introduced to Madame Hurbain, he was invited to sit at the family table and first used the ill-chosen phrase. At first Madame Hurbain thought that she had misunderstood Franz, but a little later when offering him a dish, back came the ugly words, to the hilarity of the four boys, who noticed the angry expression on their mother's face and thought it best to own up and tell her of their practical joke. Madame Hurbain's and Franz's bewilderment soon turned into a good laugh for all the assembled company.

This would not be the only time when Franz would fall victim to his friends' practical jokes. On one occasion when having spent the usual Sunday with his four friends, the youngest one, Raymond, saw him to the tram stop. When the tramcar pulled up Franz noticed on the platform of the second carriage, a very attractive young girl about his own age. He went to stand on the platform opposite her and from there carried on what he considered a very grown up conversation with his friend on the pavement, trying to impress the young lady, as only one can do at seventeen. Just as the tramcar was starting off and far enough away for Franz not to be able to reply, Raymond yelled from the pavement, "Franz don't forget to return the socks I lent you." Franz's facial expression and consternation only served to amuse his friend.

At first he had some difficulty in accustoming himself to the Belgian mentality, particularly to the sarcastic and irreverent humour which prevailed in Antwerp. He really got upset when, one day, friends at a dance school met him with the words "Good evening young man of good family, but of bad repute." He was about to put his coat on again and leave and it took the four Hurbain brothers quite a while to convince him that this was pure Antwerp humour and that no offence was intended.

After a while Franz got tired of his friends' continual teasing and sought more and more the peaceful atmosphere of Adolphe Adler's home. Franz was very impressed with the stories Monsieur Adler had to tell about himself and his family. His father, Joseph David Adler, owned one of the biggest diamond cutting workshops in the centre of Antwerp. J.D.Adler had overseen the migration of his entire family from Krakow in Poland to Antwerp. Jews in Poland had long been subject to religious persecution, which had periodically resulted in pogroms, leading to the violent deaths and physical abuse of members of their community. The year 1883 was to see one of the most violent outbreaks of anti-semitic feeling in the country, resulting in the murder of over 200 Jews. It may have been a sense of the increasing tension which resulted in the Adler's move to Antwerp, three years in advance of this event. The way had been paved by the arrival of Joseph David and Adolphe, his eldest son in 1875, at the tender age of fourteen, five years ahead of the rest of the family. By 1881 Joseph David had moved his wife, Hinde Mirel and his remaining eight children to Antwerp. On arrival his wife immediately adopted the less obviously Jewish name of Henrietta. It was here, a year later his youngest child, Edouard was born.

His eldest daughter, Breindel, had made the move to Antwerp with her husband, Abraham, Heche, Herz. She also adopted the non Jewish forename of Barbara.

At fourteen, Adoplphe had left school to enter the factory owned by his father and learn all aspects of diamond cutting and polishing. Later he also became an expert on cleaving, which is a mixture of a science, an art and a gift of nature. It consists of splitting big diamonds in two, choosing the seam of the stone and using a mallet and a special chisel. One blow of the mallet on the chisel, one fraction of a millimetre out of true and a valuable uncut stone can lose hundreds, not to say, sometimes, thousands of pounds of its value. Adolphe had the gift to be able to cleave faultlessly and his reputation went around Antwerp, when he was no older than sixteen.

The money he was earning at his father's factory, plus little extras he made by cleaving on various occasions, allowed him to take up his favourite sport, – horse riding. There was a riding school situated just opposite his father's factory. He joined it and became a very regular pupil. The proprietor noticed the young boy's natural disposition for the noble sport and soon decided to introduce him to the one and only, very select, Riding Club of Antwerp. As soon as Adolphe had joined the club he came under the influence of all the young Antwerp snobs he met there. Hearing that they all owned their own horses, he decided he could not do less and bought himself a horse which he housed in a shed at the back of his father's garden.

When the old man discovered what young Adolphe had done, without consulting him, or asking his permission, he was furious and told his son he could choose between selling the horse straight away, or leaving the house with his horse. Adolphe did not hesitate one moment and told his father, "I shall leave the house with the horse." Within a matter of days after having left the paternal home, Adolphe sold the horse at a profit, hired an attic in a house only a hundred yards away from his father's factory, bought two second hand diamond polishing mills, which he installed the best he could, and immediately got work for them. After a while he bought a few more mills and enlisted the help of one polisher and then another. Soon he had to move to bigger premises. Ten years later he was the owner of a factory bigger and more prosperous than his father's.

Adolphe had a very generous nature and one after the other his younger brothers came to call on him for help. They each in turn wanted to leave the old man and his possessive and authoritarian rules. So Adolphe found work for his brother Jacques, for his youngest brother Edouard and even for his brother-in-law, Maurice. Many years later Adolphe would recall the proud day when ten years after his abrupt departure from home, he saw his father again for the first time. It was his father who took the initial step and called on him at the factory, where he looked with pride on his son's achievements. When he came face to face with his son he took both his hands and shaking them with vigour, repeatedly said, "You are a man. I am proud of you."

Everything worked the way Adolphe wanted and as soon as he felt financially secure the thought of marriage came to him, but as he was not an ordinary man, his choice would also be out of the ordinary. One day when he had taken two of his sisters to the Antwerp Royal Theatre for a gala performance, he looked up from his stall seat at the crowd in the balconies. Suddenly, in a box on the first balcony, he noticed a most distinguished young lady, sitting together with her parents, brothers and sisters. One look at her and it was love at first sight. Turning to his sisters he explained his discovery, saying, "I wonder how I could make her acquaintance?" To which one of his sisters answered, "That is very easy, my lad, she is a school friend of mine. Her name is Cecile Roost – Strauss and, if you want, I shall introduce you to her."

One year later Adolphe and Cecile were married and four years later they were the proud parents of three daughters, Emmy, Irma, and Helene, each born at one year's interval. Adolphe was very proud of his daughters, but he had one more ambition, to be blessed with the birth of a son and heir. This unfortunately was denied to him and when twelve years after his marriage, his wife once more gave birth to a child, it was another daughter, Renee.

Very little is known of these childrens' adolescence except that they were very well looked after by a young German maid named Lisa, that they were particularly noticed in Antwerp, always walking to school, the three of them all dressed alike,with young Lisa trying to keep up with their fast pace. At school they made many friends and each time prize giving came their names were repeatedly heard as the three girls who took the first prizes in their respective classes. Three girls, three sisters, and still three completely different temperaments and characters. Emmy, the eldest, tall, slim and very good-natured; Irma the second daughter, one year younger, small, frail, and having, somehow, an inferiority complex, because both her sisters and her mother were much taller than her. As Irma would say later, this disadvantage in size did not prevent her being the first married. In fact it is more than likely that Franz became attracted to her for that reason. When speaking later of his honeymoon, Franz would laughingly explain that he had to have his and his wife's passport handy at all times, in case somebody accused, or suspected him, of having abducted an under age young lady.

It took many weekend lunches at the Adler's before Franz realized he had taken a special interest in Irma. He was then eighteen and she was five years younger. This special feeling turned out to be growing from day to day, so much so, that when two years later Franz had to return to his native country to do his military service, the farewell was heartbreaking and Franz promised to return as soon as possible. Irma soon got over her sorrow. Her school activities and the teasing of her three sisters kept her mind occupied enough to forget Franz for a while. However, they wrote to each other regularly and the romance was kept alive.

Prague, 1905

In June Franz received papers to attend a medical examination prior to his enlistment in the forces. He was to report at a local military hospital in Prague.When he presented his naked body for inspection by the medical officer, it was considered he looked too anaemic to be fit for military service. After this inspection the doctor decided to keep Franz at the hospital for further tests. Franz managed to send a message to his brother, who by then was serving as a lieutenant, to inform him of his apprehensions and to ask him if he could ensure he was not turned down for service in the army.

His brother Paul acted swiftly. Remembering that he had a doctor friend at the hospital, he got in touch with him that same evening. Franz was invited into the living quarters of the doctor. As soon as the doctor saw him in his army supplied pyjamas and dressing gown, he had a good laugh, seeing that they amply covered his thin body. "Well, young man, what can I do for you?" said the doctor. "First of all," said Franz, "could you arrange for some food for me? I have been here all day and because they want to submit me to some tests they have left me without food. I am really starving." The doctor rang a bell and when an orderly appeared, gave a few brief orders. A quarter of an hour later the orderly reappeared pushing a big trolley. In a few minutes the table was laid for two and the doctor invited Franz to partake of a very decent meal.

The young patient did not take long to polish off the food put on his plate and the drink in his glass. So the doctor soon came to the conclusion that there was not much wrong with him except for his small size and slimness. He later told Franz that he was considered fit and could get dressed. Franz had a fit of laughter saying "This is the first time in my life that I had to undress and spend several hours in bed to be entitled to eat a whale of a steak."

Three months later Franz got his call up papers and at the given time and place met the boys who for the next twelve months were going to share his army life with him. Amongst them he found his old school pal, Egon Irwin Kisch. A rumour, probably spread by Kisch, went round that Franz intended to become a regular officer, and this rumour came to the ears of the sergeant major. At the first opportunity the sergeant major spoke to Franz and told him that he had heard of his intention to become a regular officer and that he was interested to know how Franz would treat his ex-instructors, who by then would have become his subordinates. Franz seeing an opportunity to take advantage of the situation said, "I wanted my intentions to be kept a secret, but since you found out, all I can say is that I shall treat my subordinates in the same way as they treated me whilst I was their subordinate."

These words were magic and Franz was given perfect consideration by all concerned. He was given the best horse, relieved of fatigues, and made a corporal three months after joining. Three months later he was a sergeant. In the remaining six months he, with most of the boys of his class went through all the non commissioned ranks of the Austro Hungarian Army. The course finished with a period of manouevres near Sarajevo, now the capital of Bosnia – Herzgovina.

At the end of the manouevres all candidates, with the exception of Egon Irwin Kish, were posted with the rank of sub-lieutenant. Their new uniforms were supplied and they exchanged their long bayonets for a sword. At first the sword was a bit of a nuisance as it hung on a long strap on the left side of a leather belt. Many young officers, not yet accustomed to them, started to walk in a rather peculiar way, kicking away with their left leg at the cumbersome sword. One day, the sergeant major noticed Kisch, who of course, was not entitled to wear a sword, walking in the same way. When asked what he was doing, he replied he was chasing his bayonet away.

Antwerp 1908

When Irma reached the age of seventeen, Franz's parents came on a purposeful visit to Antwerp. The object was to discuss their son's future and to ask the Adler's for their daughter's hand in marriage. The Adlers welcomed the request. It was agreed that Franz must be prepared to wait another year until Irma was eighteen and accept to settle down in Antwerp. When they told their daughter of the proposal, she feverishly accepted the idea of a long engagement.

Over the next two years Franz returned to Czechoslovakia annually for his month's obligatory service as a reserve officer in the Austro-Hungarian army. After each period of military service he would resume his duties in the office of Monsieur Adler's factory, where he was joined at regular intervals by Irma and her three sisters, who were continuing their studies at the lycee they attended.

When at last their marriage was due to be arranged Franz got recalled for military manouevres. On his return, final arrangements were made and the date of the wedding fixed for 12th January, 1911. Several months of preparation were needed for an event which would not go unnoticed by the Antwerp community.

Antwerp, January 1911

On a fast train travelling towards Paris, lrma and Franz sat in a first class compartment side by side, hand in hand. They were still so affected by the events of that unforgettable day that they were completely oblivious to the presence of other passengers in their compartment. Irma was not yet accustomed to the idea of being Madame Falkenau, but Franz was quite conscious of his new responsibilities as a husband. But forgetting the present and the future for a moment, they silently remembered the past few hours.

That morning had started full of excitement and anticipation with the gathering of all the relatives on both sides at the Adler's home. Soon a long procession of carriages, each drawn by two horses lined up in front of the house. The coachmen were impressive and splendid with their top hats, beige livery, white breeches and black shining boots. Next to each coachman sat a footman. Soon the procession formed. The most distant members of the family left first. The third from last carriage was occupied by the mother of the bride and the father of the bridegroom. In the next carriage came the bridegroom and his mother. In the last carriage came the bride and her father. It took them half an hour to reach the old Town Hall in the picturesque market place.

As the carriages lined up one by one under the canopy decorating the main door of the building, crowds of friends were pushing forward to catch a glimpse of the young bride in her beautiful dress of white satin, her Brussels lace veil and the gigantic bouquet of orange blossom she was supporting with her left hand, whilst her right hand was clinging nervously to her father's arm. Adolphe Adler the proud father, very smart in his tail coat, wearing his medals, was happily smiling to all his friends, whilst entering the lobby of the Town Hall.

As is customary in Belgium, the family was lined up in the lobby, ladies on one side and gentlemen on the other. Irma and her father slowly walked between the two rows of relatives. Soon they were followed by the bridegroom and his mother and the rest of the family. The procession then reached the main staircase, at the foot of which, two ushers in tailcoats, wearing big silver chains of office, lead the wedding party to the first floor and into the historic marriage chamber. They led the bride and bridegroom to their respective chairs in front of a big oak table. At one side four chairs were reserved for the respective parents and on the other side two chairs for the witnesses. The rows of chairs for relatives and friends were in lines ten deep and ten across. They were soon filled and many friends had to stand at the back and at the sides of the hall. When those guests with seats had taken their places, the sound of the organ which had been played softly since the arrival of the wedding party, suddenly stopped. An usher announced in a loud, strong voice, "Ladies and gentlemen, please be upstanding for the the Alderman Registrar." A clatter of chairs could be heard whilst the gathering got to its feet, followed by a deadly silence. Then the ushers opened the chamber doors for the Alderman and gently closed them behind him, following his entrance. They then came to stand behind the table, three paces from him. The Alderman, or Echevin as they are known in Flemish, was Irma's own uncle, Louis Strauss.

Uncle Louis was a tall, elegant, slimly built man. His long face and aquiline features were made more sharp and pointed by a well trimmed goatee beard, silver like his hair. He had built a reputation in Antwerp as a journalist, writer, and social commentator. In time he was to become a Deputy Burgomaster of the city and represent it for seven years in the Belgian parliament. As the Echevin responsible for public works, he was to play a major role in the development of Antwerp's port. His public service was acknowledged in the city boulevarde that bears his name.

After having given a few words of friendly greeting to the future bride and bridegroom, he invited everybody to sit down. First he started to explain the implications of marriage, both the legal aspects and then his own personal views on the matter. He next asked everyone to be upstanding while the official part of the ceremony took place.

And thus on this cold January morning of 1911 Franz and Irma were married. A banquet for three hundred people followed at the fashionable Salle Hosdez. A memorable feature of the reception was the arrival, part way through the proceedings, of a noted Antwerp figure, known affectionately as 'Monsieur Cigar'. He was a street newspaper seller, who was always immaculately dressed in a natty check suit, with a brown Derby on his head and as his nickname implied, always had a cigar dangling from one side of his mouth.

Adolphe Adler had hired him to distribute to guests a specially printed magazine called 'Die Woche' containing spoof articles about the week leading up to the big day. There was also an article envisaging the year 2000 and what it might offer. Modern readers would be amused by the illustrations of large bi-planes and airships it contained.In the late afternoon the young couple caught the train for Paris. Their honeymoon trip took them to Nice, Monte Carlo, Rome, Venice, and Milan.

On their return to Antwerp they settled down in a very nice house, completely furnished at their parents' expense, with the most exquisite hand-carved furniture, in Louis XVI style. Although the house was roomy and the furniture ample, they had some difficulty in finding a place for all the wedding presents. There was enough silverware, china and glassware to supply a small hotel.

It was in this house in Rue St. Joseph that their first child, a boy, was born at four o'clock in the afternoon on 17th October 1911, exactly nine months and five days after their wedding, and named Rene Paul. One hour later a chimney fire was discovered in the house and the fire brigade was called to extinguish it. Fortunately it created more of a scare than damage, but it was perhaps a portent of the eventful life Rene was going to experience.

His birth was registered at the Town Hall in Antwerp. Under Austrian law, he took his father's nationality, but under Belgian law he became Belgian with the choice at 16 to confirm or repudiate his Belgian nationality. If he confirmed it, he would be compelled to undertake national service in the Belgian army. At his birth Rene had blond hair that grew to be rather long, but which turned black the first time it was cut. During his first three years of life he proved a lively child who needed to be carefully watched.

But the marriage of Franz and Irma was not to be the only union between the Falkenau and Adler families. In Antwerp, in November 1911, only months after the wedding of Franz and Irma, Edouard Adler, a younger brother of Adolphe, who had been born in Belgium, following his family's move from Poland, married Franz's younger sister Margarette, known to both sides of her family simply as Grete. Thus she became not only her brother's sister, but simultaneously his aunt by marriage. Similarly for Franz, it meant his new brother in law, was also his uncle by marriage.

Antwerp May 1912

A year and four months after the marriage of Franz and Irma another event was to occur which brought joy and satisfaction to the Adler family. This time it was Irma's elder sister Emmy who was to marry. As a diamond merchant, Adolphe Adler had developed contacts with purchasers for his gemstones in many parts of the world. Often these contacts relied upon the services of local traders and bankers who could arrange currency exchanges to allow him to conduct his business and who could introduce him to other traders in his own field, who could supply him with other types of gemstone, as well as pearls.

In Singapore, Monsieur Adler had established business connections with two prominent Jewish families. The Manassehs and the Nathans had interests in a variety of areas of commerce. From money changing and commodity dealing, they had expanded into property development with a large portfolio of commercial and domestic properties earning them rental income. Saleh Manasseh was an Iraqi Jew who had grown up in Baghdad at a time when it was under British colonial administration. As a result he had been able to acquire British citizenship and to arrange to have his large family of twelve children educated at English public schools. It had also enabled him to move his business interests to the far east, large parts of which were also under British colonial rule.

Monsieur Adler would make periodic trips to the far east to sell caches of cut diamonds. With the proceeds of these sales he would purchase rubies, emeralds and pearls which could then be traded on his return to Europe.It was through these contacts that two of his daughters had become acquainted with members of the Manasseh and later Nathan families. Thus it was, that in May 1912 Emmy, Adolphe and Cecile Adler's eldest daughter, was to marry Rupert Manasseh. Following their marriage they were to settle in the far east, with Rupert dividing his time between his business interests in Singapore and Malaya.

The Eagles

Adolphe Adler married Cecile Roost-Strauss
Born Krakow, Poland 1860 — Born Antwerp Belgium 1867
Died Antwerp, Belgium 1927 — Died Antwerp Belgium 1922

Emmy married Rupert Manasseh	Irma married Franz Falkenau	Helene married Edward Nathan	Renee married Marcel Roost
Emmy Born Antwerp 1890, Died Brussels 1974	**Irma** Born Antwerp 1891, Died Auschwitz 1943	**Helene** Born Antwerp 1892, Died Paris 1981	**Renee** Born Antwerp 1901, Died Brussels 1984
Rupert Manasseh Born Singapore 1879, Died Singapore 1944	**Franz Falkenau** Born Prague 1885, Died Auschwitz 1943	**Edward Nathan** Born Singapore 1884, Died Paris 1968	**Marcel Roost** Born Antwerp 1896, Died Antwerp 1965

Irene	Cecil	Rene	Georgette	Cecile	Andree
Born Antwerp 1914 Died Brussels 1995	Born Antwerp 1923 Died London 1971	Born Antwerp 1911 Died Windsor 1991	Born Vienna 1917 Died Auschwitz 1943	Born Singapore 1916 Died London 2005	Born Singapore 1917 Died Paris 1983
married	married	married		married	

George Osselaer	Susan Hall	Doris Hancock	Brendan Daly
Born Louvain 1907 Died Brussels 1965	Born London 1931	Born Gateshead 1913 Died Gateshead 2005	

The Eagles

Adolphe Aron Adler

Cecile Roost Strauss

The Adler Sisters and their children:
Back row left to right: Renee Roost, Helene Nathan (seated),
Emmy Manasseh and Irma Falkenau
The children: left to right – Irene Manasseh, Andree Nathan,
Georgette and Rene Falkenau
Front, standing: Cecile Nathan

1908 postcard showing Adolphe Adler's diamond cutting workshop

Adolphe Adler, seated front row, photographed a year before his death, surrounded by his daughters, their husbands and his grandchildren.
Back row: Franz Falkenau, Rene Falkenau, Marcel Roost, Rupert Manasseh, Irene Manasseh, Emmy Manasseh, Eddie Nathan, Renee Roost
Front row: Irma Falkenau, Aldophe Adler, Andree Nathan, Georgette Falkenau, Cecil Manasseh, Helene Nathan, Cecile Nathan

The Adler Sisters

Emmy

Irma

Renee

Helene

Renee   Emmy   Helene

Helene   Emmy   Irma

**Helene Nathan in her
Red Cross uniform 1943**

**The three surviving sisters
photographed c1970**
Left to right: Emmy, Helene and Renee

The Falcons

Sigmund Falkenau married Augusta Hock

Born Jicin, Czechoslovakia 1852
Died Prague, Czechoslovakia 1913

Born Prague, Czechoslovakia 1857
Died Prague ,Czechoslovkia 1920

Paul married Edita Katzenellenbogin   Melanie married Emile Falkenau   Franz married Irma Adler   Margarette married Edouard Adler

Born Prague 1879   Born Berlin 1888
Died Auschwitz 1944 Died Auschwitz 1944

Born Prague 1880   Born Jicin 1866
Died Lodz,Poland 1943 Died Prague 1936

Born Prague 1885 Born Antwerp 1890
Died Auschwitz 1943 Died Auschwitz 1943

Born Prague 1890
Died Brussels 1967

Born Antwerp1882

Ellen   Vera   Walter   Jiri
                                              (aka George)

Born Prague 1909   Born Prague 1913   Born Prague 1901   Born Prague 1906
Died Auschwitz 1943 Died Santiago,Chile Died Sydney,Australia Died Ultoxeter UK
                     1998   1989   1989

married   married   married

Rene   Georgette

Born Antwerp 1911 Born Vienna 1917
Died Windsor 1991 Died Auschwitz 1943

                   married

Pavel Jellinek   1) Maria Weinsablova 1) Marie Simankova   Doris Hancock

Born Bratislava 1909   Divorced 1940   Divorced 1940   Born Gateshead 1913
Died Terezin 1943   2) Margaret married 1946 2)Marjorie married 1944 Died Gateshead 2005

23

The Falcons

Sigmund and Augusta c1900

**Sigmund and Augusta
Falkenau 1911**

Augusta Falkenau

**Lieutenant Franz and
Captain Paul Falkenau**

The Falcons

Mademoiselle Gretel
Margarette or Grete Falkenau

Paul Falkenau also known in
Czech as Pavel c1908

Paul Falkenau and his wife Edita
Katzenellenbogin and younger
daughter, Vera c1918

Irma and Franz Falkenau – Wedding Photo January 1911

Louis Strauss, the Alderman and Deputy Burgomaster of Antwerp who married Franz and Irma in the Hotel de Ville on 12 January 1911

The Hotel de Ville or Stadhous in Antwerp in which Franz and Irma married in 1911

But one event was going to change what would otherwise have been a normal family life for the Falkenau and Adler families. In the three years following young Rene Paul's birth dark clouds were building up in the political skies of Europe. Unrest seemed to grow. France and Germany had still not settled their feud dating back to 1870 and the Austro-Hungarian empire had the difficult task of quelling unrest within its borders and which despite the efforts of its efficient network .of police spies and informers, it could only control by periodic shows of strength. Tensions became greater and greater and everybody in Europe was aware of the fact that it needed only a very small spark to set alight the explosive situation prevailing at the time. The spark soon came with the events at Sarajevo.

Sarajevo 1914

On the 28th June 1914, during a visit to Sarajevo, capital of Bosnia Herzegovina, the Archduke Franz-Ferdinand, son of the Emperor and heir to the throne and his wife, were murdered by Serbian nationalists. Austria declared war on Serbia. Very soon, Franz received call-up papers from the Austrian authorities warning him that if he did not answer the call within three days, his mother would be arrested and all her possessions in Prague seized. Franz was torn between two feelings. On the one side his young wife and son and his new country of adoption and on the other, his duty to his mother, more especially since her husband, Sigmund, had died in the preceding year and also his duty to the country in which he had been born.

After a lot of discussion and consideration it was suggested by his wife that he should go. She would be well looked after by her parents and he would soon be able to come back, as it was commonly believed at the time, that the conflict would be localised. It wasn't expected that this local conflict would soon degenerate into a world war. France went to the assistance of Serbia. Germany declared war on France and Britain came to her assistance. Germany then considered it imperative to invade Belgium, but Holland managed to remain neutral.

Under the Belgian laws existing at that time, when Irma married Franz she automatically lost her Belgian nationality and assumed her husband's Austrian nationality. When war was declared on Belgium, she became an enemy subject and would have been interned with her son, had she not decided, with the full agreement of her parents, to leave immediately for Holland. Needless to say, the parting was full of sorrow and tears.

Irma travelled by train to Amsterdam where she was met at the station by two of her aunts and their respective husbands. These sisters of her mother had married two Dutchmen. They had offered her and Rene Paul hospitality and had arranged for her to stay a while with each of them. They had first arranged for them to stay at Uncle Daniel Koetser's home. He was a doctor, in fact one of the official doctors of the Dutch National Railways. His home in Stadhouderskade was already known to Irma and Rene Paul as they had twice been on short holidays there. Uncle Daniel never approved of his niece marrying an Austrian. He was a tease and he taught Rene to say in French, "I am a dirty little Austrian." Irma suffered a lot from his sarcasm and this made life very unpleasant for her. These relatives had never liked the idea of Irma marrying someone from so far away in Europe and now that he had become an enemy alien, they were more critical than ever and did not make any secret of it to poor Irma.

Irma felt extremely relieved when one day she received a letter from her husband telling her that he had been refused for front line active service on medical grounds and had now been posted as an instructor to a small garrison town on the border of Austria and Hungary. He requested her to take the first available train and join him in Sopron, telling her that he had arranged a small flat for them.

Irma said goodbye to her uncles and aunts without too much sorrow and as soon as the train started on the journey she briefed her small son Rene, then aged three. Whilst having been taught to say "I am a dirty little Austrian," could have appeared very amusing to everybody in Holland, it could be very embarrassing if said in 'enemy' territory. Irma therefore warned Rene that they were going to travel through Germany where people were very naughty and would cut off their heads if they spoke French. Rene was, therefore, told he should pretend to be dumb and only express himself by sign language. The child soon realized the seriousness of the situation and sure enough, did not open his mouth from the time the train entered German territory until their final destination.

Sopron, Hungary 1914

In order to get to Sopron the train had to pass through Berlin. Austrian relatives of Franz, who lived in Berlin, had been informed of Irma's journey and were waiting to meet her at the station. Since the train took three hours to transit from one Berlin station to another on the other side of the city, via a loop line, Franz's relatives suggested that they could take Irma and Rene into Berlin for some sightseeing. They assured her that they could arrange for the sleeper compartment, with all its contents, to be safely locked during their three hour visit and that she would be able to resume her journey from the other station. Irma flatly refused to see Berlin and she and the small boy stayed in their compartment until they reached Sopron.

Franz was on the platform at Sopron station to greet them and take them to three rooms which were going to be their home for the next month. The kitchen was terribly small, but this did not matter much because most of the meals were going to be brought in anyway, by Franz's batman from the Officers' Mess. All the kitchen was needed for was to heat up the dishes brought in, or prepare drinks. The next few months were uneventful, Franz spending his mornings at the barracks, his afternoons on the barrack square and the late afternoon in one of the local cafes, where Irma and Rene often joined him.

The cafe was quite a comfortable place. It was long and narrow, with rows of mirrors on the walls. Below the mirrors and against the wall were uninterrupted lines of comfortable benches, thickly padded and covered in red velvet. In front of them were tables, with marble tops and facing them chairs covered in the same red velvet material. This provided easy seating for four to five people at each table.

On one side of the establishment four to five tables were usually pushed together, in order to make one big table, which was permanently reserved for the officers of the garrison and their wives. On the other side of the room, just opposite the officers' table, was another long table reserved for the artistes of the local opera. The artistes spent their time there between rehearsals and performances and the officers outside their hours of duty. Between 4.30 p.m. and 6 p.m. the tables on both sides were fully occupied and officers and artistes soon got to know each other, first by sight and later more intimately.

One officer, a tall, handsome, but not too intelligent, Austrian baronet, even managed to have an innocent affair with one of the young singers of the opera, but for some unknown reason this courtship had a very abrupt end and both parties looked at each other across the room with eyes like loaded pistols. On one occasion the local fair was on in the market square and on this afternoon, when both rows of tables were fully occupied, a groom came to the officers' table and handed over a big parcel to the baronet. When asked who the sender was, the groom replied that he had been instructed not to reveal their identity.

Watched by his brother officers and their wives, the batchelor baronet started feverishly to undo the parcel. Having undone several layers of paper, he finally reached a cardboard box. Inside the box were some more layers of paper. When he came to the end of the wrappings, he found a very small box, in which lay a little stone monkey, with articulated arms and legs and a spring allowing it to pop up and down. With it was a note worded as follows: "A monkey without a monocle, to a monkey with a monocle." The monkey amused him, but the baronet, who was in the habit of wearing a monocle, immediately recognised the handwriting of the young singer and this made his blood boil. He told his colleagues that he had a good mind to get up and go and slap the face of the cheeky girl publicly.

Needless to say that she and her fellow artistes had been watching the unwrapping operation from their tables and had been very amused by the expression on the face of the baronet,when he unwrapped the contents of the last box. It took Franz and his colleagues quite a while to convince the baronet that it would be very unaristocratic to debase himself by slapping the woman's face, insulting as she may have been. Franz suggested that she should be punished by the same weapon as the one she had used and he asked the baronet to let him organise it.

The following afternoon as officers and artistes were facing each other again, on Franz's instructions, a young porter delivered a parcel twice as big as the one of the previous day to the singer. She too unwrapped it feverishly, watched by her colleagues and in a disguised way by the officers' table. Having accumulated on the table a still more impressive number of wrappings, she came to the final box, in which Franz had placed a little stone goose on a bellows, which he had found at the fair. When squeezed, the bellows made a very discordant sound. With the toy was a note which read as follows: "A goose with a voice, to a goose without a voice." This certainly proved a more effective rebuke than a slap on the face would have been and the expression on the face of the young singer left no doubts as to her feelings.

Many weeks later, when Franz was orderly officer of the week, his duties took him one evening to the local opera house, which was patronised by the troops and where an officer's inspection of security and fire prevention arrangements was called for. He went back stage with his N.C.O. during an interval and was introduced to all the artistes. When it came to the young singer, she met him with an engaging smile and immediately said, "Ah, you are the officer who gave that witty reply to my message to the baronet." Franz immediately enquired how she had found out, as he had instructed the small groom to keep his identity secret. She replied, "That was very easy to deduce. The baronet had told me, when we were on speaking terms, that you were his best friend and since I knew he was not clever enough to plan such a scheme. It was not difficult to deduce that you must have thought of it."

Army life in Sopron developed into a monotonous routine. The war seemed far away and Franz, Irma and their son had almost begun to forget what their life in Belgium had been like. One day they arrived at the cafe to find the daily papers. Suddenly their memories came flooding back. The headlines, declaring a German advance, read "Belgian Army in full retreat. Antwerp taken." Irma could not hide her resentment and very tactfully the fellow officers avoided any talk of the painful subject.

Next morning, as soon as he had reached the barracks, Franz was informed that the Colonel wanted to see him at once. The Colonel greeted him cordially and said, "You have heard the good news, our allies and friends the Germans, have overrun Antwerp. They are anxiously looking for officers who know the local languages. I have noticed in your records that you have been living seven years in Belgium, so I assume you know the local languages well and are prepared to be transferred. This would give your wife an opportunity to return to her country." Franz was astonished and replied, "Sir, may I ask you if this is a request or an order?" The Colonel thought for a moment and responded rather quietly and slowly, "No this is not an order, as it is to be a temporary transfer to another country's army. This cannot be ordered and must be voluntary, but I have no doubt that you will accept the honour of serving and helping our allied friends." Franz hesitated a little before saying, "If this not an order, Sir, then I wish to refuse the honour." "And why, may I ask?" said the Colonel angrily. "Must I answer this?" was Franz's reply. "Yes, I insist," said the Colonel. Franz hesitated again before saying, "Simply because I would not dare to show myself in this uniform amongst my Belgian friends." "Yes, I see," said the Colonel. "I see what it is, – your Czech stonehead displaying itself. But we will soon break that stone head."

The interview ended abruptly and although Franz was not due for another medical examination, he was not at all surprised to hear that same afternoon that the Colonel had arranged a medical check for him for the next morning. Once more the doctor decided that Franz was not fit for active service. When the Colonel heard this he flew into a violent temper and decided to over-rule the doctor saying, "In present days people more handicapped than him have to serve in the front line."

It did not come as a surprise the following day to find Franz was to be posted to the Italian front. The only concession he got from the irate Colonel was to be allowed to take his wife and son to Vienna, where relatives and friends could look after them.

Vienna, Austria 1914

On arrival in Vienna Franz was advised by friends to take his wife and son to the Pension Adlon in Dorotheagasse off the Graben, right in the centre of the city. The boarding house was owned and run by two old maids, English born sisters, named Yeager and the place was run in a very old-fashioned way. Nelly and Elsa were, daughters of an Austrian father, but had an English mother and were on the whole more English than Austrian in their upbringing. Franz had discovered their boarding house because many officers on leave in Vienna were using it and had recommended it highly to him. Also he had realized that it would be better for Irma to be amongst people who had the same aspirations as her about the outcome of the war.

At meals all guests were seated on both sides of one long communal table and the two sisters presided at each narrow end of the table. Conversation was general and whenever the conversation died down the sisters saw to it, at their respective ends of the table, to bring in a new topic for discussion.

In the early days of her stay Irma had been informed by the two sisters that they would see to it to keep up her morale and that they would make her forget that she was in an enemy country. Later, when they knew her better they told her they had means to know and get information about the true trend of the war. They advised Irma never to discuss it in the common rooms, but to come to their private sitting room to hear the latest news.

Little Rene who did not speak a word of German when he first arrived in Vienna. could now conduct quite a conversation in that language. He had even made friends with the drivers of a cab rank just in front of the pension. Whenever Irma would allow him, he would go down to the main door, greet the cabbies who would take him to stroke their horses or even put him on the driver's seat and put the horses' reins in his hands giving him a chance of taking the carriage on an imaginary ride. After a few weeks, Rene to his mother's horror, had picked up the typical Wiener Kutshel dialect.

The sisters Yeager had received Irma with all the friendliness and attention normally due to guests, but very soon she became more than a guest and was treated by them more like a member of the family. Irma and Rene Paul were soon to meet the Yeager's widowed brother and his very attractive daughter of seventeen who on many occasions asked Irma to be allowed to take Rene Paul out on walks. Although he was only four years old then, he was already impressed by her beauty and although up to then he had never left his mother's side, he did not mind leaving her to go out with the young niece.

Rene learned his German amazingly quickly, but his mother in the privacy of their room continued to speak to him in French. Therefore, apart from being of dual nationality he soon had the mastery of two languages. His German was spoken with an Austrian accent and he heard the first words spoken in English when his mother and the Yeagers wanted to exchange information which they thought safer for him not to understand. His mother often visited the Yeagers in their private apartment to be told news of the real state of the war. Their information was reaching them from sources only known to them, but which was much more realistic and reliable than the news officially issued to the Austrian press by the authorities.

Irma and Rene Paul also paid a few visits to an open air ice skating rink where they watched the two Yeager sisters, who were keen skaters and dancers on ice, perform.

Whilst Irma was gradually settling down in Vienna, forgetting, or at least trying to forget that she was amongst her enemies, she made more and more friends who concentrated their efforts on making life pleasant for her. She even discovered in Vienna an old school friend married to an eminent professor, named Glessner, the director of one of the main hospitals and the first contact having been made she got invited quite frequently to spend the day with her friend, formerly Susanne Walk, now Frau Glessner. Susanne had a daughter of the same age as Rene. The two children seemed to play happily together, whilst the two mothers spent their time discussing their fears and their hopes in the conduct of the war.

One day when Rene Paul came back from an afternoon at the Glessners, his mother was horrified to see him sit at the dining room table holding his spoon and fork vertically upright with his two closed fists resting on the table. Irma got very angry and said, "Rene, where are your manners? Put that cutlery down." To which he answered, "If a king can do it, I can do it." At first his remark brought surprise, but on later investigation, his mother found out that he had been inspired by the sight of a fairyland painting seen in the Glessner nursery representing a crowned and opulent king, sitting in the position copied by Rene and awaiting the placing on the table of pies and other food brought in front of him by a queue of chefs.

Following his arrival on the Italian front, Franz sent on a regular basis, the only correspondence allowed, which was a pre-printed card with several types of sentences. The inappropriate ones were meant to be crossed out. By the crossing out of certain words in these prescribed sentences it was possible to arrive at quite a variation on the messages intended, so much so that Franz, who had to censure his men's mail prior to despatch, one day found a card saying "I have been ill recently and I hope you too." That must have pleased the relatives of whoever the sender was.

Franz meanwhile, although under constant fire, found that life could be boring in his isolated outpost in the mountains. He was in charge of a mountain artillery unit. The guns, of a reasonably small calibre, appropriate to mountain warfare, were carried dismantled on the backs of mules. So were the ammunition containers. These animals were fantastically robust. Usually they had an amazing sense of balance on narrow mountain paths, and it needed a really unusual event for them to fall down on the mountain tracks.

However, this happened, one day, to a mule carrying live ammunition. One of the ammunition boxes got caught by the branch of a nearby tree. The mule, thrown off balance, fell, rolling several hundred feet into a ravine. Franz expected an explosion at anytime, but when he noticed that the mule and containers had ended their fall at the bottom of the ravine, without such a detonation, he decided to investigate. To his amazement he found the mule on her back, still alive and kicking furiously and trying to get back on her legs. But the two upturned containers, on the ground either side of her, prevented her from moving.

It was quite a dangerous task to approach the kicking mule, cut off the straps holding the containers in position, then to quickly move the containers a safe distance from the mule. Several men volunteered for the job, but no one thought that after her drop and fall the mule would be able to get up unaided. This is, however, exactly what happened. As soon as the mule got free of the straps and the containers having been moved, she shook herself like a dog coming out of a pond, and that was the end of the incident. The unit veterinary officer examined her carefully and judged her unharmed.

After having pushed forward for a while in the mountains along the Brenner Pass, and facing fierce Italian resistance, the advance became held up by the condition of the weather and it was soon decided that the troops had to take up positions ready for the approaching winter. Whilst half of the unit kept watch at their guns in readiness for any Italian surprise attack, the other half was employed felling trees and using them to build huts as sleeping accommodation and mess huts. One hut divided into three rooms was built for Franz. The biggest of the rooms became the Unit Office. The next largest became Franz's bedroom, and the smallest of the three was shared by his batman, a Montenegran man called Tell and his dog, a little smooth haired terrier called Franz. The huts had hardly been completed when the winter set in and a good number of the huts were hidden under the snow.

Life became monotonous, short days in which to fulfil all the normal duties of the camp and long dark evenings and nights with no other entertainment for the men than their own conversation, card games, or for those who were able to read, books sent by relatives. Welfare in the units was very primitively organised and varied from unit to unit. Franz had always been concerned with the welfare of his men and always managed to obtain, by hook or by crook, those things his men wanted most in addition to their normal diet. Cigarettes and drinks were never in short supply, but their fair distribution was strictly controlled by Lieutenant Franz. He was liked by his men and although, in accordance with Austrian tactics of 'divide and rule' his unit was composed of men of a variety of different nationalities, languages and creeds, he managed to keep them working happily together in a harmonious unit.

It was amazing to see how these men, from various walks of life, some from the Czech lands, some Slovaks, some Hungarian, others Serbs, Croats or Montenegrans, all tried to understand each other. All had only one common enemy, apart from the one they had been forced to face and that was the Austrians, who having overrun their countries, turned them into Austrian provinces and compelled these men to fight a war, the purpose of which they did not understand, against an enemy who was not their enemy, but their ruler's.

Franz received letters at regular intervals from Irma telling him that all was well in Vienna. In 1916 the Emperor Franz-Joseph died and

Irma and Rene watched the impressive funeral from a window facing St. Stephen's Cathedral. Rene would later recollect the funeral and how his mother had hired a window on the second floor of a building on the corner of the Graben from which to watch the procession. The gigantic catafalque pulled by six black draped horses was followed by the German Kaiser and by Karl, the new Emperor of Austria.

The same day Irma wrote a long letter to her husband describing the procession and had even the audacity to defy the censors by writing that when she saw Wilhelm II marching behind the hearse she was secretly hoping that somebody would throw a bomb amongst all those crowned heads of eastern Europe. Franz didn't receive this letter until a few weeks later, because he was on his way to Vienna for one of his regular leaves. In order not to disappoint his wife, in case his leave was cancelled at the last minute, he had made it a habit never to announce his arrival and usually he would surprise Irma by suddenly knocking at the door of her room.

Franz missed the Emperor's funeral by two days, but he was determined to see the film of it at the cinema. The snag was that as the army was in mourning for six weeks, no serviceman was allowed to go to theatres or the pictures. Franz decided to infringe the regulation forbidding officers to wear civilian clothes in wartime. He got his suit out of mothballs and went to the picture house, but on his way home he nearly gave the game away. As he was walking along the Graben he had to pass a colonel and instinctively he lifted his hand to salute. Suddenly remembering he was in civilian clothes, he took off his hat and pretended to greet an imaginary friend on the other side of the road.

Leaves were always short and this one went by like lightning. When Franz got back to his unit, everybody was feverishly preparing for a move forward in preparation for a big offensive. Franz's unit started by blasting the enemy positions and the Italians retaliated by firing back. Not many men were killed, but both armies suffered a considerable number of blinded men, because each time a shell struck the hillside rocks, thousands of little fragments of stone pelted them. After two days of these artillery exchanges, information came back that the Italians were retreating and a quick advance of the Austrian forces was ordered.

Franz's unit came down from the mountains and on reaching the first Italian village, a surprise was in store for the men. They must have been so close on the heels of the Italians that in every house in the village there were tables with piping hot food still on the plates, showing the haste of the Italian retreat. Franz said later that such a thing would never have happened in the Austrian army. They would possibly have abandoned their weapons, but never their food.

Franz was lucky to find amongst the spoils an Italian guitar which he made his and taught himself to play. Later when the fighting was over and he was transferred to a training centre in the Tyrol, he was able to entertain his fellow officers by singing songs he had composed, so shortening the dreariness of long winter evenings in the officers' mess.

A few months later Irma wrote to Franz to announce that on the 8th June 1917, she had given birth to a daughter who was later to be named, Georgette Elfriede. Rene Paul's sister was born in the clinic of Professor Glessner. His mother had entrusted Rene to the care of the Yeager sisters and he proved something of a handful for them, escaping whenever he could from the pension and going down on to the corner of the street. He never went very far, usually he was found in conversation with the horse cab drivers awaiting business at the Graben end of the street. They all knew him by name and he called them by their Christian names.

Vienna, July 1917

Although he applied for special leave to see his newborn child, it took a few more weeks before Franz obtained permission to travel to Vienna. Meanwhile at the Pension Adlon, Irma was to face a new ordeal. For the last few months German officers had been coming to Vienna on leave from the various fronts and the billeting officer had tried several times to get them into Pension Adlon, but the proprietors always managed to refuse them by pretending that all the rooms were occupied. On one occasion, however, they were thrown off their guard and they had to admit that a room had just been vacated by an Austrian officer. From the first moment of his arrival in the Pension Adlon the German officer upset what had previously been a harmonious atmosphere.

Whenever he entered the dining room his loud voice could be heard from one side of the room to the other. All conversation had to stop to listen to his boastful accounts of the progress of the war and his criticisms of the Austrians. Although several Austrian officers were on leave at the pension at the time, the German went on to criticize their conduct of the war, arguing that wherever the Germans were fighting with the Austrians on their flanks, they had to deploy more troops to watch the Austrians than the enemy. The Austrian officers listened to these criticisms either with indifference or in a resigned manner, accepting the unpleasant words of a guest of their country, but no one ever attempted to stop the serpent tongue of the German.

Irma, alone of the guests, seemed to be living with her nerves on edge and had it not been for the significant looks of her two hostesses across the table, she might have exploded earlier. However after a week of the ordeal Irma could hold her tongue no longer and when once more the bragging German officer started to criticise the Austrian soldiers, she found the occasion to drop her bornbshell. In a voice as loud as the one used by the German, she shouted across the table so that everyone present could hear, "There is only one piece of good luck for the Austrians, that at the Marne they were not on your side and you still got a nice licking."

The German officer became pale with rage and walked out of the dining room leaving his plate half full and shouting that Irma would pay for these wicked words. He was never seen again at the pension. For a few days the two owners feared the consequences of this incident for Irma, as much as for the future of their hotel, but either the German officer had found it wiser not to report the incident or the Austrian authorities having been notified and knowing the usual reputation for hospitality of the Pension Adlon, had found it wiser to shelve the complaint. In any event nothing further was ever heard of the matter.

A few weeks prior to this it had been discovered that Rene Paul was suffering from enlarged tonsils and it had been decided to operate. His mother took him to the clinic. She was instructed to undress him and he was then wrapped in a white sheet. His mother's suggestion that she accompany him to the operating theatre was turned down and a nurse carried him up to the theatre in the makeshift dressing gown, but as soon as she entered the operating theatre and Rene saw the impressive row of men and women in white, he managed to wriggle out of the sheet and as naked as the day he was born, started to race in the direction of the door. It took six people to hold him and carry him to the operating table. He fought like a lion and several of the assistants later showed his mother traces of bites and scratches they had received during the struggle.

Eventually the anaesthetic mask was forced over his face and the chloroform did the rest. When, after the operation, he came out of his deep sleep, and the effect of the chloroform had worn off, he was completely changed. From the nervous and lively, rather restless boy he had been, he suddenly became quite reserved, even lazy and it was later said that he had probably suffered from the after effects of war time chloroform. The change in Rene's nature became apparent to everybody including his father when he came to fetch him.

Prague 1917

Shortly before Franz came to Vienna on leave he had been informed of the incident at the Pension Adlon by one of his colleagues who was present at the time and on his advice decided that it was time to move Irma to somewhere where there would be less likelihood of such unpleasant occurrences. Prague was indicated, firstly because Franz's mother would be able to look after Irma, her young turbulent son and her newborn daughter, but also because in the whole of Bohemia there had always been antagonism towards the Austrian masters and their German friends.

Irma was soon to find out about this. One day when her mother-in-law had sent her on an errand and had given her the German name of a street, she found that at most street corners the German version of the name had been crossed out with white paint, leaving the names in Czech only. Irma went to a policeman and asked her way in German. The policeman very rudely replied, "Go back to Berlin where you come from, then you won't need my help," and turned on his heels and walked away. The next policeman Irma saw, was asked the same question, but in French this time. The policeman, hearing it was not German, very politely asked if Irma spoke German, and gave her all the information she wanted. Naturally he was interested to know what the language was and where she came from.

Franz's mother's flat overlooked the River Moldau and Rene would spend hours on the balcony overlooking the Zofin Island and see people walking and children playing there, but only being permitted to go out to the park with his mother was an ordeal to him.

Never at any time did Czechs she met consider Irma as an enemy. She had almost forgotten that she was amongst her enemies and that there was a war on, but the stiff food rationing reminded her of it each day and gave her many worries, mainly concerning the feeding of her baby daughter, Georgette. Unforeseen events soon were to rid her of these worries.

Activities at the Italian front had been pretty brisk and had kept Franz and his unit very busy with continuous moves of positions. One day the Italians were in full retreat and the next day they would launch a surprise offensive and catch the Austrians off their guard and compel them to surrender the ground they had gained only a few days earlier. During this time, Franz's unit was constantly in action, either to support an attack or to stop, or at least slow down, an enemy advance.

As his unit had already spent two winters in the mountains, it was decided that it was time to give his men a rest. So, at the end of October the whole unit was withdrawn from the front line and Franz got posted to an Instruction Centre in the Tyrol. Several of his N.C.Os and men were posted with him, the thinking being that new recruits would benefit from their tactical experience. Irma and the children stayed in Prague until such time as Franz was moved from the front line to the instruction centre in Kramsach.

Kramsach, The Austrian Tyrol December 1917

The camp was situated between Brixlegg, Kramsach and Mariathal and in walking distance from Rattenburg, the smallest town in Austria. The main railway line from Arlberg and Innsbruck to Vienna follows the valley of the River Inn. Most trains stopped at Brixlegg and others stopped in Rattenburg. The two stations were only separated by a long tunnel which allowed the trains to pass under the foot of a high mountain.

The Colonel in charge of the camp was a Hungarian nobleman called Freiherr Von Klingspor. He lived with his wife, his two daughters and a young son on the first floor of a big old house, situated in the main street of Brixlegg. His office and the officers' mess for his headquarters was located in an old inn, right opposite his house. It, and the food there, were good at all times.

Franz had been billeted in a typical Tyrolean farm house in the centre of Kramsach. The whole of the first floor had been requisitioned for him and his batman. He had lost his old batman, his faithful Tell, but had soon been able to choose a young Czech recruit by the name of Miroslav to replace him. Miroslav prepared his breakfast every morning at the farm house, but his two main meals of the day were taken at a second officers' mess in another old inn located opposite the picturesque church in Mariathal. Franz had been at the camp about a month when one day he was summoned to the Colonel's office in Brixlegg.

While the two horses pulling his carriage were speeding along the narrow country lane leading from Kramsach to Brixlegg, Franz was anxiously thinking of the reasons for the summons to see the Colonel. Was it for promotion? Was it to send him back to the front line? Or was it a telling off for the way he was running his new unit? He was so deep in thought that he hadn't noticed that his carriage had crossed the Inn Bridge, entered Brixlegg and stopped in front of the White Deer Inn. The driver pulled him out of his dream by asking if he had to wait. Franz was shown into the Colonel's office almost immediately and was pleased by the fatherly way the old and distinguished looking man received him.

All his fears of bad news were dispelled. "I have good news for you my friend," began the Colonel. "As you probably know your previous commanding officer had recommended you for promotion and in view of your excellent record the higher authorities have granted it. I have great pleasure to be the first to congratulate you First Lieutenant Franz, and don't forget to put a new star on the collar of all your uniforms. Before I invite you to join me in a drink and lunch in the mess, I have one small thing I want to discuss with you here. When your promotion came in yesterday I studied the whole of your file and noticed that you have a wife and two young children staying in Prague. I am surprised that you have not thought of asking my permission to bring them here. After all, rationing in Prague is known to be pretty fierce and here in the country we have got everything we need. Don't you want your family to be here with you?"

"Sir," replied Franz, "there is nothing I would like more than having my family with me, but since you studied my file you will have noticed I am married to a Belgian girl for whom the fact of being amongst her country's enemies can cause a considerable strain, sometimes leading to fits of ill temper. I would not like to endanger my future by an incident she may provoke in such fits of temper." The Colonel listened carefully and after Franz had finished talking, collected his thoughts for a few moments and said, "Well, Franz, I am going to give you special leave, first to show your new promotion to your wife. Secondly, I suggest that you invite her to join us here and I can assure you that we will make her feel so much at home that she will forget that she is among enemies."

The next morning Franz was on his way to Prague. It did not take long for him to convince his wife of the usefulness of a change. Irma had not always seen eye to eye with her mother-in-law and was very glad to be removed from the control she sought to exert. It was, therefore, arranged that she would join Franz at the earliest possible moment and Christmas eve was decided on. Franz had to return to his unit straight away and inform his Colonel of his wife's arrival. He promised to be at the station in Brixlegg to meet her when she arrived.

On the agreed day Irma left with her two children, accompanied to the station by her mother-in-law and other relatives of her husband. After a reasonably comfortable journey she reached Brixlegg in darkness. The scenery for a good while had been breathtaking. The mountains on both sides of the Inn valley and the valley itself were covered in snow. Contrasting with them were the woods at the foot of the mountains. The tree trunks looked blacker than normal and the needles of the pine trees seemed greener. When darkness came, the reflections off the snow's whiteness was still more striking. The light shining from the houses or from the train windows made golden beams of light on that whiteness.

Brixlegg, Rattenberg and Kramsach are all situated in the Inn valley at a place where the two lines of mountains bordering the valley seem to separate, leaving between them a wide and fertile plain. The railway line at this point runs on a viaduct following the southern slope of the mountains. Half a mile just outside Rattenberg, a tunnel had been cut into the mountain side, in order to maintain the straight line of the tracks leading from Rattenberg to Vienna.

As the train went through the Rattenburg tunnel, slowing down to stop at Brixlegg, Irma noticed all the farms perched on the mountain side had steeply sloping roofs, hidden by a heavy layer of snow. Emerging from the tunnel it was surprising to find the railway viaduct was much closer to the side of the mountain and was practically level with houses built on the mountain side. Only the front and the sides of the houses could be seen, the rear being hidden by the slope and the accumulated snowfall. As they reached Brixlegg in complete darkness, Rene noticed the lights shining from each window and their beams extending in long streaks on the snow in front of them.

Franz was waiting on the platform and took his family to a horse-drawn sleigh, while his batman attended to the luggage. After the usual embraces, Franz lead his family down the station's stairs to the sleigh pulled by two horses. As the sleigh was pulling away from the station and passing under the viaduct, the train had started and all the lights of the carriages once more flickered on the snow leaving an unforgettable impression. Rene hardly had time to notice the noise of the bells tinkling on the horses' collars when the sleigh stopped in front of the farm in the village of Kramsach. The short journey over the Inn Bridge and through the country lanes had brought the sleigh to the front of the Missbaum farm. Irma was still under the spell of that sleigh ride through the quiet valley, where the silence and peace had only been disturbed by the horse bells. Even the usual noise of their hooves had been softened by the thickness of the snow.

Although her new residence was far smaller than the ones to which she had been accustomed to before, Irma was full of enthusiasm for it. The building, despite being small, was scrupulously clean. Balconies in carved wood surrounded the whole of the first and second floor. Access to the inside of the house was through a storeroom with a stone flagged floor. Here, little Rene's eyes were immediately drawn to a churn for making cream and butter.

The apartment on the first floor was composed of one big bedroom for Franz and Irma and a smaller bedroom for Rene Paul. In the sitting room a large area of the main wall was occupied by a form of heating typical of the Tyrol. A square structure, standing full height to the ceiling, projected out from the centre of the main wall opposite the windows, leaving deep four feet wide alcoves on either side of it. It was covered from the ground to the ceiling with green ceramic tiles, each a foot square. A wooden bench was built into the three visible sides of this structure. It was in fact a stove, into which logs were fed through a metal door in the corridor outside. The heat given off by this stove, gave the room an even, pleasant, temperature, which was well maintained by the use of double glazed windows. The kitchen was situated next to this room and was big enough to also be used as a dining room.

Although little Rene's first impressions were of a large farmhouse, visiting it again forty years later, he was struck by its compactness. The living quarters did not cover much more than the space of a modern three bedroomed house. The stables and the barn took up most of the space near the house, and the house was connected to them by a buttery, full of the utensils needed to extract cream from the milk, which was stored in churns and which could also be used for the making of butter.

Externally the house was built in brick covered with render, painted white. It had the typical pointed roof of a Tyrolean house. The first floor was surrounded by its wide wooden balcony with its beautifully carved and decorated wooden railing. The roof of the house extended on all sides, overhanging the walls and also protecting the balcony from the elements.

Franz had prepared a big decorated Christmas tree for his children and whilst putting them in the care of a nurse engaged to one of his NCO's, he prepared to take Irma for dinner to the officers' mess. As soon as Irma had unpacked, Franz suggested that she put on her best dress as they were both invited to a Christmas Eve party given by the Colonel in the Officers' Mess at Brixlegg.

"I am not going," said Irma sharply.

"You cannot do this to me," replied Franz, although not unduly shocked by his wife's outburst. "The Colonel has expressed his desire to make your acquaintance this evening and introduce you, personally, to all the officers of the garrison and their wives."

The expression on Irma's face displayed her stubbornness. "Your Colonel can order you about, but I don't come under his orders and I am not going," she said with a note of finality.

"But why not?" asked Franz, by now almost pleading.

"Firstly because I am not in the mood. Secondly because no doubt we will be expected to drink to the health of the Emperor and I shall not do so!"

Franz was still trying, without much success, to convince his wife to go, when his friend and colleague Moore arrived. Moore had promised to fetch Franz and Irma with his own sleigh to take them to Brixlegg and at Franz's suggestion had come early for an aperitif. Franz left his wife brooding in the bedroom and went to meet his friend and took him into the living room. In a few words he told Moore of the dilemma he was placed in by the obstinacy of his wife. Moore suggested that he brought Irma and introduced him and then under some pretext or another left him alone with her. He guaranteed that he would make her change her mind. Franz was a bit reluctant, because Moore, a happy bachelor, had the reputation of being a seducer, but in view of the gravity of the situation Franz did not have much choice.

He went to fetch Irma and after a brief and formal introduction left the room as agreed. Immediately Moore went to work on Irma.

"How can so beautiful and so charming a woman as you, be so stubborn and selfish?" he said.

"What do you mean?" demanded Irma angrily and immediately on the defensive.

"Your husband has told me all about your argument and I ask you very seriously to reconsider your decision as your refusal could have the gravest consequences."

Irma remained firm in her refusal. Then Moore used shock tactics.

"Alright," he said "then I shall not outstay my welcome here and I will try to forget I ever met a selfish woman, who has signed a death warrant for her husband."

A cold shower could not have had more effect. Irma's temper subsided and anxiously she again asked "What do you mean?," only this time without a hint of stubborness.

"If you refuse to go," said Moore, "the Colonel will consider it as a personal insult and could take it out on your husband. He might even decide to send him straight back to the front line. Imagine, the day after his arrival there Franz gets killed; you would never forgive yourself for having sent your husband to his death just for the sake of your pride."

Moore very soon saw that Irma's will was weakening. He managed to sway her finally by promising that he would get several sympathetic officers together at their table and that they would choose a table at the furthest corner of the dining room and that when the time came for the toast they would place themselves shoulder to shoulder, thus hiding Irma and allow her to remain seated.

By the time Franz came back into the room carrying a tray of drinks, Irma had given in. While the men had their drinks Irma left the room to get dressed. A relieved Franz thanked his friend for his successful intervention. When twenty minutes later Irma reappeared she was wearing a very attractive evening dress and Moore joyfully forecast that she would attract the admiration of all the officers and that she would also attract the jealousy of their wives. For this Irma was well prepared.

Before going to their Christmas dinner, Franz and Irma were approached by a group of villagers, who offered their services to come to the house the following day and present Rene with toys provided by his parents. In many Roman Catholic countries the feast of St. Nikolaus is celebrated on 6th December and St. Nikolaus fulfils the same role as Father Christmas. A particular custom in the Austrian Tyrol is that the festival of St Nikolaus is combined with Christmas. Whilst, in other European Roman Catholic countries, St Nikolaus is represented by a man with a white beard and wearing the mitre and surplus of a bishop, the Tyroleans represent St. Nikolaus in the same manner as Father Christmas. He is usually escorted by a boy with a blackened face representing his negro servant and by two other black faced individuals, representing demons, with horns and tails and carrying chains which they rattle to frighten the children.

One of them carries on his back a basket containing toys, the other carries an empty basket and a birch. When St Nikolaus approaches the children, he asks the parents if they have been good. After they have kissed the ring on his white gloved right hand, he instructs his negro assistant to take the toys for the child out of the basket carried by one of the demons. If the child has been naughty, then the demon is supposed to punish them with the birch twigs carried by his companion and the empty basket is supposed to be used to carry away the very naughty child, whose parents feel they must be rid of.

When Franz, Irma and their friend Moore got to the White Deer Inn, many officers and their wives had already arrived. As soon as they reached the entrance to the lounge, the Colonel left the little group he was talking to and came with outstretched hands to welcome them. To the surprise of Franz and Moore, the Colonel immediately addressed Irma in perfect French. Then he took her to introduce her, first to his wife and daughter, then to all the other guests. Whilst it was very customary for members of the Austrian or Hungarian nobility to speak French amongst themselves, it was quite unusual to hear it being used in an officers' mess.

When the time came to enter the dining room the Colonel stood up and asked for everyone's attention. Then in a loud and clear voice he said that he was asking everybody's permission to depart from the usual seating arrangements. On this occasion, as the wife of Lieutenant Franz was newly arrived and as he happened to speak her language, he wished to seat her next to him and thus make her feel more at home. Everyone signified their agreement and then made their way to the dining room. Contrary to the usual custom, they had done away with the individual tables, which had all been placed to make one big table stretching from one end of the dining room to the other.

The Colonel took a seat at the centre of the table, placing on his right the wife of the senior major and on his left, Irma, who normally according to the rank of her husband should have been at the far end of the table. During the dinner the Colonel hardly addressed more than a few words to the wife of the major, but kept up a very animated conversation with Irma, whilst Franz who was seated at the far end of the table watched his wife with considerable anxiety.

As the end of the meal was nearing and champagne was being poured in preparation for the toast to the Emperor, Irma was becoming uncomfortable with the situation and beads of perspiration were visible on her face. At the far end of the table Franz's anxiety also increased. At that moment the Colonel drew the attention of his wife, who was sitting opposite him, and gave her a pre-arranged nod. She left her seat and came around the table and stopped behind Irma's seat. Whispering into Irma's ear, she said, "If you wish to powder your nose, I shall show you where the ladies' powder room is." Irma smiled in acceptance of this offer.

As soon as the ladies had left the room the Colonel got up and proposed the Emperor's health, then the toast to their army and to their allies the Germans. By the time the ladies came back to the dining room, Franz had been requested to sing one of his latest compositions aided by his guitar and the return of the ladies had passed unnoticed. Later when told that the toasts were over Irma went to thank the Colonel for his kind consideration. "I promised your husband that I would make you forget that you are among enemies," said the Colonel "and this I hope was the first step in the right direction." It surely was and as midnight was approaching the party came to an end. As Irma said goodbye to the Colonel and to his wife, the Baroness Klingspor invited Irma to the next officers' wives' tea party, which, Irma accepted without hesitation. As all the officers and wives left the Mess they all set off in the direction of the picturesque village church to attend the midnight mass.

Next morning being Christmas day, Franz told Rene Paul to get ready for a big surprise. He and his sister would be visited in the flat by St Nikolaus himself. Little Rene, for whom everything was a new experience, had quite forgotten Christmas, when he discovered in the living room, what appeared, to his eyes, to be a gigantic tree, on which, in accordance with Tyrolean custom, hung various biscuits specially baked in the shape of stars, moons and half moons, houses, men or animals. Each was made in shortbread pastry and had a hole, through which richly coloured ribbons were placed. The biscuits were then hung from the tree by these ribbons. Also mounted on the tree was an array of candles designed to be lit to mark Christmas day. This made an everlasting impression on the young boy.

Soon after, the group composed of four men arrived at the farmhouse. One man represented St.Nikolaus wearing a red coat with a golden surplice and a golden mitre. He also wore white gloves with a big pascal ring on one finger of his right hand. In his left hand he held a golden staff of office. Behind him stood a young boy with a blackened face, also richly dressed, representing the assistant to St Nikolaus. Behind him in turn came the two horrible creatures, also with blackened faces, wearing garments made of black wool and sheepskin. Protruding from their forehead were the two horns and their footwear had been shaped to look like hooves. Symbolically they were represented as having been enslaved by the benign spirit of St, Nikolaus, their wrists manacled with metal bracelets and chains. On their backs they each carried their basket.

Rene never forgot that dramatic instant when he came face to face with St. Nikolaus, who asked him if he had been good. After getting confirmation from his parents that he had been, St.Nikolaus had handed over to him the toys brought in the good demon's basket. Needless to say that this little drama makes a lifelong impression on little children. The villagers who perform this pantomine go from house to house and get a small reward in money and in kind for their services. The toys are usually supplied by the parents and handed over to the good demon before he enters the room where the children wait for him with silk ribbons of various colours, but with red and green predominant.

But there was one gift which had been far too big to come in the basket and was brought in separately. Rene could not believe his eyes. His parents had bought him a two-seater toboggan with two unusual features. The first was that the front was completely round and streamlined. Secondly there was a handle on the toboggan at the end of which were three prongs, so that when the handle was pulled it acted as a brake.

That same day a special wartime Christmas meal had been arranged for the men at the camp, followed by sports events. The officers and their wives were present and Irma did not go unnoticed. Franz introduced many of his NCOs and soldiers, who saluted her respectfully and glanced at her with admiring eyes. After Sunday lunch, the family returned to the Missbaum farm where some of the pastries decorating the Christmas tree were removed and eaten.

On the following morning, whilst his parents were still in bed, Rene entered their room and asked permission to go and try out his toboggan on the hill opposite the farm. He was told he could, as long as he did not go on the steepest of the slopes. At first he contented himself with the lower slopes, but having become more proficient and having noticed the older boys using a longer and steeper slope, he decided he had to have a go. The snow on this slope covered a four foot wide path used in summer, which lead to the forest on the upper reaches of the mountain.

The ambitious and adventurous little boy pulled his toboggan as high as he could. When he thought it was high enough to enjoy a really long ride, he turned round, sat down, and let the toboggan gather speed. As he came around a bend, he suddenly noticed an old farmer obstructing his path. The old man was walking down hill with his legs wide open. He must have been stone deaf, as he carried on walking, despite the warning shouts of the little boy. In a flash Rene had made up his mind. First he sat back as far as he could on his toboggan. Next he applied the brake as hard as he could. He managed to direct the toboggan between the legs of the old man, so that as he lost balance, the old farmer fell and seated himself in front of the little boy on the toboggan. It was lucky that the toboggan had not very much further to go to reach the bottom of the slope.

The sledge came to a halt and and before the old man could recover his wits Rene had run away and was hidden behind a tree. The old man got up heavily, leaning on his stick, he shouted and swore in the direction taken by the child. Then he went on his way and when safely out of sight Rene came out from his hiding place to recover the precious toboggan. His fear had been that the old farmer would confiscate the sleigh and that he would have to provide an awkward explanation to his parents on the circumstances of its loss. As it was, the old man left the sleigh, which he brought home and so his parents never got to know that he had disobeyed their instructions about the high slope.

After the Christmas celebrations were over, the family started settling into their new surroundings. The following days were spent unpacking the cases and finding room for the clothing in the spacious wardrobes, did not take very long. Assisted by the wife of the landlord, Irma went around the village to find out where the various merchants and suppliers were. Some of the food was to be brought in by the batman from the Officers' Mess in Mariathal in three stacked containers, held together by a metal frame and handle.

Very soon Franz had introduced his family to several of his colleagues who, in turn, invited them to their homes to meet their families. There were several boys and girls of Rene's age and it did not take long for him to get accustomed to his new way of life and new surroundings. The incident involving the toboggan had been noticed by many villagers and Rene soon became a little hero amongst them. His popularity in the village soon increased when he joined the village school.

Although the son of an officer, he sat on the school benches next to all the local children, without receiving special favours. The only thing that made the other children a little envious was when, on a few occasions, Franz came to fetch his son in an open carriage pulled by two horses. Occasionally Rene asked his father to give one or two other boys a lift and this naturally increased his popularity. Rene's closest friend was the son of Baron Slatin, an Austrian nobleman whose father was stationmaster of the main Vienna station. Baron Slatin was a lieutenant like Franz. His wife and Irma were getting on well together and the two little boys were the same age. Both children went regularly to each other's homes until one day an incident made Rene very unpopular with the Slatin family. In fact it is the one and only occasion where Rene remembered being seriously chastised by his father.

It was on the occasion of a wedding anniversary and all the relatives of the Slatins had come from Vienna to Kramsach. About twenty of them had found accommodation in the nearby town of Rattenburg for a few days. On the day of the celebration they all gathered at the farm where the Slatins were billeted and enjoyed a meal, which by wartime standards was a feast.

As this was taking place in the late Spring, the weather had been favourable enough for an open air luncheon in the gardens of the farm. Rene had been invited to this lunch, mainly so that the young Slatin did not feel too lost amongst all the older members of the family. After the lunch, the family gathered in the garden for a souvenir photograph of the occasion. A professional photographer had been hired from the nearby town and he had brought in addition to an enormous camera on a large, sturdy tripod, background scenery, attached to an intricate framework, to stand it upright.

After this was put in place, he lined up a row of chairs and placed all members of the family into an orderly group. The children were told to kneel or sit in front of the chairs. On the chairs sat the Slatins and their respective parents, whilst the rest of the family stood behind them in two rows. The photographer took quite a long time to arrange the family group. Meanwhile little Rene who had been invited to the party, but was not entitled to appear on the photograph, was watching the proceedings, first from behind the photographer and then from behind the screen. He had been warned twice to keep away from the framework, but apart from this nobody was much concerned with the little boy. They were far too preoccupied and concerned to appear at their best for the photograph, which was going to be a reminder of a unique family occasion. The photographer had finished organizing the group and was now focusing the camera, his head and shoulders hidden under a large black cloth. Eventually he emerged from under the cloth and stood to one side of the camera, ready to actuate the mechanism which would expose the photographic plate. He called everyone to attention and then the most unexpected thing happened. Little Rene having disappeared once more behind the scenery, tripped over a rope holding up the background scenery and the whole framework collapsed, falling forward and burying the whole family under its wide canvas. Luckily no one was hurt. It was more fright than anything else that upset them.

The responsibility for all this was soon traced to Rene and Lieutenant Slatin sent him away saying, "Go home and tell your father what a naughty boy you have been." Brooding over the incident, Rene slowly started his journey home, but on his way he passed the house where his father's friend and colleague, Moore, was billetted. The young bachelor, who before being called up, had been a professional concert pianist, had managed to get a flat with a piano, allowing him to go on practicing. As Rene was passing his house, he could hear Moore play and was fascinated by his virtuosity. Rene, being very fond of music, decided to pay the young lieutenant a visit.

Forgetting about what had happened only a few minutes earlier, he knocked at his door.

"Good afternoon Herr Moore, I heard you from downstairs. Would you mind very much if I came to listen to you?"

"No, certainly not," was the answer. "As long as you keep quiet and don't disturb my concentration, you are welcome."

Rene had found him studying a musical score. Rene was offered an armchair and promising to keep quiet, was allowed to listen. Rene sat down as quiet as a mouse in a big armchair and listened contentedly to the classical music, but after a while even a music loving little boy can get tired and fall asleep. The sound of the music flowing from the piano had the effect of making Rene forget the trouble he had got himself into earlier in the afternoon and soon sent him into a wonderfully relaxed slumber.

Meanwhile outside it had become dark and Irma was very worried when the little boy did not return home at his usual time. Franz rushed to the Slatins and was told of all that had happened and how Rene had been sent home. Franz was very worried and started a systematic search. This brought him to the flat of his friend, Lieutenant Moore. Having looked for him vainly in several places, he suddenly remembered that Lieutenant Moore's flat was halfway between the Slatins and Missbaum farm. He found Rene there, fast asleep in the armchair, whilst Moore, who was so absorbed by his practice, had forgotten all about the little boy's presence. Franz found him still rehearsing and oblivious to the fact that Rene was fast asleep in the armchair.

Rene's awakening at the hands of his father was rather abrupt. He had hardly come to his senses when he felt himself being dragged home by one arm and before he could protest his father had pulled his trousers down and given him a real good hiding on his bare bottom. It was the one and only good hiding he ever got, but it left a firm impression on him.

After this life in Kramsach settled into a pattern of monotonous routine. Every morning after breakfast the horse drawn brake would fetch Franz from the farm and take him to the barracks. On his way he would drop Rene at his school. Franz's midday meal would be taken at the officers' Mess in Mariathal and dinner would be brought home for the whole family. It was brought to the table in the special tins from the Mess and would be served by Franz's batman or the nurse, Julie, married to Franz's senior N.C.O., who Irma had brought from Vienna to look after baby Georgette.

By then, Rene having joined the local primary school, was learning to read and write in German. Irma's mornings were very leisurely, but afternoons were spent with other officers' wives, either in conversation, or in more useful meetings, where the welfare of the soldiers was discussed and organised. The only events that cut across the monotony of daily existence were occasions like Easter, the Emperor's birthday celebration and other holidays.

The birthday of the Emperor was mainly a military event, starting with a church parade. Although Franz was probably the only non-Roman Catholic officer in the whole garrison, he was the one who was chosen to command the guard of honour at the church parade. Although this caused some amusement to his wife, his young son watched with pride and pleasure to see his father in his smart uniform, sword drawn, give his orders loud and clear.

All the officers, their families, the local civilian dignitaries and the villagers would stream out of the church and form themselves into small groups on the square in front of the church to watch the guard of honour coming out of the main porch. Under Franz's orders, they would come out smartly, two by two, and as soon as they had come out of the church, they would change formation into lines of four. When the whole unit was about thirty yards away from the porch, a sharp order would make the soldiers stop. Another order and they would make a quarter turn and present arms. Franz then drew his sword and facing the unit, returned their salute. Next, after ordering them to slope arms, he would instruct a junior officer or a senior NCO to take over and after returning his sword to the scabbard, he would break away and rejoin the group formed by the officers and their wives and receive the usual compliments or congratulations on the smart display of the troops under his command.

Then, as the little groups started to disperse, Irma and Rene were taken by Franz to the hotel used as the officers' mess, where all the adults would have their morning aperitif, discuss the latest war communique, whilst the children were either running about in the lounge, or when too noisy, would be told to go and play in the hotel yard, where either a batman or a carriage driver would be instructed to keep a watchful eye on them.

The lunch was usually at the headquarter's mess in Brixlegg and the children were very disgusted to find that after having had the freedom of the mess at Mariathal, their parents would drive them home where a meal would be served to them by the batman or in Rene and Georgette's case, by Sister Julie their nurse, whilst the parents went on to the luncheon presided over by the Colonel. The children would meet their parents again in the afternoon at the sports field, where sports events, mostly competitions between various military units, loudly supported by the local villagers, took place.

Easter and Palm Sunday which preceded Easter were the occasion of colourful processions and festivities which only took place in this particular area of the Tyrol. The procession formed up in the main square of the village, preceded by the local brass band in picturesque Tyrolean costumes. Players in the brass bands would wear their grey suits with short lederhosen trousers, held up by wide straps which ran from their waists to their shoulders. Over their white embroidered tunics were worn grey jackets with green lapels and rough horn buttons. Finally on their heads they wore the traditional Tyrolean hat with hen or peacock feathers on the side. Footwear consisted of nail studded boots, above which they wore green knee length socks.

The procession around the village was followed by schoolboys and girls in their traditional Sunday clothes, the girls in long white dresses, the boys dressed in their best suits. They were followed by all the young men and girls of the village in national costume.

They in turn were followed by a considerable number of men, one from each farm, carrying an upright pole twenty to twenty-five feet long. These poles of white wood were decorated with crepe paper of different colours, spiralling down from top to bottom of the pole. Some were white and red, others yellow and green or blue and red or white and yellow. Suspended from the top of the pole by four colourful ribbons was a hoop. These hoops were also garnished with the same crepe paper as the pole. Some were cleverly wrapped in chains of leaves or foliage. Neatly suspended from the hoops hung various items of produce, which were going to be part of the Easter dinner fare. It could be a bottle of local wine, or cider, or even champagne. It could be a whole smoked ham, or a garlic sausage, or a specially baked bread, shaped either in the form of a cross or a lamb. The procession was then made up of various groups of men carrying religious statues representing various saints or patrons. All the banners of the church were carried by strong men, as were the richly decorated statues of saints. Behind them was carried a statue of the Virgin Mary. This group were accompanied by men, who in true Tyrolean style, carried a hunting rifle.

The ladies also appeared in the procession wearing a traditional Tyrolean skirt made of black material, held up by shoulder straps or braces of the same colour. Beneath a tight fitting bodice, they wore white blouses with puffy, short sleeves, leaving their arms uncovered below the elbow. In contrast to the black and white of their skirts and blouse, they wore over the skirt colourful aprons, with embroidered designs of Alpine flowers. Their knee length socks were usually white and their shoes black, ornamented with metal buckles. Many of them were carrying wreaths of flowers to be placed at one or other of the shrines at which the procession would halt for a moment on its winding route to Mariathal church.

The end of the procession was no less picturesque. It consisted of a military band followed by a detachment of troops, preceding and surrounding a priest, who walked slowly under a canopy supported by four men. Walking behind him were several members of his retinue, carrying the holy sacraments, all dressed like the priest in richly ornamented surplices and vestments. Accompanying the priest and his retinue were choirboys in their austere black and white gowns, at their head one carrying the cross, accompanied by two or three choirboys, carrying and swinging at regular intervals, the silver incense burners hanging at the end of long chains. Finally behind the canopy came the mayor and aldermen of the village, the officers of the garrison and other dignitaries. On either side of the procession, soldiers marched in slow time, with rifles at their sides, bayonets attached.

The procession left the village square and by a prearranged route, went through the winding country lanes around the boundary of the village. Each time the end of the column reached a shrine built beside a crossroad, the whole procession would come to a standstill and the priest under the canopy would bless the statue. Then on a signal relayed from the back to the front of the column, the head of the procession would move off again.

When it eventually reached Mariathal church the pole bearers placed themselves on both sides of the porch in a half circle, while the rest of the procession entered the church to attend holy mass. Meanwhile during the service, the pole bearers put their poles down, resting them vertically on the ground and whilst still having to support them, they were able to engage in a friendly chat.

Members of the local band had adjourned to the bar of the gasthaus opposite the church, to recover with the help of beer, all the saliva spent in blowing their brass instruments. The military band was not so fortunate and together with the escort troops had to take up positions opposite the church in front of a convent. After nearly an hour's wait, the mass suddenly finished and all the worshippers came thronging out through the main door of the church. They jostled for good positions on the square, some behind the troops, others behind the local band, who by then had taken up position opposite the military band. At a signal given by a bugle, the bearers lifted their poles back into their harnesses. The soldiers were ordered to present arms. The band then played a hymn, which the assembled crowd sang. The priest, now dressed in a plain surplice, said short prayers in a loud voice. All the pole bearers now faced him in a half circle. The priest now proceeded to bless each pole in turn, emblematically carrying that blessing to the food at the top of the poles and to those who would eat it on Easter Sunday. Following this brief ceremony, the poles were carried back to the farms they came from and stripped of the produce, which would become part of the Easter Sunday fare.

On most of the farms the family would gather, together with their workers, around a big table in the main living room and eat the "Kaisershmarrn," which mainly consisted of a scrambled pancake, which could either be eaten salted or sweetened to taste. In the centre of the table was usually placed a decorated basket full of handpainted hard boiled eggs, which formed part of the Easter morning breakfast. On this occasion Irma and Franz kept to Belgian tradition and had hidden these coloured eggs in the house and the garden. Rene was provided with a basket and was told to hunt for them.

Easter 1918, which like Christmas, was supposed to bring goodwill to all men on Earth, was probably the last celebration in the Austro Hungarian Empire, before unexpected events changed the course of history and still more the geographical maps of Europe. For some time now there had been an atmosphere of unrest. Although the official comuniques reproduced by the national and local press were describing the remarkable victories of the Austrian army and its Allies, this information was contradicted by the news brought back straight from the fighting lines, either by men on leave, or deserters transitting through the village. It took the officers and NCOs of the local camp a good deal of effort and talk to persuade their own men that these rumours were spread by the enemy and that no notice should be taken of them.

Kufstein, Austria July 1918

It was around that time that Franz received a mysterious message from a captain who he did not know, but whose name indicated that he was of Czech origin. This message suggested that he should, as soon as possible, ask one day's leave from his unit and secretly go to Kurfstein to an address given by this officer, where news to his advantage would be given to him. Very intrigued, Franz asked and obtained permission to go on what he pretended was a shopping expedition to Kufstein and to give more credibilty to his alibi, he took Irma with him. As soon as they got to their destination, and while Irma really did go shopping, Franz went to the address given in the mysterious message. When Franz asked shyly to see the Czech captain, he was taken immediately to the first floor and taken to the captain's office. Captain Miroslav Capek met him with outstretched hands and after a cordial welcome, invited Franz to sit down. Having made sure that the doors were properly shut Captain Capek made a gesture to Franz to come and sit nearer to him. First he asked him for his identification papers, then satisfied that he really had in front of him the man he wanted to see, he explained the reason for their meeting.

Franz and Miroslav were seated close together and Miroslav talked to Franz in a hushed voice, which made Franz uneasy. But Miroslav soon dispelled the unease Franz felt in these first few moments of their meeting by telling Franz that he was a personal friend of his brother Paul, that he knew all about Franz's family and their devotion to the Czech cause. Miroslav said that he also had a complete file on Franz, describing his military career, including the incident at Sopron involving Irma.

Franz, not knowing if this was an Austrian trap, remained non-committal and listened more than he talked. Miroslav went on to explain that since Franz had always done his duty in the Austrian army without ever volunteering for anything and had only done what he was ordered to do, this was a clear indication he had acted as a good Czech, but now would come the opportunity to really show his attachment to the Czech cause.

Miroslav went on to explain that the well-known and respected Czech national leader, Thomas Masaryk, whilst based in Paris, had managed to organise a movemement that was expanding each day. Soon, he explained, all the Czech brethren although dispersed in different units by the Austrians would be drawn into a vast spider's web covering the whole of the army. He also explained that other subject nations were involved in similar conspiracies, the leaders of which, were working in close liaison. Having explained this, Miroslav went on to say that he had been recruited by a Czech major whose name he could not reveal, who was stationed in a different town. He was now instructed to await orders for further action from the major. Having managed to convince Franz of the genuineness of his intentions he made him take a solemn oath of faithfulness to the Czech cause.

He then swore the young recruit to secrecy and gave him his first, assignment. "You will go back to your unit" he said, "and work out carefully a complete list of all Czech officers, N.C.Os and men under your command. You will only have contact yourself with one Czech sub-lieutenant under your command, but only after we have first investigated him and only when we give you the all clear. You will approach him in the same way as I did with you. You will need to make him take the oath and he must promise never to reveal your name and you must never tell him from whom you receive your orders. You will instruct him on who should be approached next by him and so the spider's web will gradually expand to every Czech soldier serving under your command. As soon as the recruitment is completed I shall convey to you by the safest possible means, accurate and real information about the course of the war and you will see to it that this news cascades down to the humblest of the Czech soldiers and therefore, develops their hopes for their future and ours. Make sure that it gets known by all new recruits to our cause that secrecy and patience will be the essentials for success, and when the moment comes, obedience to our leaders will influence the outcome of the enterprise."

Franz took leave of the captain and rejoined his wife in town. She was a bit puzzled at the sight of her husband seeming to be in an unusually good mood, but with the discretion learned by an officer's wife she did not ask any questions. Thus Franz did not need to lie and his secret remained safe.

Kramsach, Austria, September 1918

As soon as Franz got back to Kramsach he went to work on the task he had been given and the day after his meeting, with Miroslav's agreement, he swore in one of his Czech lieutenants and one month later he was able to provide Miroslav with a complete list of all the Czechs under his command.

On 8th September, Franz was informed by Headquarters that Colonel Klingspor had had to deal with the death of his only son, a student aged 19 years, that morning. The young man had been suffering from tuberculosis for a while. Franz took the sad news home to Irma and they agreed to phone the headquarters in the afternoon to find out if it would be convenient to visit the Colonel and his wife and offer their condolences. When Franz contacted the adjutant in the late afternoon he could not believe his ears when told that Colonel Klingspor had himself died only ten minutes earlier. Apparently that morning, when his son died in his arms, he seemed to take the tragedy very bravely, as the soldier and nobleman he was, and he tried to console his wife and daughters. He then went to his office to attend to the most pressing duties and make arrangements for his son's funeral. He had gone home earlier than usual to prepare a list of all the relatives to be notified. It was while sitting and writing that suddenly he gasped and fell face forward onto the table. The events of that morning had been too much for the poor man and a heart attack had taken him away, three months too early to see the liberation of his beloved Hungary.

The funeral of father and son took place a few days later. They were escorted with full military honours from the mortuary to the local church and after a full mass, they were both buried in the cemetery at the back of the church. Irma went to the funeral, but Franz had been instructed to take his unit into the hills overlooking, Brixlegg and to position his artillery guns above the cemetery. A field telephone had been installed and as the funeral procession was leaving the mortuary he would be informed, and would have to order a prescribed number of rounds to be fired. He had been informed of the length of the journey and had worked out the spacing out of the shots accordingly. But when he ordered the first round to be fired, he discovered to his horror, that the ammunition depot which had supplied the blank cartridges had forgotten to insert the disc of cork which usually replaced the normal shell and simulates the sound of a detonation. As a result of this, all that was heard by those at the cemetery was a series of noises similar to those made by a firework rocket on its journey from the ground to its point of explosion. Little did Franz know that the events of the next few months would make more noise than the sound of his guns.

Between July and August 1918 visitors had brought to the village a disease, which for a while, had been causing anxiety to the health authorities of the neighbouring towns. It was an unknown virus, causing what came to be known as the 'Spanish Flu'. Numbers of people were dying after a very short and ravaging illness. The military authorities tried to prevent the spread of the disease to the army camp by putting most parts of the village and the surrounding towns out of bounds to the forces.

This did not help to improve the already faltering morale of the soldiers. Most depressed were the pure Austrians, because by then the

Czechs and the members of other enslaved countries were receiving the news through their respective organisations. The Austrians became increasingly depressed by the war communiques, which by now were acknowledging that victory was still far away. This only served to ensure that their other imperial troops felt that their hour of liberation was coming nearer.

By the late summer of 1918 the epidemic of Spanish flu was taking its toll amongst the armed forces. Soldiers were dying by the hundreds and Rene always remembered the one occasion when his father took him to the local cemetery to watch the burial of a soldier, with full military honours. The sounding of the last post, the farewell salvo, all left quite an impression, but what he remembered most was the long row of freshly dug graves ready to receive the next victims of the epidemic.

Although, by then, the soldiers were confined to barracks, because it had been proved that the epidemic had been brought by a soldier returning from the frontline and the military authorities wanted to avoid the spreading of the epidemic to the civilian population. The ugly illness still found a few victims amongst the local inhabitants. One such victim was a young girl of eighteen years and Rene witnessed her funeral. The coffin and the hearse were entirely painted white and all the wreaths and floral tributes were made only of white flowers.

The next tragedy to strike was a series of mysterious forest fires high up on the mountain sides. On each occasion, the local authorities called on the help of the army to fight the fires. Franz's unit went up and the only practical way to isolate the fire was to quickly fell trees outside the range of the fire zone and create a clearing where only grass would be set alight by the burning trees. The men would then stand in line facing the advancing fire and beat it down by digging earth or striking the flames out with the flat of their shovels. When, after three days and nights of strenuous labour, the men came down, they were all exhausted, their faces and hands blackened by the smoke and their working uniform bearing the traces of their ordeal.

The first indication of a breakdown in the military power of Austria came only a few weeks later, when it was reported to Franz that the local military police had arrested an ever growing number of Austrian soldiers who had deserted the Italian front and had been caught while trying to board trains to Vienna or the east of Austria. Soon their numbers became so large, that there were not enough police to arrest them and the cells were unable to house them. Many of them had been plundering farms or houses on their way, helping themselves to wine and food. Then drunk, like the whole of Poland, they had found their way to the trains. Nobody dared to challenge them. They had their guns loaded and at their sides and in their state would not have hesitated to make use of them.

By now, with their numbers growing, there was not enough room in the railway carriages for them all. Ignoring the regulations which reserved first class carriages for officers, they invaded every compartment, every inch of space in the corridors and every luggage van. Quite a number of them had to sit on the steps outside, at each end of the carriages and suffer the soot poured on them by the train's engine and the wind. Quite a number of the more daring ones, having failed to find any space in the carriages, climbed on to the rooves and regardless of the protests of the railway staff, decided that this was how they would complete the journey. When these trains arrived at Brixlegg, the local stationmaster ordered the men off, warning them of the danger of a low tunnel quite near. But they flatly refused to come down unless the stationmaster could provide extra carriages. When he attempted to dislodge them with the help of his staff, the men, crazy and drunk, showed that they meant business by firing with their rifles in the direction of the nearest field which resulted in the killing of several cows. The stationmaster then had no other option than to order the train to resume its journey and what he had foreseen, happened. Quite a number of men on the rooves, either because they were not lying flat or because they were not on the centre of the roof, got hit by the masonary and the ceiling of the tunnel. Their deaths were instantaneous.

Meanwhile in Kramsach, at the army training centre, the situation was also becoming critical. While the soldiers of the enslaved nations were calmly awaiting orders from their respective secret organizations to move, the Austrian officers, N.C.Os and men, could feel the tension between them and the others growing and they had one thing in mind – to run before the situation exploded.

One day Franz came home earlier than usual. He seemed very nervous and told Rene to remain in the sitting room and not to go out of the house under any circumstances. He asked Irma to go into the bedroom where they had a long conversation. When they came back, Irma told Rene that a revolution had started. That meant soldiers were coming back from the front line and using their last ammunition on any moving target they could see. She confirmed his father's instruction that Rene must stay indoors.

That same evening, Franz brought several rifles into the house and he demonstrated to Irma and to Sister Julie how to load and fire a rifle. That night Franz and Irma went to bed after placing the rifles on a chair near their bed, in easy reach and ready to meet any intruder. In fact they were disturbed by the noise of steps on the outside balcony which surrounded the whole of the first floor of the farm, but probably when the intruder saw the lights go on inside, he fled.

Next morning Franz left very early for the barracks and again came back earlier than usual. Irma and Sister Julie hurriedly packed belongings for the family's use. A little later Franz and Sister Julie's husband returned with a small ammunition cart, a two wheeler pulled by one mule. The senior NCO and Franz's batman helped him to carry the packed cases on to the ammunition cart. Then the assembled group, Franz, Irma, and their children accompanied by Franz's batman, Sister Julie and her husband, the senior NCO, left the farm for an agreed point in the village, where they met other officers' families and their transport. They soon started a long climb along what was more of a mountain track than a road. At some places the mules got stuck and the men had to push and heave to help the overtired animals. Eventually they reached the top.

The valley below them, with many richly fertile fields contrasted strangely with the thick pinewood forest or the rugged mountain side bordering the track that had led them up. The officers had hoped that in the village on the hilltop, their families would be protected from the wild plundering of the passing deserters. The movement of soldiers leaving the front had increased to the scale of a real exodus and on their way to their homes, they were helping themselves to whatever they found useful.

The villagers had reacted very quickly to this situation by guarding their stores and barns and openly displaying their strength by carrying their hunting rifles on their shoulders at all times. One problem the officers had not reckoned with was the hostility shown suddenly by the civilian population to them and their families. The farmers on the hillside bluntly refused to let them have any of their supplies, giving as a reason, the present situation and the fact that the disruption of transport might endanger their own supplies for the coming winter.

After an assessment of the situation, it was agreed that the next morning, Franz and another officer would go down into the valley and see if things had improved and whether it would not be wiser to return to the village where the officers were well known and had always entertained friendly relations with the local authorities and the civilian population.

Towards the end of the following day Franz and his colleague returned to say that the situation in Brixlegg, Rattenberg and Kramsach was improving and suggested that the families spent only the one more night in the unfriendly village on the hill top. The next morning they started their trek back to the valley at the crack of dawn and this proved to be as horrendous as the climb. Although the ammunition carts had wooden brakes operating on the wheel rims, the blocks were a bit worn out and failed to brake the cart sufficiently. To help the poor mules, who had to hold back the vehicle, some narrow tree trunks were placed horizontally between the two wheels, immobilizing them completely, and from then on the vehicle was pulled down like a sledge. As soon as they got back to Kramsach, families went back to their respective farms, whilst the officers went to the army HQ to decide on further action.

During the stay in the hilltop village, Rene had, without scruples or remorse, made himself guilty of stealing by finding. With the hope that villagers would be kinder to children than to adults, their parents had given them some money and encouraged them to call on the farmers and offer to buy some of their produce. Rene finding an old woman working in a field asked her if he could buy some of the radishes she was collecting. Her answer was, "I have no use for your money which soon will be worthless. I'd rather keep the stuff for myself or for barter."

Disappointed he walked to the next field, where he got the same response. Deciding to return to the inn, which was the family's base whilst staying in the village, he walked back through the country lane, when suddenly in front of him, he saw the old woman from the field, walking slowly in the same direction as himself. She was carrying on her shoulders a heavily loaded bag full of radishes.

Unbeknown to her, there was a hole at the bottom of the bag from which radishes dropped each time she moved. Rene had already noticed the trail she had left behind her and he picked up the radishes and gathered them in his basket. By the time he got to the inn, his basket was nearly full. These radishes, sliced and placed on top of country bread,covered with cream cheese, never tasted as good as on that one occasion.

On the morning that Franz had received precise instructions from the Czech underground movement in Kufstein regarding his future orders and that of his Czech subordinates, he was about to organize their briefing, when one of his loyal N.C.O.s came to warn him that events were coming to a head in the camp. Under the leadership of a few braver, or possibly more undisciplined men, the bulk of the Austrian soldiers had broken into the food stores.

In a matter of minutes Franz ordered his N.C.O. to openly gather all the Czechs, fully armed, in one corner of the camp. This being done, for the first time in his life, he gave them his instructions in their mother tongue. While one unit was sent to guard the ammunition and weapon stores, and make sure that no Austrian could lay his hands on them, Franz followed by the others, got to the food store where a most unpleasant scene awaited him. Hundreds of men were trying to push their way into the stores, while others with arms full of their loot, were trying to push their way out, losing a large part of their goods in the attempt. The ground was littered with precious food.

In a moment Franz assessed the situation. If order had to be restored it had to be done firstly inside the store. With the help of his men. Franz managed to undo an air vent leading into the store. Assisted by two of his N.C.O.s, he squeezed his way inside, revolver in hand, and surprised the looters. Two shots fired in the air caused panic amongst them. He then ordered everybody outside and with the help of his compatriots, turned what had been an unruly crowd, into an orderly formation. He told the men to gather around him and in a loud, strong voice told them that he understood their anxiety and their wish to depart, but that the way they had acted so far would not help anybody. He now told them to form a single line to the stores, that distribution of food would be organized in an orderly manner and that every man would receive as much as he could carry. A few minutes later some of the Czech soldiers had organized the store. One by one the Austrians walked in and at each table were given different types of food, which they fitted into their kit bags. Having obtained their supplies they quietly walked out and most of them came to say goodbye to Franz and thank him for what he had done for them.

Whilst this was going on Franz had sent one of his trusted men to ensure the safety of the wives and children of the officers and N.C.O.s billeted in Mariathal. He was soon informed that events had taken a new turn at the Officers' Mess in Mariathal and that he would be well advised to get there as soon as possible. Franz got there as fast as his horse could take him up the slopes to the village. On approaching the Officers' Mess, which was installed in the hotel opposite the old church, Franz noticed a considerable number of men of the village, all dressed in their national costume and holding their rifles at the ready. They were all drawn up two hundred yards from the Mess, facing it and ready for action.

When Franz went by they greeted him, but not with the usual respect they had previously shown to officers. Reaching the Mess, Franz heard loud arguments going on in one of the rooms. Here he found Major Baron Krelmeyer in heated discussion with the mayor and members of the Council. Franz soon discovered, that the major had placed a guard of men he trusted around the field where the army horses were grazing that morning, with instructions to shoot on sight anyone who attempted to go near the horses.

The mayor had come with a deputation to ask the Major to hand over these horses to him and his villagers, and to do it before there were too few troops to look after them properly. The Major had shown himself most uncooperative, arguing that he could not take responsibility for releasing them. The mayor was about to depart, after having warned the major that he and his villagers would take the law into their own hands and would forcibly take possession of the horses.

Franz decided it was time for him to intervene. Taking his revolver out of its holster and pointing it at Major Krelmeyer, Franz said, "Today the voice of the strongest is the one that counts. How dare you endanger the security of our families and antagonize the villagers against us, when you have a carriage ready outside to take you and your family away to safety. Well Major, you are now going to be a good boy and sit down and sign an order cancelling your instructions of this morning. After that you had better disappear with your family while I shall settle with the mayor the details of the handover." The Major did not offer the slightest resistance. Like a lamb he sat down and signed the paper. Franz having seen that he had done as he had been told let him go without another word being exchanged between the Major and himself. A few minutes later the Major's carriage departed.

Franz, meanwhile, had settled down to a bottle of wine shared with the mayor and councillors, while they discussed the method for the handing over of the horses. Franz suggested that the mayor should produce a list of all villagers and the number of horses they would require, and on delivery, everyone would sign a receipt, countersigned by the mayor and handed over to Franz. This was agreed by both parties and the mayor, on behalf of the councillors present, congratulated Franz on his well timed intervention, without which there might have been some bloodshed. He even invited Franz and his subordinates to join the new Home Guard, formed that very day with the purpose of preventing plunder and chaos and safeguarding private property. Franz accepted and was soon provided with special badges and red and white armbands to be worn over the uniform. That same morning every soldier discarded from his uniform any sign, button or badge bearing the imprint of the crumbling empire, and reported to the local authorities for briefing, but everyone also knew that their real chief was Franz, and that as soon as he spoke they would follow his instructions.

He was waiting with anxiety for a word from Captain Capek and meanwhile spent his time supervising the work and welfare of his men. A few days later the expected order came. Franz was to instruct his men to hitch-hike their way to a small village sixty miles north of Linz, where he would join them and brief them on their next duties. Those men who had only themselves to look after, left practically immediately, but those officers and N.C.O s who had their families with them, quickly returned to their billets to arrange with one or the other the safe keeping and providing for their loved ones, until they could come back and fetch them. Franz made arrangements on behalf of all of them with the mayor, who promised to look after their safety and supplies in exchange for certain army equipment, which until then Franz and his men had hidden from the villagers.

When Franz came back to the farm he told Irma that he had to leave the next day for the Czech border, but he had made provision with the local authorities that they would be looked after whilst he was away, and supply the family with food. Thus reassured Franz and his N.C.O.s took leave of their wives and children and started their journey to the agreed meeting point. He left early next morning and it took several weeks before Irma heard from him. The postal service in Austria had broken down completely and the newly formed Czechoslovakian state had isolated itself entirely from Austria, until its frontiers were definitely agreed and recognized by treaty.

Studansky, Bohemia, October 1918

Franz and one of his most trusted N.C.Os. were lucky enough to find room on a direct train to Vienna and therefore reached Linz in a few hours. From there they managed to find road transport to the assembly point. Franz and his travel companions reached the village about the same time as the first contingent of their men, Whilst they stayed on the market square to wait for the others, he went to look for the gasthaus where Captain Capek would send him a messenger with the latest instructions. After a long wait these instructions finally came. They explained briefly that Studansky, the village in which Franz and his men were assembled, had been chosen by President Masaryk as the most southerly point of the future Czechoslovak State. As from 0024 hours, on that day, they were to take up positions facing south. Checkpoints were to be established on all roads and they were to be properly guarded.

No Austrian was to be allowed to travel north unless he could prove that he belonged to one of the new border defences or could prove he was a Czech or a Slovak.

Railway lines were also dismantled beyond signals north of Linz, after they had been set to indicate danger. The army was to take control of the nearest telegraph and post offices and cut off all communication with villages south of the new demarcation line. The army, now called the Czech Liberation Army, was soon provided with new badges and national colours, lately devised by the nationalist leadership and instructions to hold and secure their respective positions until such time as Masaryk had obtained the recognition of his country and the acceptance by all the great powers of the new borders, as defined by him. Meanwhile, any attempts by the Austrians to regain control of Czech soil would have to be met by force.

But such an attempt never came. A country which had for centuries ruled other nations with a population six times its own size, was too busy licking its wounds, and the little energy that its people had left was being used to prepare their country for the huge change from an absolute monarchy into a democratic republic. A few weeks went by and Franz and his men were in full control of an area of about ten square miles and were in close contact with other Czech units. Internal communication had been well organized and allowed all the men to get news to their families within the new republic and also receive reassuring news from their relatives. The ones who were not so fortune were those, like Franz, who had left their families south of the border in the Tyrol, as all communications with that area were cut. Nevertheless Franz obtained a promise from his immediate superior officer that Irma and the other wives would be contacted at the earliest opportunity by their newly organized secret service.

The wait was long and worrying. Another two weeks elapsed and back came the news from Kramsach. All the wives and children were in good health and spirits However, Irma informed Franz that the local authorities had severely reduced their food supplies on the grounds of shortages. As the rations supplied by the local authorities were very inadequate, Irma was really worried at baby Georgette's state of health.

Having heard that the Italian army had marched down the Brenner Pass and were now occupying Innsbruck she had decided to venture to that picturesque city to try and make contact with those she considered as her allies. Taking little Rene with her, she decided to pay a visit to the Italian army HQ in Innsbruck and request their help as a citizen of an allied country stranded in enemy territory.

Georgette had been left that day in the care of Sister Julie. The trip to Innsbruck was not to be in vain. This was demonstrated when Irma returned with a large sized potato sack full of goods which the family had not enjoyed for years, such as bananas and oranges, which Rene had not tasted since the family left Belgium at the beginning of the war. Other typical Italian foods, however were completely new to him.

She found the headquarters of the Italian army was located in a large luxury hotel opposite the station. Irma told Rene some years later that she went full of apprehension to the hotel used as a headquarters by the Italians. She pretended to speak only French. Twenty minutes after speaking to the soldier on duty at the reception desk, he called an officer, a lieutenant, to whom she had to tell her story. He asked her to wait in the lounge whilst he referred her case to his superiors. She was then interviewed in turn by a captain and a major who were impressed by her frankness, her deportment, her straight answers to their questions and the insistent way she had said that the purpose of her visit could only be revealed to their commanding officer.

The colonel, when informed, was intrigued and asked that she be brought to meet him. She was not kept waiting very much longer before the officer returned and asked her to follow him, informing her that she would be introduced to his colonel. She was received very courteously by the colonel who bore a long aristocratic name. As soon as she entered the large room being used as the colonel's office, he came forward and kissed Irma's hand, inviting her and the little boy to sit as near as possible to his desk. The colonel listened with great interest to her story. She explained in a few words the whole situation. For four long years she had been living amongst her country's enemies and now more than ever they were turning against her, taking advantage of the fact that she was temporarily deprived of the protection of her husband.

The colonel quickly grasped the situation. Whether it was because he had an admiration for Belgium or because he appreciated the fact that Franz, after having been a member of the Czech liberation movement, was now an officer of an allied army, the fact remains that the colonel went out of his way to make Irma feel that the Italians in general and he in particular, owed it to her, to help her.Firstly he promised to deliver messages by the quickest means possible to the Adler family in Belgium and to get news in return to reassure Irma about their whereabouts. Next he told Irma that he would assure her safety and provide supplies until such time as her husband could return to fetch her.

Next he invited her for lunch at the officers' mess where he introduced all his officers to her. The atmosphere was excellent and when the time came for Irma to catch her train back to Kramsach, the colonel instructed his own batman to take charge of the food sack which on his instructions, had been prepared. The orderly had been instructed to fill a large bag with food and to carry it for her to the station. She was told that a similar supply would be delivered to her every week and the colonel suggested that on her next visit to Innsbruck she should come and have lunch with him. He escorted Irma personally to the station, chose a compartment for her and bid her farewell kissing her hand and requesting her to come back with her husband as soon as possible.

Back at the Missbaum Farm she unpacked the bag and could not believe her eyes. There was a quantity of various types of macaroni, sugar, precious coffee, cocoa, tea, pure cooking fat which was completely different from the donkey fat that Irma had had to use for the best part of the war and which jumped out of the frying pan like the chamois in the mountain. Pastries and sweets had not been forgotten. The first week Irma kept most of the supplies for her family and for the wives of the Czech N.C.O.'s who had remained in the village with her, but when she saw that the promised supplies came regularly each week and were more ample than required by her family, she started to barter some of them with the villagers in exchange for fresh goods such as milk, butter, eggs, and wine. This method of payment was more appreciated than the Austrian money, the purchasing power and value of which, had grossly depreciated.

Much to Irma's regret she was never able to return to Innsbruck again with her family to meet the kindly Italian colonel who had shown them such generosity, because Franz arrived back unexpectedly and instructed Irma to pack all the family's belongings and to await a message telling her that she and the children could join him in Prague. He then rushed to the station to catch the next train for Prague.

A few uneventful months went by when, finally, news came that the Versailles conference had agreed on the 28th June 1919 to the breaking up of the Austrian-Hungarian Empire. Out of its partition Czechoslovakia, Hungary, Yugoslavia, and Albania emerged as independent, and sovereign states. Czechoslovakia became a republic and its first president was to be Thomas Masaryck, who as soon as the official documents had been signed, left for Prague, where a hero's welcome awaited him.

As soon as the boundaries of the new country had been established, the duties of Franz and his men were taken over by newly appointed and freshly uniformed customs officials. They got back to Prague just in time to be fitted with new Czech uniforms and to take part in the huge parade to be inspected by the new president. New medals, acknowledging their part in the liberation of their country, were also issued. Years later Franz would still describe this unique occasion, where the most hardened soldiers shed tears of joy. He was confirmed in the rank of first lieutenant in the new nation's army and soon, having been informed that he would be stationed for a while in the new capital of the country, he sent word to Irma to pack her cases and to come and join him.

Prague, Czechoslovakia 1919

Irma and the children took their leave of Sister Julie and her husband and left without regret the village where they had known happy days, but where they had felt very unwelcome since the collapse of the Austro Hungarian Empire. A few days later they were reunited and a room was waiting for her and her children at the apartment of her mother-in-law. This was a large modern apartment in a large building next to the Opera House and facing the River Moldau. From the balcony one had a marvellous view of Prague Castle and the Charles Bridge. A few happy weeks were spent visiting all Franz's relatives, then came the time to decide on a return to Belgium.

In the spring of 1919 Franz had been informed that he could apply for his release from the army whenever he wanted, and he had also been informed that he could avail himself of the diplomatic train travelling three times a week between Prague and Paris. He therefore made arrangements and fixed the date for the family's departure, but it so happened that two days before this date, the diplomatic train, on its way to Paris, was the object of a vicious act of sabotage. While on its way through the Austrian Tyrol, a bomb placed by Tyrolean nationalists, had exploded, blowing the track away over a distance of a hundred metres and causing the derailment of the whole train. It so happened that the officers' carriage was the only one which broke away from the rest of the train and crashed down the slope of the mountain, killing all but one of its occupants.

Irma was so shocked at the news that she insisted that Franz cancel their reservations and that they should travel on an ordinary, less conspicuous train. From a journey of a few hours, this became a seven day trek. The details of this journey are lengthy and almost too tedious to recount. Suffice to say that everything that could go wrong happened, including avalanches, hours spent in carriages with broken windows and no heating. There were goods to be loaded and unloaded at every station possible, and more time spent in shunting, than in actual travel.

At some point in the Tyrol the railway tracks had been hit by an avalanche. The train stopped at a safe distance from the gap in the track, which had been created. Passengers had to transfer to a train on the other side of the gap by a narrow bridge hastily built by the army engineers. Rene was carried across that bridge by a tall Italian Besaglieri soldier and his hat, decorated with black capercaillie feathers, which seemed to shimmer with the colours of the rainbow, greatly impressed the little boy.

The other thing that impressed him was the manner in which the seating of Italian railway compartments could be converted during the night into six couchettes.

The journey involved travelling from Prague into Austria via Linz, then onto Salzburg and Innsbruck, where it was found that the blown up section of the Arlberg had not yet been repaired. Travellers were, therefore, forced to take a train over the Brenner Pass into Italy and from there to the south of France. As elsewhere, tracks were still being repaired as a result of war damage in many places and the co-ordination of the time table had been neglected since the outbreak of the war. It meant many changes of train and many long hours waiting between connections at the various stations.

As the Italian colonel in Innsbruck had kept his promise and managed to locate Irma's parents, she had received from him, prior to leaving Prague, the address at which the Adler family could be found. Her father was on his way to India, but her mother and younger sister were planning to meet her in Paris. In their message, they gave her the time and place where they would be. Irma had previously notified her mother of their original plan, then informed her by telegram of the alterations to their travel arrangements, indicating that their eventual date of arrival was as yet unknown. When Irma and Franz reached the last stage of their journey, and prior to boarding the train to Paris, Irma was lucky enough to contact her mother at her hotel and give her the correct time of their arrival at Paris Gare de Lyon station.

Paris 1919

This explains how it was that Madame Adler, her youngest daughter Renee, and the old and faithful maid, Lisa, were at the station to meet the train. This moment, which had been so long awaited by the whole family was full of tension and excitement. After their first embraces, their eyes filled with tears of joy and happiness. Little Rene did not know what it was all about, but seeing the others cry, he found it fit to cry in sympathy. Even little Georgette, who was eighteen months old by then, participated in the concert of tears. But tears of happiness are easier to dry than tears of sorrow and in this case they soon gave way to great excitement. Irma suddenly found herself, having in the space of a few minutes to answer all the questions which had worried her poor mother during all the years of separation. How had her daughter been treated by her enemies? How was it to live amongst them, completely cut off from her country of birth? Was she aware of the suffering that the immediate allies of the Austrians, the hated "Boches," had caused to the Belgian population?

Irma, had as many questions to ask, because although the family had been able to correspond through the war, through the medium of a friend in a neutral country, they had had to be very brief in their messages, mainly on account of the censors. After having told her family of all her war experiences, Irma found that her parents had also had a life full of adventure.

Her father, who at the outbreak of war belonged to an organisation called Garde Civique and which was the equivalent of the Home Guard formed in Britain during World War 11, had been instructed to go with his unit to guard the harbour installations. When the Germans advanced rapidly on Antwerp they had mainly shelled the harbour installations, scoring direct hits on oil storage tanks. Although there was a danger of these tanks exploding at any minute, the brave Garde Civique stayed unperturbed at their posts. It was only when the Germans were at the gates of Antwerp and had made it known that they considered the Garde Civique as freebooters and would, therefore, put in front of a firing squad any man found in possession of a weapon, that the officers told their men to go home and put on civilian clothes. Monsieur Adler had tried to join the army, but was told he was too old to be enlisted.

His only concern then became the safety of his family. He got a berth for all of them, including some cousins, aunts and uncles, and they left that same evening for England. The only two of Irma's family who were left behind were Uncle Louis Strauss, the alderman who had married Irma and Franz, and who was now Acting Burgomaster of Antwerp, and her cousin Marcel Roost who was only 17 years old, but had volunteered for active service. Marcel became, like Franz, an artillery officer, receiving the rank of lieutenant and serving with some distinction during the fighting on Belgian soil.

Each of the Adlers had had their share of war experiences and sufferings. Adolphe Adler had managed to take all his diamond stocks with him to London and since he was very well known to the diamond syndicate in this city, he did not have problems in obtaining the necessary funds to support his family, but as he could not foresee how long the war would last, his first concern was to find himself a job. The diamond syndicate offered him one, which would mean a few months separation at the time from his wife and daughters. His assignment consisted in taking stocks of rough diamonds produced in South Africa, but stored and distributed from London, to far eastern countries. These diamonds, which were not of the finest quality, were traded as industrial diamonds and were very much in demand everywhere, including by the enemy, to be used in certain war industries, mainly in machining the rifling of guns. He was warned that his mission would not be without danger. He was also told that to distract attention he should take with him a supply of cut diamonds to offer for sale and he would get his share in the profits of these sales.

The first trip to India was uneventful, but on the second occasion his wife had decided to accompany him. Their daughter, Helene, who had become engaged to an Englishman named Eddie Nathan, whose family business interests had led his family to take up residence in Singapore, was due to marry in October 1915. Adolphe and Cecile therefore used the business trip as an opportunity to see their daughter married in the Maygom Aboth Synagogue in that city. There they were joined by their eldest daughter, Emmy Manasseh and her husband Rupert, who had also taken up residence in the city following their marriage in 1912. Now, three years later, it was to be their third daughter, Helene, who was to marry Edward Sassoon Nathan, based in Singapore and who, apart from sharing his family's involvement in real estate, had become a successful bullion dealer. The Nathan family were to give their name to one of Singapore's main thoroughfare's.

The Nathans and the Manassehs, like that other prominent Jewish family, the Sassoons, had become a powerful force within the business communities of Singapore and Hong Kong, as well as throughout that region of south east Asia. Eddie and Rupert had become partners in a business which had been founded by Eddie's father Ezra. By the outbreak of the war it had already established a considerable property portfolio, financed largely by the profits of commodity and currency trading. Eddie was to build a considerable fortune derived not least from his dealings as a bullion trader linked to the Hong Kong Shanghai Bank.

Rupert's brother, Ezekial Manasseh became a distinguished Singapore citizen as a result of his property dealings, leading to the development of the business district and the construction of several landmark buildings. He had also made a significant contribution to the building of the synagogue in which his sister in law was to be married.

Like many British colonial expatriates the Nathans and the Manassehs retained close links with the old country, not least as somewhere to seek the education of their children. Eddie had been sent to England, where he became a boarder at Cheltenham College in Corinth House. Supervised by a master named Ivan Nestor-Schurnmann, it was specifically for Jewish boys. Although Eddie did not shine academically, – he finished thirteenth out of eighteen in his final year, he showed more promise on the sports field, gaining several caps for participation in team games as well as a string of trophies for individual sports.On the rugby field, he was a three quarter and played for the college team in 1900. As a member of the college army cadets he attained the dizzy rank of lance corporal and bugler in the Engineer Corps. In time, the offspring of these two men and their Adler sister brides, would also be sent back to Europe to gain their education.

Returning home Monsieur and Madame Adler had, for the time being, the comfort of knowing that two of their daughters were safely distant from the turmoil besetting Europe. However, for them, the trip nearly ended tragically. On the return journey, the 'Le Gange', a ship of the French company Messageries Maritimes, struck a mine off Bizerta on the Tunisian coast on 16 April 1916, and the "abandon ship" was sounded. Immediately the members of the crew ran to the life boats and took up their positions whilst the passengers, who now for many days had been drilled in such an emergency, calmly went to their cabins to collect their most precious possessions and returned on deck to their assigned lifeboat. There was no panic and although everyone understood the gravity of the situation, the information given by the officers had them realize that the sinking of the ship was not a matter of minutes, but rather of one or more hours. Even if that information was not correct, it had boosted everybodies' morale.

When all passengers had assembled at their lifeboat stations and several lifeboats had been filled, the captain ordered the first boat to be lowered, but the swell was so violent that as soon as the boat hit the water and had been released from its pulleys, it capsized. Ropes and ladders were thrown to the passengers, but most of them were drowned. After that the captain stopped the lowering of the other lifeboats, and disregarding instructions he concentrated on organising the salvage of his ship. He instructed the crew to move some of the cargo towards the hole made in the hull by the mine and to plug it to the best of their ability. Amazingly enough, it did the trick and the boat managed to reach Bizerta. The captain was later rewarded with the Legion of Honour for his actions.

A particularly sad detail of this eventful trip was the loss, when the first lifeboat capsized, of a young Englishman who was on his way home. He had spent many years in India and whilst there, he had married a young Anglo-Indian giirl who later gave birth to twin boys. The children had reached the age of three when their mother suddenly died and the father had then decided to pack up his business and home in India and to return to England. In view of the age of the children they had been assigned to one of the lifeboats reserved for the women. This lifeboat should normally have been lowered first, but as the panic among women and children was at its worst the captain decided to get the next boat down first. Thus the two boys lost their father and with him went all his assets, because he had confided to one or two passengers that he was carrying his whole fortune, converted into pearls and diamonds, in a special pocket fastened to his chest. When passengers were given details of this sad event they organized a collection amongst themselves and a quite impressive amount was placed at the disposal of the captain for the benefit of the two orphans.

The family spent a few more days in Paris, after which it was decided that Madame Adler and her daughter Renee would return to London, where they would need another month to pack and hand over to its proprietors, the house they had occupied during the four years of war. It was decided that young Rene Paul should accompany them, whilst his parents and his sister would return directly to Antwerp.

Adolphe Adler in the
uniform of the
Belgian Garde Civique

Marcel Roost, fourth from left in the
uniform of a lieutenant of artillery in the
Belgian Army 1914 – 1918

Irma Falkenau and her young son Rene
whilst staying at the Pension Adlon,
Vienna 1915

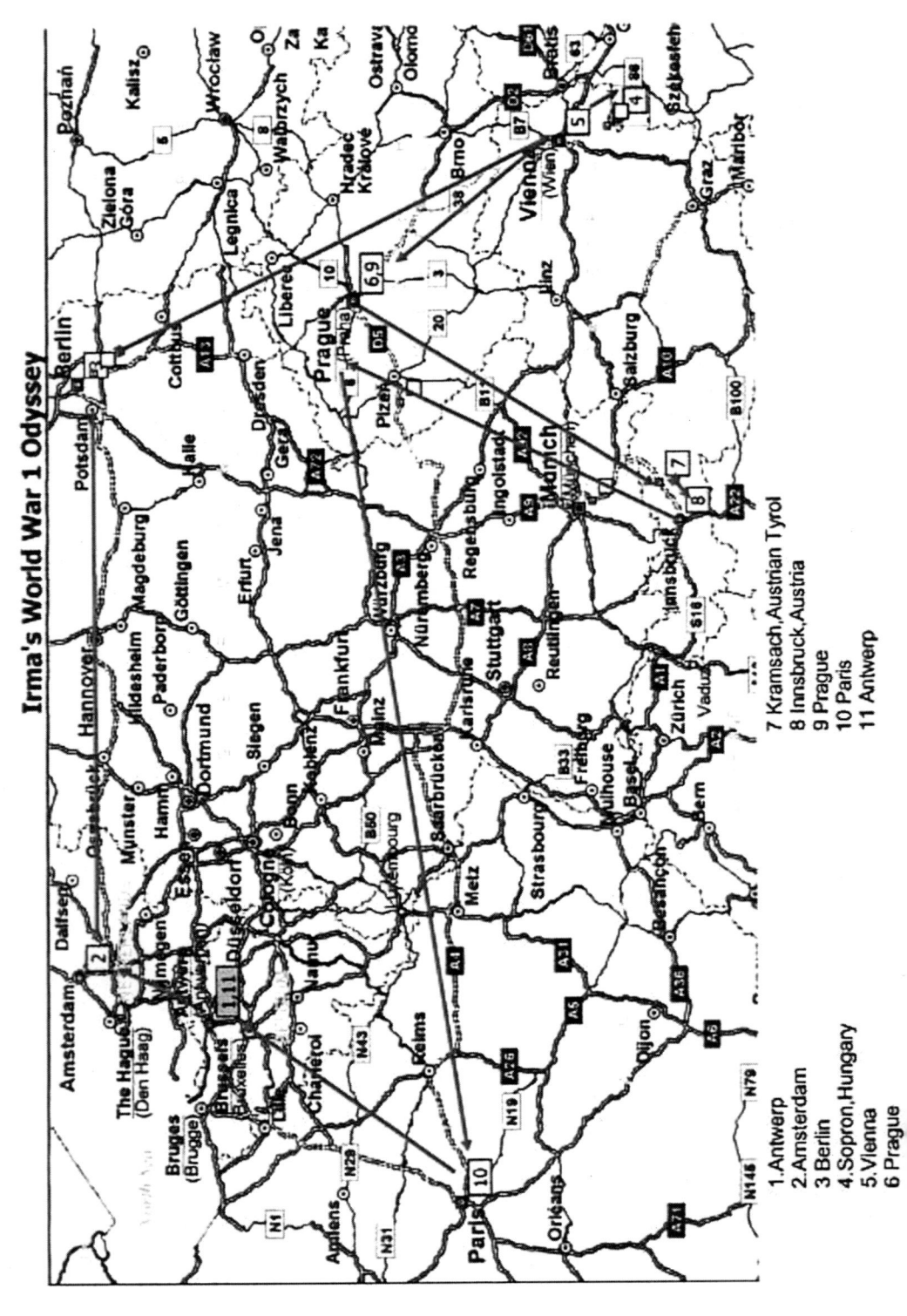

Irma's World War 1 Odyssey

1. Antwerp
2. Amsterdam
3. Berlin
4. Sopron, Hungary
5. Vienna
6. Prague

7 Kramsach, Austrian Tyrol
8 Innsbruck, Austria
9 Prague
10 Paris
11 Antwerp

82

After these few days in Paris, Franz and Irma left by train and got to Antwerp. They were very apprehensive at the state in which they would find their home after four years of absence. A shock was awaiting Franz and Irma at Rue St. Joseph. They had to spend the first few nights in an hotel. The house was still standing, although many windows were missing. The window frame on the second floor had gone altogether. This was explained by the fact that when the Germans had left Antwerp, they had tried to stem the Allied advance by an artillery barrage directed onto the city. All the windows of the house had been shattered by the exploding shells and on the second floor it was found that a German incendiary bomb had ended its journey in the bath. Luckily its trajectory had made it hit the edge of the bath sideways, thus dislodging the firing cap and preventing it from detonating.

A handyman who had worked for the family before the war, noticed the broken windows and window frames when passing the front of the house, and decided to investigate. He borrowed a ladder and climbed into the second floor window. When he found the unexploded shell he came down fast and went to consult with an artillery officer, who advised him to put it in a bucket full of water. From the description given, he said that it probably was an incendiary and told the handyman how to empty it. The silly fellow decided that it would be better to empty the shell at his own house. So up the ladder he went again and carrying the heavy missile on his left shoulder, brought it down and carried it all the way to his home where, after soaking it in his own bath for two days, he scraped the contents out.

Had the trajectory been fractionally one more inch left or right, the shell would have exploded and the house probably burnt to ashes. As it was, he cleaned out the casing and offered it to Irma as a souvenir of the lucky escape.

The house had been occupied during the four years of the war by the German forces. When they had started their retreat they had planned to remove the contents of the house and take them away to Germany. All the pieces of value, crystal, silverware and china had been neatly packed in wooden cases. Furniture had been wrapped in a canvas material. Irma was fortunate to find that although the Germans had planned to take the furniture away, the war had ended so abruptly that they had not been given time to fulfil their mischievous plan.

Although none of the furniture or the precious art works were missing, the fact that they had been packed for removal meant they now had to be unpacked. Crystal chandeliers had been completely stripped. The copper frames were lying in one corner of a room whilst all the crystal pieces had been thrown, luckily without damage, in a large tea chest. For one chandelier alone, a copy of one of the chandeliers of the Palace of Versailles, it took three men seven days to put all the crystal pieces back into position.

By the time Rene Paul came back from England, the house was back into its pre-war state and the only war scars that could be seen were a patched up hole in the bath, and a few pieces of German shrapnel embedded in the side panel of one of the wardrobes. Needless to say that the wine cellar was found empty, not of bottles, but of their contents.

Irma's parents' house had been left untouched, although it had been occupied by German officers during the whole of the war. The old cook, Dina, had stayed on the premises the whole time and cared for it like a watch dog. The only thing she did not manage to prevent was a raid on the famed wine cellar of Monsieur Adler and there too, the German wines were ignored, but 3000 bottles of his best French vintages were missing and all Dina had to show for it was a receipt from the officer who had removed them.

Two weeks after Franz and Irma had moved back into their home, a town official paid them a visit and asked them by what authority they had occupied the house of which he was custodian. It was only then that it was revealed to Irma that as Franz was Austrian, at the outset of the war, he was considered as an enemy alien and the property had been placed, in his absence, in the care of the State Custodian. During the four war years the Custodian was responsible to the occupying forces for the maintenance of the property and when the war ended he again controlled it on behalf of the Belgian Government. Franz explained to him that he was no longer an enemy, following the outcome of the Versailles Conference.

Soon after this gentleman's arrival Franz went to attend to formalities at the Town Hall to retrieve full ownership of the property and furniture which were under the control of the Custodian of Enemy Properties. He soon proved to the authorities' satisfaction that he was no longer Austrian, but a Czech citizen. Thanks to that explanation, the family was allowed to stay on condition that they applied immediately for a court order, cancelling the previous order, which in 1914 classified the property as enemy. Luckily an emergency court heard his case within a few days of his return and the documents proving that he was now a Czechoslovakian citizen and retired officer allowed him to obtain the keys of the house and as a result the requisition order got cancelled.

Franz's main concern after regaining control of the family home was to start earning his living. With the help of his father-in-law's reputation he was admitted immediately to membership of the Antwerp Diamond Club, which is the most important diamond exchange in Antwerp.

London, 1919

In London the Adlers had taken up residence in a large house in Ackroyd Road in Camberwell. The underground railway passed at the bottom of the garden and the escalator at the nearest station constituted a novelty and a great attraction for Rene. He was also impressed by the double decker buses which he had never seen before.

At the end of two months, Madame Adler, her daughter and grandson travelled by train to Harwich where they took the overnight boat to Antwerp. They were just finishing their breakfast in the dining room when they were told that the spire of Antwerp cathedral could be seen in the distance. They went up to the front of the ship, to the highest possible point on the lifeboat deck and were soon faced with a magnificent panorama. Behind two bends of the River Scheldt, the course of which the boat had been following since entering its mouth two hours before, they could now see on their left all the harbour installations of the port of Antwerp. On their right they could see marshland and fields ending with sandy beaches along the bank of the river. In the distance, in front of them the city of Antwerp seemed to be nestling around its cathedral. As their boat glided slowly around a bend, buildings became more distinct. Soon they passed the harbour pilots' building, which controlled the movement of all ships in the harbour and on the river. Next they passed the Stein Castle which has so much to do with the origin of Antwerp.

According to legend a giant by the name of Druon Antigon lived in this castle and who, from this ideal position, could observe the movements of all ships travelling upstream. He would stop the ships and demand a toll from their captains. If they refused to pay, he would imprison them in his castle and cut off their right hand and throw it into the Scheldt. However, one Spanish captain by the name of Brabo put an end to this by challenging the giant. He managed to kill him and following the giant's example, he cut the giant's hand off and threw it into the river. This event is symbolized by a statue in front of the Town Hall. On top of it Brabo can be seen triumphantly holding up the hand of the giant, whilst at the foot of the statue lies the giant's mutilated body, cast as a fountain, water springing from the severed hand. It is said that the origin of the name of Antwerp derives from these events, because in Flemish, "to throw a hand," is "hand wespen." In later times, pronunciation of the H fell out of usage and became Antwerpen. The crest of the city is represented by the castle with two hands above it on either side.

No giant stopped the family's boat, but it slowed down about five hundred yards upstream from the quay and it gradually began to manoeuvre into its berth. By now Madame Adler and her charges could clearly see the place where they were going to dock. As the boat moved nearer, Rene Paul recognized his parents amongst all the people waiting to meet friends and relatives. Next to them and also waving too, were some of Rene Paul's uncles and aunts, who he could not remember meeting before the outbreak of the war. As soon as the ship had been solidly fastened to the dockside and after the usual greetings, a fast car took Rene Paul home to the house where he had been born just over seven years earlier.

Antwerp 1919

It was quite a change for the family to speak French and Flemish again, and this time little Rene, who by now was more accustomed to speak

German, had to be warned of the unpopularity and danger of speaking it. He had returned to Antwerp from England two months after the rest of the family, it having taken Madame Adler a month longer to arrange her return than had been anticipated. The little boy had never heard English before, but with the facility only given to young children, he forgot German as as quickly as he learned it and picked up English with the same speed.

Now he had to re-learn French and Flemish and was sent to school straight away. As soon as he had settled down into the house in Rue St. Joseph his parents made arrangements for him to attend the nearest school, the Ecole Communale No 3 in the Avenue de Belgique. He was unaware then of all the problems that his parents had had to face during the time he was in London and immediately after their arrival in Antwerp.

A week after Rene's return his mother took him to his new school. At the age of eight, he now once more, had to forget the German language which he had mostly been speaking for the past five years, and now speak French, the language which his mother had only used when talking to him in the privacy of the many living quarters in which they had resided during the years of war. In addition to this, he now had to learn Flemish, which was a completely new language to him, but his knowledge of German and its similarity to Flemish made it much easier for him to learn it fast. When, after that first day at school, his mother came to fetch him, he had so much to tell her that the walking distance from the school to home had not been long enough to describe his impressions of the day.

What had impressed him most was that during the break in the morning and the afternoon in the school yard, pupils could go to a window overlooking the caretaker's flat, where he would sell them a choice of glasses of flavoured milk of a type consumed in most Belgian homes. He also had a wide range of cakes, biscuits and sweets for sale at ridiculously cheap prices.

Rene soon made good progress at the school. He liked his teachers and got on very well with his classmates. For the few first days his mother took him to school twice a day and also came to fetch him, but when she discovered that one of the boys in his class only lived a few doors away from them and went to school on his own, it was arranged that in future the two boys would walk to and from school together, without being escorted by an adult. Rene had a very busy time. The classes started at 9.00 in the morning until 12 noon and then from two until five p.m. Rene was usually home by 12.15 and during the forty minutes preceding lunch he was required to study the piano.

The usual routine was that at five minutes to one, when he heard his father come in from the office, he had to wash his hands and be ready to take his place in the dining room at one o'clock. In the later years which followed during which Rene's life was full of unforeseen events, he often remembered the days, the months and the years spent in his parent's home, where routine and a schedule for every activity of the day, were strictly imposed by his father.

His progress at school was remarkable and had it not been for stubborn Jacques Hermann, who always made sure he came top of the form, Rene would not have had to be content with the second place in the class. This went on for four years until it was time to leave the school for the Athenee which would be the equivalent of a grammar school in England.

The diamond cutting factory of Monsieur Adler had been left intact by the war, but the enemy had removed all the machinery which, with a few modifications, could be used for making war materials. Monsieur Adler's factory had been plundered of the hundred precious polishing mills it contained and as the building was now empty, he had decided to give up manufacturing and concern himself solely with the sale and export of cut diamonds. He had therefore, instructed Franz to reserve two offices on the first floor of the Diamond Club. One could be used by Franz, who by now had registered as a broker.

Antwerp 1921

Two years later Franz was elected to the management of this important exchange. The Board of Management of the Diamond Club consisted of fourteen members. One President, one Vice-President, a Secretary, a Treasurer and ten directors. These ten directors were on duty, two at a time for a week, their turn coming up every five weeks. During their week of office, in addition to the normal duties of supervising the staff and watching the smooth and normal running of the Club, they had to be available to members in a special office every afternoon of their week of duty. There they acted as mediators to any members who had a grievance against another member. It is worth noting that since the diamond trade is such a specialized one, the Belgian Government had passed a law which provided that any dispute arising out of dealings between two or more members of a diamond exchange had to be brought in front of specialized tribunals called 'Chambre d' Arbitrage' and composed of directors of the various exchanges.

Normal civil tribunals, if informed that plaintiffs and defendants were both members of an exchange had to declare themselves incompetent to deal with the case. There were five degrees of court, the lowest one being called the ' Chamber of Conciliation', the highest one the 'Appeal Court' composed of five members, a president and four members, one each drawn from the lower courts. Franz thus was quite busy every five weeks doing this voluntary work in addition to his own.

Singapore 1921

In late autumn 1921 Monsieur Adler, who by then had done six trips around the world, decided very abruptly that he wanted another trip to Singapore and Java, only this time he decided to take Franz with him. At first Franz was very reluctant to leave his wife and children for a spell of six months, but his father-in-law soon convinced him that his whole future in the diamond business could well be advanced by the experience he would acquire during his trip.

They left by boat from Marseilles and called at Port Said, Aden, Karachi and Bombay. They interrupted their journey there to call at their Bombay office. This office was managed by a retired British army colonel named H. H. Jenkins. After a few days they travelled on to Singapore where Monsieur Adler was to see his eldest daughter, Emmy Manasseh and third daughter, Helene Nathan.

Franz and his father-in-law made several journeys to the Dutch colonies on Sumatra Island, calling at Batavia and Sourabaya. Diamonds were in so much demand there that as soon as it was known that Monsieur

Adler had arrived at the hotel, people would queue in a waiting room to be able to buy the goods. Very often, after a day or so, he would have to walk into the waiting room and announce that, very regretfully, his supplies of diamonds were exhausted, but that he would replenish them in Singapore and be back the following week, promising to those who had patiently waited, to give them priority the following week. This went on until all diamond stocks in the Singapore office were exhausted and until Monsieur Adler had bought with the money thus obtained, pearls of a quality and price to satisfy the European market.

Bombay, India, January 1922

He and Franz then travelled back to Bombay. Col. Jenkins informed him that he had had to engage a new messenger boy. The fellow in question, when he had come for the interview, had brought with him a number of very flattering letters of reference, but he insisted that Jenkins should read one particular one, adding, "Read this one sir, this best one sir." The letter said ' Would be a very good servant, if he had a little more brain'. Jenkins soon discovered that this last testimonial did not lie, but he did not worry over it, as he did not really need a brainy boy, as long as he was capable of completing the various small assignments given to him. Although he was not intelligent, he had enough brains to become mischievous sometimes. On one occasion this mischievousness turned out to be tragic.

On the 21st January 1922 two telegrams reached Bombay from Antwerp, both were addressed to Jenkins, but received in the office by the Indian boy at two hour intervals. Having forgotten to hand them over to Jerkins as they had arrived, he decided later in the afternoon to give them both to Monsieur Adler, hoping to get more indulgence for his mistake from the big boss. When Monsieur Adler opened one of the telegrams it read, "Inform Monsieur Adler, his wife has died this morning." When he opened the second telegram, which in fact had been the first to arrive it said "Please inform Monsieur Adler with care that his wife is very seriously ill." The way in which Monsieur Adler learned about his wife's death gave him a very serious shock and it took Franz and Colonel Jenkins quite a while to divert his thoughts from the sad news.

When Jenkins found out what the Indian boy had done, he got into a violent temper and before Franz could hold him back, he hit the boy with a violent punch in the stomach. The Indian boy folded in two and Jenkins sent him rolling across the room. This blow could have had very serious consequences for Jenkins, because the British laws were very strict in respect of the way British residents had to behave towards the Indian population.

Luckily the Indian boy had a better nature than might have been expected. Franz having patiently explained to him the cause of Jenkin's anger, the boy was very upset, not so much for what he had done, than for the serious consequences his act could have had. Franz emphasised that the kind of news received and the way it had been delivered to Monsieur Adler could easily have caused a heart attack in a man of his age and disposition, from which he may not have recovered. The boy started to apologize to all concerned and for the rest of the week he looked after Monsieur Adler as if he was his own father.

A few days later the boy was instructed to fetch a horse drawn cab for a shopping expedition Monsieur Adler wanted to do prior to his departure from Bombay. Monsieur Adler, Franz and Jenkins sat inside the cab whilst the Indian boy sat next to the driver. When they came back from their shopping Jenkins asked the driver for the cost of the fare which, as customary in eastern countries, he started to bargain down. At one stage in the discussion the cabbie used a rude word and the Indian boy who had been standing next to Jenkins decided it was about time for him to intervene. So he punched the cabbie exactly in the same way as Jenkins had done to him a few days earlier. A policemen came on the scene attracted by the sight of the crowd which had gathered around the little group by then. Fearing that if the incident was brought to court the Indian boy would possibly reveal where he had learned to use a punch in this manner, Jenkins found it safer not only to pay the fare first demanded by the cabbie, but also to compensate him for the punch. By the time the policeman took his notebook out to take particulars, both parties could report that everything had been settled amicably. Two weeks after this incident Monsieur Adler and Franz were on their way back to Antwerp.

When Franz arrived home he found a very distressed wife. Apart from the sudden death of her mother, she broke the news that during Franz's absence their landlord had died and his next of kin had sold the house to a man who now wanted the house for his own occupation. Notice that the lease would terminate had therefore been served and they would have exactly six months to find another house. Monsieur Adler, who by now had made a nice profit on the sale of his pearls, told the young couple to look for a house of their choice and he would buy it for his daughter. After a long search they eventually found the very house they wanted in the Rue de Palais on the south side of Antwerp, not far from the Palace of Justice.

It was a typical house for an upper middle class family. The double entrance door led by twelve marble steps to an upper ground floor. This was composed of three large rooms, all of the same size and connected to each other. The room nearest the street was the salon or drawing room and was bathed in light from two high, wide, windows. This room contained rich Louis XVI style furniture. In a glass showcase and on a marble table were displayed a number of art treasures in carved ivory.

Double panelled glass doors opened into the dining room, also richly furnished with carved oak sideboards. A table was normally set for six people, but could be extended to seat twelve comfortably. The oak dining chairs had brown leather seats and backs. Lighting was provided by a very large crystal chandelier, which was a copy of one ornamenting the hall of mirrors in the Palace of Versailles. The third room was a smoking room with a wide glass door which lead to the cast iron staircase which descended into the garden.

The layout of the rooms on that floor permitted them to be used as a continuous space in which, on rare special occasions, a table to seat twenty four people could be arranged. To one side of these rooms was a corridor, with staircases leading to the lower ground and upper floors. Off the corridor was a serving room with a dumb waiter connected to the kitchen in the basement, with its still room and cellars. On the first floor was a music room and Franz and Irma's bedroom and bathroom. On the second floor were the two children's bedrooms and their bathroom. On the third floor were the servant's quarters amid the attics.

Franz and Irma liked to entertain and both of them were known to be very good hosts. They enjoyed very good relations with their neighbours. The ladies were very fond of attending the bridge parties organized by Irma and the men always enjoyed Franz's latest jokes. He could also entertain them by playing piano, the guitar or singing a few songs he had composed himself. Sometimes Irma would play the violin and Franz would accompany her. Franz had kept many of the qualities for which the people of his land of birth were well known. He had that unusual gift of being able to play any tune, either on the piano or on the guitar after having heard it only once.

Franz and Irma were to enjoy the comfort of their home at Rue du Palais from 1922 until the outbreak of war in May 1940. During the seventeen years of their existence in this house life went on quietly, pleasantly and uneventfully. The decade of the 1920s were mixed by both pleasure and pain. Irma, her husband and children would enjoy numerous holidays to visit their respective European relatives, as well as relaxing times on the Belgian coast at their favourite beaches of Ostend and Wenduine.

Antwerp 1923

In October 1923 the family of Adolphe Adler celebrated the marriage of his youngest daughter, Renee, to Marcel Roost in Antwerp. The occasion was tinged with sadness at the fact that Adolphe's wife Cecile, who had died in the preceding year at the relatively early age of 55, had not lived to see her youngest daughter married. But it still proved to be a glorious family occasion. The two sisters of Renee and Irma, Emmy Manasseh and Helene Nathan and their respective husbands, Rupert and Eddie on one of their occasional visits to Europe from their homes in Singapore, had brought their children over for the wedding. Emmy's daughter, Irene, who had been born in Antwerp in August 1914, just prior to the outbreak of World War 1 joined her cousins, Cecile and Andree, the daughters of Helene, who had both been born in Singapore and Irma's daughter, Georgette, in providing Renee's bridesmaids. These young ladies looked resplendent in dresses which were smaller copies of the bride's wedding dress. Irma's son Rene was also dressed in a satin suit, befitting his role as groomsman.

The groom Marcel Roost was the son of Emile Roost, the elder brother of Cecile Adler and therefore, Renee Adler's cousin and Adolphe Adler's nephew. Following his service in the Belgian army during World War 1, Marcel had attended university and gained a degree in law. Having followed his father and his uncle Auguste Roost into the practice of law, Marcel had decided to concentrate on commercial law, with a particular specialism in cases involving disputes over insurance claims. Early in his career he had won a high profile case concerning the salvage of a vessel which had been sunk in the mouth of the River Schelde. This was to make his reputation as a lawyer and guarantee his income in the years to come. His bride had shown early talent as a pianist and had studied at Antwerp's Conservatoire de Musique.She briefly followed a career as a concert pianist, before settling for the genteel pleasures surrounding family life.

For young Rene Falkenau the 1920s were occupied with acquiring an education and it was to be a time of unusual opportunity which was to shape the young man's interests and future career aspirations. In autumn 1922 at the age of eleven Rene had transferred to the Athenee at which he would undertake his secondary education. This single sex boys' school was state run and was organised very differently from his primary school. The classes were bigger, with far more pupils lead into class each day by senior prefects. When the boys were seated, one teacher for each subject would walk in turn into the classroom, deliver his lecture, and walk out again without any real contact with his pupils. The supervision of the pupils, – or rather the lack of it, meant that Rene soon became very disgruntled with this school and as a result of this, the first exams he took were a complete failure and he came out one place from bottom of his form.

Rene's parents became very worried and arranged for him to get private tuition from a young mathematics teacher at his school. Twice a week after the classes, Rene would travel together with his tutor on the tramcar to his home, where they would have tea and he would receive two hours of mathematics tuition, his weakest subject.Rene did not know whether it was because his teacher had a very aquiline nose or because he had very square shoulders, that the boys in the Flemish speaking classes, – Rene attended the French speaking classes, – had nicknamed him "Kapstok" which in Flemish means coat hanger. When, on one occasion the teacher was due to come to Rene's home, they were given a lift by a friend of his who had a horse drawn shooting brake and came to fetch them at the door of the school. This had been observed by Rene's fellow pupils and from the next day he was given the nickname Kapstok Junior, many of the boys having imagined that the teacher was Rene's elder brother. In the years following Rene used the nickname as his nom de plume when writing articles for the students' monthly magazine.

After classes on various afternoons and with several other boys, Rene would spent one or two hours in a bar run by a kind old lady. The bar was called Le Griffon, the French name for a long haired terrier. In fact the old lady had such a dog, over which she made a great deal of fuss. She was extremely good to the boys. She did not mind if they only bought one drink and stayed there for the rest of the afternoon, playing cards, dominoes or billiards. She knew every one of them by their Christian names and always seemed interested in their stories. The boys appreciated her kindness and behaved probably better than they would have done at home.

One day, as they were quietly playing billiards, a stranger came into the place and asked the lady to serve him a cognac. "My dear man," she said, "you know that we are not allowed to sell spirits in this place." In 1925 a law in Belgium had prohibited the sale of spirits in restaurants and bars. Only private clubs were allowed to sell it by the glass, but you could buy bottles containing as much as two litres at one time in any grocery store. This law had been placed on the statute book by a government minister who was hoping to prevent working class people from buying the stuff, by making it compulsory to buy two litres at a time. What he had not bargained for, was that workmen would pool their resources, buy the spirit, and then divide it amongst themselves. The law went as far as to prohibit the owner of a restaurant or bar from having any alcoholic drinks, other than wines or beer, in their own private apartments and for their own use, if these living quarters were, as is customary in Belgium, adjacent to, or above the licensed premises.

The stranger in the Griffon persisted in demanding to be served a glass of cognac. He pretended to being indisposed and he pleaded so well with the old lady that she believed him genuinely to be unwell. Her good heart overruled her usual prudence. She went to a copper umbrella stand in her corridor, lifted a pile of telephone books and from under them appeared the prohibited bottle of cognac. As soon as the bottle appeared, the stranger suddenly recovered from his feigned indisposition and produced a warrant card proving that he was an enforcement officer from Customs and Excise.

Rene and his school friends had been witness to the whole incident and they were angry and disgusted by the vile trick used to catch the old lady. Their anger knew no bounds and when the fellow pulled out a form to prepare a summons, in one concerted action, they all got hold of him and laid him forcibly on the billiard table. Whilst a few of the group held him pinned to the table, one went to get a funnel from behind the counter. He then forced it into the official's mouth, whilst another of the group slowly started pouring the cognac into the funnel. The best part of the contents of the bottle disappeared down the man's throat and when they found that the alcohol had taken effect, they took him out of the bar and dumped him three blocks away on the pavement. One of the boys then gave an anonymous phone call to the police to inform them of the drunken man seen on the pavement. The old lady had vainly tried to prevent their action and for one month was in fear of what might happen to her licence, but happily enough she never heard another word.

A short while after this incident and whilst Rene was in his second year at the Athenee, a new law was passed that parents no longer had the choice of deciding if they wanted the main subjects taught to their children to be in French or in Flemish. Any child born in Antwerp had to be moved to be taught in Flemish speaking classes. Rene's parents objected strongly to the idea and went to consult their uncle Louis Strauss, the former alderman and burgomaster of the city and now a member of the House of Representatives, the Belgian parliament. He told them that the law only applied to town or state schools, but that private schools were free to choose.

As a result of this conversation, Rene's parents decided to move him to the Lycee d' Anvers where, although he had to receive the number of hours prescribed by law of Flemish lessons, the majority of tuition was in French. Rene enjoyed the change, as this school was run on similar lines to British public schools. Pupils wore a blazer and cap and were organised in classes with prefects and house captains. Instead of practising sports in the dreary yard of the Athenee, this school had a well equipped sports ground just outside the city. The school was located a hundred yards away from Rene's former primary school, but following the move in 1923 to the house in the Rue de Palais, his tram journey was a bit longer and entailed one change enroute.

The boys in this school were far nicer and made him welcome from the first time he met them. The teachers too, were far more conscientious. In a word, everything seemed better about this school, but to his mother's despair, it did not make an immediate difference to his lack of enthusiasm for academic study.

The next few years were spent on the usual routines of school life. Rene showed little interest in the study of Latin, mathematics or history, but the study of modern languages and geography fascinated him. A few months prior to his sixteenth birthday he sat the twice yearly examinations and passed reasonably well and regained the second place in his form, he had previously achieved in primary school.

During the summer holidays following these exams, Rene overheard a conversation between his mother and his uncle, Marcel Roost, the barrister. They were discussing Rene's future. In fact, they had it all planned for him. When he had finished his classes at the Lycee, he was to be sent to the Universitie Libres Bruxelles, to study law. His uncle would then take him as a trainee into his legal practice, which dealt mainly with maritime law. This conversation which, if he had not overheard it, would have sealed his future. As it was, it created in him the natural reaction of a boy of sixteen, – a feeling of revolt.

As a result of what he had overheard, he deliberately sabotaged his next Latin examination, which he would need to have passed to gain entry to the university law school. His mother insisted that he should sit it again, but he flatly refused and requested to be transferred to the commercial course at his school, where time would be spent on learning book keeping, which he considered much more useful than Latin. Eventually his mother gave in and he was transferred to the commercial course, which meant that although he would stay in the same form, he would attend the commercial classes whilst the other pupils would study Latin and start Greek.

His mother was very worried about his future. She knew that he had no inclination to enter his father's or grandfather's line of business and he had not yet given any indication of how he saw his future. Irma's decision to pay a visit to Rene's headmaster, who had been her teacher of literature when she attended school, proved to be a turning point in her son's future. She told him about all her disappointments and worries and he promised her he would have a serious talk with Rene.

As a result of their conversation, Rene was called into the headmaster's office the next day. When the chief supervisor came to fetch him and told him that the headmaster wanted to see him, he became a bit puzzled, wondering what mischief he once more had been called to account for. He was somewhat surprised, when ushered into the headmaster's office to be greeted by him with a welcoming smile and to be invited to sit down next to his desk. This had never happened before. He then told Rene of his mother's visit and of his promise to help him in the choice of a career.

"Now my boy," he said gravely, "I want to have a talk with you, from man to man. Have you given any thoughts to what you want to do when you grow up?"

"Frankly no, Sir," replied Rene. "Since I still have two years to do at this school, I find it a bit early to decide. All I know is that I do not want to become a lawyer and I do not want to enter the diamond business."

The headmaster looked at him gravely. "Well, contrary to what you think, son, this is the time when you must decide, because on this will depend the specialized tuition we will have to arrange for you. So I suggest that you go home, have a good discussion with your parents and friends and in a week or two we will have another conversation."

As Rene was about to depart the headmaster called him back. "By the way, I have just been asked that our school should join a new inter-school social organization and I am giving my approval to the idea. I have also been requested to nominate a certain number of teachers and pupils to sit on the committee and various sub-committees and thus represent the school in all decision making. Would you accept to be nominated for one or other of the sub-committees?"

"With pleasure Sir," said Rene, slightly shocked at the confidence in him implied by this offer.

"Then look at this list of activities and tell me which ones would interest you most."

A glance at the list and Rene had his answer "School travel and school cinema Sir" he said.

"All right, I shall propose you for the two sub committees and let you know the result."

A week later Rene was given a memo requesting him to attend the first meetings of the two sub -committees he had chosen. At both meetings he made a few constructive suggestions on the future programmes of each section and as a result of it, was unanimously elected chairman of the pupils' sub-committee. From then on he became deeply involved in these two activities. Firstly, there came the running of the cinema club. The committee made arrangements to hire the most centrally located and the best known cinema in town, the Cinema Pathe, every Sunday morning. The aim was to show educational films, or adventure films considered especially suitable for young audiences. The only staff supplied by the cinema were the projector operator and an old caretaker, but the selling of tickets at the desk, the ushering of parents and children to their seats and the musical illustration of the silent films by a lone piano, were taken care of by young members of the cinema sub-committee.

Rene's job was to organize the weekly rota, of who did what, and supervise it was done satisfactorily, whilst the teachers' sub-committee would make the selection of films to be shown, organize the publicizing of the programme in the various schools and hear the pupils' sub – committee's comments or criticisms on the way the films chosen by them had been received by the young audiences.

The day came when Rene violently expressed his disapproval of the teachers' choice. On this occasion, after showing one or two short documentaries and one animated cartoon, they had gone on to show the dramatic film "The Fisher of Island." The film was very tragic with an extremely sad end and the sense of tragedy was accentuated by the very moving piano playing of Suzanne Van der Steen, a member of the pupils' sub-committee who, every Sunday, played the piano accompaniment to the films. The end of the film was so poignant that when the young ushers opened wide the doors of the cinema to let parents and children out, Rene was struck by the number of adults and children who displayed signs of having cried, or were still burying their tears in their handkerchiefs.

At the next sub-committee meeting he violently criticised the teachers, not for their choice of films, but for the sequence in which they had been shown. He insisted that the comic cartoon should have been shown last to counteract the sad impression left by the main film. They accepted his argument as sound and decided that the pupils' sub committee would be consulted in the future on the choice of the programme.

Rene's second area of activity, the school travel section, indirectly decided his future career. His first task consisted of helping his teacher in planning an excursion for his class. When it was found that he was good at that, the headmaster decided to get him involved with larger projects. Today such arrangements would be taken care of by specialized professional organizations, but in 1927 no such services existed and there was, therefore, far more dependence by a school of one country or town, on the help or advice and even organizational assistance, of a school in an area they wished to visit. As a result, it came about that various letters landed on Rene's headmaster's desk from colleagues in France, Holland and Italy asking for his advice and help in the planning of their school trip to Antwerp.

At first, Monsieur Henen, the headmaster, gave Rene the details of what was required and instructed him to report to him, within a given time scale, the details of the tentative arrangements he had made.

Having ascertained that everything had been duly taken care of by the sub-committee over which Rene presided, he would later simply hand over to them the letters newly received from abroad, and rely entirely on them to follow them up. This was how, for the first time in his life as a pupil, he suddenly took on the responsibilities of a teacher. In those days, professional guides had not been heard of, so he made a selection of teachers and pupils prepared to act as guides. With the help of his form teacher, he gathered all the historical and architectural information on Antwerp he could find. Then, again with his teacher's help, he prepared a selection of itineraries for the sightseeing of the city and the harbour.

As there were very few coaches in those days, most of the sightseeing was undertaken either on foot, or by private hire tramcars. For the harbour visit, Rene had arranged with the harbour authorities that one or two sea going tugs would be fitted with benches and used as excursion boats for the visit of the harbour and dock installation.

When all the technical details of these sightseeing trips were finalized, it remained to train the selected guides. For this, both theoretical and practical training was given, the delivery of which Rene participated in, alongside some of his teachers. Soon they were ready to receive their first contingent of visitors. It happened to be a girls' school from Paris. It was with pride and zeal that the young men of the Lycee d' Anvers showed these young ladies the highlights of their native city. Boys' schools from abroad were shown around by a team of young lady guides and it is certain that they must have enjoyed their visit much more than if the explanation had been given by one of the boys.

It is around this time that an organization which was named 'Les Semailles Au Soleil' or 'Sowing in the Sun' to give it an English name, came out with a monthly illustrated paper to which everyone on Rene's sub committee was asked to contribute. This was Rene's first and probably only attempt at journalism, however one of his closest school friends discovered his vocation by first starting to write for this inter school paper and he later became the top reporter of one of the leading Antwerp newspapers.

Antwerp 1927

The two events which overshadowed the happy times which the family had known during the latter part of the decade were the deaths of Irma's favourite uncle, Louis Strauss, the Antwerp city alderman and deputy burgomaster who had married her and Franz back in 1911. Uncle Louis's death was followed a few months later by that of her father, Adolphe Adler, at the not particularly advanced age of 67. A family photograph taken only a few months before his death shows the grey haired, moustachioed, proud patriarch, seated in the salon of his home in Rue Conscience surrounded by his four daughters, their respective husbands and his six grandchildren. Unlike his adored wife Cecile, he had lived to see the birth of Cecil Manasseh, the last of his grandchildren in Antwerp in 1923, during one of his daughter Emmy's periodic visits to her home city.

Antwerp 1929

Rene's two last years at school went by and he still had not made up his mind about what he wanted to become. When in 1929 at the age of 18, he completed his final secondary school examinations, his father wanted him to carry on his commercial studies. Since he had purposely failed his Latin examinations and omitted to learn Greek, the universities were closed to him, but his father wanted him to go to the Higher Institute of Commerce instead, where in two years he could get a 'Licentiate in Commercial Studies' and in three years become a 'Doctor in Commercial Science'. When Franz told Rene of his plans, he once more rebelled and told his father quite frankly that he had decided that it was about time he left the school benches and went out to earn his living. "I give you eight days to find yourself a job," said Franz, "and if you don't succeed, you will go to the Higher Institute whether you like it or not."

That same day Rene put an advertisement in a newspaper offering his services and got six replies. Armed with the cheek that only an 18 year old can carry off, he visited all six of them and before the personnel managers could open their mouths to tell him their conditions, he had informed them that he would only be interested in a job with variety and good prospects and devoid of routine. Five of the personnel managers very politely declined an offer of employment, but the sixth one assured him that he could give him a job devoid of routine. In fact, he explained, he intended to make Rene a candidate for trainee Inspector of Fire Investigation of the Schelde Insurance Company. He would first undergo a period of training in the Fire Claims' Department at the head office, in order to acquaint himself with the various forms, either of claims or of the investigation of claims. He would need to study policies and their conditions, plus the loopholes allowing the insurance company to reduce to the minimum their liability from those claims and this with the full protection of the law.

Proud as a peacock he went home to tell his father that he had got himself a job and on the Monday of the following week he started work with eagerness. At first it seemed quite interesting to prepare the claim and investigation forms, to fetch out of the archives the policy document setting out the policy conditions the claimant was subject to and prepare the file which the inspectors take with them on their rounds of investigation. After four weeks and as soon as he had proved himself to be well acquainted with procedure, he got his first thrilling chance to go out with one of the inspectors on a fire investigation and this first one had all the ingredients of a thriller.

Brussels 1929

They travelled to Brussels by train and during the journey the inspector informed Rene of his suspicion that they were investigating a case of arson. In fact, he had already received a preliminary report from the Brussels police. The fire had taken place in the small workshop of a firm manufacturing raincoats, which according to several sources of information, was in serious financial difficulties and which would have benefitted from such a fire. When they reached the premises they found two detectives waiting for them, who confirmed their belief that the fire was suspicious. The claimant was still at the police station helping the police with their enquiries. When asked the number of manufactured raincoats that were lost in the fire, he failed to give a definitive answer, but argued that according to his estimate, if a search was made amongst the rubble, it would be possible find the metal buttons used to fasten each coat and given that there were six buttons on each coat, it would be also be possible work out the number of coats destroyed.

Whether the fire was extinguished by the fire brigade faster than was expected, or whether an explosion when the fire was started brought the ceiling crashing down, the fact remained that in digging under the rubble the police found, in various places, the metal buttons, but to the dismay of the proprietor they were still attached to the cards on which they had been supplied to the raincoat manufacturer. Also found were the burnt remains of some rolls of cloth and from their position and various tests which were carried out, the police and the insurance company fire inspector came to the conclusion that both the buttons and the rolls of cloth had been deliberately thrown on the fire and that there were no manufactured raincoats on the premises. After a thorough investigation, the claimant at long last admitted his culpability and as soon as he was brought to trial, the claim file at the insurance company was marked "Case closed. No indemnity" and the actual policy was also cancelled. On many other occasions Rene had to act as clerk to the inspector and take down as dictated notes, the details of his findings, which on his return to the office, Rene had to turn into a proper report.

Antwerp 1930

Whilst Rene was busily engaged at the insurance company, work was feverishly progressing on the site of what was to become the International Antwerp Exhibition of 1930, during the following year. Every Sunday the public was allowed on the site to view the progress of the work and Rene was there nearly every Sunday. A few months before the opening of the exhibition, a school friend of his, whose father was a member of the organizing committee, asked Rene if he would join him and a few other school friends he had recruited, to act as ushers or stewards at the various functions and ceremonies which were going to take place during the exhibition. Rene accepted the offer in principle, but told his friend that although this work did not appear to clash in any way with his regular occupation, he would have to obtain his permanent employer 's permission.

At the first opportunity Rene went to see the personnel manager to get his consent. Since his work as a steward would only be in the evenings and weekends, he knew the manager could not refuse, especially considering that this was an honorary unpaid activity. The personnel manager granted his request without hesitation and went even further, telling him that if he could manage to obtain through his contacts at the exhibition first hand information on hirers of intended stands or pavilions, he would see that Rene even got free time during working hours to attend royal visits and other such events.

Rene informed the Exhibition Committee of his manager's offer and they allowed him to take back to the insurance company a complete list of the intending exhibitors. These were immediately contacted by the company's sales representatives and as a result, the insurance company sold a considerable number of policies covering buildings, the exhibited goods and public liabilities. They were extremely grateful to Rene and honoured the personnel manager's undertaking. Whenever Rene's presence was needed at the exhibition for a royal visit or other important event, they gave him leave of absence without any hesitation. In return, Rene arranged from time to time, to obtain invitations to events for any directors and the personnel manager and his family.

The opening of the exhibition took place in the early days of May and was honoured with the presence of the Belgian royal family and all the country's leading dignitaries. As the stage in the main exhibition hall was occupied by an orchestra of one hundred musicians and as many choristers, the seating arrangement of the hall had been planned in a rather unusual way. The royal dais was erected in the centre of the hall, facing the gangway leading from the main entrance to the stage. On the right of the royal dais were the seats of the members of parliament and the authorities of the city of Brussels. On the left, were all the seats reserved for members of the diplomatic corps. Facing this group, on the other side of the gangway, was the entire organizing committee of the exhibition. Opposite the royal family and to their right, were their guests. To the left of the royal family sat the exhibitors and their families.

This arrangement of the seating created a headache for the master of ceremonies, to whom Rene was responsible. Usual protocol required that all guests must occupy their seats before the arrival of the royal family, who always entered last. A further problem was created by the presence of Cardinal Mercier, head of the Roman Catholic church in Belgium. Although not a member of the royal family, it was customary for the king to invite him to sit beside the royal family on the dais. As it would have been unbecoming for him to await the royal family on the dais, a compromise arrangement had been found in agreement with the head of protocol at the palace. A small platform covered with a carpet on which an armchair had been put, was placed in the gangway in front of the seats of members of the diplomatic corps. The cardinal would then be conducted by the master of ceremonies to this seat and from there await the arrival of the royal family. As soon as the king was seated, he would request the cardinal to join him on the royal dais and this would be the time where, under Rene's supervision, ten workmen would remove the armchair, the carpet and the platform.

Although all this had been rehearsed and the time needed for the operation recorded, on the given day things did not work as planned. When the royal family was announced, the orchestra played the national anthem, everybody stood up and the royal party slowly made their way to the dais. By the time King Albert, Queen Elisabeth and the royal family had reached their seats, the national anthem had come to an end and everybody sat down. This went according to plan, but when the time came for the king to summon his steward to invite the cardinal to join him, he forgot all about it and the master of ceremonies, just as absent mindedly, had forgotten to remind the king of the agreed protocol.

When the master of ceremonies finally noticed what should have happened he instructed Rene to rush to the back of the royal dais to remind the steward of the agreed plan. When Rene got to there, he tried to draw the attention of the steward, who was standing at the rear of the dais. Not wanting to raise his voice, he found that the only way to attract his attention was to pull him very unceremoniously by the tail of his remarkable uniform jacket. He looked round in surprise and then recognizing Rene, leaned down to know the reason for his rather discourteous action. No sooner had Rene told him than he went to ask the king if he could invite the cardinal to the dais. By the time Rene reported back to the master of ceremonies, the cardinal had moved to the royal dais and Rene was able to order the removal of the small platform on which the cardinal had been seated.

The rest of the ceremony went on without a hitch, although Rene found the speeches of the Belgian High Commissionaire and of the President of the Executive Committee a bit long. In contrast, King Albert gave a short and concise speech, both in French and Flemish, congratulating the organizers on their initiative and declaring the Antwerp International Exhibition officially open.

This inaugural visit of the royal family was to be followed by many others, where King Albert, as usual, took a keen interest in all the exhibits, had lengthy conversations with the exhibitors, satisfying his curiosity by many questions, to the great dismay of the exhibition's master of ceremonies and the king's steward, whose combined planning of a timetable went completely out of the window.

Whenever such a visit took place, the royal family was conducted around the halls by the Belgian Foreign High Commissionaire, the President of the Exhibition, Monsieur Martougin, owner of a well known chocolate factory and by a good number of members of the exhibition Executive Committee. Ringing this select group and making sure that no intruder would enter the circle, was a security wall composed of members of the king's police, alternating with some of the stewards of the exhibition. Each time the king and his party moved forward or sideways, the magic circle of security moved around them. Each time such visits came to an end without an incident, notes of congratulations on the quality of the organization, were showered on those responsible for it.

Several distinguished foreign visitors honoured the Exhibition with their presence. Amongst them, were Queen Wilhelmina of Holland and the Duke of Windsor, then Prince of Wales, who came to open the British Pavilion. The President of the French Republic attended the opening of the French Week. Many celebrities, including the then well known and very attractive singer and dancer, Josephine Baker, toured the exhibition and gave the press the opportunity to give the exhibition good coverage.

At the opening of the Japanese Week an incident occurred which for the first time, but not the last, provided Rene with a narrow brush with death. The opening ceremony was taking place in the Exhibition Hall and as usual Rene was chief usher. As instructed by the master of ceremonies, Rene was walking up and down the central gangway with his assistant, making sure that every usher was at their post, to show the distinguished visitors to their pre-allocated seats and ready to be called upon by them if some problem arose. As he was pacing the gangway for the third time, Rene suddenly heard behind him loud shouts and screams. Looking round he saw something like a shadow behind him and instinctively jumped forward. With a loud crash, one of the three large light fittings illuminating the hall came thundering down only a foot away from him. It was made of a large metal awning in the shape of an umbrella, probably two metres wide, under which hung a sphere formed of pieces of glass of various colours. A small motor in the fixture made the two foot diameter coloured glass sphere, turn slowly and beam all its coloured light onto the inside of the metal awning and around the walls of the hall. The three light fittings were suspended from the ceiling of the hall by a single cable. On examination it was found that there was a defect in the cable of the light fitting that fell and narrowly missed Rene. It was Rene's good luck the awning had acted like a parachute and the light fitting came down slowly enough for people to see what had happened and shout a warning.

Another note worthy event was an open air performance of Puccini's La Boheme conducted by Toscanini, with the director and the whole cast of La Scala, Milan. They had brought along their own revolving mobile stage, which was large enough to have space for a whole market square with an open air restaurant and even a funfair, with a working merry-go-round to be used in the second act. On this occasion, the organisation was perfect and everything worked superbly on the stage and in the auditorium.

Things were not always so fortunate and on three different occasions, things did not go so smoothly. One such occasion was the selection of Miss Belgium. Rene's chief had been requested to stage that event in the Festival Hall on behalf of a leading Belgian weekly magazine which had staged the preliminary rounds of the competition in the country's nine main provincial towns. From these nine contestants, Miss Belgium was to be selected. Admission to the event was obtained by the purchase of a special edition of this weekly magazine, the cover of which had a gold serial number printed on the right hand corner. The editor of the magazine had promised to limit the issue to the exact number of seats available in the hall, around 3000 in total. Unfortunately, once the printing presses were going, somebody forgot to stop them, with the result that nearly ten thousand people turned up. The seats in the hall were not numbered and therefore, many people turned up very early, hoping to get seats close to the stage. As soon as all the available seats were occupied Rene's chief instructed the ushers to close the entrance doors. Meanwhile a gigantic crowd of people shouting, pushing, brandishing special editions of the magazine were obstructing all access to the hall.

Rene had been instructed to meet the nine contestants and their escorts in one of the main hotels in Antwerp. At the appointed time, he was to usher them to a line of cars. He would travel in the first car and direct the whole motorcade on a pre-arranged route, to arrive in front of the steps of the Festival Hall, where the young ladies were supposed to make a grand entrance, via the main central door. The journey had been timed to ensure their arrival at a particular moment. But as soon as Rene's car approached the place, he became aware of the situation and the impossibility of getting through the crowds. So he directed the row of cars to his office, a short distance away, and through an internal telephone spoke to his chief. He had already decided that the only way to get the girls in safely was to get them out of the exhibition ground and to a back door of the Festival Hall, through which supplies and stage props were brought in. The only problem was that the caretaker had gone home, taking with him the key to that door. A taxi had already been sent to collect him and meanwhile Rene was instructed to take the nine beauty queens for a ride around the exhibition site, until such time as a despatch rider notified him that the back door had been opened.

When eventually Rene and the contestants got into the hall and the public waiting outside found out that they had been deprived of even a glimpse of the beauty queens, a kind of mass hysteria broke out and the crowd nearly managed to break the doors down. Large reinforcements of police had to be called, who quickly cleared the place.

A second occasion involving mishap for Rene, was when a grand evening was organized jointly by the Federation of Paris Fashion Houses and Paris jewellers. It consisted mainly of a fashion show and in which the specially selected models from Paris would wear real jewels. A week before the show the Antwerp police were informed by Interpol that simultaneously, in Paris and in London, several known jewel thieves, who were permanently under surveillance, had disappeared and it was seriously suspected that they were making their way to Antwerp to prepare a snatch at the fashion show.

Interpol supplied their Antwerp colleagues with a full description and photographs of the known criminals and also described their mode of operation. This prompted the chief of the Antwerp police to call an emergency meeting to which everyone concerned with the exhibition's organization, including Rene and his chief, were called. At this meeting it was explained that a well organized gang had succeeded on several occasions to get away with a big haul, mainly at fashion shows. Their way of operating was quite simple. Having found the nearest electric sub-station, one member of the gang would, at a given time, cut off the electricity plunging the hall into complete darkness.

As the models usually appeared in accordance with a strictly pre-arranged timetable, the blacking out of the hall would coincide with the time a model in the pay of the gang would appear on the catwalk extending from the stage. She would know exactly where to be at the time the lights went out and she would know exactly where some accomplices would be seated alongside the catwalk. It would then be an easy matter to hand this accomplice the expensive diamond necklace or bracelets she was wearing. Following which, she would then start shouting blue murder and pretend later that she had been attacked and that the jewels had been forcibly removed from her by the gang member.

To prevent the possibility of such a crime, the most stringent precautions were agreed on at the meeting with the police. First the police, in agreement with the electricity company, made arrangements to have all electricity sub-stations leading to, or within the exhibition site, guarded by armed police. All access to the Festival Hall would also be guarded by armed police. An alarm bell would be installed and in case of a failure of the lighting in any part of the building, an alarm bell would be rung and the police would seal all doors to the place. On the stage a search light connected to a set of batteries had been installed and all girls had been warned that if the main lights went out the searchlight would illuminate the length of the catwalk and they would have to remain motionless if they did not want to run the risk of being shot at by detectives seated alongside the catwalk at carefully selected intervals.

Special care was taken in the planning of the show as to how and when the jewels were to be brought to the dressing room. Here, the girls would have to come in turn and have the jewels fastened around their necks, wrists or on their dress. Under no circumstances would they be allowed to handle the jewels. The same trained jeweller who would place the gems on each model would remove them from the girls on their return from the catwalk, making quite sure that no clever trick of conjuring had been performed with imitation jewellery substituted for the real.

It was also agreed that the Chief of Police would, an hour before the performance, give, to all heads of department concerned with the show a password, allowing them and members of their staff to enter the stage area via a door leading to the main hall.

It so happened that Rene had been given various tasks in the hall by his chief, which prevented him being present when the password was communicated. When, during the course of the evening, he wanted to go from the hall to the dressing room on the side of the stage, which he was using as an office during special events, he was prevented from opening the door to the stage by a detective. Rene explained who he was, showed the detective the key which he had to allow him to open the stage door and explained why he had not been present when the password was given. He told Rene that he knew him very well, and also of his position in the organization, but that unless he was given the password, he could not allow him through. Rene got into a temper and told him that this was ridiculous, that he had to go to his dressing room at any cost. Now the word for dressing room in French is "Loge." To Rene's surprise as soon as he had said this the detective unlocked the door and let him through. Later Rene discovered that "Loge" was the password and it was by pure chance that he had given it.

The evening went off without incident, although it was later reported by Interpol, who had sent representatives to the show, that they had spotted some of the suspected criminals in the audience and who were probably discouraged from attempting anything after the impressive display of security.

The third and final incident took place on the evening of the closure of the exhibition. Rene had been briefed to attend the final banquet and to assist the master of ceremonies before guests were seated by making a last check on the seating arrangements. There was a high table for the dignitaries of the province and the city, who were to be seated with members of the Exhibition Committee. Eight long rows of tables extended at a right angle from the high table. Rene was seated at the end of the first row, nearest to the still room, with a brief to watch the number of wine bottles coming out of the still room being served.

Rene's chief did not trust the caterer employed for the occasion and told him he had been grossly overcharged on various other occasions.

It had also been agreed that as soon as coffee and liqueurs were served Rene would go ahead of the guests to alert the person organizing the firework display to get ready. Rene's chief, who would then take all the guests to a specially provided enclosure and would then use a torch to flash a signal to him, to order the fireworks to start. However, although everything had been very carefully planned and timed, the dinner ran late, on account of longer than expected speeches and guests were still eating their dessert when they heard the noise of fireworks. Rene's chief realized what was happening and instructed him to reach the organizer of the fireworks as quickly as possible, and to tell him to stop the display.

Rene rushed out of the banqueting room and ran across the square to the nearest place from which he could reach the firework display area. A wall of people five deep blocked his way. When he explained that it was his duty to reach the organizer of the fireworks, members of the crowd decided to lift him above their heads and to pass him to the front.

He then ran in the direction of the firework display, but either because he was blinded by the glow of one lighted firework or because he was plunged into darkness the next minute, he failed to notice a stretched wire, low on the edge of the lawn. He tripped, fell forward and landed completely flat out on a muddy path. No need to describe what state his nice stiffened shirt and white waistcoat were in. His trousers and tailcoat were splattered with mud, but he managed to stop the firework display. After which had to go back to his dressing room, where he changed into less formal clothes and stayed in the part of the exhibition site which featured a reconstruction of historic Flemish buildings and had been called 'Vieux Anvers' or the 'Old Antwerp' village, where bars and restaurants provided nightly entertainment. Rene remained here until the early hours of the morning, when he watched sadly, and for the last time, the exhibition stewards escort the drunks and the stragglers to the various gates. On that last day he was given a large souvenir medal, a diploma of thanks for his services and a special paper knife which he kept preciously for many years.

Irma's brother in law, Eddie Nathan, having made a small fortune from his business activities in Singapore and the far east had decided with his wife, Helene, to resettle his family in Europe. Two daughters had been born in Singapore, Cecile in September 1916 and Andree in December 1917. For Eddie and Helene more than one possible option existed in choosing a European city in which to reside. Eddie, a British citizen had family ties with London, although he had never actually lived there. Apart from his time at Cheltenham College, he had lived entirely in the far east. He was, however, a fluent French speaker and this might have led him and Helene to settle in Belgium, most likely in Antwerp, with all its family associations for his wife. But instead Paris came to be chosen. The explanation for this owes to several factors. Paris was an excellent financial centre from which to manage, at a distance, those business interests he maintained in Singapore. At intervals Eddie would seek the remittance of income from his many investments to one of Paris's leading banks.

Each month Eddie would receive a detailed account from his agent in Singapore, detailing the rental income which had been earned on the many shop premises and houses he owned. The letter would indicate which properties were currently unlet and the steps being taken to get them tenanted once more. The agent would also list any necessary repairs to the properties and seek Eddie's approval for the prioritization to be given to work and for the sums to be expended, in the course of the work. Sometimes, as when the Singapore municipal authorities demanded improvements, for example to sanitation, through the installation of indoor bathrooms, the agent simply reported the costs of these necessary works without seeking prior approval.

Occasionally there were other matters to report, such as the cost of storing Eddie's motor launch for which he was seeking a buyer. Sadly the condition of the boat deteriorated and was eventually sold at a price Eddie found profoundly unsatisfactory. Similarly, the agent had to report that one of Eddie's mother's properties for which he had assumed responsibility, had reached such a state of disrepair that the most economic solution was demolition. This Eddie agreed to, but the agent was still required to get the best price he could for the materials salvaged from the building. After a lengthy delay in finding a buyer the agent was able to report that he had obtained a better than expected price for the materials.

A second reason for choosing Paris was that his sister, Catherine Nathan, had married into a distinguished French family, the Billottes, offering the possibility of contact with their French relatives for his wife and two teenage daughters. A further reason was that his elder daughter Cecile,would shortly be looking for somewhere to complete her education and her interests already pointed to a place at the Ecole du Louvre in Paris, where she would learn skills appropriate to someone considering a career as an archivist or curator.

Even before leaving Singapore, Eddie had become involved in a project to build a complex of exclusive apartments near the Bois de Boulogne, in the fashionable 16th arrondissement on the north side of the Avenue Henri Martin. A syndicate had been formed with other investors in the project and an architect and builder commissioned. Each stakeholder would acquire an apartment covering an entire floor of the block, served by two lifts, one giving access to the apartment's entrance, the other a service lift allowing goods delivered to the basement garage to be brought up directly to the kitchen and pantry, as well as providing access for tradesmen. Three, one room flats in the attic,provided accommodation for the cook, housemaid and chauffeur of the occupants of each apartment. In addition each apartment had it's own designated space in the basement garage beneath the complex for the owner's motorcar.

The occupants of each apartment were able to make use of the services of their architect in designing the permanent furnishings and fittings of their new home, entirely in accordance with their own tastes. In keeping with the fashion of the times, the Nathans chose Art Deco as the dominant theme of these internal features. Panels, sometimes with marquetry inlay, were used on walls, where they occasionally disguised doors leading from service areas, such as the kitchen, from public rooms such as the salon and dining room. Even electrical fittings, such as light switches, were chosen to compliment the décor on walls and ceilings. Light fittings by Lalique added the final touch of opulence to the fixed furnishings. In addition Eddie and Helene had brought back from Singapore a variety of pieces of oriental furniture from their former home amongst the old colonial style properties on Nassim Hill. Somehow traditional Chinoiserie seemed to sit well with the new found taste for Art Deco.

Two years after settling into their new Paris apartment, Eddie and Helene acquired a second property, this time of rather greater antiquity. The fifty two room Chateau d'Aunoy situated near Melun in the Marne valley had been built in 1750, replacing an earlier medieval chateau which had been destroyed by fire. Set in a 70 hectacre park, it was one of the first in France to be planned in the English style. Beyond the formal gardens, woodlands with a lake containing a small island and an artificial cave, creating a small folly, had been designed to convey an impression of natural beauty and a rural idyll. The chateau was approached down an avenue formed by four lines of chestnut trees. An unusual feature of the house was that after the reconstruction no timber was employed in the building resulting in walls over two metres thick being used to support 'Catalan vaults' or 'Saracen' and brickwork arches.

For the Nathans the chateau became an important summer retreat and they were joined here by both their immediate and their extended family. An occasional visitor was Catherine Nathan, Eddie's sister, and her husband Gaston Billotte. Gaston was a professional soldier who had trained at France's elite military academy at St. Cyr, graduating in 1895.Having made steady progress through the ranks, he had by 1930 been made commander of all French troops in Indochina and military governor of Hanoi. The couple would use the hospitality provided at Aunoy during Gaston's leave and return visits to France.

For Eddie and Helene's two daughters, as well as the children of Helene's two sisters the ample grounds of the chateau provided a safe haven in which they could play and even indulge their fantasies. The estate possessed a farm, tenanted at the time, and photographs of the family show them engaged in rural and even agrarian pursuits, normally the domain of the workers employed on the farm. The family would fish the lake, assist in haymaking, and other activities which also provided the younger members of the family with an excuse to ride the high sided horse drawn carts returning the hay and straw to the stables and barns surrounding the chateau.

The summer following the Nathan's occupation of the chateau, a grand family gathering took place. Emmy and Rupert Manasseh had returned from Singapore bringing their two children, Irene and Cecil. They were joined by Helene's youngest sister, Renee and her husband Marcel Roost. Franz and Irma had been prevented from attending by Franz's duties at the Diamond Club in Antwerp, but Marcel and Renee had permitted their daughter Georgette to accompany them from Belgium. For Georgette it was an occasion to meet up again with her four English cousins.

Gaston and Catherine Billotte were also able to attend accompanied by their son, Pierre, his wife Paulette and their young daughter, Monique who had been born almost two years earlier in Hanoi during her father's service there with the French forces. Pierre like his father, had sought a military career and had been able to obtain a posting to Indochina whilst his father was serving as commander of French forces in the country.

Apart from lavish picnics in the grounds of the chateau with trestle tables groaning with food and bottles of wine, the family were able to indulgence their appetite for competitive sports, donning their tennis whites for little tournaments, or engaging in cycle rides, with Marcel adopting a style of riding for the camera which might have inspired Jacque Tati's Monsieur Hulot some years later. In between these hectic activities they would find time to settle down to a relaxing game of bridge in the chateau's grounds. This was an idyllic period of shared enjoyment and fun.

Brasschaat, Belgium 1931

The other member of the family who had not been available to join in the family gathering at Aunoy was Rene Paul. During the winter of 1930 he had received papers requesting him to attend a medical examination prior to his enlistment for national service in the Belgian army. He attended the medical and in the interview which followed was reported to be in A1 condition, although he had mentioned that he was a bad walker and would prefer a mounted regiment. Little did the doctors know that he had done some long and tiring hiking in his school days, but he was certainly not looking forward to having to do long route marches in the army, carrying heavy kit and rifle.

In March 1931 he received his call-up papers and was informed he was to be drafted to the cavalry,- the 3rd Regiment of Lancers, to be precise. The date of joining was fixed for the 1st August, 1931. He therefore had three months in front of him. He was very pleased to know that he would join a mounted regiment and that he was to be posted to Brasschaat, which was only ten miles away from his home. But he was not so pleased to know that he had been chosen for the 3rd Lancers, which had the reputation of being a tough training regiment. When he told his father of his apprehensions Franz told him he would pay for private riding lessons for the next three months, but on one condition, that he would never reveal, when joining his squadron, that he knew how to ride. As a former army officer he warned Rene of his experience, – that those who boasted of having learned to ride in civilian life were usually given the worst horses, and teased continuously about their riding capabilities.

This proved to be true. On the day of his arrival at the barracks and after the usual formalities, a visit to the stores for uniforms and kit, a visit to the infirmary for the various inoculations, Rene and the other new entrants were assembled in the refectory where the question was put to them. "Who can ride horses?" A few boys proudly put their hands up. "Fine," said the Adjudant, the title of a Warrant Officer in the Belgian army, and he took down the names of those with their hands up. "I am pleased to see that there are a few of you who are accustomed to horses," he went on, "and since you know all about them, you will be the first ones to take turns as stable boys." The poor boys did not know what they had let themselves in for. In the coming weeks, during initial training, they would repeatedly hear the Adjudant shout "Look at these Sunday riders. Look at them, they sit on their horses like a piece of butter sits on a hot potato."

The initial training lasted six weeks. In the first week they rode a different horse, bare back, every day. During the second week they still changed horses every day, but rode sitting on a blanket on the back of their mount. The third week was the hardest, involving riding with a saddle, but without stirrups. Only in the fourth week were they permitted to ride with stirrups at full leg's length.

In the fifth week they started jumping fences and in the afternoon were trained in acrobatics on horseback, similar to what you might see performed in circuses. In place of a conventional saddle, the horse was fitted with a belt around its middle with two leather handles on top. Whilst it cantered in a circle the inexperienced young cavalrymen had to jump on and off the animal, rotate themselves, so that they rode back to front and elevate themselves, so that they rode standing on the horse's back.

When the initial six weeks training was over, they were each assigned a horse which would become their mount for the duration of their national service. As Franz had suggested, those who had boasted about their knowledge of riding were given the worst horses. In the stables, which were about 240 feet long, the horses were placed in stalls facing the external walls. They were separated by long horizontal beams attached to thick iron hinges fixed into the wall next to the horses' heads and supported at the other end on vertical wooden posts, either side of the animals' hindquarters. Finally another horizontal beam attached to the posts enclosed each stall.

On the horizontal beam was fixed a plate with the name of the horse. The plate was usually painted white with black letters. Behind two or three horses, there was also a red plate with the word 'dangerous' written in white letters. This was a warning to everyone to approach that particular horse with exceptional care. Rene got quite a shock when he was given one of the horses termed dangerous. The animal was named "Taylor." He was surprised that the Adjudant had given him this horse since he had gained the impression that he was in his good books. On several occasions during the initial training he had said, "Look at Falkenau. What a clumsy rider he was when he first joined us. Now see what we have made of him." Why had he chosen to give Rene a dangerous horse? He was soon to find out that Taylor was in fact one of the best horses of the squadron. Dangerous he was all right, but only to those he did not know. Once he knew his permanent rider, he obeyed him like no other horse did.

Usually these cavalry horses were so accustomed to move in groups that they became nervous when separated from the squadron. Taylor, however, had always been used to being detached from the rest of the squadron either for scouting duties in front of the unit or for carrying despatch riders, where speed and use of the shortest route were essential. Taylor never refused to jump a ditch or a fence and was as happy away from the squadron as amongst the other horses.

Rene's first acquaintance with Taylor had been during initial training. It was not too successful an encounter. It happened at the end of the third week of training when it had been Rene's turn to act as stable boy. Amongst other duties it meant undertaking a twenty four hour guard starting after the evening meal. Dressed in denim fatigues, wearing clogs and a No 2 great coat, Rene and three other boys would march in step into the stable under the orders of the Brigadier of the week, – a corporal is called a Brigadier in the Belgian cavalry. They would then take over from four other boys who would go around the stable with them and show them that all the equipment listed on a sheet was accounted for. It consisted of four brooms, four shovels, two barrows, two measures to pour the corn into the individual nose bags and as many bags as there were horses in the stables. They also had to count the saddles and bridles which were on their stands, attached to one of the vertical posts at the end of each stall.

The old guard were supposed to have left the stables in spotless condition and it was now their job to ensure they remained so. After a while they acquired a special sense. They could anticipate when a horse was going to soil the litter and hold a shovel behind its hind legs thus collecting the droppings before they could disintegrate on the freshly laid straw. Transferring them to a barrow was then child's play.

Their next duty was to see that the two large metal basins used as drinking troughs for the horses were filled with fresh water. In 1931 there weren't all the practical implements available today. In the absence of hoses, the filling was done the hard way. Just inside the central door of the stables, a wooden barrel was placed under a tap. When the barrel was three quarters full, two wooden poles were hooked to the side and one man in front, one at the back, the heavy barrel was moved twenty yards, placed as near as possible to the trough and then water tipped into it. This operation had to be repeated many times until the troughs contained enough water to supply forty thirsty horses.

After that, the stable boys were allowed to sleep for two hours in turn, in the loft, on the straw or the hay. During the next two hours following their rest, they had to do the cleaning, whilst the others walked up and down the centre aisle of the stables. Their duty was to secure the chains of horses that had broken loose, or to shout at the top of their voice to stop two neighbouring horses from fighting each other. After another two hours the cleaner became supervisor of the horses, and the supervisor became cleaner.

On a 24 hour guard, they therefore had four, two hour rest periods, and sixteen hours of duties. The worst part of this guard duty was the two hour turn starting at 4 a.m., because the two boys on duty, then had one and a half hours to fill forty bags of corn. They then had to place them behind each horse on a specially provided hook, half way up each vertical post, and give a final clean up to the stable before the arrival of the full troop.

Reveille was at 5.00 a.m. in the summer and 6.00 a.m. in the winter. Ten minutes later all the men of the squadron had to attend roll call in their denim fatigues and clogs in the exercise yard. Half an hour was then devoted to the cleaning and pampering of the horses. The sound of a bugle announced to the six squadrons that formed the regiment that the horses' drinking time had come and every man in turn had to take his horse to the drinking trough. Another sound of the bugle announced the time for the distribution of corn. The horses could anticipate this call, even before the men, and their reaction was immediate. Some would start looking around, others would become nervous and restless. One blast of a whistle told the men to unhook the bag of corn. A second blast instructed them to move simultaneously to position themselves by their horse's head. At a third blast on the whistle, they had simultaneously, to pour the corn into the trough.

All this was done with the sole purpose of preventing the horses demonstrating jealousy towards one another. Even so, the horses' reactions were unbelievable. Some would kick furiously sideways with their hind legs. Others pulled their ears back, the usual sign of a horse intending to bite, and exposed their powerful teeth in the direction of the horse on the left or right of them. To avoid the possibility of confrontation the men had to stay near their horse's head until most of the corn had been eaten and the horses settled back into their normal nature.

Now it was time for the men to return to their quarters, first to wash, next to go for breakfast. After eating they went back to their sleeping quarters to change from their denims into the No 2 uniform. They then tidied up their beds to the prescribed standard, with their mattress folded in two and properly lined up in the middle of the sheets, blankets and pillows.

At 7.30 the bugle would announce sick parade and all those who had reported sick at reveille would have to line up at the surgery door. One might wonder why this medical had to be so early? Maybe it was to make sure that those who were judged not really to be ill, but to be dodgers, would have been found out before the time for assembly at 8.00 a.m. This is when all the fit men had to line up once more in front of their quarters, under the command of a sergeant. They would then be marched two by two to the stables, where the next ten minutes were devoted to saddling the horses, giving a last polish to the leather or the metal chains, swords and other metal equipment.

Another five minutes was spent in taking the horses onto the main parade ground where they had to be lined up in two columns of sixteen horses. Each soldier stood to the left of each horse's head holding the reigns with his right hand. When everybody was lined up and at attention, the senior sergeant would go into the building and inform the Adjudant that the squadron was ready for his inspection. This he did very thoroughly and every man and every horse was submitted to his scrutiny.

Next they were ordered to mount and then came the lieutenant's inspection. Finally they were ordered to draw their swords and were then ready for the captain to take over the command of the squadron and order the departure for the exercise field. As soon as all the horses had left the stables for the morning exercise, the four stable boys had again to clean the litter, replace the straw, fill the top mangers with fresh hay and fill the drinking troughs.

Rene's first meeting with Taylor came after having attended to all these duties one morning. He had been ordered to be horse guard in the afternoon. As it had been a tiring morning for the horses and because the weather was good, the stable boys were instructed to take all the horses outside the stables and fasten their reins to the metal rings fixed at regular intervals along the whole length of the outside walls of the stables. They had been told that if a horse got loose from his harness or slipped its reins from the ring fastening them – at which some horses were very adept, that they had to approach the horse very slowly with both arms raised. They had also been instructed not to look into the horses eyes and when near enough, to simply catch the reins, or in the absence of reins, catch the horse by the ear and take it back to its place.

Whilst attending to his duties Rene spotted a horse which had got loose and as instructed, walked slowly towards it, both arms raised. As he was half way to it, he heard one of the older boys, who was already into the second year of his national service, shout to him "Run away, it's Taylor." Believing that the older boys were always ready to tease the new trainees and to frighten them, he did not take any notice of this warning. But, his comrade was right and by the time Rene noticed the horse's ears folded back in anger, it was charging at him and it was too late to run away. Before he could count to three the horse was right in front of him had lifted its forelegs to the height of Rene's shoulders.

The horse knocked Rene to the ground and turned away from him without actually hurting him. Taylor disappeared in the direction of the football ground and was found quietly grazing on the grass there and every attempt to catch him proved unsuccessful. He eventually came back to the stables of his own accord for the evening feed. The only other way of getting him back would have been to find the soldier who had been Taylor's rider for the previous twelve months. He, no doubt, would have been able to get hold of him in the same way as Rene later could when he had become his regular mount and had become so accustomed to him that nobody else could handle him. This had its advantages, but it could also cause serious inconvenience.

It quite often happened that when Rene returned to the barracks from an evening out, the guardroom would give him a message that his horse was loose in the stables and instructing him not to go to bed before seeing to Taylor. When he got into the stables he would find Taylor trotting up and down the central aisle and not one of the boys on stable duty daring to approach him. All Rene had to do was to call him by his name and according to his mood, he would either come to him or at least stand still and wait for Rene to catch him by the ear. Then, as meek as a lamb, he would let Rene lead him back to his stall and fasten his bridle.

Taylor had unusually slim jaws which allowed him, unlike other horses, to stretch his neck and ease himself out of his collar whenever he felt like it. The horse was sixteen years old and had been given by the German government to the Belgian army as war damage compensation.

Although Taylor worried Rene a bit at first, he was later quite happy to have him as his permanent mount because his performance on duty was so reliable. Rene noticed the difference when, on one or two occasions, Taylor was ill and he was given in his place a monster of a great heavy, asthmatic horse, called Dempsey. To get into his stirrups on this horse Rene almost had to lift the point of his left foot to the height of his chin. Dempsey was also a dangerous horse and had killed a man the year before with a kick from his powerful hind leg. That same horse was nearly the cause of his own and Rene's death.

Half way through his national service and after his squadron had completed all their basic training on horse back, on foot and with various weapons, they were divided into specialist groups. Of the thirty two men forming the squadron, six were chosen to become despatch riders or scouts. Included in the training for this role was the installation of field telephones or telegraphs, including the use of Morse telegraphic code. These men were also trained to use special pistols to fire signal flares in the air during night manoeuvres. Rene had been made one of the squadron's six despatch riders.

One day during an exercise, he had to take Dempsey across a level crossing. This particular level crossing was controlled from a distance. To warn road users that a train was due on the line, the two barriers at each side of the railway track moved from their vertical position to a 45 degree angle. Then after a pause of a few seconds, to allow traffic to clear, they came down to the horizontal position. Just as Rene had brought Dempsey over the middle of the tracks, the barriers moved to the warning position. The horse became petrified and would not move past the second barrier. Rene buried his spurs into the horse's sides, but still he would not move. By then the two barriers had come down and soon Rene could see the train in the far distance.

Although in the army the life of a horse is more important than that of a man, Rene decided his own safety came first. He jumped off the horse. By then a farmer had arrived from the direction Rene had intended to take. He leaned heavily on the barrier and managed to open it. In an instant Rene took his sword out of its scabbard and gave Dempsey a big whack on the hind legs with the flat of the weapon. In his haste he had forgotten to hold the animal's reigns and Dempsey rushed away without him. Rene thanked the farmer and then walked the several miles back to the camp. Dempsey had preceded him there by quite a while. Naturally, on his return he was greeted with sarcastic remarks by his N.C.O 's and other members of his squadron.

On another occasion when Taylor was ill, Rene found himself having to ride Dempsey. It was an occasion Rene would never forget – even down to the date. It was the 8th April, 1932, the birthday of King Albert the 1st of the Belgians. To mark the occasion a military parade was held in every large Belgian city. Antwerp being the nearest city to where Rene's garrison was stationed, it was there it had been ordered to parade.

The regiment had to be out of bed for 3 a.m. and be in the stables to clean the horses from 3.15 to 3.45 a.m. By 4.15 a.m the men had had their breakfast and at 4.45a.m they had to be ready to saddle their horses for a first inspection outside the stables by the sergeants, at 5a.m. Fifteen minutes later the two platoons making up the squadron were presented to the sergeant major. After a further fifteen minutes the lieutenants appeared, prior to a final inspection by the captain. Eventually these two squadrons moved out of the Cavalry School together with the two other squadrons housed there. At the exercise field they were joined by the three other squadrons and the regiment's band. The six squadrons forming the 3rd Regiment of Lancers was now ready for inspection by the colonel.

By 6.30a.m they were ready to start the twelve mile trek to Antwerp. In order not to tire the horses too much they would be ridden for a few miles and then from time to time the men would have to dismount and walk for another few miles. Three hours later they reached the entrance gate to what was then the fortified city of Antwerp.

Once more the troops were ordered to get off their horses and give them another brushing, including a blackening of their hooves. Next they rode slowly to the centre of the city, eventually taking up position along the wide avenue running through the city from north to south. There each squadron of thirty two riders was formed up in what was called "Battle Order." The two columns of riders having brought their mounts to a halt, now wheeled the animal's head around at right angles to the line of march, so that the squadron now formed two lines of sixteen horses abreast, with the captain and the two lieutenants having taken up position out in front of the squadron and with the sergeant major positioned centrally behind the second row.

At 11 o'clock, having stood for nearly one hour on the same spot, a sudden fever went through the ranks as they heard orders being shouted in the distance and gradually coming nearer. This was the signal that the general in command of the city and his staff had started their inspection and were approaching. When the general was two squadrons away from Rene's, the captain gave the order, "Swords out." This is when Rene was faced with the most embarrassing moment of his military career.

The command consisted of two orders. When the captain shouted "Swords...." the men had to take both reigns in their left hand, lean over to the left and ease the sword a few inches out of the scabbard with their right hand ready for the second brief order, "out." Then they had to pull the sword clear of its scabbard and in a second movement swing the sword to the right with their stretched right arm fully extended in a form of salute before bringing the blade to rest on their right shoulder with the sword pommel and their right hand resting on the thigh of their right leg.

As soon as the first order was given, Rene realized that he was in trouble. As soon as he had taken the reigns in this left hand and seized the handle of his sword with his right hand and tried to ease the sword from the scabbard the whole thing, sword and scabbard seemed to move together. Realizing that his sword was, for some reason, stuck in its scabbard, he quickly dropped his reigns onto his horse's neck and seized the scabbard with his left hand and pulled as hard at the sword with his right as he could. He managed to dislodge the sword, but was aware it had come out moments after those of the other members of the squadron. When he looked at his outstretched sword, he saw floating at the end the cause of all the trouble. A piece of cloth, used by the boy who was acting as Rene's unofficial batman, to clean the inside of the scabbard, had lodged itself inside and he had simply forced the sword in, thus causing it to jam. Now the evidence of the problem was there like a flag at the end of Rene's sword.

As soon as he saw this, he brought the sword to rest on his shoulder as quickly as he could and by rubbing the point against his uniform managed to loosen the piece of cloth,so that it fell away behind his shoulder. Luckily for Rene all the officers and the sergeant major were so busy watching the general approach that they never noticed that his sword had only been withdrawn momentarily after all the others. However his father, who with his mother and sister had come, proudly as an ex-officer, to watch Rene's performance, did not fail to notice. Franz told Rene later that he had noticed his son's plight and felt like crossing the road to come to his aid. The worst thing was that he had been so conspicuous. He was in the centre of the front line of his squadron, and with his very long body and a horse one hand higher than the others, he stood a head higher than all the others.

After this little incident, the general proceeded to inspect the infantry units lined up on the right of the cavalry and eventually approached the grandstand on which were gathered all the provincial and civic dignitaries, headed by the governor of the province of Antwerp and the burgomaster and all of the aldermen in their impressive uniforms and hats with gold braid, resembling the uniforms traditionally worn by ambassadors on ceremonial occasions. The black uniforms contrasted with the multi coloured dresses of the ladies. When the general reached them, he faced the grandstand, saluted the dignitaries and then moved his horse to the right of the grandstand followed by his staff.

As soon as he had reached this position, a rider went to inform the senior officer in charge that the parade could start. When Rene's squadron's turn came to move off, its two rows of sixteen horses smartly moved to the centre of the wide avenue. By then, many of the horses had become impatient following two hours of waiting on the spot and the troops had some difficulty in preventing them from breaking into a trot.

As soon as they had passed the general and the reviewing grandstand they had two hundred yards further to go before turning left into a much narrower street. In order to do this they had to speed up the horses to trotting pace and reduce the line from sixteen riders abreast to eight riders and then from eight to four riders. In order not to delay the squadron behind, this movement was supposed to be done at a fast trot, but the horses at the front started to gallop and soon the whole squadron was charging down the street. In view of the fact that the street was cobbled, this was highly dangerous. If one horse had slipped and fallen on the highly polished stone, it could have caused a serious pile up. Luckily nothing happened except for the shouting of the officers and NCOs in their effort to get their men to keep better control of their horses.

After all this carry on had subsided, the regiment returned to the field at the entrance of the city, where they had stopped in the morning for a last clean up of their mounts. There, a certain number of lorries were waiting with supplies for lunch. They consisted of thick sandwiches of bread and cheese and a bottle of beer for the men. The horses were supplied with a bag of corn.

Once more Rene's parents had followed the squadron and had come to see him. An NCO had told them to wait whilst he went to look for Rene. Whilst waiting they noticed a whole row of horses roped to each other. Suddenly one big grey horse started to kick out sideways at the other horses. Somebody shouted "Get that Dempsey out of the way." Moments later Franz, Irma and Georgette saw Dempsey approaching them, lead by Rene.

His father often reminded him later of the scene and said he always wished he had had a camera with him. Rene was wearing his helmet, his carbine across his back. In one hand he was holding his half loaf of bread, in the other the open bottle of beer and under one arm was tucked the reins holding Dempsey who was now peacefully following him, with his nose bag of corn dangling in front of his mouth. Franz who was accustomed to horses came to stroke Dempsey, but his mother and sister were terrified of the animal and kept it at a good distance from them.

But Rene's period of military service was to contain many lighter moments. One Such occasion was when he went shopping in town with a young, but very dashing sergeant. The sergeant asked Rene to stop in front of a chemist's shop as he wanted to buy a contraceptive. No sooner had he gone into the shop than he came out and told Rene that the only attendant in the shop was a young lady. For someone who was usually very bold and enterprising, he had suddenly become remarkably shy. Rene told him he would not mind making the purchase for him. The pair walked back into the shop. Rene told the young lady shop assistant what he wanted and she, unperturbed, asked him what size he wanted. Rene turned towards his friend and repeated the question to him. His complexion changed dramatically, becoming bright red from the tip of his nose to the back of his ears, as he hoarsely attempted to whisper the answer.

On another occasion the sergeant major, who the men of Rene's squadron had nicknamed 'Crotin', meaning horse dung, discovered the usual meeting place in Antwerp of those soldiers who were fortunate enough to own cars and were, therefore, not reliant on public transport. Two boys always arranged to take some of their colleagues in their vehicles. This meant that instead of taking the midnight bus they could stay another half hour in town. The midnight bus took one hour to reach Brasschaat, a slow walk to the barracks took fifteen minutes and that was why the normal midnight pass was extended to 1.15am for the cavalry. With a car it only took thirty minutes to do the whole journey.

Quite often they arranged for one of their friends who was travelling by bus to take their passes and since most of the time the sergeant on guard duty was too busy reading his paper or a book, it was child's play for this friend to drop all their passes with his own into the appropriate tray. At 1.15 all the passes were collected by the sergeant and checked against the list of pass holders. Anybody arriving after that time was reported to the orderly sergeant major of the week who in turn put the latecomers on a charge in their respective squadrons.

Those who had arranged to see that their passes were surrendered in time, were usually able to stay out until the early hours of the morning. Then they would enter a ground floor room, just before reveille, through a very conveniently left open window. This window faced the football pitch outside the barracks and since all the warrant officers' and NCOs' rooms were on the opposite side of the barrack block facing the internal barrack square, there was only one chance in a hundred of being discovered.

On more than one occasion Rene did not get the time to change from his No 1 uniform into his denim fatigues and had quickly to pull them over the breeches of his No.1 uniform. As usual Rene's first duty of the day was to go to the stables to groom his horse. After one of his nocturnal jaunts he had started to brush the horse in regular circles, but gradually the circles became smaller and smaller and his whole body began to lean against the horse as he fell asleep. The horse must have sensed it because he kept as quiet as a bronze statue. Luckily for Rene that he had vigilant comrades and as soon as they saw the sergeant approaching the stall, they would give his horse a little prod with their brush. The horse would move with a sudden jerk and then Rene would awake just in time, so avoiding getting himself into trouble.

Sergeant Major Esters, affectionately known to the men as 'Crotin', had suspected for some time that some of his men stayed out later than permitted. However, he had never been able to find out how and when this happened. The only thing he had discovered was the agreed meeting place for the return journey. Rene and his comrades suspected that it was a pure coincidence that he had walked into the club where they met, because if he had been tipped off, he would probably have waited until past the time allowed for a return to barracks to catch them. As it was, he came into the club, saw them all sitting together at a long table and without being invited, came to sit with them. His presence was welcomed in as much as he ordered a round of beer for the group. Conversation, however, changed quickly from barrack gossip to the most uninteresting of subjects.

When the time ultimately came for the group to depart in order to reach the barracks in time, he suggested that they should stay and even paid for another round of drinks He told the men that as he was responsible for any delay, he would arrange things with his orderly colleague. Around 3am Rene, his comrades and Sergeant Major Esters left. They had managed to make room for him in one of the cars. On arrival in Brasschaat they went straight to the garage to park the cars. 'Crotin' jumped out and without waiting for the others made his way to the barracks. To their dismay, when arriving at the guard room, they discovered that not only had the dirty dog not made arrangements to clear their late arrival, but had instructed the sergeant of the guard to make a note of their names and to record the time of their arrival. It was 3.45am.

Rene tried to reach the sergeant major's room to ask him for an explanation of his handling of the affair, but found he had already locked himself in. The next morning Rene went to see him on behalf of the little group. "Well," he said, "when I said I would cover for you, I meant you and the friends you were driving back, but there was no reason for the driver of the other car and his passengers to stay. I can make arrangements for you to come off the charge sheet, but not for the others." Rene looked at him angrily and replied with real vehemence in his voice. "No thank you very much. Either you clear us all, or we will all go on a charge and we will all be able to testify that we all had your blessing to stay, since you paid for a round for all of us, after the permitted time." Esters was silent for a few moments, then realizing that he might very well get himself into trouble, as he would have to admit having had drinks with other ranks, which was frowned upon in the Belgian Army. So, he made a tactical retreat by promising that all names would be removed from the charge book and this he managed to do.

He never forgave Rene for this defeat and often tried to catch him out. On two occasions he succeeded. Once, when having teased Rene more than usual, Rene reacted saying "Watch yourself, only mountains don't meet." The captain commanding the squadron placed the worst interpretation on that remark, considering it insubordination and confined Rene to barracks for eight days.

On the second occasion, although the charge was more serious, Rene came off more lightly. The charge read: "For having returned to the barracks under the influence of drink and having vomited through the window onto the front of the parade ground. He has also by this action soiled the uniform of the sergeant major who was passing under the window at the time." The charge was read to Rene in front of the Captain, who asked him rather severely, "What have you to say for yourself?" "Sir," replied Rene, "I contest having been under the influence of drink. In fact I only had one glass of cognac after eating some rather greasy chips at the village shop. When I got to my room, which was very warm, the mixture of the chips and the cognac made me suddenly feel violently sick and my immediate reaction was to open the window to let in some fresh air. In order to relieve the feelings of nausea, I suddenly felt I had to get rid of what was making me feel unwell and rather than dirty the room and the corridors, I thought the window was the best place."

"That is quite an acceptable explanation," said the Captain. "Did you actually see him come into the barracks under the influence of drink, sergeant major?" "No Captain, I did not see him come in" said the Sergeant Major, "but I assumed that he must have been. I recognized him as he was leaning through the window." "First charge dismissed," said the Captain. "On the second charge, I accept that this was an emergency and that you chose the best course, but please, in the future before you open your mouth, be sure that the sergeant major is nowhere under your window. Charge dismissed." The Sergeant Major was furious, but there was nothing he could do in the face of Captain Waterloos's decision.

This Captain was a jovial, good hearted man, who lived firstly for his horses. He had two of his own fed at the army's expense. He hated the guts of the sergeant major and was pleased of any opportunity to demonstrate it. He liked to drink and therefore, any charge concerning drunkenness was dismissed or got a light sentence. Only one thing the Captain never forgave a man for, was a lie. If a soldier returned late to barracks and used as an excuse, that his grandmother did not feel well before he left home, the Captain would say, "Tell your grandmother to choose another time to be unwell. Eight days confined to barracks." Had the soldier admitted that he was drinking with friends and overlooked the time, then the Captain would say, "How many glasses have you drunk?" If the man replied, "Four Captain," then Captain Waterloos would say, "Good. Next time you go out, drink three and then check the time, to see if you are able to swallow a fourth one." In the book, he would mark next to the charge, "Caution."

After the first six weeks of very hard and tiring initial training, mainly connected with horse riding, more emphasis was put on arms training.

In Rene's cavalry regiment this meant the short FN carbine, the bayonet and the long cavalry sword, which after the 1914-1918 war had replaced the lance. It was not as practical as a lance to ferret out an enemy hidden in a haystack, but it was much more effective in close combat. After one month of general training in the use of arms, every man in the squadron was directed to a field of speciality of his own. By the eleventh month of national service a soldier was supposed to know every aspect of his duties and to be able to put his capabilities to the test.

Bourg Leopold, Limburg Province, Belgium 1931

The regiment would move to the east of Belgium to a place known as Bourg Leopold, the Belgian equivalent of Salisbury Plain. Here a state of war would be simulated and the experience of the various unit commanders and of the men under their command would be put to the test. Luckily for Rene, the day after the regiment's arrival there he was posted to the Town Mayor's office. This was the best duty assignment he was given during the thirteen months of his national service and unfortunately it only lasted six weeks. But during those six weeks, he lived as if in paradise. The Town Mayor's office was run by a general who stayed in the best hotel in the little town and was not seen too often in his office. The real officer in charge was his aide de camp, a captain, who lived in the building incorporating the offices, with his wife and eighteen year old daughter.

From the outside the Town Mayor's office looked more like a large country residence and contrasted strangely with all the red brick military buildings in the surrounding area. The building was situated at the entrance of a park reserved for officers only. It was a large white painted villa. At the front was the entrance to a suite of three offices. At the back, approached through a large private garden, which included a lawned tennis court, was the entrance door leading to the private residence of the captain. One door, off the main corridor at the front of the building, also led to his private apartments. The captain had one civilian cook, who prepared food for the family and also for his staff, which now included Rene. The captain's orderly cleaned both the captain's house and the three offices. In the largest one, Rene worked with two warrant officers and a sergeant. A door led into the next one, occupied by the captain and from his office, a double door led into the general's office. Any caller had to report first to Rene's office and any visitor for the general had first to be reported to the captain's office.

As soon as Rene reported for his first day of duty, he was met by a very kindly sergeant who introduced him to the senior NCOs. One of them then started to explain to Rene the workings of the Town Mayor's office. Amongst other things he explained that the local military police and the general discipline of the camp and the town came under the jurisdiction of the Town Mayor. During the day the patrols were done by the Military Police, who in the evening, were reinforced by an army patrol of one sergeant and four to six men, supplied every day by a different army unit. These evening patrols supervised the discipline of off duty troops and ensured that they had all returned to their barracks by the appointed hour. The army patrol only had authority over NCOs and men, but the Military Police could even apprehend an officer if he could not identify himself or had committed a serious breach of army regulations.

Every morning a despatch rider brought the military police and army patrol reports to the office. Any soldier or NCO whose name had been taken, but who had not been arrested, would be mentioned on one report from which extracts were made for each unit commander, leaving him to deal with the culprit. Those arrested on minor charges, such as drunkenness, were sent back to their unit in the morning and once again a report on the circumstances of their arrest was posted to their unit via the office. For those arrested on more serious charges, reports were sent to the military prosecutor known as the Auditeur Militaire and their unit informed of their detention at the Military Police jail.

Charges against officers were usually addressed to the general in sealed envelopes and through his adjutant. Sealed information would again go to the unit commanders. Rene's first job in the morning was to help the NCOs to sort out the reports, then prepare the big envelopes for each unit. After lunch when the senior NCO had checked the contents of each envelope and sealed them, Rene had to take them to the headquarters of each unit in the camp. At the same time, he would collect the envelopes containing reports informing the Town Mayor of sanctions imposed as a result of previously notified charges. This round of the camp took him the best part of the afternoon and he usually returned to the office just in time for the evening meal.

After supper he was free, three days out of four, to go into town to have a drink with his comrades in arms. In addition, he had three Sundays in four free. The evenings and the one Sunday when he was on duty, he had nothing else to do than to answer the phone and record any messages for the captain or the general. He also knew where to reach them in case of emergency.

Rene's one other major duty, and a very pleasant one, was to take the general's horse out for a ride early every morning. He did this for one hour before breakfast. The purpose of this was to tire the horse sufficiently so that by the time the general sat on it after breakfast, the nervous animal would have quietened down and make riding it easier for the old man.

One day, about one week after Rene's arrival at the camp, a patrol report came in. Amongst various incidents reported, one read as follows: "Sergeant of the Guide Regiment came out of an establishment with his collar wide open, his cap very disorderly, on sideways. When I (Sergeant of the Guard) told him to adjust his uniform he became abusive. As I suspected him to be under the influence of drink I asked him to give his name. He refused. I then felt justified in arresting him, but several sergeants who were with him prevented me. They all managed to run away. However in the struggle, the sergeant first involved lost his cap which I recovered and send herewith. All I can say is that he was 6ft tall, broad shouldered, his hair was blond, he spoke very loudly and with authority."

As usual a copy of this report went to the colonel of the Guide Regiment, but this time the cap of the culprit was sent as well. This cap had printed on the inside a serial number which would identify the culprit. The next day a note from the colonel to the Town Mayor informed him that although the serial number identified the regiment, it did not correspond with anybody under his command at present. The number was an old one and he had sent a message to his headquarters in Brussels to find out who in the past had been given this number. Two days later the answer came. It was the serial number of Prince Charles, the brother of Crown Prince Leopold, the heir to the throne, when three years earlier he had been a sergeant at the Officers' School.

The report addressed to the general and Town Mayor also informed him that the colonel of the Guide Regiment had completed his investigation which resulted in the following: "Prince Charles, now a lieutenant in the Guide Regiment wanted to spend an evening in town with his cousin Eugene, the Prince of Ligne. As officers and NCOs were not allowed in the same establishment, he had used his old sergeant's uniform, the one he had worn whilst at the Officers' Training School." The description given by the sergeant of the patrol fitted Prince Charles and it was surprising that the sergeant had not recognized him. The report mentioned that the colonel had dealt with the Prince de Ligne and the other NCOs involved in the incident, but he left it to the general to deal with Prince Charles.

The general, somewhat embarrassed, phoned the colonel to know if similar acts had taken place in Brussels and to ask the Colonel if he knew what action had been taken in those instances. The colonel's answer was that although he was personally entitled to deal with any officers under his command, he had thought that it would impress the young prince more if he was called in front of the general and was given a good telling off by him. Rene was consequently instructed to deliver an envelope to the prince containing an order to appear in front of the general the next morning.

As the prince was not at his lodgings when Rene called, he gave the letter to his batman and instructed him to deliver it to his officer without delay. The next morning, as Rene was sitting at his desk the door opened without the usual knock and Prince Charles entered the room. Immediately all jumped to attention. The prince told them to carry on and addressing the senior warrant officer he said, "Is the old man here? Tell him that I have arrived." With unusual haste the warrant officer entered the captain's office and soon came out with the captain who invited Prince Charles into his office. From there he was brought in front of the general, who apparently, gave him a respectful royal telling off. It appears that Prince Charles was not very impressed with the telling off because when he came through the outer office in the company of the captain, he made a gesture in the direction of the general's office, which is not normally associated with royal protocol.

It was probably the first time that the prince had met the general and he took full advantage of this introduction. In fact, only a few days later, he appeared without a prior appointment and asked to be announced to the general. This was certainly not in keeping with normal army practice when an officer asking for an interview with a general would first have to channel his request via the whole chain of his superior officers. But then Prince Charles was not an ordinary officer and normal rules were soon set aside. The warrant officer notified the captain of the prince's request and the captain rushed into the general's office. The general came out himself to meet the prince and invite him into his office. Five minutes later Rene's switchboard rang and the general instructed him to get a call through to the royal palace in Brussels. At first the civilian switchboard operator at the local post office thought Rene was joking. They had often exchanged some jokes on the phone, but when he insisted that it must receive army priority she immediately gave him a line to Brussels. When he finally got the palace switchboard on the line the general asked to speak to the Aide de Camp to the King.

The King was apparently not near the phone. The Aide de Camp rang off promising to notify the king immediately and to ring back. During the wait, Prince Charles sat in long conversation with the general. Ten minutes later Rene's switchboard rang. "This is Brussels, we have a call for Prince Charles, is he available?" "Yes he is here," Rene replied. "Good. Please connect." The moment came for Rene to put the call through to the general's office and there, in person, was King Albert on the line.

Rene found out later what all this was about. Prince Charles had run out of funds the previous evening and informed his father on the phone of his problem. The king then spoke to the general requesting him to kindly advance the money to his son, assuring the general that he would be repaid the next day. Prince Charles walked out quite happy and the general was happy to have obliged the king.

On the first occasion on which Rene was on weekend duty the captain's daughter came into the office and saw him sitting near the switchboard, reading a book. "Why do you stay indoors on such a beautiful afternoon?" she said.

"Well miss, I have no choice, I am here alone to answer the switchboard," Rene replied.

"Has the sergeant major not told you about this extension switch?"

"No miss," said Rene.

"Well look, there on the side of your switchboard. Push that switch down and any incoming calls will sound a loud bell situated next to our entrance door. My father had it specially installed for times when there are no troops in the camp and nobody on duty in the office. Now you can join me in our garden."

"What will your father say about this miss?"

"I have asked him already and he has no objection. He has even suggested to my mother that you should join us for meals. My mother has, therefore, asked me to invite you. We are having tea in the garden."

"Thank you very much miss. I shall be delighted to accept your mother's kind invitation," said Rene with enthusiasm.

A few minutes later he was sitting with Captain Moreau and his family enjoying a tea which bore no comparison to the one provided by the army kitchens. After tea Miss Moreau asked Rene if he would like to join her in a game of tennis. "I am afraid miss, that tennis is not one of my strong points. My main sports are ice hockey in the winter and rowing in the summer."

"Never mind, this will be a good opportunity to learn tennis and I shall be very pleased to become your teacher."

Such an opportunity was too good to be missed and Rene gratefully accepted the offer. After that weekend he spent practically every evening in the captain's house or garden, whether he was on duty or not.

Four weeks after Rene's arrival at the camp, Miss Moreau announced that a good friend from her boarding school days was coming from Bruges to spend two weeks with her. The captain ordered an army car to pick her up at the station and he requested Rene to escort his daughter, who was to meet her friend on the platform. As soon as the train arrived Miss Moreau ran towards her friend and as soon as the usual embraces were over, she introduced Rene to Jenny. She made a big impression on him and he believed he had impressed her too.

During his last two weeks at the Town Mayor's office life became still easier than it had been up to then. Most evenings the captain would ask Rene to escort the two girls on a walk in the park reserved for officers and even when he was supposed to be on switchboard duty he would tell him to go. The captain would answer the phone himself.

By the time it came for him to make his farewells, he and Jenny had become very close friends. They exchanged addresses and promised each other to write regularly. The captain thanked him for all the help he had given during the six weeks and told Rene that if he wanted, he would arrange for him to be placed at his service again the following year, when he would return for the compulsory six weeks recall.

Brasschaat, Belgium, 1932

The last month of Rene's military service was easy, but boring. The regiment were back at the Cavalry School in Brasschaat in time to see the arrival of the new recruits who for the next thirteen months were going to take the places of Rene and his comrades in the squadron. Riding was over for them. Their job now was mainly to teach the new recruits all they had been taught themselves, thirteen months ago when they had joined the cavalry. This included subjecting the new recruits to all the naughty tricks and jokes they had been the victims of and which the new boys now had to suffer.

They had installed a black board in the refectory, on which one of them had written "The 1931 promotion. 30 messing tins for sale." The number started at 30 and was reduced daily. These thirty days appeared to go very slowly and at last came their day of departure. It started with an inventory of all they were leaving behind and payment for any missing object. The only pieces of equipment they were allowed to take with them was their No 1 uniform and cap, which they were supposed to keep in good order and free of moth incursion for next year's recall to camp.

Together with eleven other boys from his squadron, all residents of Antwerp, it had been decided that they would celebrate the return to civilian life in a dignified and memorable fashion. The father of one of the twelve boys was, very conveniently, the owner of a restaurant, "The

Old Tom," situated in one of the main streets of Antwerp. The son therefore took up the suggestion of a farewell banquet with his father and brought back a most attractive offer. His father would put at their disposal a private dining room on the first floor. He further offered a most attractive menu, including wines and champagne, at a ridiculously low price.

It had also been agreed that before leaving Brasschaat that they would all have one last drink in each of the cafes to which they used to go. This took the entire morning. During the afternoon they travelled back to Antwerp and returned to their respective homes. Managing to sober up just in time to put on their evening suits, which included a dinner jacket, known in America as a "Tuxedo," or as they are called in Belgium a 'Smoking Jacket.' In their buttonholes, instead of a flower, they wore the white tassel which for thirteen months had been dangling at the front or on top of their caps as part of their regimental insignia.

The banquet was a real success and during the dinner they decided to form an ex-service men's club. Rene was elected founder president and at the end of their meal, they had their first meeting to decide on a name for the club. Rene suggested "Le Cadre Blanc" in opposition to the "Cadre Noir," the famous elite squadron of the French Cavalry School of Saumur. This was accepted unanimously, with enthusiasm.

There being no other business they decided to attend one or two dances taking place in town. They cleared the banqueting table of all its floral arrangements and made up some small bunches that each one of them carried away. At the first dance at which they arrived, they made a sensational entrance marching in two by two. They stopped near the band stand and studied the ladies in attendance. By the time the music started, each of them had made up his mind which young lady he was going to invite for the next dance. Without hesitation they dispersed in various directions around the hall. They bowed ceremoniously in front of the lady of their choice and handed her a bunch of flowers, then invited her to dance.

It so happened that that same evening, the club for former pupils of Rene's lycee was holding a dance in another hall and he had arranged with the committee that there too, they would make a grand entrance at a given time. But there he had a surprise in store for his comrades. The band playing at that dance was formed of old boys of the school and he had given them in advance the music of their regimental march. So when they appeared in the hall the band had been looking out for Rene and started to play the regimental march. So ended one landmark in Rene's life. Little did he know then that the cavalry would soon end too.

Everything seemed so peaceful in 1931 when he first joined the army for his national service. As he was not at all militarily inclined, he did not apply to join the special platoon, where he would have started as a private. Three months later he would have become a corporal, or Brigadier in the Belgian cavalry, and in another three months he would have been promoted to sergeant, known as a "Marechal de Logis." By the end of the term, he would have been a Sergeant Major or Adjudant.

The next year he would have come back as a second lieutenant for the six weeks recall, which everyone had to do. The big snag would have been that he would have had to come back every year in the spring for another six weeks refresher course. This he was not prepared to do and this was why he never mentioned at the reporting office when he commenced his national service that he had completed his studies, to an equivalent of A level standard. He therefore started his national service as a very honorary private and finished the same. After his six week's recall, which he again did at the Town Mayor's office in Bourg Leopold, he was hoping never to wear a uniform again. Events were to decide differently.

The Chateau of Aunoy

Bought by Eddie Nathan in 1931

**Eddie Nathan entertains his sister, Catherine and her husband
Gaston Billotte at Aunoy 1932**

Family gathering at Aunoy
Back row left to right: Marcel and Renee Roost, Helene and Eddie Nathan,
Cecile Nathan, Germaine Roost, Irene Manasseh, Rupert Manassseh,
Sal Adler-Weiler
Front row: kneeling left to right: Georgette Falkenau, Emmy Manasseh
Sitting: Cecil Manasseh, Andree Nathan

Marcel Roost on the bicycle with his four nieces
Left to right: Gerogette Falkenau, Cecile Nathan, Andree Nathan
and Irene Manasseh

Rene Falkenau seen on Taylor his cavalry mount during his
military service in the 3rd Belgian Lancer Regiment

The Class of '31, Rene Falkenau can be seen in the middle row, extreme right of group, leaning forward.
Note the white tassles on the army cap which gave rise to the forming of the 'Cadre Blanc' with Rene as first president of the regimental association.

Manassehs and Nathans – The Singapore Connection

Eddie and Helene Nathan with their daughters, Andree and Cecile born in Singapore in 1917 and 1916 respectively

**Rupert and Emmy Manasseh and their daughter Irene
born in Singapore 1914**

**Ezekiel Saleh Manasseh and one of the several properties
he developed in Singapore**

Following his return from national service Rene settled back into his job with the Schelde Insurance Company, but his involvement with the organization of the Antwerp International Exhibition had created a new interest and appetite and in 1934, quite unexpectedly, he gravitated into the tourist business. He had seen a job advertised with Compagnie Internationale des Wagon Lits, the company responsible for running luxury international train services such as the Orient Express. His role was concerned with the more modest services associated with the overnight sleeper trains operating the boat-train services from Antwerp and Ostend.

For Franz, following the death of Adolphe Adler in 1927, there had been the task of building upon the reputation of his father in law as a diamantaire. In that role Franz truly was his heir, although it should be said that Adolphe's brothers, Jacques and Edouard had continued to assert the reputation of Diamant Adler when they exhibited a diamond 'plus grande pierre' of over 200 carats in an expo held in 1928. For Franz his time was divided between his office in the diamond district around the Central Station and the trading floor of the Diamond Club, one of the four bourse dealing in the sale of cut or rough diamonds in Antwerp.

At his office Franz would receive clients to discuss their needs for stones of a particular cut, quality, size and colour. Apart from supplying his brother Paul, who had taken over the management of Bruders Falkenau in Prague alongside his cousin Walter Falkenau, following the deaths of Sigmund Falkenau and the retirement from the firm of Walter's father, Emile. Franz had an impressive list of clients in Paris as well as Milan and several other European cities. It has to be said that the years following the crash of 1929 were not great ones for Antwerp's diamond traders. As the depression deepened, demand halved and had it not been for the custom he received from his brother in Prague and his regular clients, Franz might not have coped so well in these straightened times.

The Diamantclub Van Antwerpen was the oldest of the city's bourse, having been formed in 1886 by a group of merchants who routinely met for coffee and to discuss business in the Café Flora. In 1892 the 'Club' acquired its own premises on Simonstraat. By 1910 the club had been rebuilt three times in larger and more impressive premises. The impressive Flemish façade with its step gabled roof had an entrance foyer where uniformed attendants would ensure that admission was strictly limited to club members. Non members could only be admitted in the company of a member who acted as their guarantor.

The trading floor, on the first floor of the bourse, was a room resembling the long gallery of many an English stately home. Along one side were a range of large panelled windows, providing ample light to permit the traders to view the gemstones being traded to best effect. On this same side of the room at right angles to the windows were numerous trestle tables faced by benches or chairs. Those engaged in the trading of the cut stones would sit facing each other across the table and in front of them would be a square of black felt, on which the cache of diamonds being offered for sale would have been placed for examination by the vendor.

Some wholesale trades would require the purchase of an entire cache of stones of varying quality ensuring that the buyer was forced to take some stones of inferior quality in order to obtain more desirable ones. However many jewellers would be represented in the making of trades by merchants who acted as brokers. A jeweller who was making a piece which had been commissioned, would supply his broker with a description of the number and type of stones required for the piece. It would then be the responsibility of his broker to assemble the cache required. This was a tricky business which might involve the broker in a series of trades to acquire the stones needed. It relied on a great deal of trust and understanding between the broker and his client, something which might only be gained over a period of years. Once a purchaser had scrutinized the stones he wished to buy, usually with the monocular eye piece favoured by jewellers to examine the quality of the cut, the deal was always sealed in the same manner, with a handshake. Often the process of agreeing a price would take some time and could often be accompanied by cups of strong coffee or glasses of Schnapps.

The trade would be completed by the purchased stone or stones being taken to a counter set in the long back wall of the trading floor.

There behind a metalled screen, rather like that which graced traditional banking halls, a teller would weigh the stones and record details of the trade. Payment was always made in cash and would be held to the merchant or broker's account, with settlement of all accounts being recorded at the end of each trading period.

Brussels 1935

Rene was fortunate to find a job on the permanent staff of the secretariat of the international exposition which was to be held in the city that year. His experience with the Antwerp International Exposition four years earlier had stood him in good stead, but this was to be a permanent full time appointment, unlike the honorific post he had held previously as a result of his employer's generous agreement to allow him time away from his normal duties.

The exhibition was to be held in the Heysel Park on the edge of the city, not far from the royal family's winter palace, from April through to November 1935. Today it is where the Atomium, the structure built for the 1958 Brussel's World Fair now stands, symbolizing the perceived importance of the atom to mankind's future. At the north end of the long Boulevard du Centennaire, in which the Atomium stands as a centerpiece, are a series of buildings which were similarly considered a symbol of modernity when built in 1935.

Within the Parc des Expositions, the Palais designed by the Brussels architect, Joseph Van Neck, is the main building, a stark modernist piece designed to house exhibits. In front of the Palais were large pools containing ornamental fountains. In the park were the pavilions of the twenty five nations which officially took part, with five more being unofficially represented. The exhibition which had been timed to coincide with the 50th anniversary of the establishment of the Congo Free State, a misnomer in view of the fact that the exposition's theme was 'colonisation'. It attracted twenty million visitors.

Rene's office was situated in a building alongside the Palais des Exposition, where he worked in the tourism section. It dealt with the promotional publicity prior to the event and liaison with travel and transport companies bringing visitors to the park. It also handled enquiries concerning hotel accommodation and providing information which encouraged visitors to broaden the scope of their visit to Belgium. By the end of the exposition Rene knew that he had found his vocation and that travel and tourism would be his future. It was not just the enjoyment and fascination of the work. He had experienced and seen the bitterness of the first world war and its aftermath. On a visit to Germany in the 1920s he had experienced the effects of hyper inflation, recalling the purchase of a packet of biscuits at a cost of two million marks. Now with tensions again rising in Europe, he saw tourism as the future, the means to break down barriers between people and end the old enmities which had so divided Europe. To his great joy, even as the 1935 Brussels Exposition closed, preparations were already commencing for the next big expo to be held on Belgian soil at Liege four years hence.

Antwerp 1938

An unusual event occurred in March 1938. One day the front door bell of Franz and Irma's house in Rue du Palais rang. When Nicolas the butler opened the door he found a poorly dressed man with a long unkempt beard who spoke to him in broken French. The man said he was an old friend of Franz and had come all the way from Prague to see him. As Nicolas knew that Franz returned from the office every day at the same time and that it was now only ten minutes until his return, he invited the stranger to wait in the drawing room. When Franz arrived Nicholas told him of the visitor and his name, which did not mean anything to Franz. When he entered the drawing room, the man introduced himself and when Franz told him that he did not remember ever having met him, the man tried to convince him that they had been school friends in the first class of the primary school, but that the boy's parents having moved to another town, he had left the school after one year.

Franz duly asked him to state the object of his visit. The man then started to tell a long and pathetic story, the outcome of which was that whilst on a visit to Antwerp he had run out of cash and having discovered at the Czechoslovakian Legation that Franz was the treasurer of the "Beseda Volnos," the Czech welfare organization in Belgium, he suddenly had thought to seek his help. Franz told him quite bluntly that the funds at his disposal were to help any Czech resident in Belgium temporarily in financial difficulties, but that he regretfully could not use those funds to help a temporary visitor. If anyone could help it should be the Legation. To get rid of the insistent and inopportune visitor Franz gave him a small amount out of his own funds. After the man's departure Franz called Nicholas and told him off for so imprudently introducing a complete stranger into the drawing room and leaving him alone with all the precious antiques openly displayed on the table and side boards.

Exactly one week later another bearded man, but well dressed this time, stepped out of a taxi in front of the house and rang the bell. When Nicholas opened the door the man asked to see Franz and he was met with an abrupt "He is not in," and the door was slammed in front of his face. Luckily, that just at that moment, Georgette had arrived at the front of the house and noticed the incident. She enquired what the visitor wanted. He mumbled his name and said he was sent by Signore Beluschi of Milan, Franz's best customer in Italy. Immediately Georgette invited him in, whilst apologizing for the rude manners of the old butler. She entertained the visitor until her father arrived. As soon as Franz walked into the drawing room the visitor introduced himself as Signore Grandi sent by your friend Guido Beluschi.

After the initial formal greetings Franz, enquired about his friend and was told that all was well with him, but that he was very upset at the restrictions placed on their business. Franz had at the time three main sources of income. One was by acting as a broker for his brother in Prague and the other by being purchase broker for Beluschi and for another important diamond merchant from Paris. When after the first Munich conference the situation of Czechoslovakia became critical, business in the jewellery industry fell flat, and almost at the same time the Italian Government put a restriction on the import of diamonds of Belgian origin, in retaliation for the restriction imposed by Belgium, at the instigation of its farmers' union, on the import of Italian salad vegetables which were flooding Belgian markets at extremely low prices. The Italian decision hit the Antwerp diamond market bitterly hard and Franz lost one-third of his income as a result. It is probably for this reason, and also because he was known to be a persuasive negotiator

151

that Franz was chosen by the board of the bourse to represent the trade as a whole at conferences initiated, at their request, with the Belgian government ministries with a view to obtaining official intercession with the Italian Government.

Signore Grandi told Franz that he had been informed of these negotiations and that he wished to have a private talk with him about it in his office, preferably that same day. Franz suggested that the visitor should stay for lunch and after the meal they could go together to his office. Signore Grandi declined saying that he was already invited for lunch and expected within minutes by his friend the Italian consul in Antwerp, but he would be very pleased to call at Franz's office at the club soon after luncheon. Franz shortened his after lunch rest to be back in his office in good time. Since Beluschi when on business in Antwerp, used Franz's office, and since he was a great admirer of Mussolini, Franz had had a big portrait of Mussolini framed and stuck on the wall. This portrait, however, had to come down each time the Paris buyer came, as relations between the French and Italian governments were so strained. Franz would then store the portrait of Mussolini until the next visit of his Italian customer.

On this particular afternoon Mussolini was once again on the wall. When Signore Grandi arrived and was invited to sit, he told Franz, "You may not have understood my name this morning, I am the Count Grandi, Ambassador of Italy in Great Britain and I have been asked to see you in your capacity as negotiator for the diamond trade here in Belgium." What was discussed was never revealed, and all Franz ever repeated later about their conversation were the parting words they had exchanged. Franz had expressed his concern at the international situation and the shadow of another war to which Grandi replied, "I do not think we have anything to fear, the four big nations, France, England, Germany and Italy bark a lot at each other, but none of them will dare to take the responsibility to start a war." How mistaken he was. A week after this visit, Franz was given a copy of the English newspaper, the Daily Mirror, showing a photograph of Count Grandi in his ambassador's uniform, taken the previous day, as the Ambassador had officially presented to King George VI his letter of recall. Mussolini had appointed him as his Minister of Justice. Franz took the paper home and teasingly showed it to Nicholas telling him, "Look there is the beggar you nearly threw out last week."

Count Dino Grandi had studied law and economics at the University of Bologna and served in the Italian army during World War 1. As a young man he had been a socialist, but had become impressed by Benito Mussolini when they first met in 1914. In 1920 he joined the Blackshirts,and became one of thirty five Fascist deputies elected to the Italian parliament in 1921. After the Fascist takeover of the country following their 'March on Rome' in October 1922, he became a member of the new government,first as Under Secretary of the Interior and then as Minister of Foreign Affairs. He became Italy's ambassador to the United Kingdom in 1929 until his recall. Grandi would enjoy a comfortable position during the coming war. He was associated with the most radical and violent sections of the fascist movement and was constantly surrounded by members of the Blackshirts. However, in 1941 he would be posted by Mussoliini to the Greek front, which may explain why he became the first one to oppose Mussolini and be responsible for his down fall. Grandi opposed Italy's involvement in the war and in July 1943 at a meeting of the Fascist Grand Council moved the motion which was subsequently passed by 19 votes to 7 asking King Victor Emanuel to remove Mussolini from office. Mussolini was arrested the following day. Grandi fled to Spain two months later and from there to Portugal and Argentina. He returned to Bologna from Sao Paulo, Brazil, dying there in 1988.

Prague, Czechoslovakia 1938

For a long period following the death of Sigmund Falkenau, prior to World War 1, the family firm of Bruders Falkenau, had been jointly managed by Paul Falkenau as Sigmund's successor and Emile Falkenau, eldest son of Wilhelm Falkenau, the other co-founder of the business. The death of Emile in 1936 had left a gap in the management of the company and as it had always been agreed that the two eldest sons of the principals should also play a part in the running of the company, Paul had had little difficulty in agreeing that Emile's two sons, Walter and Jiri should join him in the business. As the father of two girls, who had no interest in the manufacture of jewellery Paul had been anxious to secure his own succession and as his brother, Franz, was firmly ensconced in Antwerp, there was little prospect of him asserting an interest in the firm. Bruders Falkenau was now in the hands of this triumvirate.

Over the years since its formation the fortunes of Bruders Falkenau had grown steadily. From its beginnings in the Jewish old town of Josehof in 1869, the firm had moved to newer premises in Benediktska in 1875, ahead of the redevelopment which had seen large parts of the old Jewish quarter razed to the grown, starting in 1880. By 1930 the company had acquired premises on Hybernska, in one of Prague's major shopping thoroughfares, followed in 1937 by premises on the street called Revolucni in the district of Prague 2, the city's equivalent of London's west end.

Emile's two sons had been born within five years of each other, Walter in 1901 and Jiri in 1906. Walter had married at the relatively late age of thirty one, to a non Jewish woman twelve years his junior, named Maria Weinsablova from Bratislava. In January 1936 a daughter, also to be named Maria, was born and who was later christened in the Catholic church of St. Alois in the Prague suburb of Vinrohady. Jiri was to follow his brother's example in marrying a non Jewish woman named Marie Simankova in Prague, a year later in 1934.

For members of the Falkenau family in Czechoslovakia the Anschluss in Austria, in which German troops occupied the country in March 1938, was the signal for a new and frightening period in their lives. For some time the family in Prague had received reports from the Katzenellenbogins, the family of Edita, Paul Falkenau's wife, who lived in the Berlin suburb of Charlottenburg, about the treatment of Jewish families in Germany. Within days of the German annexation of Austria, a systematic tyranny involving the arrest of all elements opposed to the Anschluss had commenced. Within a short time some 70,000 had been rounded up and sent to concentration camps, many of them Jews. News of these events flowed back from family members as well as from reports in the Prague newspapers. Already the 'Sudeten Question' was looming large on everyone's minds in the Czech capital.

Events in Germany and now in Austria had led to a steady stream of refugees entering the country. The Czech Jewish community had responded to the influx through its various welfare organizations, helping to resettle displaced families and in providing assistance for the many refugees who had decided to seek the security of neutral countries or the chance of a new life in Israel, America or elsewhere.

Immediately following the annexation of Austria on 28 March 1938, Konrad Henlein leader of the Sudeten German Party met with Hitler in Berlin. A month later on 24 April, Heinlen's party issued the Carlsbad Decrees demanding the autonomy of the Sudeten region of Czechoslovakia. President Edvard Benes sensing the threat to the integrity of the Czechoslovak state and the possibility of a German invasion ordered a partial mobilization of the Czechoslovkian army. Jiri Falkenau, a reservist with an artillery unit, was to be amongst those called up.

September 30th saw the conclusion of the Munich Agreement, and saw the great powers, Britain, France, Germany and Italy agree upon the dismemberment of the Czechoslovak state at a conference to which representatives of the Czech government were not even invited. On 1 October German forces occupied the Sudetenland and on 5th October President Benes resigned in protest. In the weeks following the signing of the agreement 115,000 ethnic Czechs and 30,000 Germans fled the Sudeten, for what remained of the Czech state.

In Prague the Falkenau family faced agonizing choices – whether to stay or whether to abandon their homeland. But how? In purely practical terms liquidating the family's assets was hardly straight forward, given that so many were seeking to do the same. By Christmas 1938, with a government sympathetic to Berlin installed, the Jewish community in Prague were preparing, with the help of a British businessman of German Jewish origin, to send the children of Jewish families to Britain.

Hurriedly organized, several of these 'Kindertransport' conveyed the refugee children to the Hook of Holland, accompanied by adult members of the British Quaker community.

It was in this climate that the Falkenau family gave consent to plans for two of its members to flee the country. This would require resources to sustain them, both to finance transport and accommodation, as well as provide sustenance until such time as they could find means to support themselves. For Paul Falkenau there was no possibility of leaving the country. Without his presence the business of Bruders Falkenau would collapse and deprive his wife Edita and sister Melanie of their sources of income. Besides which, the idea of leaving his wife and sister, both Jewish women, to face the perils which might lie ahead was unthinkable. His elder daughter, Ellen and her husband Pavel Jellinek, faced other problems. Even if today it is sometimes argued that two can live as cheaply as one, when it comes to those contemplating exile, a couple can face twice the problems of a single individual travelling alone. Ellen and Pavel who were determined not to be parted, therefore decided to stay and meet whatever hazards lay ahead together. For Paul's younger daughter, Vera it was a different matter. A single woman, now aged twenty five and well educated, there was a real possibility that if she could get to a place of safety she could rapidly find means to support herself.

For Melanie Falkenau's eldest son, Walter there were other issues to confront. Now aged thirty seven, he was beyond military service age, unless the government called for volunteers – an unlikely event now that a government sympathetic to Berlin was installed in Prague. Now that President Benes and his supporters had elected for exile, there was already talk of Czech men being organized into military units outside the country. But for Walter there was another issue dominating his thinking. As a Jewish man married to a non Jewish woman, was there a greater risk that she would face injury and harm as a result of his presence, or would she and their three year old daughter be less likely to attract the attention of the authorities if he were not present? Both his wife and daughter possessed their baptismal certificates as Roman Catholics and for that reason, he believed, might be spared the mistreatment which they already knew to be meted out to German and Austrian Jewish families. Reassured by his uncle that his role in the family business could be covered in his absence, it was not without feelings of torment and anxiety that Walter made the decision to leave his homeland.

With the assistance of Jewish welfare organizations, both Walter and Vera were to make their way out of Czechoslovakia and eventually settle in countries which had agreed to offer hospitality to refugees from the horrors unfolding in Europe. For Walter it was to be Australia, which after his arrival in Britain, had offered sanctuary. For Ellen whose route out of Czechoslovakia had taken her via Switzerland and Italy it was to be South America and Santiago in Chile which provided her place of safety.

On March 15th 1939 the annexation of the remainder of the Czech lands by the German army occurred. It did not have an immediate effect on the remaining members of the family in Prague, although it was hard to avoid noticing the wave of arrests taking place in the city, of public figures and certain members of the Jewish community. At the same time fascist organizations began a campaign of harassment against the Jewish population. Tales of beatings in the street of those whose orthodox appearance made them easy targets began to be heard, along with reports of attacks on synagogues, several of which were set on fire. As secular Jews whose appearance did not immediately proclaim their ethnic identity the Falkenaus at first thought they had simply to maintain a low profile and they would be safe. But things are not always that easy.

June saw a rapid deterioration in the situation. Under decrees issued by the new government of the Protectorate of Bohemia, all Jews were barred from engaging in any kinds of economic activity, thus making it impossible for Paul to continue to run the family business. By the following month he had been compelled to file a report listing all of the company's assets. The document listed the company directors of Bruders Falkenau as himself, Walter and Jiri, and gave their occupation as factory owners, with a company office at 15 Revolucni, Prague. The working capital of the company was given as two million, five hundred thousand Koruna, with a turnover in 1937–38 shown to be six million Koruna and with exports valued at three hundred and seventy five thousand Koruna. The company employed thirty five workers and seven supervisory staff.

Following seizure of the company's assets Paul and Edita were forced to move out of the opulence of their apartment on Myslicova in Prague's New Town and look for inexpensive rental accommodation in Vinrohady in the city's eastern suburb. Paul's sister Melanie and his daughter Ellen and her husband Pavel, soon followed his lead. For all there would be the uncertainty of how long they would have to live this way and whether their savings would be sufficient to see them through.

157

Ellen and Pavel were fortunate to be able to find an apartment on Libicka two streets away from where Paul and Edita had taken up residence on Caslavska. At least they would be able to support one another or share in their misery. From now they would have to live on their savings and any reserves of cash they could bring to hand, something made more difficult by the restrictions on the amount of money Jews could draw down from their own bank accounts.

In September fresh decrees were issued. For Ellen and Pavel it meant dismissal from their jobs. They would now be dependent upon the financial support of Paul, who fortunately, due to his personal financial assets was at least well placed to support them, as he was already doing for his sister Melanie. Since the death of Emile she had received a pension from the income of Bruders Falkenau. Now she was reliant on the charity of her brother.Amongst other privations, they now faced being denied certain rationed items such as sugar, tobacco and clothing.

Antwerp, March 1939

When Germany invaded Czechoslovakia in March 1939 Franz was extremely worried for the safety of his brother, his sister-in-law and their two daughters, one of whom had only recently got married, also for his eldest sister and her two sons, Walter and Jiri. Very soon after the invasion the Germans introduced strict censorship and the news reaching Antwerp was very limited and brief. For obvious reasons Paul and Melanie had not sought to draw attention to the departure of Walter and Vera and Jiri's call up for military service. From the wording of these brief communications Franz could guess how unhappy his relatives were, and his mood changed from one day to the next. He, who previously, in any circumstances, was always full of optimism and gaiety, suddenly became obsessed by the feeling that dark clouds were gathering and that they would affect critically his own future and that of his near relatives. The conferences of Munich and the events which followed had been watched with anxiety and as each conference ended in failure, with worsening tension.

Chamberlain had come back from Munich with nothing to show, as far as Franz's Czech relatives were concerned. Their country was abandoned. Also there were reports that the Germans were marshalling abnormal numbers of troops along their western borders. A wave of pessimism ran through the country.

Liege, Belgium April 1939

Rene who was now employed as manager of the Tourist Department of the Liege Water Exhibition, an international event at which a variety of countries were represented, had watched with a mixture of curiosity and apprehension the construction of the German pavilion. The large and imposing structure was clearly intended to signal Germany's confidence and might. All of the countries and organizations participating in the exposition had made arrangements for the workers involved in constructing their pavilions to be accommodated either on site or elsewhere around Liege, all that is except the Germans. Each day construction workers were bussed in across the frontier and returned to accommodation on the German side of the border each evening. This might not have attracted Rene's curiosity, had it not been for the fact that the coaches in which they travelled had blacked out windows. When he sought an explanation for this he was told that this was to prevent the German workers from having to view the privations their Belgian brothers were suffering. More frightening was the news that German propaganda was already hinting that Germany's armies might be used to liberate Belgians from the yoke under which they were living.

Since early May the exposition had attracted thousands of visitors. On the 15th of August, a national holiday in Belgium, there was a record attendance, but on the 16th the dark cloud hanging over Europe suddenly burst. By the 17th, the exhibition was empty as rumours of a general call up spread throughout Belgium. It was pathetic to see all the flags still flying in the exhibition, but not one soul about. Everybody was at home, with their ears to the radio.

From day to day events worsened. By the 20th August Phase D of a general war footing was proclaimed and at an emergency meeting of the Board of Executives, it was decided to temporarily close the exhibition. The next day most of the twenty nine managers, including the Managing Director, were called up. Rene was one of the few who had not been called up. Although in the past he had not been militarily inclined, when the country was in danger, he had suddenly felt that it was his duty to rejoin. When, two days later, he still had not received his recall papers, he went to the 'Gendarmerie', the Military Police post, to find out why. After a prolonged search his papers were produced. They indicated that since more than seven years had elapsed since his national service, he was to be assigned to a non-fighting unit. He was earmarked for the Army Veterinary Infirmary, IVA for short, which would only be formed in ultimate emergency, called Phase E. The latest information was that the invasion of Poland was imminent and although it took the danger away from Belgium's border, the country remained on the alert. The invasion of Poland eventually decided Great Britain and France to declare war on Germany on the 2nd September 1939. On the third of September it happened, Phase E was announced.

As the front seemed to be localized, the Belgian High Command decided to reduce the size of the army for the time being and all men in essential occupations were released. Most of the exposition directors and Rene's colleagues came back and the day after his return, the Managing Director called an emergency meeting. He explained that in view of what was happening, the Board had made the wise decision to close the exhibition prematurely. The official closing date was to have been the 15th October. When it closed provisionally on the 20th August, the press had been informed that the exhibition would reopen as soon as the situation had settled. Now another announcement went out to the effect that the exhibition would not reopen. Managers were instructed to start straight away the operation of closing and the liquidation of their respective departments.

Cannes, France, November 1939

The declaration of a state of war by Britain and France on Germany, following the invasion of Poland, had prompted Eddie Nathan and his wife Helene to consider moving to somewhere more secure from their home in Paris. If a military conflict ensued, which now seemed inevitable, then northern France seemed likely to bear the brunt of this, as it had done in the previous war. In that event the security of the

Channel ports could not be guaranteed and a possible means of escape for Eddie and his family, all U.K. passport holders, closed. A move to southern France seemed to offer their best alternative. If the conflict was contained, and the arrival of the British Expeditionary Force in September and the build up of France's military forces, seemed to offer that hope, then it might be possible to resume life in Paris fairly soon. Remaining in France would reduce problems in obtaining funds through the French banking system, as well as allow all members of the family to continue to use what had been their principal language since their return from Singapore in 1930. Equally, if the conflict were to spread, engulfing the French regions, there were still possibilities for leaving the country, either through the southern French ports, or across the frontier into Spain.

Although Eddie and Helene's two daughters, Cecile and Andree, were old enough to understand their parent's desire to quit Paris, Eddie in particular, was anxious to create the atmosphere of a relaxed family holiday, rather than a panicked retreat. The family car was loaded with suitcases filled with clothes for an autumn and winter in Provence.As they headed south they made various stops at hotels and to visit friends enroute,in the Limousin and in the Haute Pyrennees.

Eventually they arrived in Cannes on the southern French coast and checked into the Grand Hotel on the seafront, Eddie having telegrammed ahead their request for accommodation. For the next few months they settled down to an enjoyable round of holiday pursuits. For Cecile, it was bathing, when the weather permitted, with a group of friends she soon assembled around Palm Beach. Eddie had time to indulge his taste for competitive sport, with tennis as a major preoccupation. He had befriended an Arab prince named Lotfalla and they soon became a regular sight on the courts around the hotel. For the time being at least, thoughts of war could not seem further away.

Antwerp December 1939

By the 31st December Rene had completed the liquidation of the Tourist Department of the Liege Water Exhibition and after handing over to the accountants his inventories and reports, he said farewell to the directors and travelled back to Antwerp to celebrate the new year with his parents.

Rene had been living away from home for the previous five years, but now at the end of December he came back to live with his parents and sister. This was not to be for long because the following month Germany invaded Norway. Rene, who had been a keen ice hockey player for a number of years, had been asked to referee an ice hockey match between Pole Sud or South Pole, a Belgian team and a Dutch team in Tilburg on the 17th January, 1940. It was in an open air skating rink and the temperature was 14 degrees below freezing. Rene was surprised to find that the weather had not deterred the tough Dutchmen from attending in large numbers. By the end of the match, a rumour had spread through the crowd the that the Germans were massing troops along the borders of Denmark and Norway.

Ghent, Belgium January 1940

Once more an emergency was declared and by the 20th of January, Rene had received his call up papers with a railway warrant for Ghent. Being stationed in Ghent, only thirty five miles from Antwerp meant he managed to visit his parents practically every week-end. In the early days of May tension suddenly grew and in the early hours of the 10th the German army invaded Belgium. General mobilization of the forces had been declared the same morning, but the German air force managed, from the outset, to disrupt all means of communication preventing men from joining their units.

As he had been previously notified, Rene was to join the Army Veterinary Infirmary. Its location was at the cavalry barracks at Pintelaan in Ghent, very near the main line from Brussels to Ostend and half a mile away from the main station. When Rene reached the barracks he entered the office next to the guard room, where he reported to the Quarter Master Sergeant, a young man with a long beard. He told Rene that there were two commanding officers in this unit, a Veterinary Captain who was a regular in the army and in charge of the technical side of the unit and an Administration Officer who had been called up two days earlier. He was a judge of the Court of Appeal in Brussels.

There were also two lieutenants both reserve officers who had joined the day before. Rene was introduced immediately to the Administration Captain, who was trying his level best to put the right man in the right place. His first question to Rene was, "What is your veterinary experience?"

"None," Rene answered. "I can ride horses and I have my Red Cross first aid diploma."

"What is your profession?" he asked.

"Travel agent," Rene replied.

"What did your work consist of?" he went on. Rene started to list the various positions he had had since entering the tourist trade in 1934. Amongst others things, he mentioned that, for a while, he had been controller of the planning of coach movements for a Brussels coach operator.

"Well," he said, "I have the right job for you. You will be my Transport Officer and since you say that you have also been through a hotel and catering school, you will share that job with the one of Messing Sergeant. Now first of all go and see the Quarter Master who will arrange to have two red stripes sewn to your uniform sleeves. If you do your job well, you will get your sergeant's stripes within the three months prescribed."

Rene went off to see the Quartermaster who congratulated him on his appointment and then said, "By the way, would you kindly sign this receipt." Rene looked at it and it read, "I the undersigned Transport Officer, declare to have received from the Acquisitioning Authorities, six transport vehicles in good condition."

Rene eyed him gravely. "Just a moment," he said. "Before I sign this, I must verify if the vehicles are in good condition."

"Well," said the Quartermaster, "I signed for them two days ago without checking. As a matter of fact," he said in a rather confidential tone, "I don't know anything about cars. I'm a Monk at the Abbey of Orval."

"Sorry old boy, but I am not signing before I have checked the vehicles," said Rene sternly.

Very worried, the Quartermaster accompanied Rene to do his inspection. Rene rather expected the worst and he found it, especially when he was informed that the vehicles had been in the yard for the last three days at temperatures of ten to fourteen degrees below freezing. Of the six vehicles he found only two in working order. A brand new Studebaker lorry was found to have the engine block cracked right through the middle. Two had burst radiators and split battery cases. He could not establish what was wrong with the fourth one, but all four out of six vehicles had to be towed away to the Army Repair Centre, half a mile away from the barracks.

As there was very little dormitory accommodation at the Veterinary Centre all officers and NCOs, which now included Rene, were accommodated with the civilian population of the neighbourhood. He was allocated a small room in a house only fifty yards away from the barracks. All soon settled down to their new life.

Rene's mornings were employed in going for supplies, meat at the abattoir, vegetables from the wholesale market and other goods from the army store. He was usually back in time to supervise the food distribution to the men. His afternoons were spent supervising the drivers and mechanics doing maintenance on the two vehicles for transporting horses and six small vans for the use of the officers and himself.

After a few weeks, the situation seemed to improve. The immediate danger to Belgium of invasion seemed to reduce and instructions came that all men employed in essential activities such as coal miners, and railway maintenance men, should be sent home. The order stipulated that their kit bags should be left in the army stores, so that, in the case of another emergency, they would be available to the men without any delay.

From then on Rene's life took on almost a civilian character. With few military duties to occupy him, he got himself a young Alsatian dog from the Blue Cross. In his spare time he set to work to train the animal. About two months after his arrival in Ghent, he met a charming young girl called Janneke, and spent most of his evenings going out with her or being entertained at her sister's home. She had a flat in the centre of Ghent.

As there were eight NCOs in the Infirmary, Rene only had to be on duty in the office every eighth day and one weekend in eight. When the captain saw him with his new girlfriend, he congratulated him on his good taste. He even suggested that he would have no objection to Janneke visiting Rene in the office on his days on duty as long as he did not neglect to answer the phone, and do his once hourly inspection of the stables. Janneke became a very familiar face at the barracks and was soon well known by all the officers and NCOs. On one of the Sundays that Rene was on duty, she came to the barracks and spent the whole day either sitting with him in the office or on a bench at the entrance of the Guard Room, from which he could watch anybody coming in or going out. Life was relaxed and the atmosphere at the Infirmary very informal and cordial. The usual distance between officers and NCOs hardly existed, and the officer on duty was not be at all surprised to find Janneke in the office. They would even take time from their duties to hold a friendly conversation with the pair.

A big benefit for Rene was having the Quartermaster, the monk of Orval, as a colleague and friend. On one occasion when the monk was supposed to be on night duty and was going to miss an evening service, Rene offered to stand in for him until he came back from the mass. The Quartermaster was so grateful for this that whenever he could stand in for Rene, he did so. When Rene's Sunday duty came around, as long as he gave his friend time to go to the morning Mass, he would take Rene's place for the rest of the day.

This allowed Rene to take Janneke out on excursions. On one occasion they went to a place called Terdonck near Ghent where there is a large canal on which the local people organize a lively regatta in April every year. That particular Sunday was a glorious day and Janneke and Rene decided to hire a tandem and cycle to Terdonck. They got there in good time and found a good place on the elevated bank of the canal, from which they had a marvellous view of the finishing line. After the third race the sky, which had been perfectly blue and clear until then,was suddenly covered with dark clouds. Half an hour later, large drops of rain started to fall and within minutes the rain came pelting down like an Indian monsoon. Janneke and Rene sought refuge under the tarpaulin of one of the many stalls selling food and drinks along the canal bank. Five minutes later, the tarpaulin burst under the weight of the water which had welled up at its centre and Janneke and Rene got an unexpected shower, receiving the full force of the downpour.

They decided that they would have to return to town as quickly as possible and dry off. As Rene's barracks were on the way to town they went there first. He managed to find a small room where Janneke undressed and dried herself whilst he obtained the loan of new underwear, a pair of trousers and a pullover fresh from the stores, which Janneke put on, all supplied courtesy of his friend the Quartermaster.

Rene also got changed too and when Janneke appeared, everyone was highly amused to see her in army trousers and pullover, but she found it far better than having to go through the centre of the town in a light summer dress which, wet as it was, was clinging to her body. They went back to her sister's flat where she put on more feminine clothes. After that Rene saw to returning the tandem to the hire shop and the borrowed army clothing to the quartermaster's store.

During his service in Ghent, he managed to get one weekend in four to go and visit his parents in Antwerp. Franz was very worried. He had not heard from his brother and sister since the German invasion of Czechoslovakia and was fearing the worst for them. He was also convinced that Germany would, sooner or later, invade Belgium. Rene tried to convince him that the situation was improving since so many men in essential occupations had been sent home.

Cannes, Provence, March 1940

Whilst Eddie Nathan, his wife Helen and daughters Cecile and Andree continued to enjoy the hospitality of the Grand Hotel and the Mediterranean air, life had not been without its small crises. Delays in receiving funds through his bank in Paris had prompted him to dispose of the family motor car for some forty thousand francs to a Mrs. Levi Falk. Unfortunately, either the cheque issued by Mrs. Falk had bounced or payment for the motor car had not materialised for some other reason. It is highly likely that the car had been used to convey Mrs. Falk to a port from whence she could seek passage out of France to the United States and that the car had been sold on to assist in financing her passage.

In all events a letter from Eddie Nathan's friend and former business associate, George Baring, now resident in New York, but formerly a director of Baring of Paris, Ltd. makes it clear that Eddie, having obtained a court order in France for repayment of the debt, was now having to pursue the matter through a lawyer in America, which his friend had recommended. He expresses confidence that the debt will be recovered, either through simply writing to the lady or by obtaining a court order.

The letter also contains news of his own family. Having departed Europe the moment war was declared, he mentions that his mother in law is still in Vienna and that "there is no chance of getting her out." More happily he can report that his brother in law and his wife had arrived in New York, a matter of weeks earlier, bringing with them horrendous tales of the treatment being received, not simply by Jews, but by anyone who is not 100% in support of the National Socialist cause. "They are made to believe everything they are told. For instance, they are told we in America are starving." Even his brother in law had been sufficiently deceived by this Natzi propaganda – he had brought food from the boat conveying he and his wife to America, thinking his family would need it.

Paris, April 1940

Franz Falkenau had retained his Czechoslovakian nationality and had been entered in the records of the embassy in Belgium as a reserve officer. He, therefore, felt it his duty to get in touch with his embassy for further instructions. He took leave of Irma and Georgette and made his way to Brussels.

At the Czechoslovak embassy they gave him a railway warrant for Paris, instructing him to report to their Embassy in the French capital where arrangements were being made for the recruitment of a Czech army.

When Franz reached Paris a big disappointment was waiting for him. At the Embassy he was told that they had far too many officers and not enough men and that considering his age he was not wanted at present. They told him that he must look after himself and keep them informed of his movements in case they required his services at a later date.

Franz found himself a modest room at the Hotel Ellis on Rue de Grenelle, then busied himself trying to get in touch with his wife and daughter. Before parting it had been agreed to use the home of Irma's sister, Helene, as a postal address in Paris.

Ghent, May 1940

In the first days of May, Rene was once more on night duty in the office, when one of the stable boys on duty, rushed in to tell him that a mare was foaling, but as she lay so near to the wall, only the head and front legs of the foal had appeared, but were pinned against the wall. Rene immediately rushed up to the dormitory and got all the men down to the stables. They placed some wide straps under the mare and pulled her gently away from the wall. By then she was so exhausted that she could no longer deliver her foal by herself. Luckily, amongst the men there were a few farm boys who knew what to do, but they left it to Rene to cut the umbilical cord. As soon as the foal was separated, one boy rubbed it with straw, then wrapped it in a blanket and took it out into the aisle separating the horse boxes on either side of the stables. This was done to ensure that it was not hurt when the mare tried to get to her feet. Unfortunately she was completely exhausted and Rene was pleased to see the Veterinary Officer, who he had summoned at the start of the emergency, arrive. He relieved Rene of further responsibility and congratulated the men on the action taken. Quickly he gave the mare an injection which seemed to revive her and an hour later she was back on her four legs.

Whilst this drama was going on, Rene had not noticed that his young Alsatian dog had followed him into the box, and when they took the foal out into the centre aisle of the stable, the dog had followed. As soon as they had wrapped the foal in a blanket, with its long neck and head, with the large, beady, protruding eyes sticking out, the dog started licking the foal, which did not appear to be scared at all and responded favourably to the attention given him by the dog.

Later, in the afternoon, Rene went back into the stables to see how the mare and her foal were progressing. Again his dog followed him around and as he entered the box, the pup made straight for the foal who was now standing next to his mother. The mare, not understanding about the friendship that had been sealed between her offspring and the dog, was ready to defend her foal. Rene just managed to hold her head back in time. Meanwhile the dog was again standing beside the foal and licking him. As soon as the mare noticed that the dog did not intend any harm, she quietened down.

Two days later, as the weather was good, the mare and her foal were taken to the field adjacent to the barracks. Again, with his faithful dog, Rene went to visit them in the field. What followed was an entertainment which brought practically the whole Infirmary to a standstill. First the dog was chasing the young foal, still a bit unsteady on his clumsy long legs and then suddenly the chase would change with the foal running after the dog. The men could happily have watched this for hours if they had not been reminded that other tasks, not quite so pleasant, were waiting for them.

For the previous few weeks the Veterinary Infirmary had been the centre of unpleasant events. When Phase E had been declared, a military administration unit got busy with the requisitioning of 40,000 horses from their civilian owners. It would have been easy enough to requisition the animals' harnesses at the same time. Instead, this was done a few days later by another army unit and a third one tried with little success to fit the harnesses to the horses. The result was that in the following weeks the Veterinary Infirmary was inundated by the arrival of sick horses suffering from neck abscesses due to badly fitting harnesses. If the abscess was recent and not too deep, the Veterinary Surgeon would cure them. If it was deeper, he would operate, but if the abscess was too deep, and left too late to operate on, then the poor horse would be condemned and it would be slaughtered in the stable yard.

Following examination by the Chief Veterinary Officer it was often decided that only the neck of the horse was infected and he would instruct a butcher in the unit to get the best pieces of meat off the animal before the carcass was collected by the special disposal lorries. Rene, as Messing Officer, was provided with big chunks of meat and the men he had the responsibility of feeding much preferred the horse steaks to the fifth grade beef or lamb reserved by the abattoir for the forces. This was his first acquaintance with horse steak and he had to admit that he took a liking to it.

As dictated by the infirmary schedule, Rene was on duty in the office on the evening of the 9th May. The news had been particularly bad that day. There were reports of rumours that the Germans were again massing troops all along their eastern border. Janneke had stayed with Rene in the office until eleven o'clock. They listened to the radio and then she went home. After she had gone Rene relaxed, still fully dressed, on the camp bed next to the switchboard. After having made sure that the last pass holder had come in and the gates had been securely locked, he rested fitfully.

At 3 o'clock in the morning, the phone rang and a voice at the other end started to give Rene his recognition code, which allowed him to check the origin of the call. It was from command headquarters. The instructions were brief and precise: "Full emergency. Recall all officers and NCOs to barracks. Have all vehicles refuelled with full tanks. Store the maximum possible supplies of food and animal fodder. Await further instructions." This gave Rene plenty to do. To start with he had to awake all the drivers and send the vans to collect the officers. He sent other men to awake the NCOs billeted in private houses near the barracks. The six lorries went out to refuel. Meanwhile, he had switched on the radio and the news was coming in fast.

At regular intervals, an appeal was made by the radio announcer to all men who had been sent home to rejoin their units immediately. It was also reported that the Cabinet had been called together in emergency session. At six o'clock, an announcement came that German forces had violated Belgian territorial integrity, without any declaration of war and that their tanks were crossing the frontier into Belgium.

Simultaneously the Luftwaffe started to bomb all the major railway junctions and strategic points. At the same time, fifth columnists appeared from nowhere. Disguised as priests and nuns, they were running about shouting "Go away, hurry, the Germans are coming." In this way they created a panic, carefully planned, so that the civilian population would impede Belgian troops trying to organize their defensive positions.

Ghent received its first aerial attack near the railway station and although the air defences were not yet organized, the German bombs only hit a few buildings along the railway line without making a direct hit on the main railway line from Brussels to Ostend. Meanwhile in the office of the Veterinary Infirmary, the commanding officer had gathered all his officers and NCOs and in their presence, solemnly opened a sealed envelope containing orders to be carried out in the event of war. They read "The Commanding Officer will instruct his Motor Transport Officer to collect another six vehicles for the transport of horses from the requisitioning authority, bringing the effective strength of the unit to twelve vehicles. Next, seventy two hours after the declaration of war the IVA will detach three groups of three vehicles and an appropriate number of veterinary teams to areas not more than 100kms away from the Veterinary Infirmary. These three new units will be known as Evacuation Veterinary Infirmaries in short, IVE. IVE1 will be located north east of the Veterinary Infirmary, IVE2 immediately east and IVE3 south east. Each IVE should have a Veterinary Lieutenant and an Administration Lieutenant in charge, with a certain number of men to attend to wounded horses brought back to their care."

The plan was that horses requiring longer attention and which could stand transportation, would be carried to the Veterinary Infirmary in one of the vehicles attached to the IVE. It was intended that the IVEs would be ready to move to their positions seventy two hours after the outbreak of the war. Events however, proved different. It took more than seventy two hours for most of the men previously sent home to rejoin their unit. The disruption of pubic transport was such that the first one of them reached the Veterinary Infirmary after innumerable adventures and with effort, having overcome countless obstacles. As the boys arrived they had the most depressing stories to tell about the panic stricken country.

By the time the unit was up to full strength, and the IVEs were able to move forward, the Germans had advanced so far across the frontier that it was considered necessary for the IVEs to take up position nearer Ghent and for the IVA to be withdrawn back beyond reach of the German advance. Ghent was now the object of Luftwaffe attention, day by day.

On the third day of the war, they were informed that a train withdrawing a cavalry unit had been attacked just outside Ghent. German aircraft had sprayed the train with cannon fire. The train had stopped. All the men on board had jumped out, seeking protection on the side of an embankment. Some of the cannon fire from the aircraft had penetrated one of the railway wagons containing eight horses. Hit by a shell fragment, and in considerable pain, one horse had broken the chain securing the four of them to one side of the wagon. It had then jumped out of the wagon and onto the track. The poor animal did not get very far. Its legs got caught in the signalling wires and it fell beside one of the railway wagons. The other three horses jumped over the fallen animal and then rolled down the embankment. They were later found grazing in the field below. When Rene's unit were summonsed to the spot, they found that the horse lying on the side of the track had a broken leg and once more the humane killer had to be employed.

On the evening of the 14th May, the captain called Rene into his office and informed him that they would all move the next day. All the horses were to be put on a train. Rene, therefore, had to organize a convoy of horse vans from the barracks to the station. As soon as the last horse was loaded, he would have to have the lorries properly cleaned and then loaded with the men's equipment, food and medical supplies. In short, they were to remove everything that could be moved from the Veterinary Infirmary.

The captain informed Rene that the trains for the horses would be available by 9am the next day, on what was still, an undamaged siding, at the main station. The captain concluded by telling Rene that if he wanted to spend a last night with Janneke, he would have no objection to letting him go, as Rene had completed the movement planning that afternoon. But he reminded Rene, with a smile, that he would have to be back at the barracks the next morning by 7am to supervise the packing of the kitchen equipment and garage stores.

Rene's meeting with Janneke was a sad occasion. After a good meal in one of the more expensive restaurants, they decided to spend the rest of the evening with her sister whose flat and bedroom Janneke was sharing. This flat was situated above their parents' apartment. Janneke's sister knew that their friendship was more than platonic, but her parents knew nothing of that. After the elder sister had made sure that the parents had gone to bed, Janneke went with Rene to an hotel, where on many previous occasions they had spent the night together. At 6 o'clock in the morning, Rene got up, dressed and kissed Janneke goodbye and made his way to the barracks.

He entered the office at the same moment as the captain, who teasingly asked him what sort of a night he had had. Rene was about to answer him when he was interrupted by the roaring noise of planes, followed by the whistling sounds of bombs falling. Then there was the thundering, deafening sound of explosions, accompanied by the uninterrupted clatter of Bofors anti-aircraft guns which were stationed very near the barracks.

The attack had been concentrated on and around the station. The captain was chiefly worried about his loading bay, but Rene's worry was different. His thoughts were of Janneke who he had left in bed in that hotel near the station. He told the captain about his anxiety for her safety. Using the pretext of going to inspect the railway track, the captain invited Rene to go with him to the station. As they set off he turned to Rene and suggested, "Lets go via the hotel and see if Janneke is safe." When they got there Rene received a chilling shock of a sort he had never encountered in his life. There, where only one hour before, the hotel had stood, where he and Janneke had spent the night, there was now only a mountain of bricks and smouldering wood. Before he could say anything, the captain told him that they ought to go and inform Janneke's parents.

When they got to the parent's home, the captain waited in the car whilst Rene went inside. He had decided to go to the second floor first and leave it to the sister to inform Janneke's parents. He rang the door bell, really worried as to how he was going to break the news. After seconds that seemed like hours, the door opened and it was a surprised Janneke who faced Rene. With tears streaming down his cheeks, he kissed her tenderly and then told her of the agony he had gone through. She had, apparently, got up and dressed hurriedly only one minute after his departure and was half way to her home when she heard the planes attacking the station. Once more he kissed her goodbye and rejoined the captain who was overjoyed to hear the good news.

They returned to the barracks and on their way assessed the bomb damage. Back at the infirmary one of Rene's colleagues was describing his morning's adventure. "You'll never guess what happened to me this morning. As you know I have a room on the second floor of a private house nearby. Before leaving for the barracks I had a sit down on the toilet. I had just pulled my trousers on again and as I pulled the chain and the water flushed I heard a big bang and the whole side wall of the toilet collapsed, leaving the toilet exposed to the street. Imagine that," he said, with a laugh. "One minute earlier and I would have been caught with my pants down." Even desperate situations can have their comic moments.

As had been planned the day before, the convoy of vehicles started to the station at 9 a.m. Three hours later all the sick and wounded horses were aboard the special trains, eight per wagon. Several other wagons had been filled with straw, hay, corn and other fodder for the horses. Immediately after lunch, all the available men started first to clean the lorries and then load them. This took until the late afternoon when instructions came that in order not to draw the attention of the Luftwaffe, they should only move after dark. Their destination was Jabbeke, a small village in East Flanders, situated on the main road from Ghent to Ostend. They reached their destination in the very early hours of the morning and were met by their advance party. Rene was billeted with the local cobbler, who was a very hospitable man. Later that morning, he drove the captain to the railway siding. He decided to release as many horses as possible into a nearby field, which would save the supplies of fodder.

Two days later, they were instructed to move again, this time to Ostend. As soon as they arrived there, they went to see the local Town Mayor, who told them he had not been given previous notice of their arrival. After many phone calls and an hour's wait, instructions came that they should move immediately to a small village called Koekelare where there was a railway station to which the trains were being despatched. This was only a stones throw from the French border. There was no time to send an advance party, so the column of vehicles moved without further delay to their new assigned destination, whilst the Town Mayor's office promised to arrange the movement of the trains which by now should have reached Ostend station.

Koekelare, West Flanders, Belgium May 1940

As soon as they reached Koekelare the captain requisitioned the local school. One classroom became the office, and the others were turned into dormitories, and refectories, with the field kitchen installed in the school yard. Rene immediately requisitioned the only local garage as a workshop for his vehicle. Their reception in the village was not too good, the local people had had no experience of the war yet, other than having their streets, barns and fields invaded by hundreds of refugees, many of whom had come all the way from the eastern border of Belgium. These refugees only spoke French or Walloon and could expect little help from the mean Flemish farmers. The captain and his men had to adopt a stern attitude towards these farmers who were trying to find every possible excuse to prevent them from bringing their wounded horses from the trains to their fields. They even had to threaten one or two with arrest if they refused to cooperate.

As soon as they were settled down in the village, Rene was ordered to try to find out where the IVEs were now located. They had lost all contact with them since their first movement out of Ghent. Each of them had three vehicles, but probably did not know where to direct them with their loads of evacuated horses. One of the despatch riders had a motor bicycle with a rear seat. He took Rene out to hunt for the IVEs.

Making their way on roads crowded with refugees and retreating army convoys, they managed at the end of a long day's search and many stops, to locate the three units. Although originally they had been well dispersed east of Ghent, they had, through the contraction of the battle front, found themselves retreating as fast as the main Veterinary Infirmary Unit and were now only fifty kilometres away from each other and not much further from the main IVA.

Having made contact with the three of them Rene found the same situation at each. They were inundated with wounded horses. The veterinary surgeons and their staff were working non-stop, but very often out of consideration for the stricken horses, the humane killer was often the only remedy. Having assessed the situation and with the agreement of each of the commanders of the IVEs, Rene ordered that the horse transporters be loaded to their maximum safe capacity with the horses worth saving. They should move to a location equidistant from all three IVEs, where he would wait for them and then take charge of the column of nine vehicles and proceed to Koekelare.

After reaching the agreed meeting place, Rene had a long wait before all nine vehicles were assembled together. Every driver had a story to tell of how he had nearly hit some refugee's car or cart, or how he had miraculously escaped from one of the now frequent air attacks which had become only one of the hazards of this war. Now that he had them altogether, Rene got the nine drivers together, gave them a short briefing about keeping close together, despite their usual instructions, so as to avoid the infiltration of strange vehicles into their column, once he and his despatch rider had managed to clear a path for them on the crowded roads.

When the column was brought to a halt, Rene's despatch rider managed to squeeze his way ahead of the convoy. They soon discovered that the hold up ahead was due to a busy crossroad on the other side of a canal bridge. The whole of the traffic seemed to be at a complete halt. They quickly parked their motorbike and then the two of them walked along to the crossroad. They took it on themselves to direct a few drivers to move a few metres nearer to the vehicle preceding them and soon cleared the bottleneck. Next they controlled the traffic until the head of their convoy reached them. Having made sure that the last of their nine lorries had passed the awkward crossroad safely, they jumped back on their motorbike and made their way back to the head of the column. It was dark when they reached Koekelare and they had to spend another two hours finding homes for the stabling of the newly arrived horses.

The following morning Rene was instructed to go with his despatch rider to Bruges and to see if the requisitioning authorities could find them one or more lorries. When he got to the requisitioning office, all they could give him was an address where a large removal lorry was available. Duly supplied with the requisition order, he went to the address given to him. As he made himself known to the owner of the removal lorry, his wife in tears explained that all their belongings were on the lorry and that they were about to leave for Dunkirk with the hope of finding a train for Paris. Their final destination was intended to be the Belgian Congo.

Rene felt so sorry for the couple, especially as they had an old mother and several small children travelling with them. So he decided at some risk to himself to take them to Dunkirk. The journey was quite eventful.

He had never driven a vehicle of that size and he had a few narrow squeezes and near misses on the roads packed with refugees. During a hold up, he even saw in the crowd some of his old friends from Antwerp. They were quite surprised to see him handling this large lorry.

At last they reached Dunkirk. The family very gratefully unloaded their belongings and the owner of the removal firm insisted that Rene should accept an amount of money which he found far too generous. Pressing his offer, Rene reluctantly accepted the money and wished him and his family a safe journey. When he got back to Koekelare his long absence had not even been noticed.

The following morning a despatch rider brought a message from their command headquarters or CHQ, notifying them that it was now stationed in Bruges and expected to receive daily reports of the Veterinary Infirmary's activities. In fact the IVA had lost contact with the command headquarters since leaving Ghent, during which time the CHQ had moved from Brussels. A despatch rider immediately took a report to Bruges giving details of the activities of the IVA during the last few days. Back came a message from CHQ which read ' In order not to waste petrol, the Motor Transport Officer (MTO) will go on a motorcycle and assess during the day the exact number of vehicles required by each IVE. These, he will despatch on his return and preferably during the night, to avoid aerial attacks and refugees'.

The one thing CHQ had not bothered to enquire was whether the MTO had ever driven a motorbike, and the only despatch rider was now fully employed travelling up and down to Bruges. The commanding officer therefore decided that the only thing for Rene to do was to learn to ride a motorbike as quickly as possible. The despatch rider agreed to take Rene once more to Bruges, to the requisitioning authorities, who soon found him a motorbike. It was an antiquated type, with the gear change lever alongside the petrol tank, but it worked pretty well. The despatch rider gave him an hour's tuition, first in Bruges, then on the way back to Koekelare. The next morning Rene went on his own to visit the three IVEs. He covered 250 miles and saw many trees from dangerously close up.

During the next few days, the news was pretty bad. Holland had given up all resistance. The number of refugees on the roads and passing through the village was on the increase. This was adding to the already very tricky problem of food supplies.One evening the captain called all officers and NCOs together to a meeting in his office. He told the assembled group that the news was pretty grim, but that in order to maintain the morale of their men, they should give them very little information. He mentioned that he had been informed by headquarters that a very active fifth column was trying to make contact with the troops. They were specially trained to spread bad news in order to undermine the morale of the soldiers. He asked them to be on the look out for these rumour mongers and if found, to arrest them with speed and vigilance and to bring them in front of him.

The very next morning, the 28th May, Rene left his room early in the morning and crossed the village square to go to the field kitchen. In the middle of the square there was a gathering of several men nervously discussing things, whilst some of the soldiers were listening in. Rene approached the group and overheard a man say, "I assure you I have it from a good source that the Belgian forces are capitulating." Pushing his way through the crowd, Rene sternly told the man to come with him. When they were a short distance away from the group, Rene told him that unless he could substantiate what he was saying, he would arrest him. The man told Rene that the news had been given to him by a refugee priest staying at the local convent. Rene ordered the man to accompany him to the convent and to point out the priest to him.

Rene called over two of his men armed with their rifles to escort him. When they reached the convent, the doorkeeper, a nun, became very worried when she saw the four of them appear. Rene told her who he wanted to see and after an absence of a few minutes, she came back with the priest. He was duly identified by the civilian Rene had almost arrested. The priest did not deny having given the information. This put the civilian in the clear and Rene released him.

It was now the turn of the priest to be told quite firmly to reveal the source of his information. He had been visiting one of his friends billeted in a large farm on the other side of the village. A major in an artillery unit was also residing at the same farm and had just moved in the previous night. As the priest was in conversation with his friend in front of the house, a despatch rider had arrived and rushed in to deliver a message to the major. On departing the messenger had told the priest and his friend that he had brought news of the surrender.

Once more to verify the facts, Rene instructed the priest to take him to his friend. Once there, Rene demanded to see the major. When he was taken to him, he was surprised to find that he knew him very well. He had been the Assistant High Commissioner at the ill fated Liege Exhibition. Rene explained the nature of his enquiry and the major confirmed that a despatch rider had earlier that morning brought him information about a Belgian surrender. The message came from his own headquarters. Rene asked him if he was convinced that the message was genuine and told him about some of the tricks the Germans were up to.

Although Rene's commanding officer was only a captain he had, up to the arrival of the major, been the senior officer in the village and therefore, its Town Mayor. In view of this, Major Legrand agreed to go with Rene to the IVA's headquarters. Once there the two officers closeted themselves in the office. After a few minutes Rene was called in and told that both of them had concerns about the genuineness of the message. They wanted him to go with his despatch rider, each on their own motorbikes to Bruges, to the Command Headquarters and find out what was really happening.

Rene and the despatch rider, who was named Van Nuffel, got into Bruges without any hindrance. When they got to the office of the Command Headquarters, the doors were closed and nobody answered the door. They came to the conclusion that all was calm and that they had been victims of false rumours. As they were about to return Van Nuffel suggested that they make a small detour, to some friends living just outside Bruges near the main road to Brussels. He was hoping to get some news of his wife and child there. When they got there, the friends were very alarmed to see them arrive still wearing their revolvers and asked if they had not heard the latest radio announcement about the capitulation and instructing soldiers to surrender their weapons. They also told them that the Germans were occupying Bruges. Van Nuffel told them that that was rubbish, because they had just come from Bruges and there was not a German soldier to be seen. "How did you come from Bruges?" they asked. "By the western side," replied Van Nuffel. "Well, if you go a hundred yards from here to the crossroads with the main Brussels to Bruges road, you will see the German army columns making their way to Bruges."

Somewhat incredulous they their took leave and made their way cautiously to the crossroads, and sure enough, one German vehicle after another was speeding towards Bruges. They decided to make a rapid strategic retreat by the same road they had come along. When they reached the canal bridge, which they had crossed only half an hour earlier, they noticed that the bridge was already being guarded by two German sentries. They stopped a short distance away to consider their options. They agreed that the best course would be to speed over the bridge before the Germans realized what had happened. Rene went first, but as he approached the bridge he noticed that the Germans had stopped a horse drawn wagon which had come from Bruges and was now obstructing the whole width of the narrow bridge.

Assessing the situation and before the Germans had time to notice them, Rene made for a field to the left of the bridge approach followed by Van Nuffel. They now followed the bank of the canal. A little further on they managed to rejoin a path leading to the new main railway station. From there, always following the canal, they eventually turned northwards, before finally reaching the road from Bruges to Ostend. A few miles away from Bruges they caught up with a mixed column of Belgian and German staff cars. On the bonnet of each floated a large white flag. Several German and Belgian outriders on motorbikes were escorting the convoy. Each had a white handkerchief knotted to his left arm. Van Nuffel and Rene stopped a moment and without consultation, they had the same idea. They took a white handkerchief out of their pockets, fastened it to their respective sleeves and caught up with the rear of the column.

Soon they fell in behind the last vehicle. The head of the column, led by a Belgian staff car, turned to the right, away from the main road into a narrow country lane. A few minutes later the entire column halted inside the gates of a large mansion. There they discovered that this was the field headquarters of King Leopold. Rene approached one of the Belgian officers who had accompanied the German staff cars and told him about the purpose of his mission. Rather nervously the officer told Rene that the column he had followed was the German delegation coming to accept the surrender of the Belgian Army from the king. The officer instructed Rene to return to his unit and report to his commanding officer that instructions would be sent within the next few hours regarding what to do and how to surrender to the enemy. Van Nuffel and Rene drove back to Koekelaere at full speed where they duly informed the captain of what was happening.

At the same time Rene asked the captain's permission to leave the unit and take his chances by escaping to the south. He understood Rene's motives. As a Jew, Rene could not hope for decent treatment from the Germans, if the men of his unit were made prisoners of war. He could expect to be discriminated against and they had already heard rumours about concentration camps, which was probably the best Rene could hope for. Without hesitation the captain gave him his blessing to leave. He instructed one of the men to strap two full cans of petrol to the sides of the bike. He told Rene to take as much supplies of food as he could carry. One of the lieutenants, who before the war had been an Antwerp bank manager, gave Rene a note of introduction to a banker friend of his in Paris and told him that he could get any credit he needed there.

When Rene took leave of his officers, with tears in his eyes, they all thanked him for his services and handed over to him an envelope with money and a note with good wishes. On the captain's advice, Rene did not take leave of the men, it was better for very few to know about his departure.

As he left Koekelare for Diksmuide and then the Belgian border at De Panne, he wondered when, if ever, he would see Belgian soil again. As he neared the French border, the sky suddenly became dark and as he reached the canal bordering the road to Dunkirk, the rain suddenly came pelting down. Within minutes of the storm starting, he was soaking wet. When he had become an improvised motorbike rider, he had applied to the central store in Bruges for a despatch rider's equipment, but they had run out of, or lost the leather jackets and trousers which would have protected him now, during their frequent moves.All they could provide him with was a motorbike crash helmet. When he left the unit he was wearing his No 1 uniform and above it his cavalry great coat. The rain had soaked his great coat and begun running along his breeches and down the inside of his boots.

As he got half way to Dunkirk he was waived to a stop by a few Belgian despatch riders who asked him where he was heading for. He told them that he was trying to make his way south to Paris. "Don't you know that we are encircled?" one of them said. "Your only chance is to join us. One of our officers has gone to negotiate with the British to embark us for England. We are meeting him in half an hour in front of the church which you see there in the distance." Rene waited a while with them whilst several more boys on motorbikes joined them and eventually they made their way to the meeting point.

It was still raining and they sheltered under the church porch. They had quite a long wait and during this time they noticed, on the other side of the church square, an abandoned British army searchlight vehicle. Two French soldiers were busy plundering it. Having found all they wanted, they made their way towards the small group of Belgians. Rene noticed that one of them was carrying a heavy one gallon pottery jar. As soon as he noticed them, the Frenchman came and invited them to open their mouths. From the jar, now carried shoulder high, he poured rum into their waiting mouths. Then every one in turn was invited to empty their water bottles of their contents of cold coffee and fill them with rum. Rene would always remember these boys, because thanks to them and their rum, the next few hours were lost for him and with them, the anxieties of an uncertain future. It probably also stopped him from catching a shocking cold. He became oblivious of the time, but it was only several hours later, as they were absorbing the effects of the rum, lying on the steps of the church, that a lieutenant turned up and told them to follow him quickly into Dunkirk. By now the night was approaching and they all kept close together in order not to lose each other.

Dunkirk, 28 May 1940

They crossed Dunkirk and reached the harbour where British troops were embarking in a hurried fashion. The lieutenant went to see the Embarkation Officer in charge and after a long discussion came back to tell them that something had gone wrong with his plans. In the early afternoon he had contacted that Embarkation Officer who had told him that, subject to approval by higher authorities, there would be a good chance for him and his men to sail. The Embarkation Officer had suggested that the lieutenant should go and fetch his men and that meanwhile he would contact his superiors and get the necessary authorization. However, to the Embarkation Officer's obvious embarrassment, this had been refused. This was the subject of the discussion the group had just witnessed. The fraught looks on the faces of the two men had communicated the gist of the conversation to the onlookers even, before the lieutenant returned to join them.

The lieutenant suggested that the group should stay together and try their chances elsewhere. After two more unsuccessful attempts, they decided that they had better find a refuge for the night. On a nearby beach, at Malo les Bains, it proved child's play to force open a few doors on the wooden beach huts and settle down for the night.

On their way to Malo they had come across a field full of abandoned British army vehicles. Copying the French soldiers they had met earlier that afternoon, they decided to investigate the contents of the vehicles. In one of them Rene found a brand new pair of battle dress trousers. In another, having broken the padlock on a storage box under the driver's seat, he only found a bag full of French coins. Breaking the padlock under a second seat he discovered a box full of emergency rations. They were much more varied than he had ever known in the Belgian army. Tins of corned beef, butter, sugar, hard biscuits, tea, jam, in short, all that was required to stop a man from starving. In less time than it takes to explain the contents of the box, he loaded its contents into the kitbag on the back of his motorbike.

When at last, he settled down in the beach hut, he tried to go to sleep, but found his wet clothes kept him awake. So he decided to have a complete change of clothing. He took dry underwear and socks out of the kitbag, took his breeches off and replaced them with the British battle dress trousers. He then found a piece of string, fastened it between two beach huts and proceeded to carefully hang the underwear and breeches he had removed on to the improvised airer. Eventually, back in the beach hut, he rolled himself into a blanket and spent a more or less comfortable night.

Next morning, the 29th May, when he awoke and got out, he had two unpleasant surprises. First, the lieutenant and the men in the neighbouring huts had disappeared. So had the string with his beautiful breeches and underwear. As he looked in the direction of Dunkirk he could now see that what he had taken the day before to be a dark fog, was smoke pouring out from one big factory on the fringe of the town. It looked as if the whole place was on fire and gusts of wind from the sea was carrying the smoke low over the town.

He split some of his previous evening's find with the one remaining soldier, who had shared his hut and like him had been left behind. They had a quick breakfast of army biscuits and corned beef. Opposite the huts they found an old woman on the doorstep of her villa. They asked her if she would allow them to boil a bit of water in their mess tins to make coffee. Instead of that, she invited them in and she made the coffee for them.

During breakfast they told her of their plans and Rene also mentioned how his breeches had been stolen during the night. "Well," she said, "nothing is safe these days. All my neighbours have moved away and we have tried unsuccessfully to prevent soldiers entering the premises and helping themselves to the property. We decided that we'd rather die in our own house in the process of watching our belongings. We have moved our beds to the ground floor and our armchairs to the cellar. Now if you boys have any of belongings you want to be safeguarded, you just leave them here with me and you can collect them whenever you want."

They thanked the kind old lady and told her they would spend their day trying to find means of getting away to England. She wished them every success and told them that if they were still there that same evening, they would be welcome to stay in her villa. As Rene walked out to the front door, he saw several ships in the distance. At the same time an air raid was in progress. Some of the German Stuka aircraft were dive bombing the ships. Suddenly Rene saw one ship surrounded by plumes of water and smoke. A second later he heard the noise of a big explosion and saw the front of the ship sink into the water. Two minutes later the whole ship had disappeared into the sea.

Rene decided to drive back to Dunkirk, whilst his companion had other plans, so he left on his own. Backtracking via the streets he had driven through the day before, he found the ride pretty tricky and dangerous. The road was ploughed open with bomb craters and cobbles scattered all over the road surface. Tram wires were hanging limply, some in the air and others strewn across the road. Burnt out or damaged vehicles were lying all over the place. Rene could not tell if this havoc had been created during the night or if it had been there the day before, because under the influence of the rum, he had driven at speed through the town and never noticed any of these hazards. The following day, and being sober, he found it extremely dangerous and it took him a good half hour to reach the harbour.

On his way, at Place Jean Bart, he noticed the skeleton of a British army vehicle which must have suffered a direct hit and was completely burnt out. The amazing thing was that the body of the driver, reduced to ashes, was still sitting in the front seat. Nobody dared to go near it.

Rene's trip to the harbour proved to be unsuccessful and an embarkation officer told him that the only way he could get an embarkation permit would be to contact a British headquarters still in Belgium, where they would be able to check with the Belgian authorities and give him a security clearance. He drove all the way back to La Panne and contacted the first British army officer he came across. The officer told him that he did not know of any British headquarters still stationed on Belgian soil. He and his unit had been instructed to stay as long as possible on the border to protect the retreat of the last British forces coming out of Belgium to be embarked in Dunkirk. He said that he had no authority to help Rene in any way and suggested that he contact the French.

Rene drove back to Dunkirk as rapidly as he could. On his way, he came across a field where brand new British motorbikes had been abandoned. He tried one and the kick starter worked at the first attempt. Now came the tricky part. That was to find out, by trial and error, how the foot selector to change gear worked. It did not take him long to find out how the foot selector worked and after one or two stalls, and a circular trip round the field, he decided to exchange his old bike for the new one. He drove back to Malo les Bains and to the hospitable villa.

When he reached Malo he noticed that the tide had brought in a black film of sludge along the whole length of the beach. On closer examination, he found that it must have been the fuel oil of the ship he had seen sinking that morning. Several human bodies covered in the same sludge had been carried in at high tide. Would they be identified and recovered before the next high tide probably took them back to sea? The British army was too busy embarking the remnants of its forces and the French army too busy plundering abandoned cellars.

Rene noted that he never saw a British soldier without his rifle. Some may have discarded the bulk of their equipment, but they always carried their rifle. He could not say as much for the French. All they seemed armed with were two bottles of wine each.

He spent a not too comfortable night in the villa. In the middle of the night the sirens went and the German Stukas were attacking again. All the occupants of the villa went into the cellar, but Rene preferred to go and lie in a foxhole on the beach. if there was one thing he was afraid of, it was to be buried alive in one of those cellars, where he might suffocate slowly before anybody bothered to find him.

During his investigation of abandoned vehicles, Rene had found some more food supplies which he brought back to the dear old lady in the villa. He also brought her a portable radio set he had found. This allowed them to listen to the latest news. The broadcasts sounded false. In order not to discourage the sections of the French army still fighting, the broadcasts were carefully edited with the usual and now too familiar statement, "Our troops, under German pressure, have had to withdraw into defensive positions previously planned and prepared and will thus be able to cope with any further enemy attempts." They vaguely mentioned that Dunkirk had been encircled, but they said that the French were holding back the Germans in order to allow the British expeditionary forces to re-embark. This was only partly the truth. In fact, every approach to the canal between the Belgian border and Dunkirk was guarded by British anti-tank guns.

On the 30th May there had been a small attempt to regroup the French forces in Dunkirk, but this effort seemed to have soon been abandoned. Rene decided that morning to see if he would be more successful with the French, but again found himself sent from pillar to post. On his way back to Malo he had his second miraculous escape from sudden death. As he was driving his motorbike along a street, he suddenly saw a Messerschmit coming from the opposite direction. Its machine guns seemed to sweep the street and he could see the ricochet of the bullets hitting the houses ahead of him. Realizing that he was an easy target, he applied his brakes as sharply as he could and headed for the nearest telegraph pole, against which he intended to prop his motorbike. whilst trying to find protection for himself in a doorway. But as he was securing the bike against the pole, he heard the tack, tack, sound of the aircraft's cannon and there just above his head, saw two holes made by bullets that had penetrated deep into the wood of the pole. At once he restarted his motorbike and did not give a further thought to the incident.

The one discouraging aspect of the day was the constant attacks by the Luftwaffe, with only very rare interventions by allied aircraft, but whenever a few Canadian Spitfires appeared the scene changed. A few dives and attacks by the Spitfires and some of the German planes would take a hit and dive out of control into the sea. The remaining Messerschmits would disengage, only to reappear an hour later. The ground defences, although very active, with the noisy fast repeating Bofors guns, had only limited success.

Having spent another night at the villa, Rene left again on his search early next morning. Rumours spread that the British headquarters had promised to embark the French as soon as the last of their men had left Dunkirk. Rene found out that a French headquarters commanded by a general was stationed on a campsite named Le Perroquet at Bray-Dunes, half way between Dunkirk and the Belgian border. Rene decided this was his last chance and was determined to attempt it.

As he was driving in the direction of the Belgian border, he noticed that the flow of British troops had practically come to an end with the exception of a few units on foot marching in single file on the side of the road. The centre of the road was now used by retreating French troops. He saw a few old fashioned French tanks, but mostly it was horse or mule drawn vehicles. On the side of one he read, "Model 1887." These were the so called elite troops that had been sent to rescue Belgium.

Bray-Dunes, France 30 May 1940

When he reached Bray-Dunes Rene introduced himself to a staff officer who told him that only the general could decide to incorporate him in the French army. Rene told the officer that he could easily verify his identity because he was distantly related to General Billotte who, as far as Rene knew, was in command of the northern sector. The mention of this name seemed to have a magical effect and the staff officer asked Rene to wait a few moments whilst he disappeared into another room. A few minutes later he came back and asked Rene to follow him. Rene was ushered into a room, in the middle of which stood the general, surrounded by a few officers.

Rene stood smartly to attention and waited for the general to address him.

"You say you are distantly related to General Billotte. Can you explain how?"

"Certainly mon general," Rene replied summoning up all the self confidence he could muster. "General Billotte is married to an English lady whose maiden name was Nathan. The brother of this Miss Nathan is married to my mother's younger sister."

"Where does your mother's younger sister live?"

"In Paris."

"Where in Paris?"

"At 90 Bis Avenue Henri Martin in the 16th arrondissement."

The general and the other officers looked at each other and then the general said, "Don't you know that General Billotte has been killed?"

A chill ran through Rene's body. He became pale and the general must have noticed that the shock was genuinely felt, because he made Rene sit down and instructed somebody to bring a glass of water. After that he said "My deepest sympathies my friend. I am sorry I had to announce this to you so abruptly. However, I have accepted the genuineness of your explanation and I am incorporating you into the French forces."

The general explained that as Military Governor of Paris, General Billotte had been given command of the French 1st Army Group responsible for the defence of northern France. Following the German invasion of Belgium on May 10th he had ordered a counter offensive into Belgium and Holland. When Holland capitulated on 14th May he had been forced to order a withdrawal to the line of the River Escaut. The failure to halt the German offensive had resulted in General Billotte being called to a meeting with General Maxime Weygand, the Supreme Commander of the French forces and General Lord Gort, commander of the British Expeditionary Force, on 20th May. Leaving the meeting the following day, General Billotte's staff car had been involved in a collision with another vehicle. The general had been taken to hospital in a coma, from which he never recovered and died two days later. Looking at Rene, still in his state of shock, the general placed his hand on Rene's shoulder and said with a tone of genuine sympathy "You will join a company formed of isolated men under the command of Lieutenant Claus. My adjutant will give you the necessary papers and tell you where to go."

Rene thanked the general, who took the very unusual course of shaking his hand and wishing him success. He walked out of the office and back to his motorcycle. Then the most stupid thing happened. As he was kicking the starter pedal, his foot slipped and he lost his balance. The bike tilted on its side and Rene did not have the strength to hold it back. It fell to the ground with a resounding crash. Next thing, Rene found himself sitting next to the bike and starting to cry like a baby. A French officer who had seen what had happened came over and full of consideration, brushed aside Rene's apologies for his uncontrollable behaviour. He very paternally said "Do not apologize my friend, yours is a natural reaction to what you and your country is going through." For a few moments Rene went on crying like a child, repeatedly saying "This is too stupid." The officer told him to lie flat on his back for a few minutes and to relax.

Five minutes later he got up and was his normal self again. The kind officer who had stayed by him all this time, then helped him to recover his motorbike. Rene thanked him for his help, kicked the starter, the engine started first go and he did not look back for the rest of the day.

Rene's first concern now was to find the new unit he had been instructed to join. He found them in the dunes half way between Malo Les Bains and Zuydcoqte. In charge of the company was a very old lieutenant, with a long white beard, a Father Christmas like figure. He welcomed Rene and the first question he asked him was, "Can you drive a car as well as a motorbike?" "Yes, certainly I can," Rene assured him. "Good. We have just acquired a British ambulance which was abandoned. The only man in this unit who could drive brought it here, but since yesterday he has disappeared." "What do you use the ambulance for?" Rene asked rather nervously. "To go and get the food supplies for the company," the lieutenant replied, perhaps sensing Rene's anxiety that he was to be deployed as a medical orderly recovering wounded, or worse still corpses. "In fact I shall appoint an assistant for you now and tomorrow morning, first thing, you will go and fetch our supplies."

He spent a rather uncomfortable night in the dunes. Next morning the 31 May, Rene left with his assistant, who asked him to also take one of his friends with them. They drove some three miles away to the yard of a big steel works where the French supplies unit had organized stores. When they got there they were directed to a line of vehicles parked, one behind the other, in the order in which they arrived. They found that ten vehicles that had arrived before them.

As each vehicle was called from the line, it had to back up to the stores and be loaded with supplies, before the NCO in charge had to sign a receipt for what had been obtained. Whilst Rene and his companions were waiting, another of the frequent wave of Stukas flew over and dropped their bombs, incendiaries this time. This resulted in various vehicles being hit and left in flames. Once more luck was on his side. The vehicle parked next to them was struck by an incendiary and burst into flames. Rene had to quickly move his vehicle away, before the tank of the neighbouring vehicle exploded. The drivers had managed to jump clear and were trying to discover which of the remaining vehicles were travelling their way, to take them and their rations back to their unit.

The queue having been disrupted by the bombing, there was a bit of argument as to who was first in line to receive their supplies. Anyhow, after a wait of about two hours, Rene's turn came. When he handed in the indent form for six officers and sixty men, he was told he would have to go somewhere else for the officers' supplies and for the sixty men he was given six loaves of bread, six tins of corned beef, six tins of sardines and six litres of red wine. In fact there was only just enough for six men. Rene decided that he really could not return to the unit with these ridiculously inadequate supplies.

Remembering the field where he had found the abandoned British vehicles, he decided to try his chances there. Armed with crowbars, he and his two companions, went from lorry to lorry and broke the padlocks of the wooden crates placed under the seat next to the driver's and hauled out the emergency rations. He could have taken back twice the amount had he had better assistance from the two men accompanying him, but every time they heard a bomb whistle they fell flat to the ground and lay there until the danger passed.

They were now under attack from German artillery not more than a mile away from Dunkirk. Rene had already found out from experience that if you hear a projectile whistle then you are safe. It was the ones that you do not hear that are liable to hit you. He repeatedly mentioned that to his two men, but each time they still disappeared at the sound of danger.

Having loaded as much food as they could take, they made their way back towards Malo, only to find that the unit had now been moved to Zuydcoote. They made their way there and found that the men had dug themselves individual trenches in the dunes on the south side of a large building which Rene discovered had formerly been a TB sanatorium, which had now been turned into a hospital. The old lieutenant had been worried about Rene and his two men because he had already heard about the attack on the food store and since they had taken longer than expected, he had wondered if they were amongst the victims. Rene explained the reason for the delay in their returning and the lieutenant heartily congratulated him on his initiative. He was delighted with the supplies that had been brought back and suggested that whilst the going was good, Rene should make another visit next day to the abandoned vehicle park. Rene told him that he would not mind going again, but that he wanted better assistance and men with better nerves than the two who had been with him that day.

"Right," said the lieutenant. "Come and see me first thing tomorrow morning and I shall select my best man to go with you. Now, you had better go and dig yourself in because I understand that we are in direct range of the German artillery and it is forecast that they are going to tease us tonight."

His forecast could not have been more accurate. Rene had just completed his individual trench and was crouching in it when they were greeted with the most devastating artillery fire. The Germans were systematically firing salvoes raking from left to right and at the end of each barrage they would reduce their range by 10 metres and then start again, raking from right to left. When they commenced firing from right to left Rene could see the shells falling, first on the north side of the sanatorium, then onto the centre, and next to the south side near where the unit was dug in. The next salvo they could hear falling behind them in the dunes, gradually becoming fainter as the range moved further south.

Ten minutes later the sound of explosions gradually came closer and closer, until some shells exploded very near to their position. The next barrage could be seen to hit the outbuildings in front of the sanatorium. With almost mathematical precision, they knew that every ten minutes, they were in the danger zone. This kept everyone's nerves on edge for a few hours. During this period, Rene saw a few explosions very near their trenches, but luckily only one of the men was lightly wounded by a shell fragment.

Having had quite an eventful night, Rene eventually fell asleep around five o'clock in the morning. He was awoken by an unusual sound and straining his eyes saw the most devastating scene. A line of Stukas were taking it in turn to dive bomb the sanatorium, regardless of the fact that a large red cross was painted on the roof of the buildings. As the Stukas dived they made a whistling noise like a high pitched siren. Only a few hundred yards from the ground, as they levelled out and began to climb, Rene could make out the sight of a bomb detached from the underside of the plane fall down, straight on to the target, whilst the plane with the full thrust of its engines was regaining height.

As it had never been anticipated that the Germans would dare to attack an installation under the protection of the Red Cross, there were no anti-aircraft guns positioned there and the Stukas had an easy target. From where Rene was he could see that the hospital had had several direct hits and in different places black smoke was pouring out of the buildings. He could also see a chain of ambulances on the main road leading to the sanatorium.

It was now the 1st June. The weather was fine, the sky was blue, the sun was shining and the only clouds in the sky were those made by the smoke of the various fires caused by the bombing. That morning the unit moved back to Malo les Bains where the last of the British forces were embarking. The sight was unforgettable. All along the beaches, company after company were lined up on the soft sand near the promenade. A roll call of men was made and as each man was called he left the line and marched forward in single file in the direction of the sea. At the water's edge they waited patiently in the queue until somebody instructed them to go into the water, knee or even waist deep, to join one of the hundred little boats picking them up, either to transfer them to bigger ships, or possibly to take them back to England.

From time to time a squadron of Messerschmidts appeared in the sky and started to attack the ships. If one of them came too near the beaches machine gunning at random, then all the army formations and queues would disperse in a hurry and find refuge in the dunes. But the remarkable thing was that as soon as the alert was over, every man came back to his place in the files or queues, and the embarkation went on as if nothing had happened.

Later that morning the lieutenant called on Rene and told him he had found the right man to assist him on his victualling expedition. The fellow he introduced to Rene was called Albert Jonqua. He was originally from Bordeaux, spoke with a pronounced southern French accent and made Rene smile with amusement as soon as they met. He reminded Rene of a well known pre-war French comic actor by the name of Bach. This actor was small, heavily built, with a stupid looking, but always smiling, large round face. He excelled in the acting of two characters. He was always playing the role of a simple village boy in the French army or else he was well cast as a very typical village priest.

Rene had seen the actor for the first time in Paris in 1931 when he attended a play called Sydonie Panache at the Chatelet Theatre. There Bach was cast in the role of a legionnaire and Rene could not stop laughing from the moment he appeared on the stage until the curtain fell on the last act. Jonqua was the very image of Bach. Same physique, same round face, same smile, same accent and gestures when talking. He and Rene became pals straight away. He told Rene that the lieutenant had explained their mission and he was prepared to help him to the maximum. And so they left for the usual place where the abandoned vehicles were parked.

Once more they searched for food and discovered several newly arrived vehicles which had not yet been plundered by French soldiers or civilians, who had mainly concentrated on the contents inside the rear of the vehicles and had not yet discovered the padlocked box containing the emergency rations in the vehicle's cab. In one of the vehicles Rene found a two gallon drum of cooking oil. When they had filled their ambulance with as much as they could load, they decided to make their way back to Malo.

En route they suddenly saw a man hanging from a parachute slowly glide down. Before it was possible to distinguish if he was an enemy or allied airman, some wild soldiers were aiming their rifles at him and shooting. Rene and Jonqua did not stay to watch the rest of the scene, but discussing what they had seen, they doubted that the parachutist, whoever he was, touched the ground alive.

They went past a farm when suddenly Jonqua had a brainwave and made Rene stop the ambulance. He entered the farm and after a short conversation with the farmer, came back with a sack of potatoes for which he gave him a few tins of corned beef, of which they now had a surplus.

On their way back, as they were following the road on the east side of the canal, the Germans who were now so near that they must have noticed the ambulance, tried to hit it with mortar fire. As Rene and Jonqua sped on the shells were whistling above the roof of the ambulance and landing on the other side of the canal. Once more, regardless of the fact that the vehicle had very large Red Cross markings painted on all sides, the Germans did not take any notice of them. Rene increased the speed of the ambulance and all the time the shooting was going on, Jonqua was either giving a running commentary or shouting at the Germans, who were too far away to hear him. "You silly asses, you don't know how to shoot. Too long. Too short." And on he went, forgetting that if they had been able to listen to his advice, he would no longer be around to offer it. From time to time, realising the gravity of the situation, he would egg Rene on to get the maximum speed out of the motor, which he was concentrating on doing anyhow.

Jonqua also repeatedly lit two cigarettes, pushing one between Rene's lips, although until then he had never smoked before, but Jonqua insisted that it was soothing for the nerves. His commentary and his swearing at the Germans had given Rene enough relaxation not to be too concerned with the dangers they were facing.

At last they rejoined their unit on the beach at Malo, only half a mile away from the villa where Rene had spent his first days. The beach, which had been so feverishly busy the day before, was now completely empty except for a dozen horses running wild from one end to the other. The company was positioned along the dunes under a fort, the guns of which were unceasingly shooting inland at the German positions.

The officers and men were pleasantly surprised with the supplies which Rene and Jonqua had brought back and told them they had a surprise in store for them. One man, a professional butcher, had shot one of the roaming horses and had just completed the task of turning the meat into sixty six delightful steaks. The drum of oil was all that was needed to start to fry them. A fatigue volunteered to peel the contents of the bag of potatoes and to cut them into chips.A few bricks were found in the neighbourhood to build a stove in the dunes. A fire was lit with wood and other flammable material found close by and soon Jonqua had arranged that since he and Rene had brought back the potatoes and the oil, they, the butcher and the officers, should have the first servings. The entire company stood in a circle around Jonqua whilst he crouched on the ground holding the handle of the frying pan in one hand and a fork with which he was turning steak and chips in the other.

Just as the meal was about to be served, another wave of Messerschmidts appeared in the sky and seemed to fly dangerously low in the direction of the assembled company. Before they even had the time to think of taking cover, the noisy 'hell's angels' were above their heads. As they started to drop their bombs, men in the surrounding area scattered, but not this stout hearted company. They were far too concerned about not losing out on their steak and chips. They flattened themselves into the sand just where they had been standing, but the only one who did not move from his original position was Jonqua. Rene would never forget the sight of him, holding the frying pan with his left hand, and the fork in his right. Just as the Messerschmidts passed above their heads, he raised his right arm in their direction, closed fist still holding the fork. Then in his picturesque, southern accent, he yelled "Bon sang de bon sang, allez vous me laisser terminer mes frites" which translated into

English means "Good blood of good blood,(a southern French form of profanity) are you going to let me finish my chips."

His language must have impressed the Germans because they disappeared for a long while during the rest of the day. It may also have been the fact that the French had taken over some of the anti aircraft guns left behind by the British and were getting used to them and successfully conducting target practice on the passing waves of Stukas and Messerschmidts.

In the afternoon of the 2nd June, a rumour circulated that now that the embarkation of the British Expeditionary Force had been completed, the British were prepared to embark the French. This was planned for the night of the 2nd to the 3rd June. During the day all able bodied men had been instructed to move the British army vehicles from the fields in which they had been parked onto the beach. At low tide they had been moved into the shallow waters and had been placed one behind the other. They thus formed an artificial pier or sea wall. As soon as one line of vehicles was in position, another one would be started three to four hundred yards further along the beach. Meanwhile engineers were building a gangway connecting one vehicle roof to the next. The idea was that at high tide during the night, the small boats would come alongside these improvised landing piers and embark the remaining French forces on the beaches.

Whilst the building of the piers was in progress, a lonely German spotter plane overflew the scene at a height. Those on the beaches were puzzled to see that at regular intervals the plane released a small line of white smoke in the air. The reason for this soon became apparent. The white smoke was released exactly above each of the assembled piers and by use of triangulation, the German artillery could calculate reasonably exactly the range needed to hit the piers. And so they did, during the night, with some precision. Not only did their artillery systematically destroy each pier, but they prevented the Royal Navy, which had probably been notified not to risk any ships along the shoreline, coming in to evacuate those on the beaches.

Rene had parked his ambulance on the beach, halfway between two piers. He and three men slept on the bunks of the ambulance, whilst the six others had placed their ground sheets on the sand under the vehicle.

Being between the two piers, they heard the explosions on both sides of them and saw the fires caused by the shelling, but luckily not one fell near them.

Under the stress of the day and the influence of the rest of their ration of rum, they were soon fast asleep, oblivious of the dramas unfolding on both sides of them. Around six o'clock in the morning, Rene awoke, got up quietly and climbed out of the ambulance. The beach was now deadly quiet, only one or two lonely soldiers could be seen along the waterfront. He followed the edge of the beach and saw a few things which drew his attention. Three hundred yards south of their position, a motor boat probably caught by the retreating tide, was stranded on the beach. Rene recognised it as being a similar type of passenger boat to the ones used for visitors to the Paris Exhibition of 1937. Some of these had been bought from that exhibition for the one in Liege in 1939 at which he had worked. A bit further along the beach there was an abandoned rowing boat and fifty yards from it a bigger boat, which although already surrounded by the rising tide, was still resting on the sand. He only had to wait a few minutes sitting in the rowing boat and the tide got it afloat. Using the oars, he made his way to the bigger boat. When he reached it, he noticed another rowing boat tied to a rope ladder. He fastened his boat alongside it and climbed on board the larger boat.

At first sight the boat appeared to be abandoned, but as Rene went down into the captain's cabin he found a French soldier who was investigating what he could plunder. On the table there was a cash box, wide open, with various documents lying around. In the cash box was a load of British pennies. Rene asked the French soldier if he was interested in them, firstly because he wanted to find out if he had pocketed the rest of the money, secondly if he wanted to share the pennies with him. "No," he said. "I am not interested in that foreign money. What could I do with it?" "What are you looking for then?" Rene asked. "Oh, whisky or gin or such like," was the answer. Rene let him carry on his search whilst he filled his pockets with the coins, eighty of them. He also loaded his satchel with a few tins of condensed milk and other tins of food, which he thought would improve his morning's breakfast.

When he got back to the ambulance, Rene found two French officers standing beside it and engaged in an animated conversation. "Yes," he heard one say, "we should have been picked up during the night, but you can see what the Jerrys did to our piers. Now we have had it." "And what are we going to do now?" said the other officer. "Well what can we do? Just wait for the Germans to come and surrender our weapons." Rene had heard enough. Finding the old lieutenant he asked him to confirm the plans. "Yes, we are just waiting to surrender," he said resignedly. Rene repeated once more to him the apprehensions he had about the treatment the Germans would give him. "And what can you do about it?" was his answer.

"Well" Rene replied, "I have seen a lot of stranded boats along this beach, which by now must be afloat. I would like to leave the company and try my chance to cross the Channel." The old lieutenant looked at him, askance. "What a crazy idea, my poor boy. You won't get very far like that. I bet that before you are a mile from the shore, the enemy aircraft will have spotted you and will sink you."

"I'd rather take my chances on that than to just wait here to be made a prisoner," said Rene with a touch of defiance. "Well, it is up to you my boy, and good luck to you if you succeed."

Rene immediately went back to the ambulance and called a conference of the ten men who were now under his command, three Belgians and seven Frenchmen including the famous Jonqua. He told them the details of his conversation with the old lieutenant and of his intentions "And what are you boys intending to do?" "You order us and we will follow," was the answer. "Right then, take only the essentials with you. I have seen one or two possibilities to get us away," said Rene trying to exude a false confidence.

First they headed in the direction of the Paris Exhibition boat, which was now afloat. They noticed that there were two men on board. Just as they were getting near it they heard the motor starting. Shouting to the men on deck, they either did not hear or did not want to hear them, and made their way straight for the high sea. They then made their way in the direction of the bigger boat, which Rene had visited in the morning. The rowing boat was still there and Rene and one of the men went to investigate if the motor on the bigger boat could be started. When they got on board they found that there was no motor and that this was purely a sailing boat. They reported their disappointing discovery back to the others. Since no one knew how to handle sails, they were forced to abandon any attempt to use this boat.

They then agreed that the best option would be to recover the ambulance and drive into Dunkirk to see what they could find there. Rene was driving the vehicle, and going through the town required a watchful eye and the skill of a rally driver. He zig zagged his way amongst bomb craters, the wheels sometimes only half touching the tarmac, passing hanging tram lines, avoiding the bodies of dead men and horses lying here and there. At last the harbour was reached and Rene drove to the north side as far as he could, gradually making his way in the direction of the sea. At last they came to a bridge which had been elevated upwards on the side of a lock. This was as far as they could go. After consultation with the others it was agreed that they would patiently wait in the ambulance whilst Rene, accompanied by the faithful Jonqua, would walk across the lock gate and further into the harbour to find out what their chances of embarking might be.

They walked a short distance in a westerly direction and reached a stone pier leading to a basin separated from the sea by a strong wall. On the left of the pier were the dunes and on the right another dock forming the entrance basin and stretching for half a mile in an easterly direction. Alongside the southerly side of the pier they found only one boat moored. It was a Belgian fishing boat from Ostend. They went on board to investigate the possibility of starting it, but soon realized that the crew that had abandoned it had sabotaged the starter unit. Whilst they were busy looking at it a French naval officer came to enquire what they were doing. He told them that he had sent for some naval engineers to repair the damage, which in his opinion was not very serious. He promised he would take them with him to England.

As they were talking another fierce air raid was in progress and the Luftwaffe was now concentrating on the north side of the harbour. As soon as the raid was over, Rene sent Jonqua back to alert the others. The naval officer left with him. Whilst Rene stood on the pier near the fishing boat, he suddenly saw a sea going tug coming from the east dock and slowly manoeuvring to glide around the head of the pier. He noticed that the ship had the Belgian flag flying astern and that it was a tug from his home town of Antwerp. He ran to a point where the tug had practically come to a standstill alongside the pier and shouted to the captain in Antwerp Flemish "Hey Skipper, can you get us out of here, we are three Belgian and eight French and we would like to get to England." "Wait for me where you are," he said. "You see the big ship on your left, I have to pull it out of the sands. As soon as I am finished, I shall come back for you."

The tug started moving stern first in the direction of a small steamer that Rene had not even noticed. It was stuck in the sands and he saw one of its crew throw a mooring rope to the tug. He did not watch the rest of the operation. He walked back to the fishing boat and was now anxiously looking along the pier to see if the naval officer and his men were coming back. Then, with lightning speed events began to move. The steamer was pulled clear of the sands, docked alongside the pier close to the fishing boat. Rene lost sight of the tug and never saw it again, but suddenly coming along the pier in his direction, he spotted two endless lines of French officers and soldiers approaching at running pace. The queue seemed to start somewhere in the dunes.

Using two gangways, they started to crowd onto the steamer. Within the space of a few minutes, 1,200 men had been embarked. By now the last men had been embarked and one gangway had been withdrawn, near the other one stood a naval officer. Rene was about to ask him if his ship would take the fishing boat in tow when he shouted to Rene, "Well, don't you want to embark? If you don't hurry, you will have missed your chance." Just at that same moment, Rene noticed his little company of men at the head of the pier, but they had been stopped by two French military policemen. Impatiently Rene waved them on. Thankfully, the military police let them through and they came running along. Rene saw the last of his ten men safely aboard and one but last, he embarked. He was followed by the naval officer who had already released the mooring ropes holding the ship alongside the pier and who now instructed two sailors to pull in the gangplank.

This French paddle steamer, named the Rouen, had before the outbreak of war, served on the route between Dieppe and Newhaven. It was licensed to carry 350 passengers. At the beginning of the war it had been requisitioned by the French Navy as a hospital ship, but had now undertaken several evacuation trips. This, the very last one, had started the day before, when all the men Rene had seen running from the dunes had been embarked. A wrongly executed turning manoeuvre had sent the ship onto a sand bank. The 1,200 men on board had been taken off the ship in the hope of making it possible to refloat her, but this had not worked. So the only alternative had been to wait for the high tide and find a tug to help in her salvage. This was what Rene had seen successfully undertaken.

The crossing was uneventful until mid channel. Most of those aboard were standing, sitting or lying wherever possible on deck. Suddenly the engines stopped and men on the port side shouted that distress signals were coming from a small boat now only a few hundred yards away. This had led to a throng of men moving from starboard to port to see what was going on. From the bridge the captain shouted through a megaphone, waving his arms and ordering the men to return to the starboard side as the ship was now listing dangerously to port. Then the Rouen made a half circle and picked up the two occupants of the small boat in distress.

Another hectic moment came when the ship was in sight of the white cliffs of Dover. Suddenly they saw their ship receive signals semaphored from an admiralty launch speeding towards it. The ship's engines stopped, and their monotonous rhythmic noise was followed by a deadly silence. Once more the captain spoke into a megaphone and warned everyone that the ship was over a minefield and that their safety depended on remaining as quiet as possible. The ship glided along very slowly whilst the admiralty launch came alongside and a pilot was hoisted aboard.

Dover, England 3 June 1940

There was a visible sigh of relief from all on board when at last the Rouen entered Dover harbour mouth. As they passed the two lighthouses at the entrance to the docks, they could see dozens of people along the quayside, moving about in readiness to berth the ship. It took a little longer to disembark than embarkation had taken. Once ashore the troops were directed by police and army officials to a waiting train. A few minutes later they were on their way. Their first stop was at Folkestone, where an army of Womens' Voluntary Service members were waiting for them. Through the windows big trays were handed to the men. On each tray were four cups of tea, sandwiches, chocolates, fruit and Horlicks tablets. These were new to Rene and he developed something of a taste for them.

Also new to him were railway carriages with tables, which on the continent would only be found in restaurant cars. They took several hours to reach the outskirts of London where the train was diverted by a loop line to join the main line to Southampton. On this loop line was a viaduct, somewhere near Lambeth, overlooking some yards and archways. During a pretty long wait there, people had gathered below and were trying to work out the nature of the uniforms of the troops on the train. Those, who like Rene spoke English, and there were a few who could, told the onlookers what nationality they were. Some of the spectators disappeared and re-appeared a few minutes later with musical instruments. They started to sing and dance to entertain the men on the train during the long wait. When at last the train started again they cheered the troops as if they were royalty.

A few of Rene's colleagues were so touched that tears came to their eyes. So as not to show his emotions to his men, Rene went out of the compartment into the carriage corridor, where left on his own, he started to cry like a child. This was a natural reaction after the days of strain and uncertainty he had gone through. It was possibly also caused by the anxiety of not knowing what had become of his beloved parents and sister, from whom he had not heard since the invasion of Belgium. When the train reached Southampton a fleet of army lorries was waiting at the station and the men were taken to a transit camp installed on a nearby common.

Southampton, England 3 June 1940

First, all the French soldiers were told to deposit their rifles and any ammunition they were still carrying. Next they were directed to tents. Rene managed to squeeze in with his men, although only ten were supposed to occupy each tent. When Rene had sent Jonqua back in

Dunkirk to fetch the others, he had asked him to collect his kitbag and bring it along. In his hurry, Jonqua had forgotten to do so. It was only after the departure of their ship that Rene had asked Jonqua for it and it was then discovered that he had left it behind in the ambulance. As a result Rene only had the clothes he was wearing and not a piece of equipment. This gave Rene a few problems, because the evening meal was served in messing tins and he had to wait until one of his men had finished eating to borrow his implements and go for his own food.

The night of the 3rd to 4th of June was the first peaceful night Rene had had in eighteen days. The Luftwaffe was still too busy trying to slow down the embarkation in Dunkirk and had not yet started active operations over England. During the journey from Dover to Southampton, Rene had been surprised at how detached everybody seemed to be about the realities of the war. Here you could see little groups playing cricket, others in shorts playing tennis. Nothing appeared to look like what they had just left behind and the only defensive war preparation they saw were a few brick walls being built in a hurry near the station. He was told that these were anti-tank defences in case of an invasion. This made Rene and his men laugh because the walls were so thin that a German tank would just have driven through them.

After breakfast, Rene went to see the camp commanding officer to find out what the score was and what was intended for them now. He told the commanding officer that he believed there were only three Belgians, amongst the 1200 odd French troops that had been evacuated. "What do you intend to do?" he said. "Well, I came for your instructions Sir," Rene replied. "As far as I know," said the commanding officer "the French troops will be returned to their country as soon as a ship is available. Therefore you have the choice of two alternatives, either stay here or re-embark with the French." "Could I see the Belgian Consul to get his advice?" Rene asked. "Sure, just go and see him and then give me your decision." "Do I need a pass to go to town Sir?" "Not at all, just go and if you are stopped by the military police, just tell them that you are on the strength of the transit camp and that they can ring me to verify that."

Rene rejoined his two men and their first visit was to a hairdresser on an estate alongside the common. They were each given a shave which they badly needed. A hot towel around their shaven faces made them feel alive again and appreciate the blessings of civilization. Very obligingly the hairdresser offered to let them into his living quarters where they undressed and had their first decent wash for at least a week. After that, he directed them to town.

Their next visit was to the Belgian Consul. They discovered that he was only an Honorary Consul. He did not show much enthusiasm when he saw them come, probably expecting that they had come for money. Rene asked him if there were any Belgian forces in England? His answer was, "No. If you really want to fight on, you had better go back to France. On the radio I have heard that the Belgians are reforming in and around Paris." What the Consul was not to know and which Rene only found out many years later, was that a whole Belgian unit, nearly the strength of a brigade had landed in England and had been sent to Tenby.

As they left the Consul's office, Rene's two countrymen decided they wanted to go shopping on their own. This suited Rene admirably. He was longing, for once, to only have to make decisions for himself and himself alone. As he was walking along the streets, people were looking at him, children were stopping him in the street and asking him "Did you come out of Dunkirk soldier?" As soon as he said yes, they made him sign their autograph books. Girls were waving at him from office windows. In short, everywhere there was a hero's welcome.

He went into a Woolworth's shop to buy a first aid box, but as he went to pay, the girl on the counter said "You don't need to pay. The other girls and me are offering it to you." Rene protested that he was willing to pay, but they just would not accept his money.

He still had on him the eighty pennies found on the ship in Dunkirk and he had not been able to spend a single penny. The hairdresser in the morning had refused to accept any payment and this seemed to happen everywhere. On his way he was stopped by two young ladies who asked him where he was going for lunch. He told them he had no definite plans so they insisted that he should go back with them to their home. Their parents, they said, would be delighted to entertain one of the brave survivors of Dunkirk. In the face of such a warm hearted invitation, he could not refuse. He accompanied the two sisters to their home, which by coincidence was very near the transit camp.

Having met their parents and partaken of a very nice lunch, their father suggested that they should all go together to the pictures. The main feature did not make much of an impression on Rene, but what interested him most was an extended version of the newsreel, which showed the beaches of Dunkirk. Here strangely, he found that the noise of the screaming German bombers and the noise of the explosions were much more frightening in the cinema than they had been in reality.

After the pictures they went back to the home of his newly found friends and had supper. Later that evening he went back to his tent, only to find that several of his men had also had the same experience as himself and had been impressed by the hospitality shown them by the British.

In the morning, after breakfast and following discussion with his two countrymen, Rene went to see the camp commanding officer and informed him of the outcome of his meeting with the Belgian Consul, which was that if they wanted to go on fighting, they must rejoin the Belgian forces in France. Rene informed him that that was what they wished to do. The commanding officer complimented them on their decision and told Rene that as soon as a ship was available he would personally see to it that they would be amongst the first to embark.

The next two days were spent almost like the first one. People were stopping them in the street, and inviting them to their homes to get from them a first hand account of what it had been like to be evacuated from Dunkirk.

During Rene's first day at the transit camp on 4th June, a group of French sailors and soldiers, around one hundred and fifty in all, had arrived. He met some of them next morning and spoke with them. They told him they were the last ones to come out of Dunkirk. They had found a sailing boat on the beach at Malo les Bains and got it afloat, just as the Germans were making a careful first appearance on the promenade. From the description they gave Rene of the boat, he was convinced that they had taken the sailing boat he and his men had investigated, but did not dare use on account of their lack of sailing skills. He realized that they must have been the very last ones to come out of Dunkirk.

Another two days were spent in Southampton. On the morning of the 5th June, Rene was called into the office of the commanding officer and told that they would be embarked for France that same evening. He told Rene to report around 6pm at his office with the two other Belgians. As instructed, they arrived at the command post at 6pm prompt and were assigned to a coach full of French officers. Prior to that they had taken leave of the eight French soldiers who, up until arrival at the camp, had been Rene's responsibility. Saying farewell to Jonqua was hard and there were the usual promises about looking one another up once the war was over. Neither doubted their ability to survive, or so they pretended.

When they got to the docks an Embarkation Officer came over to their coach and called out, "The three Belgian volunteers please." Rene and his two companions followed him to the ship and he took them straight to a nice three berth cabin. As they settled down in it, they had left the cabin door open. They noticed one or two French officers looking into their cabin. Soon they could hear a big argument taking place in the corridor. The French officers were complaining to the Embarkation Officer that they were six to a cabin, when certain lower ranks had been given a three berth one. They were trying to get Rene and his companions moved. The Embarkation Officer told them very firmly that he had had instructions from his superiors to reserve that cabin for the three Belgian volunteers and that he had no power to alter that decision. Then he came to see Rene and asked him to keep the cabin door shut to avoid further trouble and recommended that if they left the cabin, that they should lock it.

Cherbourg, France 6th June 1940

The crossing went without a hitch, although they were informed next morning that the captain had changed course several times during the night to avoid a German submarine which had been picked up on the ship's sonar detectors. They landed in Cherbourg in the early hours of the morning and their first impression was one of a town in panic. Cherbourg had had its first aerial attack by the Lufftwaffe that morning. The attack had been mainly concentrated around the harbour and as they disembarked and made their way to the station, they noticed the extent of the damage. The two Belgian soldiers, who up until then had always been very dependent on Rene, suddenly decided that they now wanted to demonstrate their independence. When he suggested that they make their way to Paris, they decided that they were not in a hurry and intended to stay for a while in Cherbourg. So he left them and went to enquire about trains to Paris. On account of the conditions which now existed, the number of trains had been greatly reduced and the timetable had become very erratic.

Rene was directed to a train which would leave within the hour. When he got to the platform, he found that the train was already completely full with people tightly packed in the corridors. In many carriages, people were sitting on the steps situated at each end. The doors had to be left open so that they could sit on the floor of the corridor with their feet dangling out, balanced on the external step. Rene was wondering whether they would be allowed to travel like that. Finding that the situation was the same all along the train and that there was only one end of a carriage where there was a step which was not yet being used, he decided to take a chance and occupy that precarious position. At long last the train started to move and nobody in authority seemed to be worried about the open doors and passengers with legs hanging out of the carriages.

After a few stations, the situation seemed to change. Rene found that most of the passengers were residents of Cherbourg, who frightened by this first air raid had decided to find refuge inland, but it soon became clear that none of them intended to go as far as Paris. So, after five or six stops, the train became almost empty.

He was able to find a comfortable compartment where he was joined by a few French officers. A conversation soon started and he found out that like him they had been evacuated from Dunkirk and shipped back from Southampton on the same ship as himself. The train made many stops, including some at branchline stations on secondary rail lines, with the result that it took the whole day to reach Paris.

Paris 6 June 1940

When at last the train arrived at the Gare du Nord, Rene immediately made his way to the office of the Military Rail Transport Officer, who enquired where he had come from and what his further travel instructions were. Rene gave him a quick outline of where he had come from, but told him that he was now in search of a Belgian unit that he could join.

To this the lieutenant in charge of the office said, "Well, it is a bit late to go anywhere tonight. I shall give you a voucher which will allow you to get a meal at the army canteen on this station. Another voucher will allow you to spend the night at the dormitory installed in one of the waiting rooms. Tomorrow morning, after breakfast, you can go to the Belgian Embassy and there you will find out where to join." "Thank you very much lieutenant," Rene said. "Do you think that before reporting to the Belgian Embassy I could call at my aunt's address here in Paris?" "Sure. Why not? Just go ahead." "Yes, but should I not get some sort of a pass from you?" "No, that is not necessary. You are in uniform. You have your identity papers. That is all that is needed."

"Thank you very much for your help," Rene said and went off to get a meal at the canteen and a night's sleep in the dormitory. The sleeping arrangements here were certainly not as comfortable as the cabin on board the ship, but he slept soundly all the same.

Next morning, 7th June, he got up early and walked out of the station in order to find out how to reach his aunt Helene Nathan's apartment in the Avenue Henri Martin, near the Bois de Boulogne. He was standing in front of the station when suddenly the sirens sounded to announce an air raid. He did not take much notice of it. He needed to cross the road to catch a bus, but as he attempted to do so, he suddenly felt a gendarme catch him by the arm and he was pushed in the direction of the entrance to the Metro, the Paris underground. Rene told him rather sullenly that in Dunkirk, where he had just come from, you did not bother with shelters. But there was nothing doing. Whether or not he wanted to, he was given no option, but to go down into the Metro.

The alert did not last long and he made his way to Bis Avenue Henri Martin. When he got there it was only to hear from the concierge that his aunt and her family had left for Cannes in the south of France. He took a note of their forwarding address at the Grand Hotel. As he was writing the details in his notebook, the concierge told him that a relative of Madame Nathan from Belgium had called there the week before and before Rene could ask who this was, she took a piece of paper from a pigeon hole and handed it to him. He immediately recognized his father's handwriting. On the paper he had indicated that he was staying at the Hotel Ellis in Paris. Rene thanked the concierge for her help, left a message with her saying that he was going to the Hotel Ellis, in case his father should call back.

Off he went in the direction of the hotel. But at the Hotel Ellis he was told by the manager that his father had left two days before on receipt of a message from his mother. She had asked Franz to join her and Rene's sister Georgette at a place called La Roche-Posay, near Chatellerault on the edge of the Loire Valley. The manager gave Rene the address of the hotel where they were going to stay, then he invited him to have breakfast in his dining room.

Rene had just about finished eating when a young boy dressed in a white overall, of a type French butchers wear, came in through the door of the restaurant followed by a policeman. He looked searchingly around the dining room, then saw Rene and pointed him out to the policeman. They both came straight over to Rene and the policeman asked him for his identity papers. Rene produced them and handed them to the gendarme. He was then asked to produce his marching orders.Rene told him he had none and explained why. The gendarme looked rather suspiciously at some of Rene's army papers which were tinted brown as a result of having got damp in his wallet when he had been drenched in Dunkirk.

By then the hotel manager had come back to see how Rene had enjoyed his breakfast. He assured the zealous policeman that contrary to what the young butcher's boy had assumed, Rene was not a spy or German parachutist. Rene's Belgian motorbike crash helmet had been mistaken for a parachutist's helmet by the boy. The hotel manager told the gendarme that Rene's father had been staying at the hotel until two weeks earlier and had a genuine Czechoslovakian passport. This puzzled the gendarme. How could a Belgian soldier have a father with a Czechoslovak passport? Rene's explanation only partially satisfied him and he asked Rene to accompany him to the Rue de Grenelle police station.

There Rene was interviewed by a sergeant to whom he had to tell his whole story all over again. The sergeant decided that he could not take the responsibility of releasing Rene and that the CID should be called in. He telephoned the CID office, but apparently the officers he wanted were not available, so in a very kindly manner, he asked Rene to take a seat on a bench at a table where off duty policemen came to read their papers or eat their sandwiches.

Every time one of them came to sit down, Rene was questioned at length about the events he had lived through during the last few days. Paris had not yet tasted the sufferings of war. Apart from one or two air raid alerts similar to the one earlier that morning, which had frightened the population a bit, no damage had been reported so far. Whilst Rene sat in the police station he had noticed a long queue of people waiting in the corridors. He was told that they were coming to get a priority certificate to be evacuated from Paris. This certificate was given to elderly people, to invalids and families with small children. At lunch time he was asked if he would like a meal and was told that if he had the money to pay for it, he could get a meal brought in from a restaurant across the road.

After what proved to be an excellent lunch, Rene still had to wait whilst the sergeant continued to try to find somebody available in the CID to make a decision about what to do with him. Eventually, around five o'clock in the afternoon, Rene lost patience and started to shout at the sergeant and anybody around him, telling him that this was no way to treat him. After all, he had volunteered to return to France to carry on the fight, not sit around at their behest. He also told the sergeant that he wondered if he would be so duty conscious in a few days time when the Germans would undoubtedly enter Paris, or whether he would like so many of his Belgian police colleagues Rene had seen, abandon their posts and run faster than anybody else. Rene omitted to say that this applied mainly to the Belgian Gendarmes or military police. But his shouting did produce rapid results. Another phone call and within minutes two CID men appeared.

Once more he had to repeat his story to them. Without further ado they told him that they would take him to the Belgian Embassy for further identification. "If your rather too zealous policeman had not stopped me, I would already have been to the Embassy this morning," Rene remarked tersely. "Well corporal, we only do our duty, If you knew the number of fifth columnists we have had to deal with in the last few days, you would understand the purpose of our precautions." They escorted Rene by Metro to the Belgian Embassy. During the journey they told him how the fifth column had been active, how they had arrested German spies dressed in priest's cassocks and even dressed as nuns. To Rene this all sounded rather familiar.

When they got to the Embassy they were taken into the office of the Belgian Military Attache, a Captain Ausloos. He first examined Rene's papers and declared them to be genuine. Next in front of the two CID men, he started to shout at Rene, mainly criticising the state of his uniform. This was simply too much for Rene, who recognized a spit and polish officer, but without his recent experience of combat. Looking Ausloos straight in the eye, Rene shouted back at him that if he had been through what he had experienced in the last two weeks, he would possibly also have an unusual uniform. His reply was, "If anybody during the 1914-1918 war had lost one piece of his equipment he would have been court martialled for it." "Then your 1914-1918 war must have been a picnic compared to what we have gone through. I am anxious to see in a few days time, when the Germans approach Paris, whether you will still be in your No 1 uniform with all your medals on." At this Ausloos quietened down and after having thanked the CID men for bringing Rene there, he watched them leave.

Now in a much more sociable frame of mind, he asked Rene to sit down and to tell him how he had come to exchange his cavalry breeches for a pair of British battle dress trousers. Having listened to what Rene had to say, he told him that he would send him to a French barracks known as "Laserne des Tourelles," where he would have to await further instructions.

Rene arrived there that same evening, but found the situation there rather disorganized. He was told that next morning, after breakfast, he would be free to go where he wanted to, but he had to report at the barracks for each meal. He was fitted with a new pair of Belgian army trousers, given a new kitbag, rucksack and replacement of all the equipment left behind in Dunkirk.

On the morning of 8th June, he went into town and visited the bank whose address he had been given by his lieutenant when he left Belgium. At the bank he was asked if he needed any money on loan. Rene told them that he had enough at present. The bank representative invited Rene to call on him if ever he was in need of any help.

Nothing further happened that day, but next day at lunch time the duty sergeant told Rene that after his meal he had to go to the Belgian Embassy to see 'his friend' Captain Ausloos. When he got there he found the captain to be really friendly. Again, he invited Rene to sit down and told him that the strength of the company at present at the Tourelle Barracks was 40 men. He was the only NCO available, so he was putting him in charge of these 40 men. "Here is a railway warrant to travel tomorrow morning to Malestroit in Brittanny near Questembert. I am giving you five francs for each man, to pay for a lunch en route. Please sign this receipt for 205 francs." He then took out his wallet from his pocket and gave Rene an additional 100 francs from it. "There you are," he said, "to buy yourself a drink and to forget about our quarrel on the day we first met." Thus provided, Rene went back to the barracks to make sure that the duty sergeant had made all the transportation arrangements for the next day.

Rennes, Brittanny 10th June 1940

On 10th June Rene's company were taken by army lorry to St. Lazare station to catch a train for Rennes. There they would have to change trains to get to their destination. As they got off the Paris train, they noticed on the platform opposite, a stationary train. Each carriage had a Red Cross marking. French ambulance orderlies were disembarking wounded German prisoners. Most of them were stretcher cases. The orderlies lined them up on the platform as they eased the stretchers from the train. Suddenly, whilst Rene and his men were watching this operation, they heard shouts at the end of the platform and an angry crowd of civilians prevented from invading the platform by a handful of military police.

Rene's company made its way to the exit and soon found out the reason for the anger of the crowd. News had just come through that Italy had entered the war on the side of Germany. The reaction of local people to the news might be thought typically French. They took to the streets. Angry, they wanted to take their revenge by lynching the wounded German prisoners. This was only just prevented by the rapid and firm action of the military police.

Rene and his little company had arrived in Rennes around lunch time, but there their problems started, as he wanted to take his men to a restaurant near the station. He was told that all the restaurants in the town were out of bounds to soldiers. They all then walked to the nearest French barracks where they were told, "Sorry, we have no authority to feed Belgian soldiers, you must look elsewhere." Rene sent his men back to the waiting room at the station, whilst with the assistance of one man, he found the address of the Belgian Consul in the town. Once again, he was only an Honorary Consul and not very helpful at that. Rene told him about his problem and all the consul could say was, "Well, I cannot do very much for you. I shall give you five francs per man out of my special funds and you will have to buy your food somewhere." Once more Rene had to get angry and shouted at him "Look here my man, I don't need your money. I have plenty on me, but the shops won't sell to soldiers, the restaurants are out of bounds, the French army won't have anything to do with the Belgians. Now are you our representative in this town or not? I demand that you use your influence with whoever you see fit, to arrange to feed my men and I refuse to leave this office before you have found a solution."

Rene's stern attitude brought him out of his complacency, particularly after Rene told him that he was keeping a list of all the people who had been helpful or unhelpful, so that they got their just desserts once the war was over. These words prompted him to reach for his phone. He made a few calls with no results. At long last he managed to get hold of a refugee centre quite conveniently near to the station and from the conversation that followed Rene understood that they would be prepared to break the regulations and feed his men.

Back to the station Rene went and followed by his forty lads, headed to the refugee centre. There they were given a very clear, to his mind, watery soup and two slices of bread with a bit of meat pate spread on it. It was not much of a meal, but it was better than nothing. In the late afternoon, they reached the Belgian camp at Malestroit and checked in. Later that same evening, Rene was called into the commanding officer's office and told that after he had checked their records, he had found that Rene and two of the men should never have been directed to his camp. As the three of them belonged to cavalry regiments and not to the infantry they would have to travel to Montpellier where Belgian cavalry units were being reformed. He told Rene that he and the other two men should spend the night at his camp, but he would have marching orders and railway warrants ready early next morning, so that they could catch the first train.

Rene's understanding of the geography of France was very poor at the time. He had heard of Montpellier, but had no idea where it was. He went to the station that same evening and consulted a railway map. There, to his surprise, he found that Montpellier was right down south near the Mediterranean Sea. Next morning, the 11th June, he got into the CO's office and met the two boys who's names were on the travel warrants and who would be his travelling companions.

On their way to the station, Rene told them about his study of the railway map the previous evening and since their warrant did not specify any particular route, he suggested that they should travel to Tours, then south via Chatellerault, where he would be able to ring La Roche- Posay and find out if his parents were still there. Both boys agreed with this plan. Like Rene, they were not in a hurry to reach their final destination.

One of the boys named Drusson said, "I agree to stop in Chatellerault, but I noticed on the map that our route brings us down via Poitiers and Angouleme. I have relatives in Angouleme. If you give me a chance to call on them, they may have some news about my parents. I haven't heard from them since the beginning of the war."

As planned they took a train to Tours, changed there and got to Chatellerault in the early evening. From the station, Rene rang the hotel where, according to the information obtained in Paris, his parents were supposed to be staying. When he got through to the reception at the hotel, he was told that his parents had moved to another hotel in the town, but that relatives of theirs were still staying there. Did he want to speak to them? "Sure," Rene said. "Put me through to them." A few anxious moments of silence, during which Rene was trying to figure out who the relative could be. A few minutes later he recognized the voice of his uncle, Marcel Roost, the barrister from Antwerp. "Rene-Paul, where are you speaking from?" he said.

"I am at the station in Chatellerault."

"Are you wounded?" was his next question.

"No, I am quite all right."

"Good. What are your plans?"

"To come and see my parents. I have found out that a bus leaves Chatellerault for La Roche-Posay in fifteen minutes and I hope to get a seat on it."

"Good," said Marcel excitedly. "Meanwhile I shall inform your parents of your arrival. If you have any problems about transport, please ring me back and I shall arrange to send a car from here." He did not have any problems and forty five minutes later Rene and his companions got to La Roche-Posay where his parents and other members of the family were waiting anxiously for him at the bus station.

La Roche Posay, Vienne 11th June 1940

Their mutual emotion at this happy reunion was understandable. Apparently, as soon as his uncle had finished talking to him on the telephone, he had rushed across the village to the hotel where Rene's parents were having their evening meal. He rushed into the dining room, went to their table and all out of breath simply said, "Rene-Paul," then stopped to recover his breath. Rene's mother looked at him anxiously and said "Killed?" "No, he is on his way from Chatellerault and hopes to be here soon," said Marcel exultantly. The shock was such that Irma fainted and had to be carried to her room, but by the time Rene arrived in La Roche-Posay, she had completely recovered.

With the whole family and his two men they went back to the hotel. During their meal he heard from his parents how, after many adventures, they had arrived at La Roche-Posay.

His father told him how, as a reserve officer in the Czechoslovakian army, he had reported to his embassy in Brussels. Then with many others of his nationality, he had been redirected to Paris, where they told him that they had too many officers and not enough men, and in view of his age, they released him from any obligation to undertake further military service.

215

His mother and sister had travelled by car with his uncle Marcel and aunt Renee, the latter having done the driving. They had much to tell him about their journey through crowded villages, on busy roads obstructed by the constant stream of refugees running away from the German advance. There were also the problems of finding food and petrol on their journey and the continuous alerts caused by the appearance of the Luftwaffe.

They had all managed to enter France before the Germans had reached Dunkirk. A diary kept by Georgette had chronicled the course of their journey. Leaving Antwerp on May 12th, two days after the German invasion of Belgium, they had travelled to the seaside resort of La Panne. Four days later they had driven through the night to reach Boulogne. The following night they had slept in the car at Neufchatel en Bray, before arriving in Rouen the next day, the 18th May, where they rested for some twenty hours. Setting off again through the night, they came to the Loire and rested in a chateau's grounds, before arriving in Tours on 20th May. Finally on the 21stMay they had reached the safety of La Roche Posay, the small spa town south of the Loire valley, where Rene had now found them. They had chosen La Roche Posay as their destination because they knew Paris would be far too crowded and because Irma's sister had a very good friend in La Roche Posay, who she had visited several times before the war and on whose hospitality she knew she could rely.

After his meal Rene had to tell his parents at length about all his adventures since the day Belgium was invaded. He told them how, a few days after the first bombing, his unit was faced with the care of five hundred wounded horses, how they got pushed back day by day, until they reached the coast. He told them how he had been put in charge of the transport of his unit, how he had been given one hour to learn to drive a motor cycle and gone for a 200-mile drive on busy roads the next day. He told them how he had been sent to reconnoitre the position of the enemy on the morning of the 28th May, how he had driven through German check points and got back to his unit, to inform his commander that Belgium was capitulating and that they had been ordered to surrender their weapons to the Germans. He then described how, with the permission of his C.O, he had left his unit to drive to Dunkirk and spent five horrible days there, waiting either to be embarked or to be killed. Luckily for him he had been embarked with 1,200 French troops on the one, but last boat, leaving Dunkirk, landed the same afternoon in Dover and reached France three days later via Southampton and Cherbourg. In Paris he was given the address of his parents in La Roche Posay and reported at the Belgian embassy for further instructions.

After a three-day wait he had been put in charge of a party of forty men and told to escort them to a little place in Brittanny. He was entrusted with a rail warrant and money to buy the food on the journey. When they reached their destination, all the men with the exception of two, had been taken from Rene's hands. He was then told that since he and the two others belonged to cavalry regiments they would have to continue their journey to Montpellier. Rene had looked up a map and when he found that their route to Montpellier was passing only three miles west of La Roche Posay, he agreed with his travelling companions to break their journey for twenty four hours and that was how they had got there.

The hotel had one treble room available and Rene shared it with his two men. The next day they went for a walk and then sat down on a bench in the public gardens. They had not been there five minutes when they were approached by two civilians, who told them that they were Belgian CID officers attached to the Belgian Government now in exile in Poitiers and that they were checking on the movement of all Belgian military personnel. They asked Rene what they were doing in La Roche-Posay. Before answering them Rene asked to see their warrant cards, which they produced and he then told them why they were there. Once more, in the manner of typical Belgian officialdom, they told him that they should have travelled south without stopping. Rene barked back at them in the same way as he had done with Captain Ausloos and with the French police. This seemed to have a salutary effect. They suddenly became much more agreeable and even polite.

They explained that so many Belgian soldiers had lost their regiments and were roaming around France without means of existence and that therefore their job was to find them and direct them to reorganisation camps. Rene told them that they were not lost, not without means of existence and knew to which camp to go and that they would be doing that the next morning. Satisfied, the two CID men walked away and Rene spent the rest of that day and the night with his parents at their hotel.

Mourmelon, France, 12th June 1940

For Captain Pierre Billotte, son of General Gaston Billotte, the day did not go well. He was commanding a squadron of B1 tanks belonging to the French 41st Tank Battalion. During the preceding month he had already distinguished himself in the fight to halt the German incursion into northern France. On 16th May, in the wake of the great tank battle around Sedan, he had been involved in destroying several German tanks and forcing the retreat of a number more. But today things were to go very badly. His squadron had fought until the very last of their tanks had been destroyed. Pierre had been forced to evacuate his own burning tank, but not before he had been wounded in the head. Incapacitated and unable to evade the German attackers, he had been taken prisoner. Soon he would be taken as a prisoner of war to Oflag 11D in Pomerania, eastern Germany

Poitiers, Vienne 12th June 1940

It was with anxiety in their hearts that Irma, Franz, Georgette and the rest of the family took their leave of Rene when he went on his way to Montpellier. Little did he suspect that in less than a week his parents would be submitted to another big ordeal. He left with his two travelling companions for Poitiers, the next leg on their journey south. It was to this city that the Belgian Government in exile had moved and the city was swarming with Belgian civil servants. He was amused to find that the traffic at street crossings was being controlled by Brussels policemen.

As he and his two companions walked through the streets. trying once more to find somewhere to eat, they passed a captain of the Belgian Gendarmerie or Military Police. Rene either did not notice him or pretended not to see him, but he suddenly heard a voice behind him saying, "Corporal, stop a minute." All three turned around and there they were facing a fat gendarmerie captain. He had thick, dark and long moustaches. He was wearing a splendid black uniform with silver and red beading and nicely polished knee high cavalry boots and well cut cavalry breeches.

"Don't you know that you have to salute an officer?" he shouted at Rene. "Sorry Sir, I did not see you," was Rene's reply.

"Stand at attention, when you speak to me and what type of a Punch and Judy cap do you wear?"

Rene still had the French army cap he had found in Dunkirk. No one had been able to provide him with another in Paris. All this was shouted at him in front of the two soldiers. Knowing King's Regulations, Rene asked the captain to walk a few yards away with him from the other two men.

When they were out of hearing range of the two soldiers, Rene reminded the captain that he was in breach of regulations by telling him off in front of lower ranks in the manner he had done. This resulted in him becoming more aggresive and ordering Rene to accompany him to the Town Mayor's office where he would have him put under arrest and court martialled. Rene shouted to his two men to go to the station and wait there for him and if they did not see him within the hour, to look for the Town Mayor's office.

That office was just around the corner and the captain went into an office, ordering Rene to sit down in a waiting room. He came out of the office after a few minutes, told Rene he would appear in front of the Town Mayor, who would decide what to do with him. Then he disappeared. When, after a few minutes wait, Rene was led into the Mayor's office, to his surprise, the Town Mayor turned out to be an old acquaintance of his. It was Monsieur Janne, who Rene had known when he was Chief of Cabinet to the Minister of Public Works and who he had had a lot of dealings with in connection with the Liege Exhibition. He greeted Rene as a friend, shook hands and asked him how he happened to be in Poitiers. Rene briefly told him about the reasons he was heading south to Montpellier. When it came to the incident with the captain, Monsieur Janne read out the report quickly scribbled by the captain, who was claiming that Rene had been rude and insolent, including being insubordinate, which were grounds for a court martial.

Rene paused before responding and then lowering his voice said quietly, "If reminding the captain that he was infringing King's Regulations is an act of insubordination or rudeness, then naturally I am due for a court martial, but knowing my rights, I wish to enter an official complaint against him, for having rudely shouted at me in front of the men in my care."

The Mayor smiled and asked, "Where are your two witnesses to this?" "At the station, I have told them to wait one hour for me, and if I did not return, to report here," Rene replied.

"When is your next train south?" Janne asked. "In exactly forty minutes from now."

"You'd better hurry," he said. "Pleasant journey. I hope we will have a drink together after the war, when I shall tell you how I have dealt with the captain."

Forty minutes later Rene and his two travelling companions were on the train to Angouleme.

Angouleme 12th June 1940

When they reached that picturesque town they found that the station was down in a valley, but that the town centre was at the top of a steep hill. When they reached the top of the street leading from the station to the centre of town, they found a promenade on their right overlooking the lower town. Whilst Drusson, the man who had relatives in Angouleme, went to enquire how to get to their address, Rene and the other boy found a bench overlooking the delightful Charente valley. They agreed that Drusson should go alone to find his relatives and they would sit on the bench and wait for him.

Behind where they were seated was a covered market. Rene went to investigate what he could get for lunch for himself and the boy who had remained with him. Soon he returned with a large and very long loaf of French bread, four dozen oysters and a large bottle of local red wine. Rarely had they enjoyed a meal so much.

Whilst they were waiting they were able to observe the lower road coming from the north directly from Paris. A rumour had circulated that German columns had by passed Paris and were speeding down south. In fact they only entered Paris two days later on the 14th June, but Rene and his companion were not to know that at the time and they anxiously watched the Paris road in case the Germans should make a surprise appearance. What they would have done in that situation, God only knew. However, they were relieved that nothing appeared on the horizon. Two hours later Drusson rejoined them and back to the station they went. Trains by then were few and far between. They reached Toulouse that same evening and decided to spend the night there.

La Roche-Posay, Vienne 15th June

On the 14th June the Germans had entered Paris and without wasting any time they carried on their advance to the south the next day. When Franz and Irma awoke on the morning of the 15th, unusual noises in the street prompted them to look out of the window and to their utter amazement, they saw French troops install guns at the mouth of a bridge which was less than a hundred metres away. They dressed in a hurry and went to find out what was happening. They were told that the Germans were expected to reach La Roche Posay within the next few hours and that the French army had been instructed to block their advance by blowing up the bridge over the river leading to the south. Engineers were busy placing the explosives, but just in case the German advance reached the town before their work was completed, two guns had been placed at the south end of the bridge with the intention of blasting at short range the enemy spearhead as soon as it appeared at the other end of the bridge.

Franz's family once more gathered all their belongings with the intention of leaving town to the south, but before they were ready to go they heard the bridge being blown up. They also heard several artillery rounds, which appeared to whistle past in both directions. Suddenly they realised that the French troops, who had succeeded in blowing up the bridge and in slowing the enemy advance, had now been instructed to make a tactical withdrawal to new positions further south. The noise of the troops moving had hardly died down when the temporary silence that followed was interrupted by another kind of noise. The German scouts had reached the north side of the bridge and reported to their main unit the extent of the damage caused by the explosion. With typical German efficiency the main unit had then sent forward a team of sappers with the most up to date equipment to open what was left of the bridge and to allow their vehicles, including tanks, to cross safely. Within four hours of entering La Roche Posay German troops had occupied every available space. Once more Irma was amongst her enemies.

The German soldiers appeared to have been briefed to be very friendly and to converse with the local population. Although Irma did not give them any encouragement, several soldiers started a conversation as she was going about her shopping. They pretended to be puzzled why people were always running away from them. Irma explained that people in France and Belgium had not yet forgotten the cruelties performed by the German invaders during the 1914-1918 war. That was why the younger generation were fighting them, whilst the older ones were running away from them. The German soldiers immediately tried to explain to disbelieving listeners that the German Army of 1940 was different and that the civilian population had nothing to fear.

Montpellier 16th June 1940

During the day following their departure from Angouleme Rene and his two men had gone on, but not very far. The next three days were spent passing unfamiliar and nameless towns. All Rene knew was that they reached Montpellier on the morning of the 16th June, having spent a very uncomfortable night in a dormitory installed in the waiting room of Bezier's station. When at last they reached the army camp at Montpellier, very primitively installed in a big farm, they were received by their officers like a dog in a game of skittles. They were greeted with words which they were to hear repeatedly in the coming days "Why did they send you here? They know that we have too many men already and not enough supplies."

"Well," Rene said. "if you don't want us here, I can easily rid you of our presence. Just give me a pass and we will make our way to Nimes, where I shall try to locate some relatives and stay with them until you need me."

This seemed to please the officer in charge because he immediately made a very loose warrant saying that Rene could go on a special mission to Nimes. His two travel companions were included in the warrant. They were given a week's subsistence money in advance and off they went, after having spent only one night at the inhospitable camp.

Nimes 17th June 1940

In Nimes they went straight to the Prefecture. There Rene enquired where he could find the address of somebody staying in Nimes as a refugee. The usher on the ground floor directed him to an office on the first floor. There he explained that he was trying to locate his uncle and aunt who were Belgian refugees and who were known to be intending to stay in Nimes. He was asked if his uncle and aunt were likely to stay in a private house. "No I don't think so, they are more likely to be staying in an hotel."

"In that case you are at the wrong place my friend. We only hold the register of those refugees in private houses. People staying in hotels are registered at the Aliens Police Office located in the town." After having received information on how to get there, Rene walked down the stairs to the ground floor entrance.

As Rene approached the porter's lodge, to his great surprise, he found himself facing the very aunt and uncle he was trying to find. The surprised porter was rather taken aback by the demonstration of joy taking place in front of him.

After the embraces were over Rene's uncle, Rupert Manasseh, who was a British national, told him that according to the latest radio reports British-French relations were breaking down and that he thought it safer to make his way to England. He had tried to ring the British Consul in Marseilles from his hotel, but had been told that for any calls other than local, the Censor's permission had to be obtained. The Censor had his office on the 1st floor of the Prefecture, next to the office Rene had just come from. Back upstairs they went. Rupert had to show his passport to prove he was really British, then the Censor told him to go to the main post office where instructions would be given to let him ring the Consul.

At the post office, they went to the desk number given by the Censor, but were told by the clerk that there was a delay and that he would call them as soon as he got through to Marseilles. They went to sit on a bench opposite the counter and had not been waiting very long when they saw a neatly dressed man, go to the desk and talk to the clerk who appeared to point in their direction. The man made his way towards them and said "Are you the gentleman wishing to contact the British Consul in Marseilles?" "Yes," replied Rene's uncle.

"I am his representative here in Nimes. I regret to say that we cannot do anything for you here or in Marseilles. Our advice is that you should find your own way to Bordeaux and report as soon as possible to the Consulate there, when arrangements will be made to ship you to England."

The instructions were precise, but did not offer any help as far as getting to Bordeaux was concerned. They had noticed that very morning that all trains coming from Marseilles were as full as a London tube or Paris Metro in the rush hour. People were even riding on the steps of the carriages, as Rene had done between Cherbourg and Paris. Since his uncle's family was composed of four people, plus thirteen pieces of luggage, the train was out of the question.

They then started to tour every car hire firm and every garage in town, but everywhere they went they got the same reply "Sorry, we have no car available to take you to Bordeaux and if we had, we would not let it go that far because we would be worried about getting petrol to return to Nimes."

By the late afternoon, they were still without a result and by then uncle Rupert was really worried. Rene suggested that he should go back to his hotel, spend a restful night and be ready by 6am. He told him that he did not know what he would find, but that he had a feeling he would find a solution.

With his two travel companions, Rene went back to the station and every time one of them saw a likely vehicle stop, they would rush to see the driver, find out where he was going to, and enquire about the possibilities of hire. The answer was always negative. Around 3 am, they saw a flat lorry, with low sides and carrying a French army field kitchen stop a few yards from them. They soon found out that the driver was heading for Narbonne. Yes, he would take seven people and thirteen cases. Yes, he would wait until 6am, but not much longer.

Up until then they had been so nervous about finding a solution that they had forgotten to eat. Now with a saviour, they went to an all night restaurant and had a meal. The rest of the night was spent lying on the floor of the lorry. Just before 6am they called at Rene's uncle's hotel. The whole family had spent a very bad night, full of anxieties and were waiting for them. They were overjoyed to hear that they had a solution as far as Narbonne and started to load the luggage. Then uncle Rupert, who was rather thinly built, went to sit next to the bulky driver. Aunt Emmy who was rather on the plump side, sat at her husband's side and Rene had to push the door hard to close it safely. In later years they often talked jokingly of that journey in which his poor uncle got sandwiched between his ample wife and the fat driver. Rene, his two cousins and his two men sat on the open lorry, scrambling around and holding on to the field kitchen and whatever space was left was occupied by the thirteen pieces of luggage.

During the journey Rene's uncle tried to induce the driver to take them all the way to Bordeaux, offering him a handsome sum of money for it. The driver turned it down flat, but guaranteed that in Narbonne he knew a taxi driver who would be prepared to take them further. In Narbonne the taxi driver accepted to proceed to Bordeaux. Rene's uncle and his family occupied four of the five seats available. The thirteen pieces of luggage were placed in the boot and on the roof rack and Rene was offered the fifth seat, but turned it down as he could not leave his two men. He promised that they would find means to follow them and they arranged to rendezvous at the British Consul's office in Bordeaux. The uniformed threesome stood on the main road out of Narbonne and thumbed a lift.

Castelnaudry, Langeuedoc, 18 June 1940

Not very long after the taxi's departure, a smart car driven by a young man stopped and they embarked. He drove at 90 kilometres an hour, which considering the condition of the road and the capability of the car, was very fast. They expected to catch up with the taxi at any moment, and would have, had they not been stopped at one of the numerous checkpoints that the French had established along all the major roads.

This particular one was in the centre of Castelnaudry and manned by French gendarmes. They asked to see the driver's papers, which were in order, but when it came to those of Rene and his men, they scrutinised them at length, then made them get out of the car instructing the driver to carry on without them. When asked the reason for this, the gendarme replied, "From today we have instructions that no Belgian marching orders, or pass, or warrant is valid unless it is countersigned by the French Military Authorities. We are holding you until there is a train back to Montpellier and we shall escort you back to your camp."

Taken to a local gendarmarie, Rene and his companions were locked up in a cell. They were never searched, never deprived of their kitbags, but they were pushed into the cell and the door locked. Rene found this situation ridiculous and not very long after banged on the door asking to go to the toilet. The toilet was located very near the cell and the gendarme instructed Rene to leave the door open, whilst he stood guard over him in the corridor. Then suddenly somebody summoned the gendarme to a room at the back. As quick as lightning Rene bolted out, saw the gendarme had left his bundle of keys in the door of the cell. In a trice, he turned the key, told his companions to grab the kitbags and together they ran out into the street. As luck would have it, a large lorry with a trailer had stopped close by. One by one they jumped into the trailer which had a back board and two pieces of tarpaulin enclosing the rear.

Seconds after they jumped in, the heavy vehicle started to move. As it was gathering speed, they could see, through a slit in the tarpaulins, the two gendarmes rush out of their headquarters and look around in the street, trying to puzzle out where they had disappeared to. Rene had to suppress the spontaneous rush of laughter he wanted to emit in response to the look on their stupid and worried faces. He had enjoyed the adventure and was already calculating that they would possibly reach Bordeaux that same evening.

What they had not bargained for was that after moving through various streets the lorry suddenly took the opposite direction to the one they wanted and there they were back on their way to Montpellier. Further amusement was in store for them when they saw the surprised look of the driver when he saw them emerge from the trailer when he stopped in Montpellier. Before long they had reported back to the Belgian military camp.

Montpellier 18 June 1940

By then, the wind had been taken out of Rene's companions' sails and they decided to stay at the camp and await events. Rene had already decided that he was going to make his way to Bordeaux. The camp commandant after hearing Rene's story sent him to the Belgian headquarters to obtain a pass for Bordeaux. Once more he was in luck. The officer who greeted him at the headquarters was an old acquaintance from Antwerp. He was a lawyer and had done two years training at the office of Rene's barrister uncle, Marcel Roost.

Again Rene explained the motive for his plans. His friend quickly assessed the situation and suggested that in order to avoid any complications he would ring his opposite number at the French headquarters, tell him that he was sending Rene on an administrative mission to the Belgian HQ in Bordeaux and asked his authority to do so. Having received the OK over the phone, he issued Rene with travel documents which he then had to take to the French HQ to be endorsed with their official stamp.

Bordeaux 19th June 1940

One hour later, he was on his way to Bordeaux by train. As soon as he reached his destination, he went straight to the offices of the British Consul. The Consul told him that his uncle and his family had left the previous day for Bayonne, to be embarked there. He doubted that there would be any chance for Rene to reach them in time as they were due to sail that very morning for England. Now Rene was in a dilemma. If he went to Bayonne and found they had left, he doubted that the British authorities would give him any priority over their nationals. It would have been a different matter if he had been part of his uncle's party.

So, Rene decided that he should report at the Belgian headquarters in the city and see what they could do for him. The officer who he met there, told him that there was no hope of embarking in Bordeaux. There were still two ships idle in the harbour, but the port authorities did not dare to give them clearance to sail because the harbour entrance was blocked by magnetic mines, dropped by parachute by the Germans and no one in France yet knew how to deal with them. He advised Rene that the best course was to stay a little longer in France, and await events. In fact, he needed an NCO to take charge of nearly forty men he was sending down south of Bordeaux, to a place called Faleyras near Sauveterre de Guyenne in the heart of the famous wine country known as "Entre Deux Mers." Once more travel documents were issued and Rene was taken to the station where he was introduced to his new charges.

Faleyras 19 June 1940

The journey to Faleyras only took just over an hour. When they got to their destination, Rene expected to find either a town or a village, but in fact there was only a very small country station building with a long straight and deserted road leading to the village located over two miles away, He decided it was useless to expect the men, loaded with their heavy kitbags, to walk that distance. He instructed a lance corporal to stay with the men in the station waiting room, whilst he walked to the village and requested transport for them and their luggage.

He started along a straight road, but after about two miles further, there was a sharp bend. Another few hundred yards and he reached a massive building constructed in red brick. There was a high outer wall encircling the building and a wide entrance with heavy iron gates, painted black. A wide courtyard separated the outer wall from the building. The impression that Rene had was that he had reached some typical French army barracks. Near the gate and leaning nonchalantly against the outer wall was a civilian. He wore blue workmen's clothes, a cloth cap and rubber boots.

Rene went over to him and said "Excuse me, are these army barracks?"

"No my friend," he replied, "this is the wine coop. Would you like to visit it?"

For a short moment Rene's thoughts were about his men waiting at the station, but then he came to the conclusion that they were seated in reasonable comfort in the station waiting room and that a quarter of an hour would not make all that much difference, so he gratefully said, "Yes please."

In the course of conversation, Rene found out that the man in the cloth cap was in fact the manager of the coop. He could not have found a better guide. First he was shown the vessel into which the tipper lorries poured the freshly cut grapes. From there, on a conveyor belt, they were driven through a series of rollers and the juice extracted, whilst the pips and skins continue on the conveyor belt to be heaped up at the end of its run.

Then he was shown the room in which storage tanks are lined up and in which the grape juice undergoes its fermentation. Then it was explained, that after four weeks, it is passed through pipes using compressed air into a settling tank on a high tower. From this tower it is filtered down through a layer of very find white sand, looking more like chalk than sand and called "Blanc d' Espagne." All the impurities of the fermentation remain in that layer of sand when the wine is collected in another storage tank. It is then called 'Must'. After having rested for a few more weeks the wine is cleared of the last deposits remaining at the bottom of the tank. The wine is then carried to the various bottling plants by railway or tanker lorries.

The coop manager now led Rene up onto the second floor of the building, into an immense hall, the size of a large ballroom. Situated between the first floor they were standing on and the ground floor was the final storage tank into which the freshly filtered wine was trickling through a two inch wide pipe. An opening, one metre square, in the middle of the hall floor, allowed the wine to fall into the top of the tank. From this tank an outlet pipe could be run to the railway tank wagons. The outlet pipe was located a foot above the base of the tank leaving space for any remaining residue in the wine to settle and accumulate and later be scooped away.

From the hall on the first floor a door led into a laboratory. Rene's host led him into an adjacent storage room with rows of shelves on which were neatly lined up a series of 'Dame Jeanne'. These gigantic flasks sat in straw baskets, looking like enormous bottles of Chianti. Each was separately labelled and contained samples of wine of different vintages. Having explained how the wine was made, the manager of the coop went on to explain what distinguished a poor, an indifferent, or a very good wine. To illustrate the point, he brought down one of the bottles and filled a glass.

"Here, try this 1935, that was quite a good year, just enough sun and rain to get the right grapes.1938 was not so good a year, it rained too much," and down came a bottle of the 1938 and another glass was filled. And so it happened that in the space of twenty minutes, Rene sampled twenty years of wine production.

After that he felt quite happy, but nothing more. Then, his host carrying a beer glass, took him back to the centre of the great hall, there where the 'must' was trickling without interruption into the large tank. He rinsed the glass with must from the tap on the side of the tank, then filled the whole glass and offered it to Rene, encouraging him to drink it all. As the must is the wine before the sediment has settled, this eventually white wine, had an opaque milky green colour. It was nice and sweet and easy to drink, but treacherous too.

Rene did not remember anything after having had that last glass. All he could recall is that the next morning he awoke in a strange bed. It was near 9 am and he was told to hurry up and get dressed, as he was required to appear in front of the Colonel, who was his new commanding officer. He had no idea how he had found his way to the headquarters. He was told that he just managed to explain where his men were waiting and then collapsed.

Later that morning he appeared in front of the commanding officer, who very sternly said, "Well corporal, that was a disgraceful way to appear in front of your new unit commander. How do you justify your conduct?"

Rene started by apologising. Then he went on to tell the Colonel exactly what had happened the day before. He seemed to listen with close attention, then as Rene came to the end of his account, the Colonel said "Are you quite sure that that wine coop exists? Was it not a figment of your imagination under the influence of drink?"

"My Colonel," Rene replied, somewhat abashed, "I can assure you that until I reached that wine coop, I was as sober as I am now."

"Before I believe your story, I want to see that wine coop. Do you think you can take me there?"

"Sure sir, whenever you want," Rene volunteered almost eagerly.

"You'd better sort your men out first. They have spent the night in a barn, because we had not enough accommodation here. You had better see the town clerk who will tell you what farms need help and you can then distribute your men amongst these farms. That will give them accommodation and food and possibly some pocket money, which will help our very depleted supplies of cash. You should be finished around four this afternoon. Come and fetch me to go to the wine coop."

"Right sir" Rene said and about turned and marched out quickly, pretending he had not heard the Colonel's final remark which was, "As for last night's conduct, I shall wait until this evening to decide on your punishment."

Rene spent the rest of that morning getting the men settled. He also got himself a job at the Chateau de Sauveterre to start the next morning, spraying copper sulphate on the vines.In the early afternoon, Rene went to the coop and was met by the manager who greeted him with a smile. Rene's response was, understandably, rather cool.

"Well," Rene said. "You are a nice fellow. You got me nicely drunk yesterday."

The manager smiled again. Rene went on undeterred "Now I am in trouble with my Colonel who does not want to believe my story. He does not even believe that the wine coop exists and has demanded that I bring him this way this afternoon."

"Good," said the manager, "bring him along and I shall put him through the works. My name is not Durand, if by the time I have finished with him, he still wants to punish you."

So, that same afternoon, at 4pm, Rene went to fetch the Colonel, who had decided to take his adjutant with him. When they got to the coop, the manager was waiting for them at the gate and invited them in. In the same business like way as he had taken Rene around, he started to explain to the two officers, the intricacies of producing a good wine. Again the manager led the way to the settling tank and from there on to the laboratory store room.

Here the ritual started again and twenty years of wine were sampled. The officers not being any more qualified wine tasters than Rene, drank every glass, instead of taking a sip and spitting it out, as an expert would have done, or rinsing their palate with a drink of water between tastings, another expert's practice, to take away the taste of the wine just sampled before assessing another one.

Rene carefully abstained this time and the Colonel several times after the fifteenth and successive glasses, raised it in his direction and Rene could read his thoughts without hearing his voice; "You see little boy, you could not take it, but we can." Had the Colonel been able to read Rene's thoughts he would have known that his performance up until then had not impressed him. Rene knew that the real test would come when the Colonel downed the glass of 'must' and what he had expected, did happen.

A few minutes after having drunk the 'must', the Colonel and the adjudant were in the same condition as he had been the day before. Helped by the manager, they practically carried the two officers down bodily and then pushed them into the manager's car. This was when Rene found out how he had reached the headquarters the day before. The manager had taken him there. Needless to say that after that Rene never heard anything more about being on a charge. In fact, following this incident he never saw the Colonel and the adjudant again.

Sauveterre de Guyenne, Gironde 21st June 1940

Next morning, Rene went to work in the vineyards of the chateau. A big copper drum was fastened to his back by two shoulder straps. From it came a hose connected to a metal tube, the end of which, had a spray nozzle. This was to spray the copper sulphate on the growing vine and kill any possibility of infection, mainly of the vine pest, Philoxera.

Work started in the fields at 7am and went on until 12 noon. Then the workers went back to the chateau for lunch. A couple of Belgian refugees were working in the Chateau, the wife as cook, the husband as handyman. She warned Rene that their meal would be very poor by Belgian standards, because the old lady owning the place was very mean and kept a strict control on the purchase of food. The cook was right and after the meal Rene still felt hungry.

Since work was not resumed until 3pm, Rene decided to go and have a snack and a beer at the bar in the village. When he entered the establishment there was dead silence except for a radio giving the latest news. Everybody was listening intensely. The reports on the situation were very bad. The invading forces seemed to have advanced rapidly and the radio commentator did not even appear to minimise the gravity of the situation.

Over the next three days Rene continued to visit the bar. On the next Sunday, before going to the bar Rene went to the local church with the rest of the men and was disgusted at the sermon. The priest seemed to exhort everybody to accept whatever might happen.God had sent them these trials and if the Germans invaded this place, then they must accept the situation with good grace and do nothing to upset the invading forces. Marshal Petain knew what he was doing and if he decided to surrender, then they must accept his decision without criticism.

The sermon was utterly defeatist and what was worse to Rene's ears, was that the priest tried to put the blame for the present situation of France onto King Leopold of the Belgians, who according to him had capitulated without warning and without allowing France to disengage the best of their troops. Events had proved that the priest's accusation was wrong. In fact King Leopold had had a meeting with Britain's Admiral Sir Roger Keyes, and General Billotte, representing the French forces of the north on the 21st of May, at Ypres. The King had informed the two representatives that he had put his last reserve regiment into the line and that if the Germans broke through, he had no other alternative than to surrender.

General Billotte had suggested a plan by which the French forces within the Dunkirk pocket would attempt a counter-offensive which would compel the Germans to reduce their pressure on the Belgian front and allow the King to regroup his forces. The plan was accepted by all parties concerned and General Billotte left the conference by car to travel to Dunkirk to give instructions to the local commander. It was during this journey that he was unfortunately fatally injured in a car crash. It took the hospital two days to discover the plan in his uniform pocket and by the time it had been transmitted to field commanders, the British forces had started their evacuation and the French did not believe themselves capable of organising a large scale offensive on their own, so that after three days, when the king saw that nothing was happening to relieve the pressure on his front, he decided to capitulate.

Rene was so disgusted with the priest's sermon that he waited for him after the service at the door of the church. Rene would have happily bet that no one had ever shouted at the priest the way he did. He told him that if these were the best troops that France had sent to Belgium, then he wondered what the rest of the French army was like. All he had seen were a few tanks dating back to 1918 and horse drawn wagons with painted plates declaring they were an '1894 Model '. His shouting had attracted several villagers who were listening in silence. Some of Rene's men had also joined the crowd. The priest thought it prudent to make an evasive apology and disappeared.

La Roche Posay, Vienne, 24th June 1940

On the seventeenth of June it had been broadcast that Hitler was meeting Marshal Petain in the railway carriage at Compiegne, in which the armistice that marked the surrender of the German forces at the end of World War 1 had been signed. A few days later the details of this meeting were publicised together with the decisions and agreements reached there. They had agreed on an immediate cease fire and defined a line of demarcation to which the Germans would advance. It had been agreed that an area south of a line drawn from east to west across the centre of France would be left unoccupied and run by a government under Petain and approved by the Germans. The area north of that line would come under German military control, together with a narrow zone extending the length of the Atlantic coast. Having heard that the deadline for free movement between these two zones was the 25th of June. Franz, Irma and the rest of the family hurried away from La Roche Posay on that very day.

Sauveterre de Guyenne, Gironde, 24th June 1940

Rene had again gone to the bar at lunch time. As usual all ears were tuned to the words coming out of the radio. Faces were grim and tense. Some had crowded around a map that the manager or owner of the bar had fixed on a wall. Having missed the beginning of the news, one of the regulars whispered to Rene the latest information. Marshal Petain had met Hitler in Compiegne. An armistice had been signed after the Germans had agreed that France should be divided in two. Unoccupied France would be the south and known as Vichy France where the Marshal would establish his capital.

The Germans had demanded to be able to occupy an area a bit further south than their present line, choosing in most cases natural frontiers such as rivers to separate the two zones. When the list of counties to remain occupied by the Germans was read over the radio and after consulting the map, Rene found to his dismay that the area in which they were, would be occupied.

He left the bar in haste and made his way to the farm used by the Colonel as his headquarters. When he got there the farmer told him that the Colonel, his wife and children, the adjutant and his family and all the staff had left immediately after the news for an unknown destination. Swearing like a trooper Rene went back to the chateau where he was handed an envelope. In it was a note from the Colonel saying that since he was short of transport and Rene and his men were the last arrivals, he could not take them, but he was leaving a railway warrant to enable them to travel safely to the south.

By the time it took Rene to get his men together and march them to the station with their heavy kitbags on their shoulders, they arrived to hear that the train for Toulouse had left ten minutes earlier and that there were no other trains before the next day at the same hour. Disgusted, they went into a cafe opposite the station where they sat down to discuss the situation and their plans.

Some wanted to stay there and await events, others suggested that they should wait for the train the following day. Rene's own view was that they should find their way out of the department by any means possible, to the first town in unoccupied France. This was not met with approval by some and with criticism by those who were in a hurry to get back to their homes and thought that by staying in the occupied zone, they would have a better chance to be sent north. Rene finally suggested that those who agreed with his plan should accompany him and that the others were free to stay there.

As the group split, Rene found he had gathered less than half the men outside the café. He was approached by a farmer who had overheard the discussion. He offered to take them in his lorry to the next town where, according to him, military columns had been descending from north to south during the previous night. He said he knew the local Transport Officer personally and was sure that they would be helped by him. Rene's men scrambled into the lorry. He went back into the cafe to see if he could convince anybody else to join them, but to no avail.

When they got to the next town the farmer dropped them in front of the town mayor's office on the main square. By that time the town seemed to be deserted. Rene was introduced by the farmer to the Army Transport Officer who told him that as far as he knew, all French military units which had not been cut off by the German advance, had moved south, but he added, if Rene waited there a while there might still be a few belated units to come through. He promised to instruct the first one that came through to take Rene and his men. They were bound to stop in the square because there was a petrol station operated by the army there.

Rene and his men did not have to wait very long and soon there appeared a column of about twenty petrol tankers, all lined up on the square. The Transport Officer went to ask them in which direction they were going. They had spent the day dodging the German advance. They were all full of petrol and had instructions to make for Toulouse.

The Transport Officer called all the drivers together and told them they had to take Rene's group of Belgians with them. Some displayed a bit of temper at that decision, but did not disobey. It meant that many had to fix their personal belongings and suitcases, which up to then were in the cab, on the empty seats, outside on the wooden plinths along the tank. Rene saw that all his men were aboard and then clambered on the last vehicle.

By now it was getting dark and the moving column went very slowly because there was a complete blackout. They could only just make out the shadow of the vehicle in front of them. At one moment, Rene's driver lost sight of the preceding tanker and he noticed that they were crossing a bridge. On the other side of the bridge they entered a small town. By now the driver had become worried and stopped to listen if he could hear any of the other vehicles in front. There was a dead silence. Getting more and more worried and noticing that not a light was shining in the main street, he knocked at a door.

A frightened woman came to open it. She told the driver that she thought they were the Germans who were due to arrive any moment now. When he told her that they were on their way to Toulouse, she said, "My poor boy, you should have stayed on the other side of the river and followed the road south. You had better turn round and cross the bridge. On the bridge officials have placed a big white flag showing where the German advance has to stop."

As the old woman was talking to them, they suddenly heard in the distance the characteristic sound of tracked vehicles approaching. They jumped back into their lorry's cab. Rene had never ever seen a driver turn a large size vehicle in a rather narrow street at the speed this driver did. He had just turned the vehicle back in the direction they had to take when bright lights started to shine at the end of the street behind them. They did not wait to see who it was, although it seemed obvious that this was a German advance party. The Germans must have noticed them, although they had no lights on. The approaching vehicles appeared to flash their headlights in the hope that the French tanker would stop.

But Rene's driver did not oblige. On the contrary, he accelerated and they had soon past the white flag on the bridge, denoting the demarcation line between the two zones of France. It was only the next morning that Rene realized how fortunate they were, that the enemy had not tried to stop them in a more drastic way. At the back of the tanker they found traces of bullets which had been fired, but to their enormous relief had not penetrated the heavy back plates of their lorry. What they had taken for flashing headlights had in fact, been the discharge from fire arms.

Had the Germans used larger calibre weapons, their vehicle may have met the same tragic fate as one of the tankers, where the driver and one of Rene's men had been fired at. They had perished in the flames when their vehicle exploded. Rene only heard about this hours after arriving in Toulouse. It took him some time to find the other tankers and drivers and his men.

The men were all waiting together in a cafe opposite a large vehicle park. Once more Rene decided that the men should wait there whilst he went to find the Belgian military authorities. Teasingly one of them said "We hope there will be no more wine coops on your way," as the others roared their approval of his joke.

After finding a local Belgian consul he was told to take his men to the Parc des Sports, a large sports ground on the outskirts of Toulouse. When they got there in the early evening, they got the same welcome as in Montpellier and Faleyras. "Why do you come here? We have too many men and not enough supplies." Very reluctantly, they were given an evening meal, then told that the only place where they could park themselves would be in the cabins used as changing rooms in the covered swimming pool. Rene allocated a cabin to every one of his men and then took one for himself. He spent one of the draughtiest and coldest nights of the war there.

Next morning Rene reported to the camp commander who once more told him that he was short of supplies and suggested he should find a solution for the men. To this Rene replied that it was quite easy to arrange that in a small place like Faleyras, but a different matter in a large city like Toulouse. He did not mind finding himself a job and ridding the camp commander of his presence, but he did not see how and why he should find jobs for the men. That was, after all, what the camp commander and his staff were there for.

During his short stay at that camp, Rene uncovered some disgusting goings on. Rene suspected that with the blessing of the commanding officer, there was a black market of Belgian army equipment, including bicycles, being sold to the local population.

Since he had been given the option to fend for himself, he obtained a pass to town and first went to discover if there was a refugee registration centre. This was with the hope of discovering the whereabouts of his parents. He was told that in the forecourt of the university, blackboards had been installed,on which daily lists of arrivals were pinned. Next to it was another board on which individual messages could be pinned telling some of the refugees where to find their relatives.

Whilst looking at the board his attention was drawn to several foolscap pages headed 'List of Students of the University of Brussels. Arrived by coach in Toulouse." Rene had a look at this list which was in alphabetical order and there at the top of the list he found 'Adler. Roger from Brussels. Staying with Madam....'. There then followed the name, address and telephone number. Roger Adler was a cousin of his and he immediately went to phone him. Roger was very surprised to hear Rene's voice and arranged to meet him later that morning at the university.

Meanwhile Rene went to the post office and sent two telegrams. One was to his parents at La Roche-Posay which was now occupied by the Germans. The other was to his aunt, Helene Nathan at the Grand Hotel in Cannes, informing her where he was and requesting her to relay the message if she heard from his parents. Franz and Irma having received the telegram from Rene on that same day, telling them that after reaching Montpellier he had been transferred to Toulouse and giving them his contact address, wired back to say that they were making their way to Cauterets in the Haute-Pyrenees.

Rene met Roger Adler around lunch time and they went for a meal in a small restaurant in the covered market. A dear old lady noticing his uniform asked him why he was not getting his food from the Belgian Army. Rene explained that their headquarters was short of supplies and that all those who could afford it, had been told to buy their own food. She felt so sorry for him that she decided to give him two steaks and only charged him half price.

At dinner time Rene went back to his uncomfortable swimming pool cabin, but his cousin told him he would ask the lady where he was staying if she had a spare bed or mattress. They met again next morning, first to look at the board at the university for any further news of family members and next to go to the post office to see if there was any reply to Rene's telegrams. Rene was overjoyed when he was given the telegram from his parents telling him that they were leaving La Roche-Posay that very morning and asking him to join them at the Hotel Excelsior in Cauterets in the Haute Pyrenees, if at all possible. He and Roger had listened to the radio that same day and it had been announced that as from the next day, nobody would be allowed from the occupied zone into Vichy France without a permit from the German Military Authorities. Rene was desperately relieved to find that his parents had managed to get out just in time.

Two hours after Franz, Irma and Georgette's departure from the occupied zone all communications between the two zones were abruptly interrupted. Luck once more had been on their side. They reached Cauterets that same evening, after stopping an hour in Lourdes. In Cauterets they found several members of the family and they settled down at the Hotel Excelsior.

Another announcement by the Vichy Authorities informed refugees that as from that day they were no longer allowed to move from one department into another without a permit, to be obtained at the Prefecture. In view of this and in view of the fact that his cousin had had no news of his own parents, Rene suggested that they should travel together and join his parents. Rene asked Roger to go to the Prefecture to get a permit for both of them whilst he went to the military headquarters to get a leave pass. This was easy to obtain. The Belgian military authorities were only too pleased to see him go. It was one mouth less to feed and the only thing they asked of him was to keep them informed of his address. They also recommended that he should travel in civilian clothes. Rene was given the back pay owed to him by the army, with which he bought himself a pair of grey flannel trousers, a rusty coloured jacket and a raincoat.

Returning to his cousin's residence, he found the young man practically in tears. He had had a very rough reception at the Prefecture, where he had been refused the transit permit. Suddenly to conceal the short comings of the French military, the radio and the press were reminding everyone that what had happened in recent days was caused by the Belgian capitulation. This had led to a sudden wave of anti-Belgian feeling reflected in the attitude of the most insignificant little clerk at the Prefecture. His cousin had been told that, "As from today, we do not allow Belgian refugees to move, as we want to make a census of how many we are saddled with." Probably this exercise was being done on the instructions of the Germans. Rene told his cousin firmly, "If you think that this is going to prevent me from travelling, then they and you don't know me very well. Let us leave all our belongings with your hosts. We shall travel only with the clothes we have on us, and we shall carry a raincoat under our arms."

And so they did and by 4pm they had left Toulouse by tramcar taking them to the southern end of the town. When they reached the terminus of the tram line, they noticed, a hundred metres further along the main road leading out of Toulouse, a police check point. It did not take them very long to find a field lined by hedges, which allowed them to go around the police post without being seen.

They re-emerged a few hundred yards further along the main road and started to thumb a lift. Soon a car stopped and the driver invited them to get in. En route they explained the purpose of their trip and how they had bypassed the check point. They asked their driver to drop them off at a reasonable distance from the next one. "That won't be necessary," he said. "I am a doctor and the special badge I display on my windscreen will allow us to pass unhindered through at least three check points." They both blessed the good fortune that had delivered them that doctor. When he finally reached his destination and dropped them off, they were over sixty kilometres away from Toulouse.

Next a brewer's lorry picked them up and took them to just before the next check point. Again using a route through the fields they went around the check point and once more a car driver gave them a lift, so that three hours after having left Toulouse, they had reached the town of St Gaudens, eighty kilometres from their departure point. The scenery was beautiful and they decided to have an evening meal in a restaurant overlooking the valley and facing a row of mountains in the background. After supper, as it was still light and early, they decided to try their luck and get another lift. Once more they did not have to wait very long. This time the car that stopped was driven by a very fat, round faced man with a well trimmed and thick upcurled moustache. During the journey he started to question them at length and Roger and Rene looked anxiously at each other wondering if they had fallen into a trap of some sort. The man looked very much like a gendarme or a policeman on leave. Luckily, they soon found out that he was in fact the mayor of the next village. He suggested that they ended that day's journey there, because although the next town called Montrejeau was only nine kilometres away from his village, it was the last town of the Haute Garonne department. He suggested that if they had an early start next morning, they might be able to pass Montrejeau before the gendarmes manned the check point. He offered to drop them at the local cinema, which he very proudly said, had on his initiative, been turned into a military transit centre, but where civilians would also be admitted.

St. Gaudens, Haute Garonne, 26 June 1940

When they entered the cinema they found that all the seats had been removed and stacked on the stage. The empty floor had then been strewn with a thick layer of straw on which men of all nationalities, colours and creeds, were lying, one next to the other. There was not much empty space left and the smell emitted by all these bodies was terrible.

After looking around they found an iron ladder leading into the projectionist's cabin. To their surprise they found it to be empty, except for two large projectors, but there was ample space between them and the walls. Down they went, found a fresh bale of straw and by concerted action, pushed it up the ladder and into the cabin. It did not take them long to break up the bale, spread it over the floor and settle down for the night.

Around three o'clock in the morning, Rene was awoken by his cousin pushing him and asking him to stop tickling him. Rene protested that he had been fast asleep and had not touched him. A few minutes later Rene felt himself being tickled around the neck and told Roger, "Because you think I tickled you, there is no need to retaliate." Roger assured Rene he had not touched him. Rene got hold of his electric torch and soon found the cause of the trouble. Two mice were caught in the beam of his light. As they stood up, they also felt that they had been bitten in several places, most likely by fleas.

So they decided to get out of the place. Quietly they sneaked out onto the road and away they went in the direction of Montrejeau. Roger was a very good harmonica player and he started to play well known military marches as soon as they were on the open road. Rene accompanied him by singing and this gave them the necessary tempo to complete the journey in two hours. From time to time the noise they were making awoke dogs in distant farms, but their music and the dogs barking were the only noises that broke the silence of the night.

As they reached the entrance to Montrejeau they found along the road side an animal trough with a spout, out of which there was a continuous flow of water. They practically stripped, had a good wash and examined their clothes to make sure that they had got rid of the fleas. Thus refreshed, they decided to cross the small town like red indians on the warpath. One of them went a distance on the main road to the first crossroad. Seeing that all was clear, he signalled to the other to come along and this was how they crossed the whole town unhindered. When they passed in front of the Gendarmerie, they found that everybody was still asleep there. As they were coming to the last building in the town, they found it to be a brewery. Just as they reached the gate, a brewer's lorry drove out. They asked the driver where he was heading for and it appeared he was going to Tarbes, so they asked if they might have a lift. The only two seats were occupied by him and his assistant, but he saw no objection to them standing on the steps running along each side of his open cab.

During the journey they explained their problem to the driver. In a most helpful manner, he said "Well you passed the first hurdle and that is to get out of the Haute Garonne. We will soon come to Lannemezan which is the first village on this road in the Haute Pyrennes. Now on the top of the main street there is a control post manned by two gendarmes we know. We will tell them that we picked you up at Madame Giles who lives in that village and they won't know that you came from the neighbouring department."

When they came to that village, the lorry drove slowly up a steep hill. As they were half way up the hill, they saw the two gendarmes walking in the same direction and pushing their bicycles. They were heading to the control post on the top of the hill. Without slowing down the lorry driver passed them and shouted a good morning to them. Without waiting for their reply he carried on and dropped Rene and Roger just before entering Tarbes. They stopped in the town for a quick breakfast, before making their way to the outskirts of the town on the main road to Lourdes.

They had been waiting a few minutes when they saw a man on the opposite pavement stop, look at them and then cross the road in their direction. Approaching them he asked, "Are you Belgian refugees?" They answered in an evasive way, thinking that they were facing another policeman in civilian clothes.

"I am a Belgian refugee too," he said. "What are you doing here?"

"We are returning to our parents in Cauterets."

"Are you waiting for the bus?"

"No, we are trying to hitchhike."

"My poor boys, you would have a long wait if you rely on that, there are very few cars passing this way."

"Never mind, we are not in a hurry." Rene replied.

"Why don't you take the bus? There will be one in ten minutes time."

Roger rather offhandedly said, "Thanks for the information, but we still prefer to wait for a lift."

"Look here my boys, if it is a question of money, let me give it to you."

"Thank you very much, but we have enough money on us," Rene assured him.

"Never mind that. Let me give you the fare. It is a kind of superstition. My own son is somewhere here in France and by giving you this money, I am hoping that somebody else will do the same for him, wherever he is."

"Alright then," Rene said. "I shall accept it as a loan." The man gave him his address in Louvain and Rene promised to return the money to him after the war.

"That is not necessary. Consider it as a gift from a fellow countryman," he insisted.

Whilst they were waiting for the bus he stayed with them and told them how he had been separated from his young son and how worried he was about him. Their bus came and they bid farewell to their generous countryman. As they boarded the bus they found it to be packed and they were obliged to stand in the aisle between the two rows of seats. It was one of those very old fashioned buses with a celestory roof with a centre section a foot higher than the roof on either side and with opaque windows set in the raised panel on each side. The bus was too crowded to bow down to look through the windows and standing as they were, practically back to back, they could not see outside.

This was, without a doubt, the most uncomfortable part of the journey. The only advantage of being so closely packed together was that the bus passed two check points without hindrance. When the gendarmes saw the crowded bus, they never attempted to board it and limited their activity to asking the driver if he thought he had anybody on his bus who should not be there. The answer he gave was, "No, all my passengers are regulars."

Lourdes 26 June 1940

And so they reached Lourdes by eleven o'clock without any trouble. They then decided that since it was not certain if they would ever get another opportunity, they might just as well spend an hour visiting the Basilica and the famous shrine, the Grotto, where the Virgin Mary appeared to Bernadette Soubirau.

Having visited the shrine, they decided on a trip to the top of one of the two mountains, accessible from Lourdes by cable car. These were built to accommodate around twenty passengers with only a single car making the journey in either direction. When they approached the cable car station, they were just in time to see the car moving away. By then it was 12 o'clock, midday. They enquired about the next cable car and were told that the service was suspended during lunch hours and the next one would not go up before 2pm. They then rushed across the road to the station of the funicular railway, but there again they had missed the last morning train and the service was suspended during the lunch hours.

Very disappointed they walked down to the main road which lead to Cauterets. They noticed in front of them a check point manned by some French air force boys. A car which they recognised as a Brussels taxi, which were all of the same type and painted in dark red and green, the colours of the city, was stopped at the checkpoint. Rene approached the car and opened the front passenger door opposite to where the driver was sitting and to where the soldiers were examining his documents. In Flemish Rene asked him where he was going to.

"To Cauterets," was the answer.

"Can you give us a lift?" Rene asked.

"Yes, jump in," said the driver without any hesitation.

"We would prefer you to wait for us a few hundred yards from here," said Rene.

"Why?" asked the driver. "Because we have no permit to travel," replied Rene shooting the driver a knowing look, accompanied by a slight shrug. To this the silly man turned to the soldiers who by now had returned all his papers and said "These are two countrymen of mine, they have no travel permits, can I take them?"

Luckily for Rene and Roger the soldiers were quite decent and their sergeant said, "We have no objection, we are only here to check on cars, but your countrymen better be careful in Pierrefitte where the control is done by gendarmes and they may not be so easy."

During the journey to Pierrefitte Rene thanked the driver for having taken them, but gently ticked him off for his foolishness at the check point. "Now when we get to Pierrefitte," Rene said, "just show your own papers and let us do our own talking for ourselves." Meanwhile he had agreed with his cousin on a strategy. When they got to Pierrefitte, as expected, they were stopped by gendarmes who examined the driver's documents at length. When they asked for Rene and Roger's papers, they handed the gendarmes their Belgian identify cards.

"Where have you come from?" one of the gendarmes demanded.

"Lourdes," Rene replied affecting a quizzical tone, as if enquiring why he should be asked.

"Where are you going to?"

"Cauterets."

"Where is your travel permit?" said the gendarme, again in an authoritarian manner.

"What travel permit?" replied Rene, his brow creased in affected incomprehension.

"Don't you know that you must have a travel permit to move from one town to another?"

"Since when?" asked Rene

"Since yesterday," replied the gendarme, adopting a gentler tone.

"Well we left Cauterets the day before yesterday to visit Lourdes and there was no question of a permit." Rene attempted to appear contrite.

"Where do you stay in Cauterets?" the gendarme asked.

"At the Hotel Excelsior with my parents."

This seemed to satisfy the gendarme who returned the identity cards and said "Right, get back to Cauterets and don't move out of there without a permit."

Cauterets, Hautes Pyrennes 26th June 1940

Twenty minutes later they were at the Hotel Excelsior where Rene's parents and sister had spent their first night in unoccupied France and had a lot to tell him and Roger about all that happened since he last saw them in La Roche-Posay. They told him about being in the village during the preparation of the defences on the bridge over the River Creuse by the French and how they heard the shelling on both sides of the bridge. Then they had seen the French troops withdraw very fast and soon they had fallen under German occupation until the day they travelled south. Rene had to tell them at length about the trip from Toulouse and also about his movements since he had left them two weeks before on his way through La Roche-Posay.

The next few days were spent in a very leisurely fashion. They made a few walking excursions into the Pyrenees. Rene already had a feeling that one day he may want to cross the mountains into Spain and he wanted to acquaint himself with the area.

A good part of the mornings were spent reading the papers. Two quiet months were spent on excursions. The only thing that was spoiling, what under other circumstances could have been considered as a pleasant holiday, was the war news abundantly put out by the Vichy press. The news appeared worse than ever. The headlines read in large print. "The invasion of England is a matter of weeks, possibly only of days." The

French press was echoing at length all the propaganda provided by the Germans. Long descriptions were given of the damage inflicted by the Lufftwaffe on London and on Coventry. Now Rene's parents were mainly worried about the fate of Irma's sister Emmy and her family, who with Rene's help had managed to sail for England.

As soon as Rene had got settled down in Cauterets he had sent a note to the commanding officer in Toulouse to provide him with his address. During the second week of August, Rene received a marching order and a railway warrant instructing him to report in Lunel near Montpellier. Once more he took his leave of his parents and sister and of his cousin Roger and travelled to Lunel.

Lunel, Languedoc, August 1940

When he reported at the Belgian headquarters, he was told he had two alternatives: Either to be sent back to Belgium on a repatriation train leaving the next week, or to be demobilised on the spot. He chose the latter and was given his discharge papers and 750 French francs.

A few days later Franz and Irma received a letter from him explaining the choices he had been given when he reached his unit. He told them that he had chosen the second alternative and had been given 750 francs demobilisation pay and had used some of it to buy a second-hand bicycle for 180 francs. The army had provided him with camping equipment, blankets and cooking utensils. The commanding officer had told him, "Take as much as you can carry. Take whatever you want, then the Germans won't be able to take it away." He had enquired about a bicycle, but he was told that they had all been disposed of. Probably they had been sold to civilians, as he had seen done in Toulouse, so instead he had been compelled to buy one.

In a nearby bicycle shop he had found a second hand ladies' bicycle in very good condition. Having bought it, he then went back to the barracks where a mechanic fixed two ordnance luggage panniers front and back to the cycle. They were a large type, about thirty six inches square. He was provided with four rigid bags which clipped onto the panniers, alongside the wheels. On the top of the rear pannier he strapped four neatly folded tent sheets and on top of them two blankets, a large ground sheet and a sleeping bag. The whole pyramid at the back of the bicycle was nearly two feet high.

In the two side bags at the rear, he had carefully packed his best clothes. The only pieces of uniform he was permitted to retain were a pair of khaki trousers and a pullover of the same colour, but his army jacket was kept at the camp. In the two at the front, he had placed cooking utensils, including a spirit stove and a bottle of spirit. On top of the front pannier he had a large bag containing all the poles, guy ropes and tent pegs needed to erect a four sheet tent. Having been allowed to take as much equipment as he could carry, he was also provided by the army with some rations for the journey.

He had decided to spend the rest of his demobilisation money on touring the south of France cycling and camping. He gave his parents an approximate itinerary and timing, telling them to write care of the local post office. Lightly dressed with only a pair of shorts, a sleeveless pullover, his shirt, underwear and a pair of sandals, he started his touring journey.

His first destination was Nimes, where, although he had spent a day there, he had not had a chance to see the historical buildings and sights of which the town is full. He pitched his tent in a field at the entrance of the town and did his sightseeing on a much lighter cycle he had hired. During that day, he met a young Belgian architect, who had also been demobilised in Lunel the previous day and after exchanging information about their plans, they decided to travel together. They left Nimes after having spent two nights there and travelled to Avignon. After another two days in Avignon they cycled on to Aix en Provence. The going was hard. They were both carrying an abnormally heavy load. In fact, Rene weighed his cycle on a public scale and found that he was carrying 40 kilos, approximately 80 lbs of goods. Going uphill they had to walk and push their bikes. Going downhill they went at the speed of a motorbike.

In Aix they stayed a few days, mixing with university students, meeting many Belgian refugees. Rene had expected a letter by then from his parents at the post office and on the third day, one was received. They told him that for the time being they were staying put in Cauterets and suggested that during his intended trip along the Riviera, he should

Rene's Campaign - May and June 1940

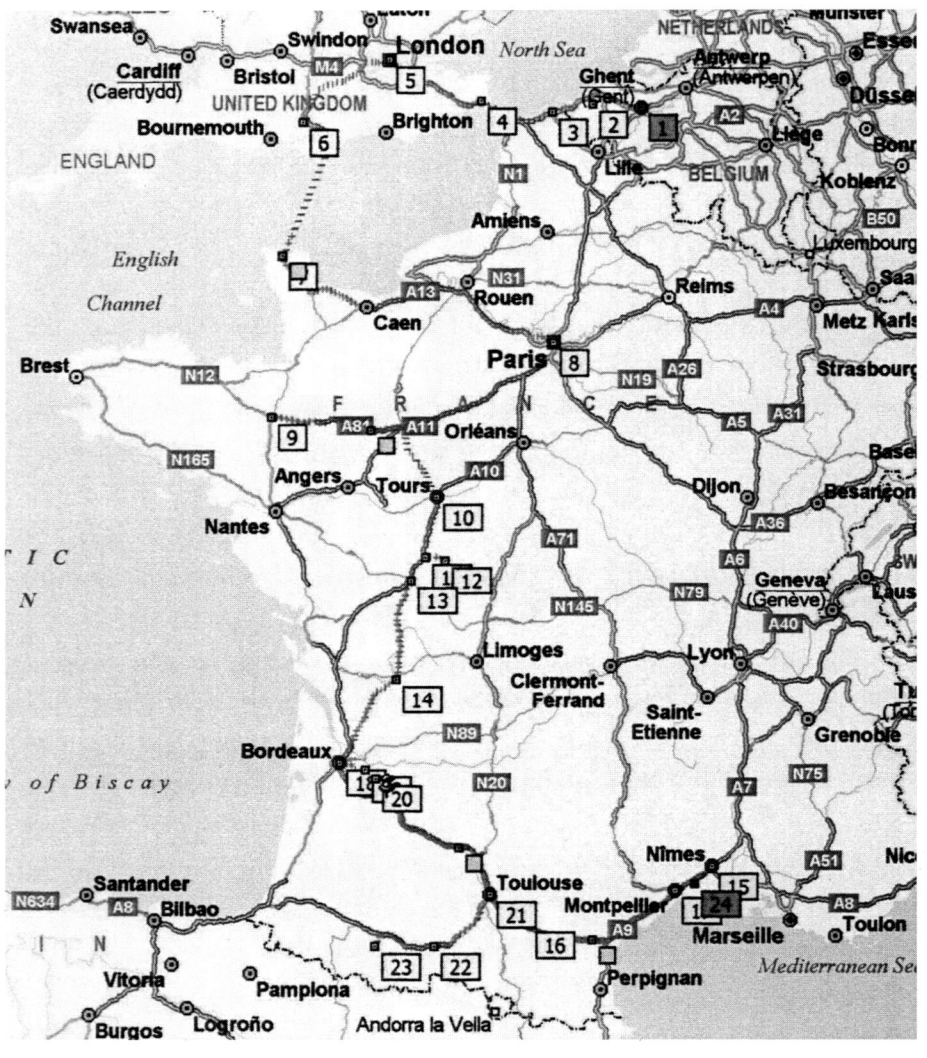

1. Ghent	13. Poitiers
2. Koekelare	14. Angouleme
3. Dunkirk	15. Nimes
4. Dover	16. Castelnaudry
5. London	17. Montpellier
6. Southampton	18. Bordeaux
7. Cherburg	19. Faleyras
8. Paris	20. Sauveterre de Guyenne
9. Rennes	21. Toulouse
10.Tours	22. St. Gaudens
11.Chatellrault	23. Lourdes
12.La Roche Posay	24.Lunel

look out for a reasonably priced hotel or boarding house where they could go and live during the winter.

Starting from autumn, Cauterets is terribly cold, as the little town is in a dip between high mountain ranges and gets a very limited number of hours of sunshine. Since his parents had not been able to take any winter clothes with them, it was a wise decision to trek to the Riviera. This would certainly limit the need for the purchase of winter clothes for them.Having received the expected letter, Rene and his travel companion decided to move on that same day to Marseilles. This was a short and easy run, since the road from Aix to Marseilles is a long and regular slope, they practically freewheeled to the centre of the city.

Marseilles, August 1940

After a short drive through the famous Cannebiere and a quick look at the harbour, they followed the coast road in an easterly direction. They soon reached a sandy beach. On it had been built one of those typically French bar and restaurants, constructed of timber, called Quingette. They went inside, had a drink and asked the proprietor if there were any restrictions to camping on the beach. As far as he knew, there were none and he immediately,and very kindly, told them that there was an outside tap which they could make full use of for their ablutions or to take water for cooking. He even suggested that if they camped in sight of his establishment, he would keep a watchful eye on their belongings whilst they were cycling into and around Marseilles.

Although they had been warned before reaching Marseilles that it was dangerous to drink the tap water there, Rene's travel companion did not take notice of this. The result was that on the second day of their stay, he suddenly had a serious bout of diarrhoea, so much so that the next day he decided to go to the nearest hospital for advice. There it was decided that he should be admitted for observation. In the doctor's estimate, he would not be discharged for a week.Rene decided that he was not in a hurry and wrote to his parents about his change of plans.

He spent a leisurely week in Marseilles during which he got a reply from Cauterets. His father suggested that he should visit an old lady friend of the family who was a permanent resident in Marseilles. He went to see the old lady, who through her sister living in Geneva, gave Rene news that some members of his family, whose whereabouts he had not known about until then, were safely living in Geneva.

When Rene's travel companion was discharged from hospital, he decided he was too weak to carry on the journey and as there was a repatriation train leaving for Belgium the next day, he had decided to book himself on it. Rene found out after the war that the train never reached Belgium. In fact, when it reached Paris all the refugees were taken off the train and interned at a football ground, because the train was needed to transport German troops to the west in preparation for an impending invasion of England. Later when the invasion was called off and trains were again available, the Nazis decided to send all the inmates of the sports ground to workers' camps in Germany. Rene's friend never returned from this trip.

Left on his own, Rene decided to continue his leisurely journey and made his way along the coast road to Toulon. The weather was beautiful, the scenery unique and he was spending very little of the remainder of his demobilisation pay. In fact all he had to pay for was bread and meat. Whenever he stopped in a village or at a farm, people noticed the pyramid of luggage on the back of his cycle. On the back of it he had attached a small Belgian flag. This attracted people's attention and they came to talk to him. When many of them offered him gifts, such as a bag of potatoes or vegetables, fruit, or sometimes even wine, he was never too proud to accept them. Sometimes he offered to pay, knowing full well that all they would accept were his thanks. Some days it was too hot to eat in the middle of the day and he was quite content with a few wild figs growing alongside the road.

Toulon, September 1940

At Toulon he pitched his tent once more on an isolated beach. After a reasonably comfortable night in the tent, he awoke as usual around 6 o'clock in the morning. Only dressed in bathing trunks, he made straight for the sea and was very surprised to find that at that time in the morning the temperature of the water was much warmer than the air. He stayed a few days in Toulon, visiting the town during the day, returning to his lonely spot in the evening to prepare himself a meal over the little spirit stove. It usually consisted of a piece of meat floating in a very thick vegetable soup in which he had also boiled a few potatoes, tomatoes, peppers and onions.

From time to time some lonely person taking a dog for a walk, or some young lovers who had taken advantage of the isolation of the place, passed in front of his tent; some just looking at him and at his installation with curiosity; others stopping and starting a conversation. Since he had no valuables and he could rely on the honesty of people, he left his tent unattended every evening. He dressed up and then cycled into town to visit a cafe or a dance.

One morning, when as he did every day, he had taken his dip in the Mediterranean, he had the shock of his life. As he was coming out of the water, he suddenly noticed a quantity of black spots on his skin. At first he wondered if he had caught a disease. Then on closer examination, he discovered that the small black spots were drops of oil. He got rid of them quite easily, because the quantity of each spot was minimal, but an hour later the tide had brought in an oil slick so thick that he knew that for many days there would not be a chance to bathe in the sea at that spot. So he decided to move further east.

This brought him to St. Tropez and then St. Maxime. He followed the whole coast via St Raphael, Cannes, Juan les Pins and Nice to Monte-Carlo. Then he made his way back to Aix en Provence, this time using, the mountain route via Grasse-Draguignan. The whole trip took him one month. He covered 690 kilometres and still had some army pay left at the end of it.

As he had promised his parents, he had been looking around for winter quarters for them and had found an inexpensive, but nice, boarding house in St Raphael. He had corresponded with his parents about it and they had asked him to make a definite reservation for the second week in October. They arranged to meet on a given date in Aix en Provence with the result that his return trip via the heights became rather hurried.

After meeting his family they travelled together by train to St Raphael. Rene, of course, embarked on the train with his precious bicycle and all his camping equipment. In the following days the cycle became very useful to his mother when she went on her shopping expeditions. Living

Rene's Cycle Tour - Summer 1940

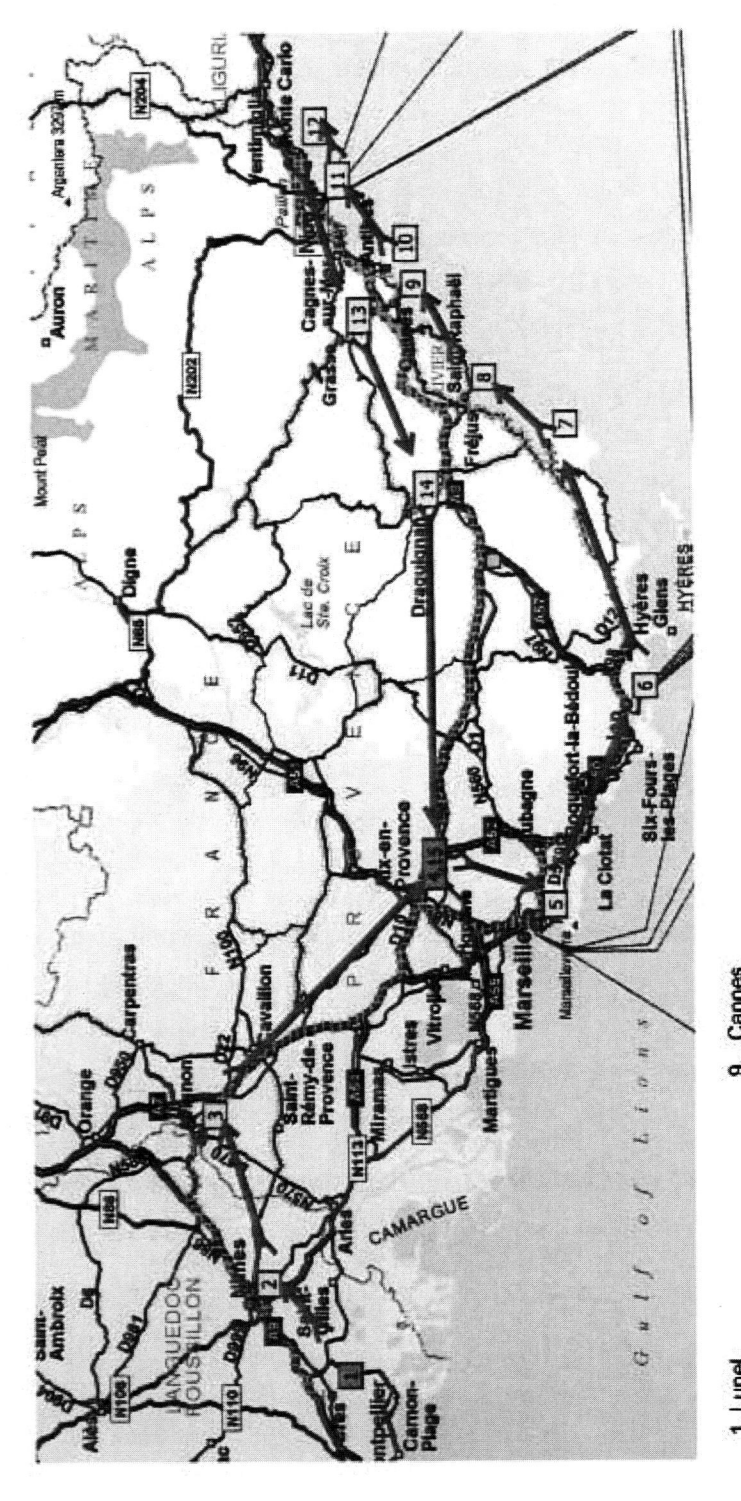

1. Lunel
2. Nimes
3. Avigbon
4. Aix En Provence
5. Marseilles
6. Toulon
7. St.Tropez
8. St.Raphael

9. Cannes
10. Juan Les Pins
11. Nice
12. Monte Carlo
13. Grasse
14. Draguinan
15. Aix En Provence

in the boarding house was a real luxury for Rene, after his weeks under canvas. His parents had a very nice room facing the sea, whilst Rene and Georgette had two rooms on the side of the building facing the street, but by leaning out of the window they could also see the sea.

At first their stay was like an extended holiday. To sleep in a comfortable bed, to be served breakfast in bed, not to have to worry about shopping or preparing a meal, – what more could one ask? The only thing to spoil their bliss was the uncertainty of the future. How long would it last? How long would his parents be able to afford this kind of expense? Although they had taken a goodly amount with them, there were limits to their assets.

Cannes, November 1940

Franz, Irma and Rene were not alone in wondering how long their assets could sustain them, given the uncertainties of the situation. Eddie Nathan, Helene and their two daughters, Cecile and Andree had briefly joined other members of the family at the Hotel Excelsior in Cauterets during the summer, when hotel rates on the Mediterranean coast were at their highest. Now when rates in the Hautes Pyrennees were increasing to capitalise on those still seeking to enjoy winter sports in the region, they headed back to the Grand Hotel in Cannes, where they could not only take advantage of the cheaper low season prices, but also the warmer coastal climate. Doubtless Eddie's credit at the hotel remained good, he was after all, a client who possessed significant assets and resources, whenever he could access them. But as a letter which reached him at the hotel indicated, accessing them had become a significant problem as the war progressed and the German advance into northern France disrupted normal commerce in the country. The letter also paints a graphic picture of the travails of the countless refugees seeking to evade the conflict and in particular of the difficulties of those looking to quit the country.

Lambs Club,
130 West 44th St.,New York, N.Y.
11 November 1940

Mr. E.S Nathan,
Grand Hotel,
Cannes, France.

Dear Eddie,

Your letter dated August 1st, written from Haute Pyrennes,has reached me a few days ago, evidently held up at the border all these weeks. Prior to receiving your letter I made very effort to locate you and the family. I was able to get a permit from the Military at Biarritz for a 3 day visit to Bordeaux where I had to go in reference to my papers, and there made an attempt to locate Mother and Kitty,which I understood was about 40 kilometres from Bordeaux, but the Military authorities would not allow me to leave Bordeaux on account of the bombing and I was compelled to leave without even finishing my personal business,to return to Biarritz. The only hope I had of locating you was taking the chance. of sending you a letter to the Bank At London,to the Chateau and to the apartment in Paris, and I am happy to say that I met with results by receiving your letter.At the present moment I haven't any idea where you are, in Cannes or whether you left for some other part of the unoccuppied territory. I readily understand your position with the family,and your financial condition, having your money and rents blocked by the Germans, plus inability to get any funds from English banks. I shall not dwell longer on matters pertaining to and on what you can and cannot do, but shall give you briefly my experiences from the 10th of June.

On the afternoon of the 10th of June,I received a hurried telephone call from my friend Mr.Marchand, of the Prefecture of the Police, telling me to leave immediately as the German Army was bombing in and around Chantilly. I immediately went to my bank to get money to leave, only to find at 10 minutes to 3, the bank was closed and already gone. I then proceeded to my hotel to get 2 or 3 thousand francs to get out of the danger zone,only to find that they were evacuated, and not having enough money to pay off the help. So there I was absolutely stranded with 35 francs in my pocket.

To make my story short, it took me 12 days to get from Paris to Biarritz, as you know, normally, it is just over night. I have had very unfortunate experiences enroute, both by the civilian and military authorities, as I was travelling without any visas, no money, and had handcuffed to my arm a briefcase containing over two and one half million Gulden of Amsterdam merchandise, belonging to an old friend of mine of Shanghai, and this has cost me untold trouble and annoyances, subject to being shot immediately for looting with the definite accusation of being strong 5th Column, but fortunately my friend who was with me, being French., plus my American passport, was able to clear myself from all the obstacles put in my way. The result of these trying experiences brought about a very strong; case of upsetting my nerves which was aggravated by 8 days of steady crying, known as hysterics, and I was under the continued treatmentof having pecures given to me by the French Military doctors enroute to Biarritz. Of course on my arrival at Biarritz, I was an awful sight, not eating, not sleeping, 12 days growth of beard, and all that goes with this kind of living. When in Biarritz naturally I knew everybody, and it, didn't take me long to get whatever money I required to get to New- York, but the unfortunate thing was my nervous condition plus the absence of the visas, sortie Spanish and Portugal Visas, and I am happy to say that in due time I received these by agreeing to coming home as a refugee in a convoy with 800 others as a prisoner of the U.S. Government. Under the blanket visas which the U.S.Government furnished with the Spanish and Portugal Governments. I am again happy to tell you that for the 10 days I had to wait in Bilboa, Spain, I went in to the Used Motor Car business, selling the cars of the refugees who were with us and did very well, and in Lisbon, as I had to wait there 3 days to get the boat, I went into the money changing business and exchanged the francs that these 800 refugees had, buying dollars at 108 and selling them to the refugees at 125.So you can draw your own conclusion how successful I was, and therefore the bad times I experienced before reaching Spain had been offset by my motor business and money changing business. Since I arrived in New York I have had several elapses of my nerves, and had several pecures, but now I am happy to say that I am comfortably normal and am again my old self, For the last 3 weeks I have started dancing regularly and am enjoying life on the whole.

As to my future plans, it is my intention to stay here for a few months as I am anticipating taking South America very seriously, and it may be that I may open offices here and one in Buenos Aires.I received a letter from Miss Fremda who is with her mother, father and sister stuck somewhere in Toulouse and I am thinking very seriously of sending her my Power of Attorney in the event that she can get to Paris to take over my business and do whatever she sees fit to raise some money for herself and family. I don't know whatever else I can write, but do let me hear from you, at once, telling me your plans and what if anything I can do for you. If you have any ideas of coming over here, I might suggest that you ask for a visas in transit to get to Singapore. In the event you are thinking of doing anything like this, write me clearly on anything you want done.

Hoping that you and the family well, under the circumstances,

I am

      Sincerely,

Copy to Mr. Edward S.Nathan Lloyd's Bank, London, England.

PS Do tell me a little about Pierre, Paulette and the children

The Pierre to whom Eddie's correspondent refers, is Pierre Billotte. Unbeknown to Hilly, Pierre is now a prisoner of the Germans and has been transported to a P.O.W. camp in Pomerania on the Polish frontier. Happily, Paulette and the children have found safety with other members of the family in the south of France.

St. Raphael, Provence, November 1940

After a few weeks, Rene decided he could no longer be a burden to his parents. His father had insisted on paying his expenses at the boarding house in St.Raphael. So one day under the guise of an excursion to Nice, Rene went to pay a visit to the Belgian Consul there. The Consul, a Monsieur Lamotte, was an extremely nice man and Rene explainedthe family's situation to him. He took Rene into an office next door to his own, where he was introduced to a Lieutenant Dubroux, an ex Belgian Air Force Officer, now a civilian and attached to the Consulate, specially to deal with refugees. Dubroux immediately told Rene that he could employ him. He needed an inspector of refugees. The amount he offered Rene was not fantastic, but it would allow him to be independent. He also fixed an amount for Rene's travel expenses, obtained a permit to allow him to travel without hindrance between two departments and gave him a brief outline of his future duties.

They consisted mainly of checking on certain refugees obtaining allowances from the Consulate, to make sure that they were living at the addresses given by them within the jurisdiction of this Consulate. He also suggested that since Rene was living in St Raphael and would make it his base of operations, he should contact all the station masters between Toulon, the limit of their territory and Cannes, as well as those nearer to St.Raphael and Nice and inform them of his name and address. By doing so, he could also request them to pass the information on to the railway staff under their control. This would allow them, if a new refugee arrived in the Var or the Alpes Maritimes, to direct them to Rene.

Very happy, Rene went back to St Raphael and told his parents about his good fortune. The next day he went to see the station master at St Raphael and told him the reason for his visit. On his advise, Rene went to see the Chief Engineer of the area, who was also in charge of personnel. The Chief Engineer, Monsieur Ruelle was most welcoming and immediately volunteered to send an official circular to all concerned, thus saving Rene the bother of numerous telephone calls and journeys. He had been given a week to complete this first task and then to report back in Nice for further instructions at a pre-arranged date and time. Having had his task simplified by Monsieur Ruelle, Rene decided to have a few more leisurely days. What better way of occupying himself than to go fishing?

Rene had previously bought fishing tackle and tried his hand at catching fish. However, he had never been enthusiastic about it before. He could not see what pleasure people could find in spending hours watching a float bobbing on the water's surface. In the south of France fishing was quite different. Sitting on a pier you could see deep into the water, so clear and pure that you could see the fish approach your line and be caught. Naturally it demanded more careful concealment of the hook. But you had a more interesting view. You saw the fish approach the bait and you could see straight away when it was caught, as it exposed its silvery flanks whilst trying to disengage itself from the hook. A swift pull and you had your catch.

After a week Rene went back to the Consulate in Nice. By then the Consul had been notified that he was no longer allowed to call his office a Consulate. The official title of his office was now the 'Centre for Belgian Refugees'. Rene was given a list of refugees in the two departments and was told to visit as many as he could and make an assessment of those who needed financial help and of those who had independent means. He was also told to make the acquaintance of the man who up until then had been the Belgian Vice Consul in St Raphael. His name was Monsieur Misson. He was Belgian born, but had lived for many years in France and owned a large corner shop in the main street opposite the Post Office. One half of his shop was an estate agency with the English name of King and the other half was a travel agency, which was a Thomas Cook and Wagon Lits sub-agency.

During the following days Rene met Monsieur Misson, his wife and his charming daughters, before setting off on his mission around the two departments. As he was travelling by public transport and the centres to be visited were sometimes quite distant from one another, he could not always return to St Raphael the same day. After a few weeks of these journeys, he reported to Nice that he had completed his survey and handed in his report.

Next he was told to go back to St Raphael and await further instructions. A few more weeks elapsed during which his main activities were fishing, sunbathing, swimming and in the evening, playing bridge with his family. He had been told in Nice that he should keep his ears open in case he heard of any means to leave St Raphael by a clandestine route and should he hear of anything to report immediately to Nice. It was whilst investigating such a possibility that he met a local fisherman called Pastorelli. He said that he had been contacted by British submarines which had surfaced suddenly during the night in front of his fishing boat. He had been paid to disembark special agents and re-embark some people leaving for England.

At first Rene took his story with a pinch of salt, but after a while he realised that the fellow seemed to be genuine. Rene listened to his stories, but gave him the impression of being uninterested Nevertheless he brought all the information back to Nice, telling Lieutenant Dubroux that if there was any truth in the fisherman's story, he would like to attempt his own departure for England.

A few days later, when coming back for lunch to the boarding house, Rene found a message asking him to call on a Monsieur Detal at the nearby Hotel des Algues. When he got to the hotel that same afternoon, he asked for Monsieur Detal at the reception desk. After a phone call to his room, Rene was asked to go up. When he entered the room he was met by a young man of about 25 years of age, small, but strongly built who welcomed him. They shook hands and by way of introduction he said "I am coming to see you on the recommendation of Lieutenant Dubroux in Nice. He tells me you would like to get to England." Rene answered evasively, because by then it was well known that the Vichy Police had organised a team of agents provocateurs.

"Before I tell you about my plans for you I must ask you a few questions," Detal said

"Go ahead," answered Rene.

"According to your file provided by the Consulate in Nice, you have said that you lived in Antwerp, Brussels and Liege."

"Yes, that is so," replied Rene.

"Where did you go to school in Antwerp?" Rene mentioned the schools he had attended.

"Good. You say you finished your studies at the Lycee d'Anvers. Can you name a few boys in your form who were British born?"

"Yes certainly. There was Bob Creighton, Eric Thornton, Bob Snowdon and Terry Hughe," offered Rene.

"Correct. Well you are the Rene Falkenau we are looking for. I have been parachuted in from England to organise an escape route for Belgians wanting to join the Belgian forces in England. One of your schoolmates, I cannot mention who, had heard of your presence here. He wants you to stay for a while to organise the sector between Toulon and Monte-Carlo and in due course we will arrange for you to get to Britain, but for the time being, we want you to work for us here. I shall come at regular intervals to bring you instructions and funds for your activities. Now the first thing I want you to do and be very careful how you go about it, is that I need maps, preferably administrative maps of this area and also maritime maps giving details of the sand banks in the vicinity."

As by this time Rene had made many friends in many walks of life, this was not too difficult a task. He had had to be very careful and selective in his choice of friends. At first sight they were just Frenchmen, but the art was to detect who was pro-Vichy or pro-German and who was pro-British. It was possible to be one and not the others. For instance, the lady running the boarding house was pro-Vichy, pro-Petain, but very anti-German and as equally anti-British. Rene had already discovered that everybody connected with the French navy, and that applied to almost everybody living in Toulon, was anti-British. But on the other hand, there were many people who, although admiring Petain, were pro-British. Some even believed that Petain was playing a subtle game in secret agreement with the British. This was to be disproved when the attack on Mers El Kebir took place. On that occasion, all those who were anti-British showed their cards, whilst the others just philosophically said that such a confrontation was unavoidable.

Amongst his most reliable accomplices Rene had found a customs officer called Denis. He was a native of the north of France and as such, much more pro-British. Through him, within a matter of days, Rene got the necessary maps. Through attempting to join up two of these maps Rene made a strange discovery, which was to prove of great help to future operations. Checking the maps used by police and customs to define the boundaries under their surveillance, he found that there was an area of approximately three kilometres between the zone on the map covering St Raphael and the zone extending around Agay, which was unsupervised. One day he asked Denis to take him to the limit of his boundary and they both cycled to it. Next Rene asked him to contact a reliable friend in Agay to show them up to where he had instructions to patrol. Sure enough, it confirmed Rene's theory that there was a no mans land of three kilometres. When he drew Denis's attention to it he said "Yes, I know and don't you make anybody wise to it, because it would only mean three more kilometres of cycling for us and the area we cover is long enough as it is."

It was certain Rene would keep that valuable information to himself. What he had discovered was an especially excellent area for embarkation or disembarkation. The Cape of Dramont, with the bay of the same name, were within that no man's land.It was possible that during the day time the authorities relied on the lighthouse keeper on top of the Cape of Dramont to keep a watch on this area, but this would be completely inadequate at night time. So when later Rene was instructed to examine a likely place for a submarine to approach the coast to embark or disembark people, he was able to suggest the Bay of Dramont.

The maritime maps of the area showed that south of a rock on which there was another small lighthouse, was a deep channel between two large sand banks. Next, Rene was instructed to go to sea and make depth tests to find the exact depth of the sea bed and chart the sand banks. With the help of his friend, the fisherman Pastorelli, and under the guise of laying the net, which in fact they did, they also took measurements with the help of a piece of lead at the end of a thin rope. Rene was also helped in this task by a man specially sent from Nice to assist him.

For Rene these night time trips were a real ordeal. He was a very bad sailor and as long as the motor boat was heading out to the open sea he was alright, but as soon as Pastorelli stopped his engine to cast the net, and the boat bobbed around on the currents, he became as sick as a dog.

Even when the sea was calm, the Mediterranean still has a pattern of short intervals between waves lapping a boat, which many cannot stand. And Rene was one of them.

By the time these nightly operations were on the go, the severity of the food rationing had begun to make its impact. Whereas in England, rationing still allowed everyone a sufficient diet and people could even save on their rations by eating in a restaurant, in France the rationing was so severe that even to eat in a restaurant, you first had to produce your ration coupons. People were issued with several pages of small stamps every month. Each page had a different colour and the colour scheme defined what use the stamps were put to. One colour of stamp was for meat, about one thin slice a day, another for bread, about two slices a day, whilst another stamp was for 'matieres grasses', which normally referred to butter or cheese, but now meant two ounces of 'greasy goods' and now included, either butter, oil, margarine or cooking fat. Sugar was also rationed. Chocolate was only available to children and elderly people. One packet of cigarettes was allowed every five days or a packet of pipe tobacco every ten days. The fact that the ration of cooking fat had been set at two ounces a day meant that people very soon knew what it was to be hungry, because although they could get a good quantity of vegetables such as tomatoes, egg plants, peppers and courgettes, there was too little fat to cook them in. One or two hours after eating, the sensation of hunger reappeared.

The only way to stop that feeling was to eat a 'Bouchie Royale'. It was the invention of a clever merchant from Marseilles who, understanding the rationing regulations and also the price controls on figs, dates, almonds and other products from the French colonies, had imported all three from Africa straight to Marseilles. Then in large mixing machines, he had blended figs and stoned dates, with almond paste added to them. When this concoction was forced out of machines in the form of a long sausage, one inch thick, it was then cut into strips three inches long, wrapped in silver paper and sold at three times its value. Since it was neither figs or dates or almonds the authorities could not find a basis for rationing it. But again, the trouble was that one hour after eating this concoction, you still felt hungry.

Although in France generally there was no shortage of food, the distribution system had broken down. The railways were completely under German control and even in Vichy France, with the help of the Petain government, they had obtained the maximum number of goods wagons. These wagons were used to carry goods arriving in Marseilles from north Africa. These goods followed the coast to Ventimiglia and from Italy were carried on to Austria and Germany. The Germans, naively hoped to deceive the Allies by this routing, but reports regularly reached England on the content of the wagons and their movement. The only reason which prevented the Allies putting an end to this movement was to delay what eventually took place, which was the occupation of the whole of French territory by the Germans.

Petrol was also in short supply in the unoccupied zone. This was why many cars and lorries had been converted to carry a large cylinder burning wood which captured a gas which the engine could use when introduced into its cylinders in place of petrol vapour. These vehicles were slow, dreadful to maintain and very often in trouble if the wood used was too wet to produce the right gas. This lack of transport meant that both German and Vichy authorities did not allow the movement of livestock or animal feed from one department to another.

The two departments in which Rene was permitted to travel were rich in citrus fruit, lemons, oranges and tangerines, also melons, tomatoes, egg plants, and grapes, but had very little livestock. Olives, which were plentiful in the area could have provided sufficient olive oil to satisfy everybody's needs, but here again the whole of the crop had been handed over or sold to the German Armistice Commission. There was a glut of chickens in the area around Bresse in Burgundy, but very few could be found on the markets in the south.

One of the few occasions when Rene really could eat a good complete meal, was when he chose to travel to Nice around lunchtime and make use of the restaurant car on the train. This train travelled all the way from the north and took on supplies all along the route and when some of the attendants learned that Rene was an ex-Thomas Cook and Wagons Lits man, they usually provided him with a bumper meal, sometimes on the house.

In Nice, he always went to eat at the same restaurant, the Cyrano, where he was known to one waitress who never asked for his ration coupons. In St Raphael he had to surrender the best part of the coupons to the old lady running the boarding house. In October she had been so welcoming, but now that the winter was over and that the prospects of holiday makers coming from the big cities within the unoccupied zone were good, she was not so friendly anymore. One day when Rene came back to the boarding house, his parents told him that the old woman, using the argument of the increased cost of living, wanted to increase their rent by an unreasonable amount. Rene went to the Hotel Hermitage at the top of the road and found that they could have full board there for far less than the old woman wanted to charge. So the family all moved to the Hotel Hermitage.

Whilst staying there Rene made the acquaintance of a French officer, a captain, who was on leave. He was interested to hear of Rene's version of the Belgian campaign and of the retreat to Dunkirk and subsequent events. Rene told him about finding a sailing boat in Dunkirk and not being able to use it. The Frenchman's immediate reaction was "Then this is one thing you have to learn." "I would very much would like to," said Rene showing an uncharacteristic enthusiasm for the idea of being on the water. "Well, I think I can help you there," his acquaintance replied. "A friend of mine, a naval officer, who has a villa in St. Maxime, owns a sailing boat. He is away on a mission in North Africa and he has offered to lend it to me for a month. As a matter of fact, I am going to St.Maxime tomorrow to fetch the boat and if you wish to come with me, you would be a great help."

Rene agreed to the suggestion and next evening they took the coastal train to St.Maxime. They arrived there around supper time and made their way to the villa. It was the last building on the road leading out from St Maxime to St Tropez. Through a metal gate at the end of a high hedge, they found a well laid out narrow strip of garden with ornate flower beds. Five yards from the hedge was a white washed building, against which a well trained purple Bougainvillea was growing. The building with its red tiled roof had been visible through the hedge from the road. It gave the impression of being a large bungalow.

The French officer rang the doorbell and a maid came to open the door. After they had made themselves known, the maid told them that the lady of the house had given her instructions to show them to their rooms. After they had settled in, she would show them the restaurant, only two doors away, where her mistress was waiting for them. Only when they entered the house did they discover that this was not a bungalow. They had entered by the top floor of a four storey villa built into a cliff and facing the bay of St Tropez. The fourth floor was the servants' quarters. On the third floor were the guests' rooms. Their hosts had their rooms on the second floor. The first floor had a large dining room, lounge and private bar with a wide balcony terrace, stretching the whole width of the villa. The ground floor, practically at sea level, was divided into two parts. On the one side there was a kitchen and its store and utility rooms, and on the other a boathouse, with a ramp giving direct access to the sea. Next to this ramp was a short jetty and sea wall, providing protection for the boat's mooring.

Rene was amazed, to say the least, by the quality of the furnishings in the bedrooms. The whole of the furniture was finished in white lacquer. In his room he found a large double bed with built in bedside tables at each side. Behind the low headboard was a built in, well stocked library. Two bedside lamps, as well as the central chandelier, were controlled by switches on each side of the headboard. There was even a bell push to summon the servants. Next to the bedroom was a spacious bathroom with bath, toilet and wash basin in pastel blue.

They did not waste much time unpacking, since they had hardly brought anything with them. They had only taken what was necessary for one night. A few minutes later the maid showed them the way to the restaurant. There they found their hostess, the wife of the other naval officer, sitting with a good number of people, all apparently friends and neighbours. She came to greet the captain, with whom she must have been on very friendly terms, since in true French fashion, they kissed each other on both cheeks. The captain introduced Rene to her and in turn she introduced them both to all her friends.

Amongst these was an American gentleman called Bill Travers. Bill was about forty years old, of average height, but rather stockily built. He was a jovial type. He spoke French without an accent and Rene found out later that he spoke German similarly well. The conversation concerned the main topic of the day, progress of the war. Within minutes Rene could sense that most of the people present were anti-British in the way they discussed the events at Mers El Kebir. Rene carefully abstained from taking part in the conversation and so he noticed, did Bill Travers. A little later their hostess suggested that it was time to go for their meal.

A table for four had been reserved for them. The captain sat next to their hostess, Rene sat opposite her and she invited Bill Travers to join them. During the meal, whilst the captain and the lady were reminiscing about previous encounters, Bill Travers started to question Rene at length about how and why he came to be in the south of France. Rene answered with some reservation. Partly he was suspicious of the fact that for an American, he spoke French too well. When he heard that Rene was an inspector of refugees, he asked him if he had any contact with Belgians other than refugees, who were living in the area. Rene told him he had met one or two, mentioning Monsieur Misson, the well known Vice Consul in St Raphael and another Belgian he had met by chance, the owner of a garage in St Raphael. Travers then asked him if he knew that garage owner well, because he said he had always found Belgian garages and mechanics to be more reliable than the French. Rene told him he had only met the garage owner once or twice, but Travers insisted that he would like Rene to introduce him to the man. Rene gave him his address in St.Raphael and Travers said he would contact Rene in a few days.

After a rather too rich dinner, they walked back to the villa and settled down in their respective rooms. The captain, before retiring to his room had warned Rene that he would give him a knock at 5 a.m, as it was essential for them to start their journey by 6 a.m. In fact they both spent a very bad night. In Rene's case, the intense rationing seemed to have resulted in his stomach having reduced in size, and his being unable to digest the abnormally large meal in which they had partaken. The result was that he had violent indigestion, which kept him awake until the early hours of the morning. He had not been asleep very long when he was awakened by loud banging on his door.

The captain asked him to rush because it was 6am. By the time he had washed, got dressed and got the boat ready, an another half hour had elapsed. When Rene rejoined the captain on the pier, he told him that he had overslept, because like Rene, he had had indigestion which had kept him awake the best part of the night. At first Rene did not see what all the fuss was about. After all, their time was their own.

He was soon to learn, to his cost, the difference that one hour of later departure made. They had caught the morning wind which was taking them in the direction of St Raphael. During the journey the captain taught him the essentials of handling the sails. Rene thought that they were making good progress, but the captain looked worried as their watches ticked on. He soon revealed the reason for his anxiety. If they did not reach the cape, which he pointed out in the distance, by 9 o'clock, they would be in trouble. By 9 o'clock, when they were only a few yards away from the cape, the wind suddenly dropped and their sails were hanging useless along the mast, like a handkerchief held between two fingers. From the bottom of the boat, the captain quickly retrieved two pairs of oars and handing one pair over to Rene, instructed him to take up position to row.

They both started to row and row, but seemingly without any result. They appeared to remain anchored to the same spot. By then, in addition to the aftermath of his indigestion, Rene became violently sea sick. The captain, without displaying any compassion for his state, started to shout, "Come on boy, don't feel so sorry for yourself, go on rowing. If you don't help me to maintain our position we will soon be pushed back into St Maxime."

They went on rowing for two hours. At 11 o'clock, as the captain predicted, as if timed by a magic bell, the wind picked up. The sails filled with the westerly wind and within minutes they had passed the cape and were pushed in the direction of St Raphael which they reached an hour later. Now Rene knew why the captain had made so much fuss about the delay of an hour. Had they left St Maxime at 5.30 a.m. they would have been on the easterly side of the cape by 9 a.m. and even without wind, the incoming tidal currents, which were deflected by the submerged rocks forming the extension of the cape, would have carried them in the right direction. As they were still on the wrong side of these rocks, those same currents would have worked to carry them back to St Maxime.

Now that the captain had the boat anchored in St Raphael harbour, he gave Rene the opportunity to spend all his spare time with him, teaching him how to handle the sails and how to catch the right wind. They also went on some fishing expeditions. This involved the use of six sets of long rods, three on each side of the boat, each trailing a long piece of fishing line, at the end of which was fastened a shining piece of twisted metal with a hook at its end. As the boat progressed, trailing this arrangement of rods and lines, the pieces of metal flickered from side to side giving the impression of a small fish playfully moving in the water. They looked so real that the voracious herrings or mackerels mistook them for tiny sprats and gluttonously swallowed the bait. They sailed for several hours without a catch, then suddenly a tug at the end of one of the lines they were trailing and they knew they had a catch and that they were above a shoal. From then on they could not work fast enough to pull in each of the six lines in turn, unhook the fish and throw the line out again.

Within minutes the bottom of the boat was full with large silvery mackerels. The hotel manager was quite pleased to see them come back with that haul of fish, enough to feed his whole hotel. He never offered to buy it, probably knowing that they would have refused payment, but he offered them each a bottle of wine to go with the fish he had cooked for them.

A few days later Rene had another visit from Lieutenant Detal. He had come to pay him his monthly salary and expenses. He also brought him fresh instructions. The 'no man's land' along the Bay of Dramont had been accepted by London as the best place for embarking and disembarking clandestine passengers. There was no problem about disembarking them, but embarking them created one problem. They needed a safe place to await the ship or submarine. Although London was able, by specially coded messages read over BBC radio, to warn that the visit of a ship or submarine was to be expected within the next few days, no precise details could be given on exact dates and times. The vessels used for such purposes were usually on their way back to Gibraltar for refuelling or re-arming after they had finished their attacks on enemy positions in the eastern Mediterranean. The time required depended on how soon they contacted their enemy target and how soon they ran out of ammunition.

There was therefore, a time lapse of several days between the signal alerting them to the appearance of the submarine and its arrival.It was essential to find a safe place, where the intending departees could wait without being detected. Rene was asked to look for such a place within the 'no man's land'. He had discovered a villa about four hundred yards away from the coastal road leading from St Raphael to Cannes. From its appearance, the villa was unoccupied, because all the wooden shutters at the windows were closed. Rene went to see Monsieur Misson in his capacity of estate agent and when he described the villa and told him the purpose of his enquiry Misson said, "You are in luck my friend, this villa belongs to one of my clients who is in the occupied zone and I look after the villa for him. If you can guarantee that no damage will be done and that good care will be taken of the house,I shall let you have the keys. If my client knew the purpose to which his villa was to be put, I am sure that he would approve of my action."

Now that Rene had the villa, he had two more duties to attend to. First to find, by some devious means, a way to get food supplies. Secondly, a way to stock petrol for the various sorties they would have to make with Pastorelli's motor boat. The petrol ration he was getting for fishing purposes only allowed him three trips a week. Once they were operational, they would need to sail seven days a week.

The first item on the agenda, food, was solved pretty easily. Rene had met a young man from the north named Patrick d'Halluin in St Raphael. Soon after they had become very good friends and Rene had discovered Patrick's pro-British feelings, He had been appointed chief of a para-military organisation known as 'Compagnons de France'. Under the cover of this youth organisation, the Vichy authorities got together young men of military age and gave them military training. Camp drill was done openly, but arms drill was done very secretly, with the hope that when France was liberated, these young men would form the backbone of a new army.

d'Halluin had invited Rene to visit him at his camp in Draguignan and as he knew Rene could be trusted, he gave him all the details of his organisation and even hinted that he could be of great help to the work Rene was doing. He had already made several useful contacts at the Prefecture in Draguignan which would enable him to accept any

Belgian Rene sent to him and provide them with French identity papers and ration cards. He also put Rene in touch with a Belgian, who had managed, goodness only knows how, to be enrolled in the small French army that the German Armistice Commission had allowed to exist. One artillery battery was located near Draguignan and that Belgian boy had been put in charge of the food store. Within a week Rene had got, through him, all the food needed to be stored in the villa.

Around the same time the office in Nice had sent Rene a young man from his home town of Antwerp. Guy Corbisier was to become Rene's assistant in future operations. Whilst Rene had managed to get some cans of petrol through the Belgian garage owner in St Raphael, there was not nearly enough for their requirements. Corbisier offered to deal with that problem and he succeeded pretty well. During his expeditions, he took some risks, managing to avoid police road blocks, travelling on a moped with a bag strapped on his back and in it a large petrol can.

Day by day, hour by hour, they were preparing for the big day The Nice office had sent Rene a reconnaissance party of two Belgians. One was the Chevalier de Thiers, owner of the Liege newspaper, 'La Meuse', the other was a friend of his by the name of Timmermans. Both lived on a large estate on the outskirts of St Maxime. When they came to see Rene on an introduction from Lieutenant Dubroux, they revealed that they were instructed to examine Rene's preparations because they would be responsible for the evacuation to Britain of the Belgian Minister of Defence, General Denis.

General Denis was with the Belgian government in Poitiers, when Rene had passed through the city. He had then moved with the government in exile to Bordeaux. When the government decided to embark for England, he had decided not to join them, because, he said, he wanted to look after the Belgian Forces scattered throughout France. But it was known publicly that that was not the real reason. He had left his girlfriend somewhere in France. She was much younger than him and he had lost her during the exodus. He had been trying to trace her and had eventually found her in Nice. Suddenly he decided that, reunited with her, he wanted to rejoin the government in London. It was for his escape that all the preparations were being made.

De Thiers and Timmermans accompanied Rene several times on bicycles from St. Raphael to the Cape of Dramont to ensure that the road was clear. Not once did they get challenged either by the police or custom officers. This was thanks to Rene's friend, customs officer Denis, who had obtained for him schedules of the patrols by customs and police officers. All was ready now and all they had to do was to await the signal from London.

Meanwhile Rene got a telephone call from Bill Travers telling him that he was coming to St.Raphael the next day and wanted to see him. When Travers arrived he cane straight to the point. He had noticed during their meeting in St Maxime that Rene had not taken part in the discussion or voiced an opinion about the events at Mers El Kebir. He, as Rene had probably noticed, had also abstained from being drawn into the discussion. Travers then revealed to Rene that he was working for the US Intelligence Service and that he was travelling regularly on missions between the occupied and the non-occupied zone.Rene was rather surprised at this admission and asked him how he managed to pass from one zone into the other. The one thing that convinced Rene that Travers could be genuine was that he told him that it was a man called Pere Mathieu who saw him through. Rene had heard that name mentioned several times by some of the boys who had escaped from the occupied zone and he knew that Pere Mathieu was also working for the escape line.

Bill Travers went on to tell Rene that on a number of occasions he had undertaken to deliver messages to Lisbon for transmission to the allied intelligence services, but recently the Spanish police had been suspicious of his numerous trips and had searched him and his car thoroughly. What he wanted from Rene was an introduction to the Belgian garage owner.He had devised a plan which required someone to weld a false bottom to a petrol tank and he would then hide important documents in special flat canisters inserted between the double lining, then travel to Lisbon to deliver the documents.

Still on his guard, Rene told Travers it would be better if he first approached the garage owner to see if he was prepared to help. This would give him time to get in touch with Nice and verify Travers's story about Pere Mathieu. He promised Travers he would contact him in St

Maxime. Two days later Nice informed Rene that Travers was known to them and that he could go ahead. The garage owner had, on Rene's assurance that Travers was genuine, also given his consent to help.

Rene rang Travers and the same day took him and introduced him to the garage owner. They very quickly agreed to collaborate, a word not used much in France at the time, because of its unfortunate connotations. To seal the agreement, the three men went to have a drink. They sat down at one of the open air terraces in front of a harbour cafe. There Bill told them a most amazing story about his trips to occupied France.

One day he had gone to the line of demarcation to see Pere Mathieu, to ask him to arrange for him to be smuggled through. He got a complete refusal from Mathieu to get him across. The Germans did not have enough border police to control the whole of the demarcation line, but to give the impression that it was well guarded, they continually moved their men from one area to another, with the result that they were always leaving a gap somewhere. The underground movement was so well organised that as soon as the Germans moved their border troops they knew where the gap was and used it as a crossing point.

But at this time, the Germans had brought in extra troops and there was no gap. Pere Mathieu told Travers that he would not dream of risking his life at that moment and endanger the future of the organisation. "You could pay me a million and I still would refuse," he had said. "This is only temporary and the Germans cannot afford such a large deployment of forces for very long. I suggest you go back to Paris and as soon as there is a gap again somewhere, I shall contact you in the usual way."

Travers had no other alternative than to travel back to Paris. He waited several days, but still no news came from Pere Mathieu. By now he considered that he had almost reached the limit of the time available for the important information he was holding to get through, if it was to have any value for the US Intelligence service. This made him decide to take an extra risk. He had heard of a French girl working for the Allies, although employed by the Gestapo. Through one of his reliable contacts, he got introduced to the girl and explained his problem to her.

"How soon do you want to leave?" she asked.

"The sooner the better," was the answer.

"Well, there is a train leaving at 19.00 from the PLM station. Be there five minutes before and I shall join you on the platform one or two minutes before the train's departure."

Travers got to the station in time to buy his first class ticket, very worried in case the man at the ticket office asked to see his permit to travel. But he was given his ticket for St Raphael without any questions. He chose a seat in a crowded first class compartment. He placed his pigskin suitcase in the luggage rack and then stepped back down onto the platform, near to the door of his carriage. The next few minutes felt like hours, as he anxiously watched the entrance to the platform for the appearance of the girl. The possibility of betrayal had crossed his mind and he would not have been surprised if instead of the girl, two black leather coated Gestapo men had appeared.

Astonishingly and luckily for him, just as the train was about to pull out, the girl came running down the platform. She had timed her arrival precisely to the moment when the train was due to depart. As the conductor was waving his flag and blowing his whistle for the train to leave, she reached Travers, handed him an envelope which he quickly put into his inside pocket. With a kiss on his cheek, she shook his hand, as he leaned out from the top of the carriage steps and the train began to move out of the station.

Travers went straight back to his compartment. The presence of other and possibly suspicious travellers did not allow him to have a look at the papers he had just received. All he did was to tear the envelope, whilst still in his inside pocket and ease the papers out for when he would need to show them. When the train reached the line of demarcation, several officials boarded.It was usual for two men of the Military Police or of the Gestapo to check the passports and visas. They were then followed by two other men wearing the usual uniform of German customs officials. But on this occasion, the police examining passports were delayed in the compartment next to the one occupied by Travers and the custom officials came in first. They asked if anybody had anything to declare and received an answer in the negative from those in the compartment. Not satisfied, they looked suspiciously at everyone, then at the luggage racks. Their attention was drawn to the pigskin suitcase.

"Whose is that?"

"Mine," said Travers.

"Right, bring it down and open it."

They searched thoroughly through it and did not find a thing. Then puzzled by the silk lining inside the case, they undid it again with a penknife. They had just finished forcing the locks, when the passport officials arrived. Travers was the last one to have to show his documents. Anxiously he produced the paper out of his inside pocket. One of the police officers looked at it, passed it to his colleague and then suddenly both officials clicked their heels, saluted respectfully and went away. The two custom officials who had watched the scene became pale and said, "But sir, why did you not say that you were a Gestapo official?"

Travers, quite calmly said "Because I wanted to see if you did your duty conscientiously. Very good men, I congratulate you."

The two customs officials then proceeded to repair the mess they had made of the case and unsuccessfully tried to close the locks. They even went to the bother of finding string to hold the case together. This was the closest that Bill Travers had ever been to real danger. Rene only saw him once more after that day.

Life went on in St Raphael with Rene busily making new contacts every day. Guy Corbisier was still hunting for petrol and bringing it back to their hideout can by can. Then suddenly, although General Denis had not appeared, Rene got a message that the arrival of a submarine was imminent and would he go to sea every night for the next six days?. He alerted Pastorelli who owned a fisherman's cottage in the Bay of Dramont.

The next six nights became a real ordeal for Rene. As before, all was well as long as the boat was proceeding under the full power of its engine. The trouble started when the engine stopped. As they went to sea under the guise of laying the nets, they had to do just that. There were 700 metres of them, which they slowly lowered into the sea. This in itself was quite a tiring operation. The nets, about two metres wide, were fitted with cork floats on one side and lead weights on the other to ensure they would hang in the water in an upright fashion. Whilst Pastorelli was rowing in a zigzag pattern, Rene was helping the fisherman's wife to ease the lengths of net behind the boat and into the water. At each end of the seven hundred metre net, a rope extended to a large square of cork into which had been inserted the neck of a wine bottle. This wine bottle, floating upside down on top of the cork, had a piece of string with a piece of lead attached, hanging on its side. As the cork bobbed on top of the waves, the lead on its length of string struck the bottle which sounded like a bell. This had a double purpose. First, to attract the fish, which were attracted by the sound waves, and secondly to allow Pastorelli to locate the cork in the dark when a few hours later they had to recover the nets.

It was during this operation and as they advanced very slowly, powered only by the oars, that Rene again became violently sea sick. Even the old sailor's cures did not help. Pastorelli had managed to illegally obtain extra supplies of bread and gave Rene quantities of the soft part of the loaf to eat to settle his stomach, but he still suffered a terrible excess of bile and vomited all the bread as soon as they started laying the nets.

When this task was completed, the engines were started again and they moved further into the open sea where the submarine was supposed to meet them. Once again the engines were stopped and they floated on the crests of the waves, like the two large cork floats they had thrown overboard a few minutes earlier. Once again Rene was violently sea sick and Pastorelli's main concern was that he should not make too much noise, so that he could hear if any unexpected intruder came, instead of the expected submarine.

For six nights they scrutinised the darkness hoping to see the anticipated blue light of the submarine. On the last day, when Rene had reported to the Nice office that no contact had been made the night before, he was told that a message from London had just been deciphered calling the operation off for the time being. But only two days later Rene was informed by his headquarters that the visit of a Polish officer was impending. Rene was asked to brief him on all the details of what had been achieved so far. As expected, two days later a Lieutenant Roswadowsky came to see Rene, who supplied him with all the details he wanted.

About the same time, the German Armistice Commission had increased its activities and Rene and his comrades were seeing, practically twice a week, a beautiful Mercedes Benz open topped car stopped in front of the Hotel Excelsior, whilst the two officers and the driver were enjoying the local French cuisine. On one occasion Rene had just returned with a supply of groceries and although short of all essentials, he decided to sacrifice two lumps of sugar for the cause. Seeing that the staff car was unattended and that the midday sun had chased everybody but himself from the sea front, he quickly opened the petrol tank and dropped the two lumps of sugar into it, put the cap back and cycled in the direction of Cannes on the coastal road, which he knew to be the usual route to be taken by the Mercedes.

Fifteen minutes later the car driven by a soldier with two German officers sitting in the back seats, came past him in a hurry. A few miles further along the road he found the Mercedes alongside the kerb with its bonnet open and the driver examining the engine. He clearly did not know what had caused the car to break down, but Rene cycled back to St Raphael, knowing that his sugar lumps had not been wasted and that the German officers would have a very long wait. After that incident, the driver was no longer allowed to leave his vehicle and had to remain in his seat whilst the officers were having their meal.

Rene mentioned what he had done to Custom's Officer Denis and together they devised a new scheme. Whilst Rene looked inquisitively at the front of the German car and the driver watched his every movement, the young son of Denis managed to sneak behind the car unnoticed and drop the sugar lumps in the tank. This compelled the Germans on their next trip to have two soldiers with them. One sat in the driver's seat, whilst the other walked around the car.

Life went on with every day bringing something new. There were a good number of newly arrived Belgian soldiers in the area, who contacted Rene and he would arrange for their stay, until they could be sent further in the direction of Spain. His instructions were to keep them for a day or two in St Raphael. During that time he had to submit them to a long interrogation and he had to take down on paper every detail of their escape story. Most of them had managed to escape unaided from a German prisoner of war camp or from a labour camp. Other men, like Rene, had managed to evade capture by the Germans. The distinction between evaders and escapers was later recognised in the award of campaign medals, with escapers generally accorded greater recognition than those who had merely evaded capture.

As soon as they reached either the Dutch or the Belgian border, they were picked up, at great risk, by a member of the local escape organisation, who would hide them in the nearest farm. There they had to give at length the details of their escape from Germany. This statement having been taken down was sent to a secret location used by the escape organization. During the following night the escapee was led to believe that he was on his way to freedom, but in fact he was taken, under cover of darkness, in a large circle, only to arrive at a farm close to the one in which he spent the previous night. There, once more, he had to retell his story, which was taken down on paper in precise detail. This operation was repeated during several nights, each time the fellow was questioned and all the statements went to the one place, where they were carefully read and compared. Only when the man in charge of the sector was satisfied that all the accounts tallied was the man moved, always under the cover of darkness, to the next sector of his journey south. But, wherever he was taken, he was made to retell his story.

Some of these escapees managed to get as far as the unoccupied zone, when suddenly a discrepancy was discovered in their story. Immediately on instructions from the sector headquarters, the man, wherever he happened to be, would be submitted to an intensive interrogation next to which his previous questioning would be a pale image. In several cases, due to the perseverance of the interrogators, the man broke down and at last admitted he had been planted there by the Gestapo, to uncover the escape route. Needless to say that the man was never given a chance to report to his masters and his journey ended abruptly, there where he had been discovered.

In the early days, when an escapee reached Rene's sector and he got the 'all clear' to send him further, he would escort him as far as Toulon, where the agent covering Marseilles to the Spanish border would take him off Rene's hands, but suddenly in the summer of 1941 a message came through that something was going wrong on the Spanish side of the route.

Rene was instructed to investigate the possibility of organising an escape school. This he did with the help of his friend Patrick d'Halluin, who created a special section in his "Camp de Compagnons de France" in which he incorporated all Belgians arriving now. As he had promised, he got them French identity cards, ration tickets, a uniform and he got together a special team of instructors. Some specialised in map and compass reading, others in astronomy and he even found a linguist who taught the intending escapers, a basic Spanish. The men were subjected to an intensive training in compass and map reading and astronomical navigation, They undertook long marches and climbing exercises at night and in the strictest silence to test the skills they had learned. The woods and hills near Draguignan were an excellent area for such exercises.

Rene later discovered that the change in the way the escape route was organised was due to the fact that in the early days, the organisation had had the cooperation of a Spanish police officer who was helping the men get across Spain. Unfortunately his activities were discovered and nobody knew what had become of the officer, with whom all contact suddenly stopped. When it became apparent that it was no longer possible to count on his help, French and Spanish guides were employed and paid a good fee for taking the men across the Pyrenees.

However, it was soon discovered, thanks to a boy who managed to return to France and was a member of the escape organisation, that these guides were betraying their charges. They were getting an equal sum to that which they were being paid by the escape route, for every escapee caught by Franco's police entering Spain. They would lead them across the Pyrenees and into the first farm on Spanish soil, where the men were picked up by the local police and transported to the infamous Spanish concentration camp of Miranda de Ebro. It was following the discovery of what had been happening, that Rene was instructed to organise the escape school.

As soon as a man was judged to be ready, he was given a folding bicycle, French and Spanish currencies, some rations for the road, maps and a compass. Then he was sent on the next stage of his journey. By this means, many men succeeded in reaching Portugal, passage to Britain and freedom. Others after succeeding in crossing Spain from one side to the other, were stupidly caught a few yards from the Portuguese border. Having reached what they thought to be Portugal, they had been over-confident and careless. This cost them a stay of several months in Miranda.

Whilst working to build the organisation to assist evaders and escapers, an incident occurred in St Raphael which was to affect Rene's future work for the organisation. One morning a train coming from Marseilles stopped at St Raphael station and a parcel destined for Monsieur Ruelle, Chief Engineer of the French Railways in the area, was thrown onto the platform. As the parcel hit the ground, it split open and revealed its contents. They were forged clandestine papers printed in Marseilles, and Ruelle was responsible for their distribution to the underground movement and the escape organisation in Rene's sector.

Unfortunately, at that time two members of the Vichy Police were scouting the platform. As a result, the forged papers were discovered, Ruelle was arrested and a search made of his office. There the Vichy police seized a diary containing a large number of names and addresses. Rene's was amongst them, because he had visited Ruelle when he took on the position of Area Supervisor for Refugees working for the Belgian Consulate. As a result Rene was visited by the Vichy Police, to whom he had to explain how his name came to be entered in Ruelle's diary. They seemed satisfied with his explanation and went away. However, Rene had the feeling that he was now being watched. He reported the incident to Nice and it was suggested that he should disappear for a while.

Roquebrune, Provence, October 1941

A few days later, he was instructed to hand over his area to Corbisier and was given the address of a wine grower in the Roquebrune area where he should go and stay for a while. His parents had by then found themselves a flat in a house in Grasse. Making sure not to be followed, he paid them a quick visit and told them where he was going. When he got to the farm in Roquebrune, he found that he was going to work with thirty young girls from the Nice area. There were only four men including himself, employed at the vineyard.

This was the grape picking season. The girls were employed to cut the bunches of grapes from the vines and fill large baskets with them. The men had to carry the baskets from where the girls had filled them to the end of the row of vines, where after standing on an upturned crate, used as a step, they tossed their load into a metal tip lorry. For this work, girls were paid 25 francs a day, plus board and lodging. The men got 45 francs, all found. In addition to that, every morning before starting work, they were allowed to fill a two litre bottle of wine, four pints approximately, for their own use and every second day they were given a half litre of Marc. Marc is a colourless alcohol made from the distillation of grape skins and pips after they have been recovered from the press. Mixed with other ingredients this Marc is turned into brandy, but many Frenchmen drink it in its natural state.

The men, who for the next six weeks were going to be Rene's workmates, made full use of the Marc. At breakfast and during the morning break they usually laced their black coffee with it. Rene did not like the stuff, so he found a buyer for it on the black market and for half a litre he got 450 francs, the equivalent of ten days wages. Rene only drank one litre of wine every day and at the end of the week, he took whatever he had saved to his parents, who he visited every weekend in Grasse.

Work at the vineyard was hard, but it had its compensations. Rene never ate so much during the whole of his stay in France, than during his stay at the farm. There did not appear to be any shortage of food there. The old lady owning the place was extremely nice and generous to her workers and more specially to Rene, when she heard that he had been through Dunkirk. Her own son had been there, but had been less fortunate than Rene. He had been made a prisoner of war.

Work started in the early morning until lunchtime, then after the traditional siesta, it commenced again at four o'clock, until darkness fell. In the morning, carrying the baskets was quite easy. The men had been provided with padding to strap on top of one shoulder. Every time a basket was full, one of the stronger girls would seize the basket by one handle, a man would take the other and with the girl's help, he would swing the basket onto his shoulder and walk a distance varying from ten to one hundred yards, depending on where the basket had been filled, to the lorry where its contents were deposited. When the lorry was filled to the brim, the men had to remove their socks and shoes, lift their trouser legs as high as possible above their knees and climb into the tip lorry to compress the grapes and allow a few more baskets to be loaded.

In peace time transport of the cargo by lorries would have been assured, but as there was a shortage of petrol, horses were used to pull the tip lorries and there was quite a distance to the wine coop where the grapes were sent for pressing. This is why the men had to compress the grapes to ensure as many could be transported on each trip as possible.

Rene found it was quite an unusual feeling to bathe his feet in grape juice, but what was not so pleasant was the discovery, when the men got off the tip lorry, that the heat of the sun evaporated the juice on their legs, leaving only the sticky sensation of the sugar. There were no washing facilities in the fields and they had to go on working until sunset, when they went back to the farm. There at a water pump, with a hard brush, they scrubbed off the sugar and red discolouration from their feet and legs.

After dinner the workers usually organised their own entertainment in the form of impromptu acting or singing and what often happened afterwards in the barn will not be described here. Rene wished his time at the vineyard had not gone so fast.

Lodz Ghetto, Poland, October 1941

Many miles away from the tranquillity of the farm at Roquebrune another member of the Falkenau family was discovering that the ability to labour might prove the key to survival. Melanie Falkenau, Franz's sister had been plucked from the home she had occupied in Prague since the German occupation of her country. Now on 31 October 1941 she was amongst the 20,000 Jews to be deported from the German occupied territories to the Lodz ghetto.

The ghetto had officially been established on 8 February 1940.At this time 164,000 people had been concentrated within an area of 4.3 square kilometres in the oldest part of the city, of which only 2.4 kilometres were habitable. In April a fence went up surrounding the ghetto and on 30 April 1940 it was ordered closed, effectively sealing it off from the outside world. From now on none of its occupants would be permitted to leave and only other Jews and gypsies, would be admitted as residents of the ghetto. At first some residents believed this would protect them from the violence they had experienced outside. They were soon to discover that without access to arable land on which to grow their own food and with the German authorities strictly regulating the supply of food to the ghetto, how harsh conditions would become.

The Judenrat, the Jewish Council of Elders, headed by its controversial leader, Chaim Rumkowski had negotiated a deal with the German military authorities in which work undertaken in the ghetto would be paid for by the supply of food. However the amount of food was never stipulated, with the result that those in the ghetto capable of work, often laboured for twelve hours a day, only to receive the minimum rations needed to sustain life, thin watery soup and meagre rations of bread. By early June 1940 ration cards had been issued and by December all provisions were rationed. Starvation soon became a feature of ghetto life.

It was into this increasing tide of human misery that the news of the arrival of twenty thousand more ghetto inmates was delivered. Melanie Falkenau was to arrive on the last of five transports, each containing a thousand Jews, which had been ordered by Reinhard Heydrich following his appointment as Reichsprotektor of Bohemia in September 1941.

Even the manner of her transportation in a railway cattle truck each containing almost one hundred people cannot have prepared her for what was to come. On arrival in the ghetto she was allocated to Flat 56 at 7 Sulzfelder Strasse. She would not have been its sole occupant. Rooms in the 31,271 apartments within the ghetto were occupied by an average of three to four people. Living and sanitary conditions were primitive. Only 725 apartments had running water, there was no sewerage and no coal or wood to provide heating.

The record of her presence in the ghetto, lists her as Melanie Volkman, although her date of birth and the address from which she was deported in Prague leave little doubt as to her identity. Was this a transcription error or was she attempting to conceal her identity to protect other members of her family still in Prague?

Some time after her arrival in the ghetto Melanie was moved from the apartment on Sulzfelder Stasse to another address. It could hardly have provided an improvement in her living conditions. 29 Franz Strasse became known as 'The Collective Prague IV'. It had been the Mariawits Parish School, but in autumn 1941 the Jews deported from Prague were housed here following the liquidation of all schools in the ghetto. The building was crowded with displaced people. Hundreds of bunk beds made of unplaned planks of wood were put in the large and smaller rooms. The bunks were placed so close together that it was only possible to pass between them turned sideways. All the corners of rooms, the space under the bunk beds, between the bunk beds, and on the bunk beds were occupied by bags, packages, bundles, bed linen, laundry hung to dry, pots, canned food, plates and clothing. In this living hell, it was astonishing that there was any space left for the people.

For those like Melanie, who had lived in relative comfort and affluence, the shock must have been unbearable. In common with all the recent arrivals the only comfort she brought with her were the clothes she had been allowed to take and the small quantity of food she had managed to horde in the harsh conditions of rationing in Prague. Neither would provide comfort for long. Many of the deportees had brought amounts of cash they had managed to conserve, only to discover it was worthless in the ghetto and could not even be exchanged for the currency the Judenrat had issued. It seemed as if in all this hopelessness things could not get worse. But they could.

St. Raphael, Provence, November 1941

After six weeks in Roquebrune the grape picking was about to finish and Rene was instructed to get back to St Raphael and resume his duties there. Corbisier was pleased to see Rene back and they were both kept reasonably busy with the handling of new arrivals. The only worrying thing was that Lieutenant Detal who used to come regularly to give them fresh instructions and pay, had not been seen and was now two weeks overdue.

Making sure not to be shadowed, Rene rushed to Nice. At the Refugee Centre, Lieutenant Dubroux could give no explanation for the absence of Detal, but he agreed to give Rene an advance on loan for Rene and the men under his control. A few days later he was visited in St Raphael by another officer sent by Dubroux who informed him that Detal had been arrested and that he was taking his place. He had already refunded the advance from Dubroux and gave Rene and Corbisier their money for the month in advance with fresh instructions.

When Rene's parents moved to Grasse he had left the Hotel Hermitage and had moved next door to Hotel Diana which was run by a Belgian widow and her son. They became very good friends. When, after his return from hiding, Rene found that his men had not been paid, he used part of what he had earned in the vineyard to help them to meet their immediate needs. This had left him short of funds and unable to anticipate that Nice would come to his aid, he went to look for less expensive accommodation. When he told Madam Osee, the Belgian hotel owner, that he was leaving, she was very upset and asked him if he did not like her hotel. Rene explained that on the contrary he had been very comfortable there, but that due to unforeseen circumstances his Belgian refugee's allowance had not been paid and that owing to this, he could no longer afford to stay there.

"Never mind," she said. "You stay here and don't worry, the war cannot last for ever. You will repay me after the war." After such a kind offer Rene could not do otherwise than stay.

As soon as he got fresh funds from Nice and from the new agent, he was able to repay her in full.As Christmas 1941 approached Madam Osee suddenly received a quantity of requests for bookings from people from some of the unoccupied cities such as Lyon and Toulouse who wanted to spend a week at her hotel. When Rene heard that she was about to refuse some bookings because the hotel was full, Rene offered to vacate his room. He had had an offer from Customs Officer Denis to occupy a vacant room in his house.

Two more months went by without much happening. Rene used to get up very early in the morning and take his fishing tackle to the harbour or to a little pier near the beach. Sunrise and sunset were the best times for fishing. It is usually just before the sun climbs on the horizon that the fish appear from under the rocks and look out for their breakfast. Some of the fish are so voracious that Rene did not even need to use his fishing rod. He had what is known in French as a spider. It is a ball of lead with upward pointing hooks all around it. Above the lead is a ring in which a bit of bait is squeezed. The "Suvereau" which are the size of a sardine, but which have the shape and appearance of a mackerel, are so gluttonous that a whole shoal of them would immediately surround the spider. By quickly pulling the line in Rene found that at least two fish were caught each time. Some were hooked by their gills, some others were caught by the tail. They constituted an excellent breakfast. Occasionally Rene was lucky enough to catch an octopus. He would bring it back to Madam Denis who would prepare an excellent meal of octopus stuffed with rice covered with a home made tomato sauce.

One of Rene's less successful and more expensive fishing adventures was the day he decided to go fishing on the small pier. He was holding the rod and looking into the water. It was much later that morning and the combination of the heat of the sun and the dazzling water made him fall asleep. When he awoke, he found that he had dropped the fishing rod, which was now floating in the water a short distance away. He removed his shoes and socks, lifted his trousers above his knees and waded into the water, standing on a large flat stone, he tried to reach the rod, but it was still out of reach. Looking into the clear water he saw another flat stone two feet nearer to the rod. But depths seen from above the water can be very deceptive and the stone on which he wanted to step was much deeper than the one he had been standing on, with the result that he fell into the sea, neck deep.

The worst of it was that he had just been to fetch his ration of cigarettes, which got soaked. Also his watch, which was not waterproof, had to be taken to the watchmaker and cleaned at great expense and all he had found at the end of the rod when he recovered it, was a tiny fish which was not worth eating. The most serious loss was the packet of cigarettes, because although he dried them in the sun, the sea salt had made them unsmokable. Rationing meant he was only allowed one packet of twenty five cigarettes every five days. The loss of this packet made Rene decide to get a packet of dried raspberry leaves from the chemist which he started to smoke in a pipe. He rather liked the taste of this unorthodox substitute for tobacco, but everybody else kept well away from him, because the smell was thought unbearable.

In January 1942, a new escapee arrived. It was a man who had come all the way from a German prison camp. He had quite a lengthy story to tell about some of his more unsuccessful attempts at escape, but with perseverance he had, at last, succeeded. Having managed to get out of the camp on his last attempt, he managed to get to the nearest railway marshalling yard undetected. There he found a locomotive temporarily abandoned by its crew, but under full steam. He managed to hide behind one of the high smoke deflectors on the side of the boiler. It was his good fortune that the engine pulled a goods train which ended its journey near Cologne. He waited until the engine moved to another marshalling yard and under cover of the night got out of the yard.

He now found that he was on the wrong side of the Rhine. He found a bridge, but when he got to it he discovered too late that it was a toll bridge. He spoke reasonably good German. When asked for his toll money, he explained to the attendant that he had had his wallet stolen and was trying to make his way to his home in Aachen. He gave a fictitious address. The attendant let him through, but suspicious, phoned his colleague on the other side. By the time the man reached the other side of the bridge, a police car was waiting for him. He was ordered to get into the car and was driven away.

At this point the tough, but rather adventurous life that this man had had began to prove invaluable. As a child he had been brought up in an orphanage. On one occasion all the boys had been taken on an afternoon outing to a circus. They had been introduced to the performers outside the ring. He had expressed his admiration for the trapeze artists. He had almost reached the age of sixteen when the boys were allowed to take up a job. His enthusiasm was noticed by the leader of the circus troupe who put him to the test and offered him a job. He continued to work in the circus for three years, but was forced to give up owing to an unfortunate fall. This didn't prevent him from going on practising many of the skills and routines he had learned as a tumbler in the circus.

Whilst he was being driven away in the police car, he suddenly remembered the details of an escape he had seen in a movie in Brussels, just before the war started. In it, they had shown in slow motion how a man managed to roll, shoulders first, out of a fast moving car, without injuring himself. This gave him his inspiration. He waited for the moment where the car had to slow down at a sharp bend. He had also found an area offering the right conditions for hiding, so in less time than it takes to describe his actions, he pushed the rear door open and rolled out of the car onto the side of the road. By the time the screeching of the brakes told him that the car had been brought to a stop, he had already picked himself up and raced away.

He knew he could not be far away from the Belgian border. Gifted with a good sense of direction, and the experience acquired during the previous unsuccessful escapes, he made progress literally by leaps and bounds, ducking like a fox where necessary, jumping forward like a deer to the place which he knew to be safe. His efforts and persistence gave him his reward. He reached the approach of a farm where he could hear the people talking and although the dialects along the border sound very similar in German or Flemish, certain words he heard told him that this farm must be on Belgian territory. However he decided to keep hidden until dark before knocking at the door of the farm. This would give him a better chance of escape if he had been mistaken about the border. But his good luck held, he had reached a Belgian farm. The farmer was a member of the underground movement running the escape route and made him tell his story in detail. It seemed so suspicious and improbable, that in accordance with the drill laid down by,the escape organisation, the man was taken on a long circuitous march under cover of the night

After the second night he realised what was going on, but could not get an answer when he asked why he could not be taken down south. After six days of circling and repeating his story, he was cleared and from then made a fast journey to St Raphael. Rene sent him to Draguignan after the usual formalities and he was one of the men he later met in England.

Prague, 30 January 1942

Paul Falkenau and his wife Edita had already experienced the heartbreak of seeing Melanie, Paul's widowed sister, taken during the roundup of Prague Jews in the previous October. She, along with the other deportees, had in the official language of the German Protectorate of Bohemia been 'evacuated to the east' for 'labour'. Those like Paul and Edita who faced transportation to Theresienstadt were given a different justification for their enforced departure from their home city. They were to be 'transferred to a ghetto for the elderly.' Among those who qualified for this seemingly better treatment were Jews who had served in the Austrian army in World War 1 and either been decorated or injured in combat. It is likely that Paul's age, – he was sixty three and the fact that he had been decorated during his military service, had spared him and his wife from suffering the same fate as his sister.

Theresienstadt had been constructed as a fortress and garrison town between 1780 and 1790 on the orders of the Austrian emperor Joseph 11 and named after his mother, the Empress Marie Teresa. Following annexation of Bohemia and Moravia, the Germans used the town as a military base until the summer of 1941,when it housed around 3,500 soldiers and 3000 civilians, most of whom worked for the military. In October 1941,as they planned the deportation of Jews to the east, the Nazis decided that Theresienstadt should become a transit camp or way station for the Jews of Bohemia and Moravia. The military personnel and civilians were relocated and the fortress handed over to the SS. First Lieutenant Siegfreid Seidl was appointed commander of the planned camp ghetto. In November 1941 Seidl had ordered the leaders of the Jewish Religious Community in Prague to provide a thousand of their members to adapt the barracks in the town into a 'settlement for Jews'. They even described it as a 'spa town' where elderly Jews could retire in safety. By means of this fiction the Nazis hoped to divert attention from Theresienstadt's primary function – to contribute to the 'final solution'.

In a space previously intended to house 7000 Czechs, over 50,000 Jews from Bohemia, Moravia, Austria and Germany were incarcerated. Food was scarce and in 1942 almost 16,000 died either of starvation or disease. Medicine and tobacco were strictly prohibited and their possession punished by hard labour or even death. Single men and women were forbidden to meet or to communicate with a gentile without permission, however married couples often remained together and were able to sleep together in the same quarters, perhaps the only luxury Paul and Edita would enjoy during what was to become their 14 month detention in Theresienstadt.

Theresienstadt supplied the German war effort with a source of Jewish slave labour. Amongst the tasks allotted to prisoners was the splitting of mica mined locally and the making of boxes or coffins. Others sprayed German army uniforms white to provide camouflage for troops fighting on the Russian front. Theresienstadt also served as a sorting and redistribution centre for clothing and underwear confiscated from Jews sent to the extermination camps further east. The baggage taken away from Jews was sent to Theresienstadt where it was sorted, repackaged and sent to various cities all over Germany for the use of people who had been bombed out of their homes and were short of clothing.

Other forms of work were often undertaken by inmates of the camp to improve their own living conditions. There was no water supply in Theresienstadt and the wells that there were, were soon contaminated with typhoid fever. For that reason a number of the wells were closed and the inmates set to work to extend water pipes in order to provide clean, or at least sufficiently clean drinking water. It also provided water for the flushing of toilets, reducing the risk of disease. Inmates also created their own fire service and relied on the water supply system to staunch fires. Such were the conditions under which Paul and Edita were now forced to live.

St. Raphael, Provence, February 1942

Rene never expected that he would have to take the same route as the many evaders and escapers he had assisted in getting to England from occupied France. It all happened in mid February 1942. One morning at 3 o'clock he was awakened by a knock at his door. When he opened it he stood face to face with Customs Officer Denis. Next to him stood Monsieur Brash, the Chief of Police of St Raphael. He told Rene that he had had a phone call from the Surete in Vichy instructing him to arrest him. No reason had been given and he had asked for written confirmation of these instructions. He was also the last man Rene would have expected to help him. Rene always distrusted him because he knew him to be Alsatian and suspected him, therefore, to be pro-German. Rene's surprise was understandable when he told him he had come to warn him, so that he would have a chance to disappear.

Rene did not waste much time. Packing his belongings into two cases, he left by an early train for Nice. As previously instructed he reported to Lieutenant Dubroux and within an hour he had been supplied with a passport which had a visa for China, a faked visa for transit of Spain and a transit visa for Portugal. He was provided with a medical certificate declaring that he was unfit for military service. He was also given funds, a first class railway ticket for Lisbon and a letter of introduction to the escape route's agent in Pau who would decide when Rene should cross the border into Spain. This timetable provided just a few hours for Rene to go and say goodbye to his parents in Grasse.

Lieutenant Dubroux was sure that the news of Rene's disappearance from St Raphael would take at least two days to reach Vichy and by then he would have left France. Before taking his leave of Lieutenant Dubroux, Rene was given a list of addresses of people to see in England. Dubroux also made Rene memorise an entire long sentence which did not mean much to him, but was apparently a coded message. He instructed Rene to pass this message in person to a Captain Clarke at the War Office and to let nobody else have it.

Rene spent a few hours with his parents and his sister in Grasse and they decided to accompany him on the train journey as far as Aix en Provence. For the rest of his life he could still see them in his mind's eye standing on the platform waving him goodbye. They tried to look cheerful, but he could see that all three had tears in their eyes. As soon as the train had taken him out of their sight, he sat down in his compartment and started to weep like a child. Little did he know then that he would never see them again.

When after a few changes Rene reached Pau, he was met at the station by a local agent of the escape route who had booked a hotel room for him under an assumed name, in case his name had been passed to the local police. He also provided Rene with a set of documents, including an exit permit. He told him that a first class sleeper had been booked for him the next evening, a Saturday, to depart from Canfranc on the Spanish border. This would take him as far as Madrid. Then he gave him a detailed map of Madrid and showed him where the Belgian Embassy was located in relation to the railway station. He told Rene to spend as much time as possible memorising the map. He said it would be essential for him to walk out of the heavily guarded station in Madrid, without hesitation and without arousing suspicion. "Once you are at the Embassy, "he said. "you are more or less safe, but follow their instructions scrupulously for the rest of the journey."

The journey to and from Canfranc, was uneventful and when Rene got to Madrid, he walked out of the station mingling with the crowd and avoided passing near to the Guardia who stood two by two, rifle slung from their shoulders, near the entrances to the platforms. Out of the station, he turned left and found that he traced his way to the Embassy without problems.

There he was met by a Monsieur Crener who told Rene he had been notified to expect him. He then told Rene that he had made arrangements for one of his staff to take him to a safe place where he would be able to spend the rest of the day until his departure from Madrid that same evening. He was taken to a hotel called 'The Gay Lord', near the Puerta del Sol. There he was introduced to the owner, a Senora Mansard. She offered him a delicious meal in her very elegant restaurant. Then, she took him by taxi to her villa, situated on the outskirts of the town. He spent the rest of the afternoon relaxing in her large garden and listening to what Senora Mansard had to tell him.

Apparently there was a Belgian priest in Madrid who had organised his own escape route. He was in continuous conflict with the Belgian Embassy and some of his activities seemed rather dubious. He appeared to be well in with the Spanish authorities. Always seeming to have ample funds, he was spending much of his time and money in places usually not visited by priests. She asked Rene to convey to London her concerns about the priest as well as the information she was able to give about him.

When the time came to leave for the station, she again ordered a taxi and instructed the driver to first go past her hotel. She asked Rene to wait in the car whilst she went to fetch a large parcel containing a very substantial packed meal. She handed this over to Rene at the station after she had seen him to his sleeper compartment.

Once more Rene reached the Spanish frontier without problems and here he transferred to a Portuguese train. It was by the standards of the time a most modern train, a metallic colour, streamlined and very luxurious inside. Rene had breakfast in the restaurant car and was told that an observation carriage with bar was available at the rear of the train. He went there and sat down to drink a glass of beer. Soon a man came to sit next to him and they started a conversation. He had been warned not to speak to strangers whilst getting out of France and through Spain, but now that he was in a friendly country he did not see any harm in speaking to strangers. Rene revealed that he had just come out of France without giving any details of how he had made it. His travel companion was mainly interested to know of living conditions in Vichy France and how much Rene knew about the activities of the Vichy Police. The two men had many drinks together and by the time they were approaching Lisbon, they had become the best of friends. He then revealed to Rene that he was a member of the Lisbon International Police, what in Britain would be termed a Customs and Immigration Officer. He told Rene that Lisbon would probably be made out of bounds to him, but he gave him his visiting card and suggested that if he came to see him at his office the next day, he would provide him with a pass that would allow him to move freely in Lisbon.

Lisbon, February 1942

When Rene reached Lisbon, he went straight across the square opposite the station to the Hotel International, where a room had been reserved for him. When he sat down to his first evening meal at the hotel, his eyes swelled at its size. The way people at neighbouring tables were partaking of this meal amazed him. They ate in one meal, what he in France, would have had to be content with for a whole week. Through the long months of privation, with the exception of the time he had spent at the vineyard, his stomach had shrunk and he only managed to eat samples, mere morsels, of the very attractive food that lay in front of him. Rene knew that Belgians were reputed to be big eaters, but they seemed to make pale figures next to the Portuguese.

When he sat down to his first meal at Hotel International on the corner of the Rossio, the head waiter very apologetically informed him that due to the war, there was a restriction, limiting guests to only one dish of meat. Rene ordered the table d'Hote menu, which read:

He asked the head waiter where the restriction was, to be told, "In peace time, we would have two courses of meat. The first one would be white meat such as veal or pork, the second one a red meat such as roast beef or steak."

The meal Rene was served was far from a restricted meal. First they covered his table with hors d'oeuvre dishes, each succeeding one more appetising than the last. He could help himself to as much as he wanted and had he not been careful, this would have been a full meal on its own. The soup was very rich. He was served two shrimp croquettes, but only ate one. He cancelled the fish and had only one slice of beef leaving four or five slices on the serving dish.

A tray with a variety of cheeses was then placed in front of him and he was free to help himself to as much as he wanted. Pastries for dessert were supplied with the same generosity and the head waiter noticed that Rene had only taken one piece. He seemed surprised that Rene turned his offer of more down flat. Rene noticed that the Portuguese at the tables next to him did not leave much to return to the kitchens.

After a good night's rest, very much needed after two successive nights on the train, he got up early to have a first look at Lisbon and locate the Belgian Embassy. He reported there at opening time and was introduced to the Attache, a Monsieur Rotschild. He knew all about Rene's progress and informed him that as soon as he heard from London, he would send him on his way. He warned him to be very careful about who he met and spoke to in Lisbon, as the city was infested with German spies. He then handed Rene over to one of his assistants. This man called Jabot, was a most unpleasant character. Rene was told later that he was an ex-gendarme and as Rene had previously had brush ups with his kind, he took an instant dislike to the fellow. He gave instructions to Rene in an overbearing military manner, instructing him to take the first boat across the Tagus to a place called Costa de Caparica. He informed him that the Hotel Praia do Sol was specially reserved for Belgians. He told him to get there and stay there, adding that if he came back into Lisbon before he called him, he would get into trouble with the International Police.

When Rene got to the Hotel Praia do Sol, he found that the same day, a contingent of thirty men and two girls, the first to be released from the Spanish concentration camp of Miranda di Ebro, had just arrived there. The stories they had to tell about their experiences at the hands of their Spanish captors were most unpleasant. The girls had probably suffered the worst, the more unpleasant conditions. Because there was no concentration camp for women, they had been sent to a women's prison in Madrid. They had spent several months locked up, sixteen to a large cell with just a large hole in the centre of the floor, where without any privacy, the prisoners had to attend to their natural needs. Washing facilities were also very primitive and the two poor Belgian girls, both volunteer nurses, from a good middle class background, had now to live amongst thieves, prostitutes and even murderers. Not only were they subjected to the ill treatment of their jailers, but they were also forced to submit to indescribable indignities from their fellow inmates.

The men had also had unpleasant times, but as they were a large group of the same nationality, housed together in barrack type huts, they found it easier to withstand the ordeal of their captivity. All the men of various nationalities had one thing in common. Their one aim was either to help each other, either by sharing the Red Cross parcels that some of them got from Canada, or use some of the contents of their parcels to bribe their Spanish guards into supplying them with some goods which were otherwise unobtainable. Some attempts at escape had taken place, but proved to be unsuccessful.

This contingent, the first of many, had been released by the Spanish government in exchange for goods supplied from the Congo by the Belgian government in exile. Rene had his first meal together with this group at the Hotel Praia do Sol and discovered that they were all suffering from the same trouble as himself. Their stomachs, through lack of food, had shrunk to the extent that they could only take very small quantities of food at each meal. It was aggravating to see all that nice, rich food, but not dare take too much of it for fear of the consequences.

The day after his arrival at the hotel Rene ventured into Lisbon and went to the office of the International Police. There he met the Immigration Officer with whom he had travelled two days before and as he had promised, he gave Rene a pass allowing him to move freely in Lisbon. When he got back to Costa a message was waiting for him, asking him to call the following day at the British Embassy in Lisbon. There he was met by the Military Attache and by a doctor. Many questions were asked and he was submitted to a thorough medical examination. He was then told he had to stay for a while in Portugal, but that he would be flown to England as soon as possible. He was again given a warning about the dangers of circulating in Lisbon. When he confessed that he had been given a police pass, the attache seemed very surprised, but never asked how he had managed to get one. However he again warned Rene about the places known to be visited mainly by German spies.

For nearly three weeks after that Rene and his Belgian confederates had the leisurely life of holiday makers. Their main pastimes were eating, walking, swimming, sunbathing on the beach, watching the local fishermen departing or arriving in their very colourful boats or see them pull in their nets. In the evening after dinner, they sat in the lounge telling each other all that had happened in their lives since the Germans had invaded Belgium. When that subject was exhausted they backtracked to pre-war memories going as far back as school days.

At the end of March, Rene decided to go to the Belgian Embassy to find out why he had not yet been sent to England. When he got there he was met by Jabot who shouted at him that he had no right to come there without permission. He had just come back from Costa, where he had collected all the Belgian contingent and had embarked them on a ship called, ironically, the 'Rene-Paul'. This ship was plying between Lisbon and Gibraltar and had just sailed away. He told Rene he was supposed to be on that ship.

Jabot told him to go back to Costa and await his pleasure there. Instead of that Rene went to the British Embassy and asked to see the Military Attache. When he saw Rene he was very surprised, because he had informed the Belgian Embassy himself that he had reserved a seat for Rene, more than a week before, on one of BOAC's planes. A vehement telephone exchange took place between him and Monsieur Rotschild at the Belgian Embassy, who was apparently not aware of the fact that Rene had not departed for London and promised to investigate immediately and report back.

The Attache and Rene did not have very long to wait. Monsieur Rotschild's findings were that Jabot had sent one of his friends in Rene's place and this explained why Jabot had been so anxious to despatch Rene to Gibraltar. The British Military Attache informed Monsieur Rotschild that he would personally arrange Rene's departure for the next day. Rene was told to go back to the Belgian Embassy. When he got there he saw Jabot and looked defiantly straight into his nasty eyes. He never said a word, but disappeared leaving an orderly to take Rene into Monsieur Rotschild's office. He told Rene that Jabot had provided the excuse that he could not be found at the hotel, the evening prior to his flight and therefore he had given his seat to a friend. Rene assured Monsieur Rotschild that these were pure lies, because he had not missed one evening meal at the hotel and had spent every evening in the lounge. Apologising to Rene, Rotschild said, "You will have been told by the Military Attache that you are flying tomorrow. You will take a taxi to the ferry and I shall send a car to pick you up at the Tower of Belem landing stage. You will have the time to report here, collect and sign for a diplomatic bag which we want you to take to London."

Rene spent the last night at Hotel Praia do Sol all alone. Next morning he crossed the Tagus from Trafaria to Belem and found the embassy car waiting for him. Monsieur Rotschild gave him a passport duly endorsed with an entry visa, an air ticket and a large brown bag, the size of a kitbag, tightly closed by a thick string. To it was attached a label claiming diplomatic immunity for its bearer and finally the knot was covered with a thick layer of sealing wax in which had been imprinted the seal of the Belgian Embassy.

The car took Rene to Sintra Airport. The departure lounge was very small. At each of the four corners of the hall a door led to the administration offices of the airlines. At one corner was BOAC, opposite it the Portuguese airline, the other two corners were respectively occupied by the German and the Spanish airlines. His check-in was very fast and he was taken with his bag to the aircraft, before the other passengers.

Although he looked forward to this journey, he was a bit apprehensive. He had only flown once before in a three seater light aircraft. This was in Antwerp before the war at a charity afternoon organised for the Red Cross. Several light aircraft owners were taking the pubic on joy rides above the city. The money thus collected was given to the Red Cross. Rene was at that time an active member of the Red Cross and had helped in the organisation of the afternoon. Just before closing time he had been offered a free ride in one of the aircraft. In those days passengers were not strapped in, only the pilot was. As they were circling above Antwerp, the pilot asked him what he thought of his first flight. Rene replied, "There is really nothing to it." To demonstrate that, on the contrary, there was more to flying than Rene's answer implied, the pilot suddenly rolled the aircraft like a barrel and Rene found himself out of his seat and hitting the ceiling. The pilot had a good laugh. Rene did not. He later found out that the pilot was known in his native town of Ghent, as 'the flying fool'. This was Rene's first experience of flying and now he was going to experience his first flight in a commercial aircraft.

When he boarded the aircraft, he was given a seat half way along the port side behind the wing. The plane was a DC3 belonging to KLM and the crew was Dutch. His diplomatic bag was placed in front of the seat next to his own. So he knew that he would have nobody to talk to during the journey since the seat next to him could not be occupied. The air hostess showed him how to fasten the safety belt and soon the aircraft took off. As they were about to land in Porto, Rene suddenly saw part of the wing appear to split and flop down. He had never heard of flaps before and wondered if the plane was disintegrating. However it made a safe landing and when he shyly mentioned his worry to the hostess, she had a good laugh and explained the purpose of the flaps to him.

After a half hour stop in Porto, during which he was allowed to stay in his seat with his precious bag, the plane took off once more and he could see for the first time in his life the sea in all its immensity, which he only now fully appreciated from a height of 9,000 ft. When they came nearer to the coast of England, the stewardess came to close the blind on each window and it gave Rene a strange and worrying feeling as they were swaying and coming down for the landing approach. The plane made a perfect landing and it was only when he came down the aircraft steps that Rene found out that they had landed in Bristol.

He had been told to wait until all other passengers had gone. Then an airport employee came up and carried the diplomatic bag for him. He saw the last of the passengers go to one building, whilst he was taken to another one. On this short walk across the apron, he noticed the strict security arrangements in force with several policemen and army personnel supervising the movement of the passengers.

Bristol, England, March 1942

Rene was led to a large room and ushered in. At one end four people were sitting behind a long table. One was a civilian, the other three in uniform represented the navy, the army and the air force. The civilian asked Rene for his passport and started the questioning. He had to explain at length what he had been doing in the last few months. Sometimes the civilian was interrupted by one of the officers who asked a more specific question, relating to their particular service. Rene noticed that as he was giving his answers, they were marking some cards. At the end of the interview, Rene mentioned his last meeting with Lieutenant Dubroux and told them about the message he had to deliver in person to Captain Clarke of the War Office.

The interview came to an end and he was ushered to the main lounge where he rejoined the other passengers. They had gone through Immigration and were offered tea, whilst waiting for transport to town. The official who escorted Rene introduced him to a Captain Grisar. He was wearing a Belgian uniform and sat in the lounge and also had a diplomatic bag placed near him. After the usual exchange of courtesies, he told Rene that he was travelling regularly between England

One Family – Three Uniforms 1940 – 1945

Gaston Billotte, Commander
of the French 1st Army died
in an accident May 1940

Captain Pierre Billotte,
promoted to Colonel in 1941 and
general in 1944. Chief of Staff to
General De Gaulle, leader of the
Free French Forces

Rene Falkenau in the uniform of
the Belgian Brigade or the Brigade
Piron as it became known after its
commander Colonel Jean Piron

George (Jiri) Falkenau in the unifrom of the Czech Independent Brigade.
Seen with his wife Marjorie who he married whilst stationed
in Britain in 1944

Refugees In Southern France

The Grand Hotel Cannes 1940
Eddie Nathan (far right) and his family enjoy a relaxing game of tennis
with Prince Lotfalla and his family.

**Rene and Georgette Falkenau and their cousin Roger Adler,
with whom Rene had spent part of the summer of 1940 on a cycling
holiday along the Cote d'Azur**

Late autumn 1940 at Cauteret in the Hautes Pyrennees and already the need for warm winter clothing is apparent. Franz and Irma Falkenau with their children Georgette and Rene.

Grasse, Provence late autumn 1941 and the strains of life as refugees in a foreign country are beginning to show on the faces of the Falkenau family. In only a few short months Rene will be gone, having made his escape to England, leaving his family behind

Rene's Escape From France - February 1942

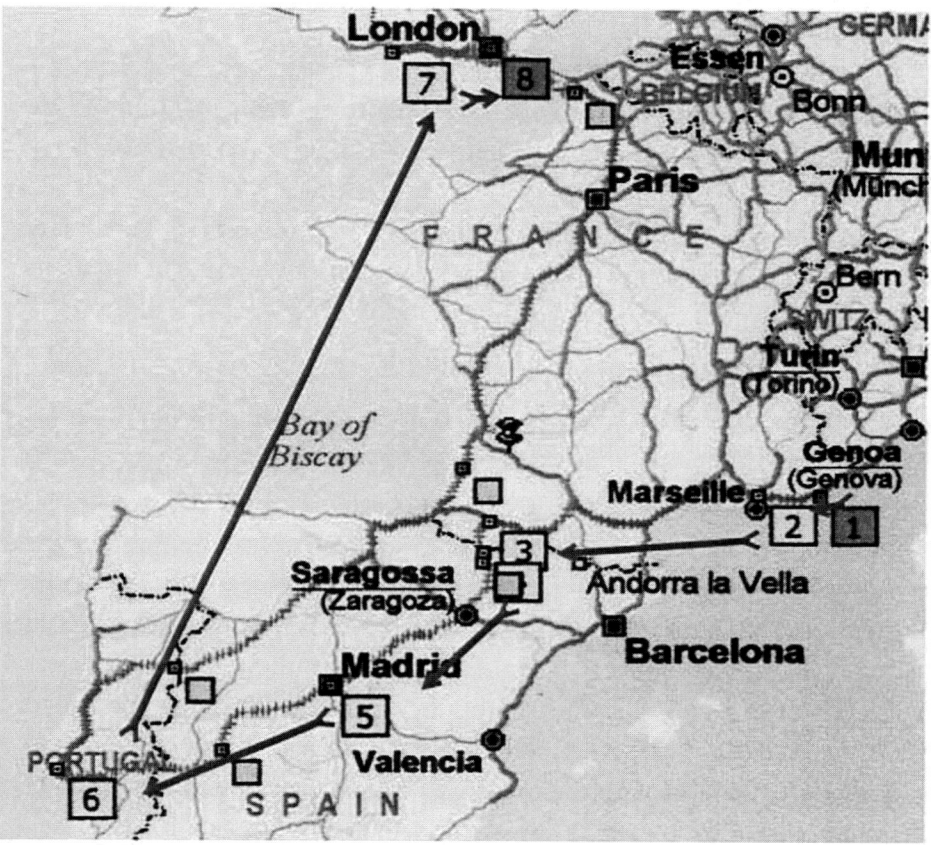

1. St.Raphael
2. Aix En Provence
3. Pau
4. Canfranc
5. Madrid
6. Lisbon
7. Bristol
8. London

and Gibraltar, conveying the diplomatic mail there and back. After they had had their tea, they were both taken to an army car and driven to Bristol station.

There their driver introduced them to a representative of Scotland Yard. He informed them that he was escorting them to London. He told them that he relied on their honour as Belgian officers not to try to leave him or to contact anybody during the journey. He also warned them to be careful of their conversations on the train as there were many spies about. The train journey was quite pleasant. Around half way their escort took them to the restaurant car and paid for their meal.

London, England, March 1942

At Paddington Station an army truck was waiting for them and they were driven in a completely blacked out vehicle across the town, over a Thames bridge in the direction of Camberley. As they reached the gate of what seemed to be a park entrance, their truck was stopped by a sentry. Having shown his papers, the driver was allowed to proceed and stopped the vehicle in front of a very large building. Again a sentry asked for his papers whilst aided by the Scotland Yard man, Rene and Grisar got out of the truck and unloaded their baggage and the two diplomatic bags. Meanwhile the driver had rung the bell on the side of the porch and two men in black uniforms with royal crowns on each lapel came out, took their luggage and they were asked to follow them whilst their police escort took his leave of them.

One of the uniformed men now accompanying them told them to leave all their belongings in the entrance hall and to follow him. From a nearby corridor they were taken into a large and comfortable office. A gentleman left his desk to bid them welcome. He invited them to sit down. He appeared to know Captain Grisar and asked him how things were in Gibraltar. He then asked them both to sign a paper on which was printed a sentence to the effect that they promised, on their honour, not to get away or contact anybody outside until they had been cleared by the authorities. A receipt was given to them for the diplomatic bags, with a promise that they would be delivered without delay to the Belgian Embassy.

They were then led back to the main entrance hall. The uniformed orderly then instructed them to take out of their suitcases, what they needed for the night, their pyjamas and toilet requisites, which he examined. All their luggage was then put under lock and key in a nearby store room. Next they were taken to another store room where they were given a pair of sheets, a pillow case and three blankets. Thus provided, they followed the orderly up a flight of stairs to the first floor. Through a doorway they came into a large dormitory with two long lines of double bunks, all occupied. At the end of the room another door led to a landing, a further door and another dormitory as long as the previous one, through which they went from end to end. Once more on the other side of a door they found another landing the shape of which showed them they had reached the corner of the building, which they had now traversed along its length from end to end.

Turning at right angles, they came to another door on which a board indicated "Officers Only." They found themselves in another dormitory, but with only single beds this time. At the end of this dormitory they were taken into a room in which there were two beds. The orderly opened a door opposite it and showed them a bathroom especially for their use. Rene was a bit surprised at such VIP treatment, but Captain Grisar told him that this was the room usually reserved for diplomatic couriers. He also told Rene that they might occupy this room for quite a number of days. "You see," he said, "we are Friday today, tomorrow is Saturday. They may or may not see us for an hour or two. Sunday they are all away playing golf and tennis. I then expect them to keep us here at least three to four days until our reports have been studied by higher authorities."

They made their beds and went to sleep. Next morning at 7am an orderly came to awake them and tell them that breakfast would be served at eight o'clock and that they had to be available for the examiners from 9 o'clock. After having a good warm bath, they got dressed and made their way through the long row of dormitories. As they came to the landing separating the two long dormitories, Rene could see to his right a staircase and to his left was a large window from which he could see into a gigantic dining room already busily occupied. For the first time in his life, Rene became acquainted with a large English breakfast.

After their meal, they returned to their room. Just before nine o'clock an orderly came to fetch Rene. After a long walk he was led into a room on the ground floor. Just as at Bristol airport, there was a long table with five officers seated behind it. The officer presiding stood up and said, "Mr Falkenau?"

"Yes Sir." "I am Captain Clarke." He shook Rene's hand and invited him to sit down on the only chair placed opposite the table. "I understand you have a message for me. Will you say it slowly to allow the shorthand typist behind me to take it down."

Rene slowly repeated to him the message which he had learned parrot fashion before leaving Nice. This done, Captain Clarke started to ask Rene a lot of questions about the situation in the south of France. One or two officers sitting on his right also fired questions at him, but when the officer on his left addressed Rene, he had the surprise of his life. Rene recognised he was an old school friend of his and up to then he had not noticed him. Rene made a movement of surprise, but he remained unperturbed. He thought to himself, "Ah, now that he is a captain, he is too proud to acknowledge me." So Rene simply answered his question.

When the interview was over, Rene was told he could go back to his room. He had hardly been there more than a few minutes, when the orderly came back to fetch him. Back he went through the long maze of corridors. He was taken back into the same office in which he had been interviewed only minutes earlier. The long table was now empty, but at the back of it several officers were sitting at their large individual desks, with their secretaries in ATS uniforms, sitting and typing opposite them. Beside each desk was a chair for visitors.

As he entered the room, his old school friend beckoned him to come and sit next to him. In the same rather stern way as he had addressed Rene before, he took a cigarette box from the top of his desk and said "Have a cigarette." Then pointing to a wooden block on his desk on which was inscribed Captain Tremayne, he said, "You see this. This is my name. If ever you have known me under a different name before, forget it and never mention it. Is this clear?"

"Yes Sir," Rene replied. Then suddenly Tremayne's expression changed. He became all smiles and the friendly Eric Thornton Rene had known before the war. "Well Rene, I am pleased to see that you made it. I was a bit worried about you. I was kept informed of your activities in the south. In fact, I was responsible for your enrolment in Operation Gypsy."

It was the first time Rene had heard that the organisation he had worked for, for more than a year, had the code name "Gypsy." Tremayne went on, "Yes, I did send you the poor Lieutenant Detal, who recruited you. He has not been as lucky as you and as far as we know, he is locked up in a French prison. Now I have a few more questions to ask you, mainly concerned with the service you have had to leave. I have then arranged for you to be interviewed by the navy, the army and the air force who each have questions to ask you relating to their service areas. All going well, you should be out of here by Tuesday."

Contrary to the forecast of Captain Grisar, Rene found himself being interviewed the whole of Saturday, Sunday and Monday and by Tuesday morning, he was given his passport and clearance papers. Meanwhile on Saturday afternoon, the Welfare Officer had come to see Rene on Eric's instructions, first to bring him a supply of Canadian 'Sweet Corporal' cigarettes. Next he informed Rene that Eric had told him that Rene was a good organiser and speaker and that he should be asked to direct and compere a variety show which was planned for that Saturday evening. Rene readily agreed to this invitation.

Considering that there were only two hours in which to rehearse, the show made up only of local talents, was quite a success. So, on Tuesday morning Rene left the 'Patriotic School'. This was then the name given to this building where he had spent the last three days. Today it can still be found standing as it was in 1940, but it is now called the Emmanuel School. Every war time alien will remember the Patriotic School. For most it was a portal leading either to the opportunity to rejoin the armed forces of their native land and continue the struggle for its liberation, or for those unable to do so, to refugee status in Britain. Some found it to be a transit route to Wandsworth Prison and a few even concluded that journey at the end of a rope.

Before he left the Patriotic School, as the place in which he had been interrogated was known, Eric had given Rene his private telephone number and had told him to ring as soon as he had settled down in

London. He suggested that they should meet one evening. A taxi took Rene to the Belgian Embassy in Eaton Square. There he was told that in view of his age, – he was 31 by then, that he did not need to rejoin the forces if he did not want to. He could remain a civilian and the British authorities would probably find work for him in a factory or elsewhere, but if he rejoined the forces, he would be considered as a volunteer. So Rene volunteered, but on condition that he was first allowed to spend a week in London.

Through the embassy, he found out that his uncle Rupert and aunt Emmy Manasseh,who he had helped in 1940 to reach England, had been staying at the Hotel De Vere in Kensington. He went straight from the embassy to the hotel. His aunt's surprise when she saw Rene, quite overwhelmed him, as they embraced and greeted one another. In conversation with his aunt, it transpired that his uncle, Rupert Manasseh, had returned to Singapore, where his brother, Ezekial and other members of the family were still residing. He had gone back in order to safeguard his business interests in the colony and thereby ensure a possible means of financial support for members of the family in Europe.

The fall of Singapore to the Japanese only weeks earlier was a matter of grave concern, particularly as she had not heard from her husband since. She could only hope that the civilian population, although enemy aliens in some cases, would be viewed as non combatants and not subjected to harm on that account.

Rene's arrival coincided with the arrival of two other distant members of the family. One was the husband of his cousin, Irene Manasseh, Lieutenant George Osselaer, who had managed to get away from Belgium and found his way by the usual route. The other was a distant cousin, Colonel, formerly Captain, Pierre Billotte, the son of General Gaston Billotte, killed near Dunkirk and whose name Rene had invoked in his bid to join the French forces in Dunkirk.

Colonel Billotte had had a very adventurous escape. Following being taken prisoner by the Germans when his tank had been hit, he was first taken to a military hospital, for the treatment of his head wound. When he had recovered, he was transferred to the officers' prison camp in Pomerania near the Polish frontier. He managed to escape at the third attempt and ended up in Russia. Captured a second time by the Red Army and due to Stalin's non aggression pact with the Germans, he was taken to Moscow and placed in a local prison where he had to share a cell with a Russian who was insane and tried once or twice to strangle him. He had to keep a constant vigil and when he wanted to sleep, he had first to knock his cell companion unconscious before he dared take a much needed rest.

This ordeal lasted for several months until the German invasion of the Soviet Union in June 1941 resulted in the Russians allying themselves with the western powers. Pierre Billotte was then released with many other allied officers and having been promoted to Colonel was appointed military attache of the Free French in Moscow. In 1942 he was recalled to London, having been flown to Teheran, and from there to England, where he became General de Gaulle's Chief of Staff. It was following his arrival in London that Rene was able to have a short meeting with him at the Hyde Park Hotel where he was staying.

A few days after his departure from the Patriotic School, Rene phoned Eric Thornton who invited Rene to meet him that same evening for dinner at the Piccadilly Hotel. After an excellent meal, considering that England was in the second year of war, Eric took him to the Astoria Ballroom in Tottenham Court Road. It was a strange place, entered by a long corridor into what was the ground floor of the building. The dance floor was on a lower level, giving the impression of a large oval opening surrounded by a balustrade, from where it was possible to look down on to the dancers below on a floor which was in fact located at basement level. Two winding staircases led to the lower floor.

They found themselves a table near the balustrade from where they could observe what was going on below. The dance floor was crowded mainly with members of the three branches of the forces, male and female. There were very few civilians. Eric took a special interest in a few civilians and pointed a few out to Rene, both male and female, who were under constant observation by his service. They had been observed to always dance with members of the allied forces rather than with the British and were suspected of collecting information for the enemy.

From time to time, Eric came back to the subject of Vichy France and asked Rene more questions. One of the names Rene had given him at Patriotic School was of a Frenchman known to be fraternising with the German Armistice Commission and inviting them to parties in his villa on the Riviera. He was one of the escape route's best sources of information. Rene warned Eric that this man was in real danger of being bumped off by the French patriots. "That is a risk he has to take," Eric said. "He would be in bigger danger if the French knew what he is really doing. They talk so much and could not keep his secret."

As they were talking a British lieutenant in uniform, with two young ladies, came to ask permission to sit at their table. Up to then Eric and Rene had conversed in French. Now Eric leaned over and said to Rene in a quiet voice, "Let us watch our conversation now, – les murs on des oreilles, – walls have ears." Looking at the two girls with the young officer, Rene smiled and said to Eric in Flemish "Is it not stupid that these two nice girls are with that snotneus," – a Flemish expression meaning a nose where the drop of milk still hangs. "They would just do for you and me." Then to Rene's amazement the British officer said in pure Antwerp Flemish "If you look once more at these two nice girls, the snotneus will give you one on the jaw." Apparently Rene's shocked expression must have been quite funny, because both Eric and the officer had a good laugh at his expense.

When the hilarity had receded Eric said "Don't you recognise him, he is my assistant and was present at your first interview in our office." Rene appreciated what he viewed as a practical joke and felt the need to respond in kind. "I must say I had been far too busy watching Captain Clarke and his kilt and the ones immediately next to him." He was soon to appreciate that Eric's little ploy had a more serious purpose. "Let this be a lesson to you" said Eric. "Even when speaking Flemish in London, you have to be careful what you say." Rene never forgot the lesson.

Chelmno, Poland, March 1942

In late 1941 the overcrowding in the Lodz ghetto had been substantially worsened by the arrival of 20,000 deportees from the territories under Nazi control. Melanie Falkenau had been one of these deportees. By 10 December 1941 the Nazis had instructed the Judenrat, the ghetto's Jewish Council to draw up lists of 20,000 people to be resettled to labour camps elsewhere. Initially the Judenrat managed to bargain this number down to 10,000, but in time this number was exceeded several times over. Amongst the first to be deported were the Roma people who had been sent to Lodz in the previous year. To increase the pressure on the 'Evacuation Committee' drawing up the lists, food supplies to the ghetto had been restricted during the winter months and the promise of a meal for those being 'evacuated' was intended to make the receipt of the 'wedding invitations', as they became known, more palatable for those being selected for deportation. Those selected were told that they were being sent to Polish farms to work.

The Nazis had chosen the village of Chelmno as the site for an extermination camp late in 1941 and by 8 December it had become operational. Chelmno was just over 200 kilometres north west of Lodz. From Lodz deportees were carried by train in closed cattle trucks to the village of Kolo. There they were taken either by truck directly to Chelmno or in the open carriages of a narrow gauge railway to Powercie some eight kilometres on foot from Chelmno.

Chelmno had been chosen, not only because of its rail links to Lodz, but also because it contained two buildings which could be used to handle the deportees. The first was an abandoned palace which had been renovated and adapted to receive its intended victims. Near the palace was a church and a granary, together with several outbuildings which could be used to receive deportees before they were moved to the palace. The other advantages of the site were that it was on the edge of the village and a little distant from the main road. Nearby was an area of forest. All combined to make it less accessible to unwanted onlookers. Also the River Ner flowed past the church and although it was not deep, it made escape more difficult and provided a barrier which was easy for guards to patrol.

On arrival, the 'evacuees' were herded into the courtyard of the palace, where they were addressed in a most reassuring manner by the camp commandant. They were then led to the hall of the palace. There their hand luggage would be handled for them, each piece numbered and its owner's name recorded for forwarding to their final destination.

Before they could be sent on to their new workplace their clothes had to be disinfected and they had to be washed in the bath house to prevent risk of infection. They were taken down a corridor in groups of 35-40 to two rooms where they were instructed to undress. They were then ushered down another brightly lit corridor, on the walls of which were inscribed 'To the bath house.' The same inscriptions could be found on a stairway leading to a basement.

Now suddenly the atmosphere changed. Armed members of the SS brutally pushed the prisoners towards a ramp at the back entrance of the palace. Any who attempted to stop were violently pushed in the direction of the ramp which led downwards to a vehicle. When the vehicle, a large van with a specially strengthened floor, was full of occupants, the rear doors were closed and locked, preventing any means of escape. The driver then connected the vehicle's exhaust pipe to a vent which had been installed in the floor of the vehicle to allow carbon monoxide fumes to enter the space in which the trapped occupants were confined. Once they were all dead, the driver drove the corpses to the forest in which large burial pits had been excavated. Here the bodies were thrown into the pits by Polish forced labourers, dowsed in petrol and set alight. Within fifteen to twenty minutes the bodies had been rendered to ash and the pits were ready to receive their next victims. By April 2nd 1942, some 34,073 people had been transported to Chelmno and killed. Melanie Falkenau was amongst the group of elderly Prague Jews sent to Chelmno between February 23rd and April 3rd 1942.

London April 1942

Rene had offered to return to France and was prepared to undergo parachute training. First he was sent to Harley Street for a thorough medical examination. Next he went for an interview at an office in Edgware Road. The interviewer was a Captain Hardy Amies of the War Office. He told Rene it would take some time before a decision was taken and suggested that meanwhile he decide on either working as a civilian or joining the British forces. Rene told him he had already joined the forces and that he was in fact at the end of a one week's leave. This seemed to upset Captain Amies because he told Rene that having signed a volunteer's agreement, the Belgian military authorities would not release him. They were very short of NCOs and would probably object to his return to occupied Europe. However, if ever Rene decided to desert the Belgian army, then he would see what he could do.

Two days later Rene went to a building next to the Belgian Embassy and was provided with a uniform. He explained that although all his papers indicated that he was a corporal in Belgium, he had in fact already been put on the promotion list to become a sergeant. His promotion had been due to take effect on the 17th May,1940,but since the war started on the 10th, the order for his promotion had not come through. "Sorry," came the answer. "We have to take you in as a corporal, but you can write in to a special commission who will decide on your case."

The next day, prior to being posted, Rene was informed that he was joining a squadron of armoured cars, currently stationed in Pembrey, near Llanelli in south Wales. Before leaving London Rene had dinner with his aunt, and cousins at the De Vere Hotel. His cousin's husband, Lieutenant Osselaer, was there too. When Rene revealed that he was joining the armoured car squadron, Lt.Osselaer told him that he was joining the same squadron as second in command. He told Rene that in the interests of them both, it would be better if he did not tell anybody that they were related. This, Rene promised to keep secret.

Pembrey, South Wales, April 1942

By train, Rene travelled from Paddington to Llanelli, where an army van took him to nearby Pembrey. The men were living in Nissen huts on a golf course. After the usual introduction to the commanding officer, Rene was posted to the first platoon consisting of two Daimler reconaissance or scout cars, two Humber armoured cars and two motorcycles. His lieutenant was called Lanksweert, a very nice man, who when nervous stuttered terribly. He told Rene that the first thing he was going to do, was to give him experience of riding in an armoured car. He called in Sergeant Hasschoen, one of the men who had been through Rene's hands in the south of France and instructed him to take Rene for a ride around the Welsh countryside.

Rene had also been told that he was going to be driven by the best driver in the squadron. When operational, the officer in command stood on the right in the turret of the armoured car and his No.2, who would also act as gunner and radio operator, on the left. Their heads and shoulders protruded above the turret through two circular openings and could be seen from the outside. Each of these openings in the revolving turret, could be closed when the vehicle went into action by shutting two metal half covers, one half hinged to the front of the opening, the other to the back. Once the turret covers were closed, both the commander and his No.2 were seated in the cramped confines of the turret. On the front of the turret were mounted a gun and a machine gun.

The space behind their seats was entirely occupied by very elaborate radio equipment. At the flick of a switch it was possible to either be in touch with the Squadron Commander or with the Platoon Commander. A third position was for intercom conversation between the commander of the armoured car, his No.2 or the driver, hidden down below them, between the petrol tank and an ammunition box.

The Humber armoured car sat very high on its wheels. The suspension was very soft in order to protect the delicate radio equipment and the body of the armed car had a tendency to sway. The fact that the driver was taking bends at 40 miles an hour, increased the feeling for those inside that the top of the turret seemed to lean in the opposite direction to the bend they were taking.

As they were coming down a narrow lane, they suddenly came to a crossroad. On the other side of the crossroad, was an eighteen inch high bench on each side of the road. For some obscure reason, the driver pulled his vehicle over far too much to the left of the road and his wheels hit the bench throwing the vehicle slightly out of control. He then proceeded to put his brakes on sharply. Whether the vehicle simply skidded or whether its brakes were not properly adjusted, Rene wasn't sure, but the fact was that the two nearside wheels bit sharply into the bench. The heavy 7 ton armoured car was knocked completely off balance and fell on its side.

Having had a lot of practice of falling whilst playing ice hockey, or whilst riding horses Rene had always been taught to relax and let himself go when he felt he was going to fall. This he did once more here. He was thrown like a projectile onto the bench on the other side of the road. But when he recovered from his flight, he was astonished to discover that he had sustained nothing more than a scratch on the forehead. Sergeant Hasshoen had tried to hold himself back in his turret, but the front hatch cover was not properly secured and fell back onto his hand breaking three fingers. Next he had tried to jump clear, but had left it too late and his foot got caught under the heavy turret as it hit the ground. The driver although shaken was unhurt. Rene and the driver had to quickly lift the vehicle with the aid of a jack and release Sergeant Hasschoen who was then rushed to hospital. He had three broken fingers, two broken arms and all the toes of his left foot were in a very bad state. At the hospital, there was a big argument between two doctors over whether or not to amputate the five toes. Luckily for Hasschoen, they eventually decided not to amputate and three months later he had recovered and was back in service.

It was only when Rene submitted his report on the accident that he discovered that the so called best driver in the unit had only driven this type of vehicle for a week. For a first experience of an armoured car, it was a pretty rough one.

The next day Rene took a ride in one of the scout cars. This was a two seater vehicle, very strongly protected by armour plating in front. The driver was seated at a slight angle rather than sitting square to the front of the vehicle The idea behind this was that if, during a reconnaissance, the scout car approached any enemy position, the driver only had to kick his clutch and the vehicle would halt abruptly, then could easily be driven at speed in reverse. A speed lever allowed him to pre-select the speed. From the way he was seated, the driver could steer as easily driving in reverse as driving forward. The drawback Rene saw with this vehicle was its bad exhaust system, causing fumes to collect inside it. Every time he took a ride in a scout car he suffered violent headaches afterwards, from carbon monoxide inhalation. On one or two occasions, Rene was also invited to ride a motorbike.

A week after his arrival at the squadron Rene was joined by Lieutenant Osselaer, who took up his position as second in command. From then on Rene faced difficulties in the conduct of his daily duties. Rene was convinced that George Osselaer had never forgiven the fact that he had once told his wife that he had a very poor opinion of regular officers in the Belgian army. This remark had been made to her well before she had met her husband, but soon after they got married, she had told her husband about it and this was why, to Rene's mind, from the moment he arrived in Pembrey, he seemed to take a sadistic pleasure

317

in belittling his cousin by marriage in front of his immediate superiors. Lieutenant Osselaer understood army regulations too well to try to do the same thing in front of Rene's men, but they had to suffer as a result of this feud. He would always find fault with them and then blame Rene for lacking authority and control over them. If it had not been for the kindness of a family named Evans who regularly invited Rene to their home, and boosted his morale he would have deserted the army there and then.

London, May 1942

This month saw the arrival of several more members of the family in Britain. For Eddie Nathan, his wife Helene and two daughters, Cecile and Andree, the journey via Spain and Portugal had been similar to the one taken by Rene almost three months earlier. Apart from the obvious fact that the war was becoming more protracted than might originally have been imagined, there was also the fact that life in the south of France was becoming more difficult. It wasn't simply the food shortages, there was also the fact that access to Eddie's reserves of cash, which had been a source of difficulty for some time, had now been made more difficult by the fall of Singapore. It meant that remittances of income from his properties in Singapore, which Eddie had found means of channelling through accounts in neutral countries, had dried up. The Japanese occupation had also scotched any ideas of returning to the far east, by any means which could have been contrived, in the difficult conditions of the time.

So a move to the United Kingdom and London in particular, seemed the obvious answer. Here, Eddie's British citizenship would guarantee automatic right of entry, unlike the USA which friends had encouraged him to toy with. He had an existing bank account in London with sufficient funds to see the family through for a time and in any case his credit was good amongst friends in the London business community. In addition he had already seen the determination of other members of the family to make their contribution to the war effort. Too old for military service himself, he nonetheless volunteered himself as an air raid warden on his return to Britain and was soon undertaking air raid patrols in Kensington and Chelsea.

Helene too decided it was time to do her patriotic bit. She immediately enrolled with the Red Cross and became a nursing auxiliary. It would not be long before one of their daughters also found a means of contributing to the war effort.

Soon they were joined in London by Renee, the youngest of the Adler sisters and her husband, Marcel Roost, the Antwerp lawyer. Their departure from France had been altogether more complicated. They had been in Bayonne on 21 June 1940, the day on which Rupert and Emmy Manasseh had sailed for England and had almost certainly hoped to accompany them. But whereas Emmy had benefited from her marriage to a British citizen, both Renee and Marcel as Belgian citizens, had been declined entry visas to Britain. Instead they had been obliged to remain in France and seek other means to leave the country. Nor had they been passive in that attempt.

Having sought refuge with a family friend in Marseilles in September 1940, they had managed to obtain a transit visa for Portugal the following February. But without an entry visa to another country, the transit visa had been unusable and they had been forced to delay their departure from Marseilles. On 2 March 1942 they had eventually secured an entry visa to China, but it still took them until 23 March to obtain an exit visa from France. Six days later on 29 March they arrived in Valencia and from there they were able to gain entry to Portugal. On 7 April 1942 British consular officials in Lisbon granted them the option of a three month stay in the United Kingdom. However it still took until the 25 May for them to arrange a flight, – not to England, but to Shannon in Ireland. It was from Eire that the couple found means of obtaining passage by sea which finally brought them to Southampton on 29 May 1942.

For Marcel and Rene there now came the question of how to justify their continued residence in the United Kingdom. For Marcel the obvious answer was to offer himself for military service with the Belgian forces in Britain. Marcel had already served with considerable distinction as an artillery officer in the first world war, winning both the Belgian Order of Leopold and the French Legion d'Honneur. Although at almost 46 he would have been considered too old for frontline service, his previous military service and his legal training and background made him most suitable for use as a staff officer.

Accordingly he was awarded the rank of lieutenant colonel and soon commenced his role as Deputy Chief of the Belgian Surete or Secret Service in Britain. In this capacity he would play a significant part in the training and deployment of agents into occupied Belgium to organise resistance and to gather intelligence for the Allies. He would also have assisted in the analysis of intelligence reports coming out of Belgium in cooperation with the British Special Operations Executive, charged with implementing clandestine operations in the occupied countries and with the American OSS which also had its own intelligence network. It seems improbable that someone holding Marcel's position within the Belgian Secret Service should have taken part in missions into enemy territory, but after the war it was always rumoured that Marcel had been parachuted into Belgium on a number of occasions, returning to Britain by submarine. What is certain is that following the war, having separated from Renee, he took up residence with a woman who had been a member of one of the resistance groups he helped organise. In time the official records may help us understand his role better.

Umberslade Hall, Warwickshire July 1942

After a few weeks in Pembrey, Rene's squadron was moved to a large private house in the Midlands, called Umberslade Hall. It was a large 17th century mansion surrounded by a gigantic deer park. The owners had moved into some gardeners' bungalows allowing Belgian troops to be billeted in the mansion. It was approaching the 21st July, the Belgian National Day. Volunteers were asked to organise a special lunch followed by afternoon sporting entertainment. In the evening an ENSA show would be put on in the hall and would also include a number of variety acts by the men of the brigade. Rene volunteered to supervise the table arrangements and the serving of the lunch where officers, NCOs and men exceptionally, would be seated together. Rene also volunteered to direct and compere the evening show. To the displeasure of Lieutenant Osselaer the commanding officer complimented Rene both on the floral arrangements and table settings and for the organisation of the variety show.

Cecile Nathan having attended an interview at Bush House, Aldwych for a post in the Political Intelligence Department of the Foreign Office on the 21st July, had received confirmation of her appointment. Her letter of appointment indicated that she would be "working in the country at a salary of two pounds and five shillings a week all found." The letter also indicated that she would be "granted two day's leave a fortnight, with free transport to London on those days." She was asked if she was prepared to start work the following Monday, 27th July, and in the event that she was, to report to Bush House for 1pm prompt, in order to catch the car to the country.

The Political Intelligence Department was a covername for the Political Warfare Executive which had been formed in August 1941 as a clandestine body created to produce and spread propaganda, both to undermine the morale of the enemy and boost the morale of those engaged in resistance in the occupied countries. Its staff were drawn from the Ministry of Information, the propaganda arm of the Special Operations Executive and the BBC. Its main base was at Woburn Abbey with offices in London at Bush House.

Its activities included the production of radio broadcasts for transmission to the occupied countries and leaflets, postcards and documents which could be dropped or smuggled behind enemy lines. There was also a considerable task in analysing information coming out the occupied territories, including information gleaned from newspapers, POW interrogations and other material which came into its hands.

Cecile was ideally placed to play a role in the work of the Department particularly in relation to its work in France and Belgium. A fluent French speaker, she had recent knowledge of conditions in France, as well as familiarity with life in Belgium. Her closeness to the French exile community in London cannot have been a disadvantage, particularly when her cousin was Colonel Pierre Billotte, a member of General De Gaulle's Committee of National Defense and one of his closest aides. Relations with Britain's French allies had not always been easy and having someone with some understanding of their thinking may well have proved helpful to the Department's work. One of the people with whom

Cecile seems to have developed an association was Maurice Buckmaster, who headed up the French Section of the Special Operations Executive, sending secret gents into France and who later wrote to her in a personal capacity when she eventually left the Foreign Office.

Prague, August 1942

Only two members of the family remained in Prague following Paul and Edita's deportation to Theresienstadt in January. Their elder daughter Ellen and her husband Pavel Jellinek had lived in rented accommodation on Libicka, only a street away from where her parents had previously lived. They had watched helpless to intervene as first Ellen's aunt Melanie and then her parents had received their orders to report to the collection point near the main railway station which, would lead to their deportation. Now it was their turn. They were ordered to report on 10 August. The official postcards that her parents had been permitted to send would have given little clue as to the conditions in the camp. The fact that there had been no word of Aunt Melanie for so many months was troubling. All that Ellen and Pavel had to hang onto was that they were together and that they were still relatively young – she was only thirty three and Pavel not quite forty one And of course there was the possibility of being reunited with her parents.

But what they could not have allowed for were the conditions in Theresienstadt. If conditions in Prague were hard, those in Theresienstadt were harsh. On their arrival they were to discover that thousands had already died due to the shortages of food. As autumn gave way to winter, thousands more would die. Weakened by hunger, many victims would succumb easily to disease.

Nottage, South Wales, August 1942

Whilst in Umberslade Rene had managed to use his free time in the evening to go horse riding. A farmer in the neighbourhood had a dozen horses, but not enough staff to exercise them. He came to see the commanding officer and told him about his problem. The commanding officer asked all the ex-cavalry men to volunteer and instead of spending their evenings in the local pubs to go riding. This Rene enjoyed immensely, but unfortunately by the end of August, his unit had to move once more.

This time they were posted back to South Wales and stationed in a small village called Nottage, near Porthcawl. Whilst there, they were sent on intensive training and took part in manoeuvres with British units and the Home Guards. One of the exercises in which Rene's unit were involved resulted in their having to play the part of German invaders pushing forward an attack towards Cardiff. Their first opposition was to be encountered in Caerphilly where they would face the Home Guards, who were defending the approach to Cardiff. When they got to Caerphilly Castle they found that no 'enemy' was waiting for them. However, they received instructions not to progress, to hide their vehicle and progress on foot to the outer wall of the castle.

Rene had chosen a position behind the low outer wall, from where, without being seen, he could stop any enemy advancing by any of the three streets that converged at a junction. His men placed their machine gun behind the low wall on the grass, whilst young children, very puzzled by their activities, came to look at them from the pavement side of the wall. One little boy aged between seven and ten asked what they were doing there. They told him they were waiting for the enemy, represented by the Home Guard. "Where will they come from?" he asked. "We don't know, but it can be from any of the three streets in front of us," Rene answered.

After consulting with his playmates he suggested that one of them would go into one street and two others cover the other streets and they would report to Rene as soon as they saw any signs of the Home Guards. Sure enough, about ten minutes later, one of the little boys came running back to tell Rene that he had seen a load of Home Guards disembarking from a personnel carrier and coming in the direction of Rene's company.

Rene's men hid their heads below the wall and asked the little boy to tell them when the Home Guards emerged on the square. On the little boy's signal Rene's company threw half a dozen thunder flashes over the wall and before the Home Guard could recover from their surprise an umpire decided that their unit had been wiped out by grenade blasts. It was only a little later that the small boy who had organised the look

323

out party, came back and found out that Rene's unit were representing invading Germans. His face was a real picture. With a grave face he said, "I really should not have helped you." Rene could see from the expression of the poor lad that he felt terribly guilty, as if he had really betrayed his country. Rene and his men gave the boys some sweets and told them not to worry. They had planned the whole thing they said, to show them how careful they had to be.

Having taken Caerphilly, their next target was Cardiff, also defended by the Home Guard. There Rene paid dearly for the fact of disobeying two orders. The first one was to remove their black berets and wear their steel helmets. The second one was to close the turret on the armoured car. Rene disregarded both. The result was that at a cross roads a very zealous Home Guard tossed a half brick in the air in a way that resulted in it falling back inside the turret and right on Rene's head. Luckily it was the flat side that struck him and as his beret was made of pretty thick material and his skull very hard, the damage was reasonably small, although painful for a few days.

The company's stay in Nottage was clouded by one fatal accident. One of the men, who had previously served in Belgium's Foreign Legion and who had gone through many dangers in order to reach England, was stupidly killed whilst trying out a new type of scout car. Unlike the scout cars the unit had previously used, which could travel in reverse as soon as the crew encountered enemy fire, this vehicle had four wheel steering, which allowed it to turn around in a complete circle in the narrowest of roads. Unfortunately something went wrong as the legionnaire came down a steep hill from Bridgend. The steering suddenly jammed and the scout car hit a tree. After an inquiry into this fatal accident, this type of scout car was withdrawn from use.

Whilst in Nottage Rene again had trouble with his distant cousin, Lieutenant Osselaer. Rene asked for a private interview with him, at which he asked the lieutenant to explain why he was so anxious to make life difficult for him. Lieutenant Osselaer replied that he was angry at the fact that Rene had not kept his promise not to reveal that they were related. Rene assured him that the information had not come from him, but he remained unpersuaded. It was only a bit later that Rene discovered that it was a boy in the squadron, who was also from

Antwerp and knew Rene's family well, who had spread the news that Osselaer and Rene were related.

Rene again reached the stage where he became completely discouraged. He asked for a posting to a different company, but his cousin opposed it and the commanding officer upheld his cousin's advice. Luckily for Rene, Captain Waterloos, who had been his commanding officer between 1931 and 1932 when he had done his national service, was now in London. Rene knew him to be the assistant to the general commanding the Belgian forces in Great Britain. Rene rang him from South Wales and briefly told him about his problem. Rene told him that he had reached the stage where he was seriously considering deserting the army. Waterloos promised to obtain Rene's posting to a new company, and sure enough, two days later an order of posting came from London, which neither the commanding officer, nor his cousin could oppose.

Moreton Paddocks, Warwickshire, October 1942

He was posted to Moreton Paddocks in Warwickshire, where he joined an RASC unit. The commanding officer there was a Captain Wintergroen, an extremely nice man, who had already been informed of Rene's situation. The first thing he said to him was "I hope you will enjoy your life in this unit. We are all members of a happy family and you are welcome here."

Little did Rene know that two days later would be a double landmark in his life, both military and civilian. This was a Friday and in the morning he was called to Captain Wintergroen's office. He told Rene that he had carefully studied his file and that he had been the victim of a gross injustice. He should have been taken on the strength of his service as a sergeant. He had no power to alter the ministerial decision, but since he had been asked to send some of his NCO's to a course for promotion to sergeant, he had put Rene's name down for a course starting the following week in Leamington Spa. The course would last six weeks and at the end of it, Rene would come out as a sergeant, subject to having satisfied the examiners.

That same Friday evening, the Almoner had organised a weekly dance. Twenty WAFs, – members of the Womens' Air Force Service and twenty ATS, – the Auxiliary Territorial Service, made up of women conscripts and volunteers, had been brought in by personnel carriers from nearby stations. When Rene entered the dance hall the dance was in full swing. At one table he saw a lonely ATS and he asked her for a dance. During the dance she told him she had not been feeling very well and, therefore, had not volunteered to come that day. Seeing that there were not enough volunteers, she had been sent against her will. Rene didn't know what attracted him to her. Was it her nice soft voice? Was it her sweet eyes, looking at him like a frightened deer? Was it her slim and charming body? He did not know, but it was love at first sight.

They sat and danced together for the rest of the evening. The only other person he danced with was her sister, who was a corporal in the same ATS unit as Doris Hancock. Both girls were interested to hear how he came to be in England and they told him that they had both been born in Gateshead, County Durham. Although Rene knew of Newcastle by name, he never knew that opposite Newcastle on the other side of the River Tyne was a town called Gateshead. Doris told him that her father had been mayor of Gateshead for the last two years and was an alderman responsible for the health services of the town. Rene told her about his great uncle, Louis Strauss, who for many years had been an alderman in Antwerp, responsible for the harbour organisation which developed the city's port facilities.

The evening went by so quickly. Doris and Rene arranged to meet each other at the next dance, which would take place exactly one week later. Before the following Friday he found he had been posted to the sergeant's course, which as he had anticipated, meant being sent to Leamington Spa. This would have disrupted his plan to meet Doris again. But happily for him, as he thought at the time, the course was now being held at his home base in Moreton Paddocks.

However, unhappily, one hour before the dance he was told that he had to take part in a night manoeuvre. Reluctantly he got ready for it. Wearing his army denims, a balaclava cap with his face all blackened with boot polish and in full equipment, he had just five minutes before the beginning of the manoeuvres to go to the dance and tell Doris the disappointing news that duty had come before pleasure. He told her he was hoping to be back in time for the last dance. Little did he know what he had in store that evening.

A lorry took about thirty troops quite a distance away. Rene wasn't sure how far they had travelled, but he was convinced they had covered some distance. There, they were dropped, divided into several teams and instructed to find their way back by the shortest route, with the help of compasses and maps. Rene was leading a team and since they were supposed to be making a reconnaissance in enemy territory, he chose to place the men in an inverted V formation, which involved the men advancing two by two, with the two columns tapering to the rear of the formation, where Rene took up his position. After giving them their direction, he sent two scouts forward through a field and then gave the signal for the other men to follow.

It was a pitch dark, moonless, night. From where he was advancing he could just see the shadow of the two men immediately in front of him. At one moment he had the impression that the man on his left had stopped moving. He went forward and tapping on what he thought to be the man's shoulder, said, "Come on boy, what are we waiting for." On closer examination he found that he was tapping the haunch of a placid horse. Luckily for him, the horse seemed unmoved by the experience.

Half way through the march, the rain suddenly came down in buckets. They eventually found themselves on the edge of the camp. By then, it was 2 o'clock in the morning. To add to their ordeal, somebody had removed the little bridge used to cross over a stream separating the field in which they stood, from the site of the camp. Rather than adding several miles to their journey, they decided they had no other option but to cross the stream at this point. The rain had increased the height of the water considerably and they soon found it lapping around their hips.

Their CO had, at least, been very considerate. When they got back soaking wet to their Nissen huts, they found that a good strong fire was burning in each of them and a large warm meal was served within minutes of their return. The only thing that aggravated Rene was the fact that he had missed the last dance of the evening with Doris. He did not know exactly where she was stationed and he was wondering if he would ever see her again.

One week after the night manoeuvre, Rene was rushed to the unit's infirmary with suspected yellow jaundice The doctor who diagnosed it asked Rene many questions to discover the origin of the ailment.

Eventually he came to the conclusion that there were two possible causes. It could have either come about as a late reaction to his being underfed in Vichy France and then too rapidly being overfed in Portugal, or it could have been the result of a fright Rene had received just a week before, following a not very practical joke performed by his room mates.

On that particular day Rene had had a tiring morning's exercise. After lunch and during the rest period, he was lying flat on a bench in the middle of the Nissen hut. As the bench was not long enough his feet were resting upright on top of a pail of coals. One of his colleagues had decided to create some amusement by fastening two thunder flashes to the soles of Rene's shoes. A thunder flash is a kind of firecracker used during military exercises to simulate the noise of an exploding grenade. These thunder flashes, having been lit, exploded separately. The first one detonated and awoke Rene suddenly, making him lose his balance and fall off the bench. Before he completely awoke and realised what had happened, the second thunder flash exploded and it was thought that this could have resulted in the bout of yellow jaundice.

For the first few days Rene was very well looked after at the infirmary by the only Belgian nurse, a Madame Bloch. She was the wife of the captain in charge of Rene's course. It was approaching Christmas time and it was thought that he would be better looked after in hospital, so an ambulance took him to the emergency hospital in Stratford on Avon. What an ordeal it was on Christmas day, for Rene to see all the patients in neighbouring beds eating the typical Christmas fare, whilst he was reduced to milk and bread and butter.

During his stay in Ward D, the emergency ward, he was very well looked after by a young nurse named Miss Platt. She was a small blonde with a very pretty face, whom he had nicknamed Sonja Henie, because she moved very gracefully and quickly through the ward as if on skates, just like the famous Dutch figure skater. She seemed to like Rene and he had to admit that he was not indifferent to her. He only regretted that his stay there was too short. He saw Nurse Platt once or twice after his discharge from hospital. He even invited her to shows at the Shakespeare Memorial Theatre. When he returned to the NCO's School, which had now moved to Leamington Spa, he again met Doris, his ATS and soon forgot about Nurse Platt.

The course lasted three months. At the end of it, as is usual in any British army course, instructors and pupils had a farewell dinner together with a Colonel Branders, presiding over the proceedings. After the dessert was served and the usual toasts drunk and speeches completed, Rene asked the permission of the Colonel to read a page of poetry he had composed, intended to be humorous and in which he had mentioned every instructor and pupil and funny incidents that had happened during the course. This met with unexpected success, hilarity and applause. Little did he know that these few lines would change the whole of his future military career. As he sat down, he was told that the Colonel wanted to speak to him.

First he congratulated Rene on his comic piece of poetry. Next he said "And where are you going tomorrow?"

"Back to my unit in Moreton Paddock, Sir!"

"I have different plans for you, I want to keep you here as an instructor. I need people like you to boost the morale of the troops. I shall phone the Ministry in London tomorrow and request your transfer." Rene had no alternative but to accept and thank Colonel Branders for placing such confidence in him.

Leamington Spa, Warwickshire, December 1942

Rene had already heard rumours that things had not gone too well in Leamington Spa. A few weeks before his arrival, there had even been a small revolt resulting in several men being found guilty of indiscipline. The general feeling of the men was that all the drills and exercises were without any practical purpose, as they would never be called into action. The next day Rene saw all his colleagues from the course depart, whilst he had to stay and await further instructions. At the end of that morning Rene was called into the Colonel's office. The meeting was very informal. The Colonel told Rene to sit down whilst he was putting in a second telephone call to London.

A few minutes later having spoken to Rene's friend, Captain Waterloos, he told him the news that not only had his transfer been agreed on, but an important decision had been made by the commission deciding on ranks. The Colonel must have informed them that Rene had come second out of forty in the recent exams. So they had decided that he had been wrongly attached to his unit as a corporal and should have been made a sergeant. In view of this, it was decided he should receive the difference in back pay between the rank of corporal and that of sergeant from the time he joined the Belgian forces in Great Britain. Also, through his newly acquired seniority, he was immediately eligible to become a First Sergeant. It was with this rank that he was introduced by the Colonel to the Regimental Sergeant-Major.

His name was Bob Vitali and quite a character. His father was Belgian, but married to a Corsican woman and Vitali certainly had the vivacity of the Corsicans. He was very gifted, amongst other things, an excellent violinist. He took a liking to Rene the first day they met and decided to appoint him as one of his two assistants. This meant that one week in three Rene had to deputise for him in getting up early every morning. He then had to make sure that the sergeant and corporal of the week were up and had called the men. Next, he had to supervise the distribution of the men's breakfast, after which he would inspect the troops on parade and order the salute to the flag.

The duties for the two other weeks were shared with Vitali himself and with First Sergeant Knaepen, a fat and strong farmer from the French speaking part of Belgium. Knaepen and Rene shared rooms at the Masonic Rooms in Leamington Spa, whilst Vitali, who was married, had a flat half a mile away. From then on life became monotonously repetitive. During the two weeks between his sergeant major's duties, Rene was an instructor, either at the Sergeant's School or at the Campion Hill Camp, where new recruits were trained. The one thing that Rene enjoyed best during these days was the real friendship and understanding which existed between officers and their NCOs. The NCOs also worked in harmony between themselves.

As Rene had always had a liking for animals he accepted one day a gift of a puppy dog. It was a smooth haired terrier bitch, black and white spotted and he called her Micky. She grew very quickly and became a real army dog. He soon had her trained to follow him everywhere, including the troop inspection and the flag parade. She always walked one foot distance behind him and if he stopped to inspect a man's uniform more closely, she would stop and wait. As soon as he had carried out the inspection, she would follow. Then when Rene faced the men to order them to close ranks, she would sit beside him, facing the men. He would then order the salute to the flag, make his about turn, to face the flag and salute whilst the flag was hoisted and the bugle played. Micky would by now be sitting beside him, facing the flag. There was, however, one problem. Micky, like all dogs, was allergic to the sound of the Belgian last post. As soon as the bugler played it, she would howl and her howling was echoed by all the dogs in the neighbourhood. Therefore, to prevent the men from collapsing with laughter, Rene had to lock Micky up in the Unit's office in the evening. Even then she could be heard howling.

Micky soon became very fat and Rene had to request the men not to give her any food outside of her normal feeding times. Micky had befriended the company cook, visited him at a definite hour once a day and then found Rene in the bar or in his room. She knew that the NCO's dining room was out of bounds to her and she would never attempt to enter it. She would wait for Rene, either in the corridor, or in front of his bedroom.

The only breaks in the monotony of the daily routine of army life came when a contingent of new recruits arrived. One such party composed of Belgians who had never seen Belgium, arrived from Canada. Most of these were second generation Belgian born boys, having acquired their parents' nationality, either in the USA, South America or Canada. As their fathers had kept their Belgian nationality, they, although born abroad, were Belgian citizens and as such had been called up. They went for six weeks training to a camp in La Joliette, Canada. After that they were shipped to England and were sent to Leamington Spa. Here, ill feeling arose when they found out that the arms drill they had learned in La Joliette was useless and they found they had to be taught a completely new drill. Many expected that immediately after reaching England, they would see action and their enthusiasm was seriously dampened when they found out that, for the time being at least, the parade ground was their only theatre of operation.

One over zealous Belgian consul had even gone so far as to recruit non-Belgian citizens, promising them that they would join the Belgian Air Force on arrival in England. Instead of that, they were found unfit for the air force and posted to Leamington Spa. Here they began a sit down strike. They were brought in front of the Military Prosecutor who had to admit that he had no jurisdiction over them, as they were Colombian citizens. As a result of this, the boys demanded to be repatriated and claimed damages from the Belgian government in exile. This happened at a time when, for reasons of security, nobody was allowed to leave England.To avoid further trouble, the government decided to have the Colombians moved to London, where a hotel was provided for them. Then officials tried to induce them to help the war effort by working in a factory, but they flatly refused. Meanwhile, the Belgian government had to foot the bill for their stay at the hotel.

Another contingent of Belgians arrived after either escaping or being released from the French Foreign Legion. Every one of them had a story to tell, long enough to fill a book. Some had made several attempts to escape, but each time had been caught and been brought back to the offices of the French Deuxieme Bureau for interrogation. The methods used were as sadistic as the ones used by the Gestapo. The men were stripped, tied spread-eagled across a table, then either burnt with cigarettes or electrodes were applied to their genitals. All this was to make them reveal who had helped them to escape. In most cases, they had left unaided, on their own initiative, hoping to reach Tangiers, the international port. One thing is certain and that is that these men had learned in the Foreign Legion how to be tough. They were excellent marksmen and very reliable in action, as Rene was to find out later.

Whilst in Leamington Spa, Rene regularly visited two canteens organised for the forces. There he met Doris the ATS again and they started to go out regularly together. Another pleasant surprise for Rene was the discovery that not far away, units of the Czechoslovakian Independent Brigade had been stationed. Having made various enquiries, it did not take him long to establish that his cousin, Jiri Falkenau, who had now adopted the more Anglicised forename of George, was amongst the 3324 men who had been evacuated from French ports on the west and south of the country, following the repatriation of the British Expeditionary Force at Dunkirk. Shipped back to Britain in July 1940, they had originally been assembled at Cholmondeley near Chester with the aim of incorporating them into British army units, but when it became apparent that there were sufficient men to justify it, they had been formed into the Czech Independent Brigade and moved to bases in the Midlands to receive training. This happy conjunction meant that it was not long before the two cousins were meeting socially in their off duty periods. George, like Rene, had made the acquaintance of a nice English girl, who he was to marry in 1944.

Walton Hall, Wellesbourne, July 1943

In June 1943, recruitment commenced amongst the NCOs for volunteers to train to become Civil Government Officers who would be responsible for the administration of the liberated countries. Rene was not particularly interested and did not apply to attend the training course. However, when it was decided that this course was to be held at Walton Hall near Wellesbourne and that a Messing Officer was wanted, he applied for the job for the sake of a change of scenery.

Walton Hall was a big mansion, requisitioned by the army. The students were accommodated in Nissen huts built near the hall in the surrounding park. Rene found he had a very nice room all to himself on the first floor of the hall and immediately below his room, on the ground floor, was a store room used by the hall's owners to store the kill from the local hunts. The walls were covered with white tiles. Hooks inserted in the walls, on two sides of the room, were used to hang venison. Under them were cupboards with marble slabs on top of them. Rene chose this place as his main food store room and in the place of the usual venison, the army's big carcasses of meat were hung.

Twice a week, Rene drove to Stratford on Avon where, with the help of one driver, he collected supplies from the RASC,- the Royal Army Service Corps and the NAAFI, – the Navy, Army and Air Force Institute stores. Every time he went to Stratford he paid a visit to Corporal Bertha Elliott, Doris's sister. Soon after he had made her acquaintance in Moreton Paddock, she had been transferred to the RASC in Stratford. She was living with five other ATS girls in a requisitioned villa near the RASC depot. Doris also managed to come a few times from Leamington to Stratford to meet him.

Rene was responsible for the Officers' Mess and the NCOs' mess, which included those attending the training school, in all approximately 300 men. The Colonel in command liked good food and with his blessing, Rene quite often broke Kings' regulations. The only vegetables the RASC could supply were cabbages and peas. Rene decided to travel to Evesham taking surplus corned beef and other goods supplied by the RASC. There he went from one farm to another and offered his surplus goods in exchange for fresh lettuces, carrots, cauliflowers and even asparagus and cucumbers. This allowed him to plan menus very similar to the ones his men were accustomed to in Belgium.

Again, thanks to the fact that the Colonel liked his food so much, Rene had been able to get transferred to the kitchen any man, who in civilian life, was connected with food preparation. He had a professional butcher brought in from the transport unit, a pastry cook who had previously been employed on weapons' maintenance and he even found a chef, who before the war, had worked in a hotel on the Belgian coast. Thus organised, his task was easy, – bring in and control supplies, compose the menus for the three messes, officers, NCOs and troops, and make sure that the food was ready in time. Sometimes he had to chase up the Orderly Sergeant of the week to get him to bring in the men for the potato peeling fatigue, or the cleaning of vegetables on time. These duties were usually done in the evening by the men punished with CB, – being confined to barracks. Otherwise, he had an easy life and was more or less his own master.

A few days before the 21st July, the Belgian National Day, the Colonel discussed with Rene his plans for that day. In the morning, there would be a parade and a church service, then a lunch with the officers, NCOs and men, all eating together. In the afternoon there would be sports competitions in the grounds of Walton Hall. The local civilians would be invited to watch the events and then they would be invited to partake of a buffet in the great hall, followed by a dance. The Colonel asked Rene to make sure that there would be enough drink available for the occasion. So instructed, Rene went from one brewery to the next, telling them why he required large supplies of beer. All of them gave him the maximum possible.

Inspired by the idea of showing the British civilian what Belgian cuisine was like, his men worked wonders. In fact they worked through the whole night preceding the 21st July, with the expected result. The lunch was a real success and the buffet was as good as any provided at any of the functions he had so often attended at the three international exhibitions where he had worked before the war.

On one side of the great hall, a long table with three tiers on top of it, had been installed. White bedding sheets, fresh from the factory, were used as table cloths, hiding the wooden framing forming the three tiers surmounting the table. Floral arrangements on that table had been left to one of the more artistic colleagues. Large trays with a variety of open sandwiches, real Belgian pastries and cakes, made the whole buffet look most attractive. At the other end of the room, a well stocked bar had been installed. The first drink, sherry or port, was given free, as well as soft drinks. Spirits and beer had to be paid for, but it did not prevent hosts and guests from clearing the bar before the evening was over. The music for the dancing was provided by a Belgian army band. They kept the couples swinging until the early hours of the morning.

A bad surprise was to await Rene the next day. When the corporal responsible for the bar came to render his account. Rene found a discrepancy of six dozen bottles in it. The corporal protested his innocence, but was unable to explain the discrepancy. On closer examination of the receipts the corporal had signed for when the supplies were brought to him from the stores, Rene found that his account agreed with what he had signed for from the suppliers. This put the corporal in the clear.

However, Rene soon found that these receipts did not agree with the ones signed for by a sergeant who had been responsible for a fatigue of six men carrying the crates from Rene's store to the great hall. The sergeant and the six men appeared in front of the commanding officer. After a tight investigation, the sergeant admitted that whilst the crates were taken from the store, he had stayed at the door of the store room having a friendly conversation with the store keeper. He was certain that the number of crates he had signed for had left the store. Now the mystery to be solved was, what had happened to the six missing crates between the store and the great hall? A search led to the finding of three empty crates in some bushes near the hall. Three more were found in an empty room in the tower of the hall. The other finds in that room were a mattress on the floor and a lady's bra.

This left little doubt as to what may have happened in the tower, but it still remained to be found out how the crates had got there. After a lengthy interrogation of the six men who had made up the fatigue and despite their initial denial of guilt, they eventually admitted that they had taken advantage of the fact that the long corridor leading to the great hall turned at a right angle, someway beyond the storeroom. As soon as they had turned the corner and were out of sight of the sergeant, they had opened one of the windows and since they were at ground floor level, it had been easy to pass the crates out of the window to some of their friends waiting outside. The six men took the full rap, each getting eight days confined to barracks, as well as having to pay for the missing bottles. Some of them will have taken back more vivid memories of that National Day than the rest of their comrades.

Leamington Spa, England, September 1943

At the end of the summer, Rene went back to Leamington Spa. His meetings with Doris became more frequent and in mid-September they decided to announce their engagement and ask their respective commanding officers for permission to marry. As soon as Doris made it known to her commanding officer that Rene was Belgian, she was given a long lecture on the dangers of marrying a man of a different nationality. She was made aware of the fact that once the war was over, that Rene might want to return to his own country, where she would have to go and live with him and probably would have problems in adapting herself to this new way of life. She answered that she knew all that and was prepared to take that risk. The CO then said she would only grant authority for a marriage after a period of three months. Meanwhile, she posted Doris to another ATS unit in Droitwich, hoping that this separation would make her forget Rene. Little did she know that this action only increased their mutual desire to show the army that they knew what they wanted their future to be.

Birmingham, England, October 1943

Although they were unable to see each other during the week, Rene and Doris met every weekend, when not on duty. They had found that Birmingham was the most convenient place to meet. Doris took nearly the same time to get there as Rene took to get from Leamington Spa. Near New Street Station were two adjoining army hostels, one for women, one for men. Rene was allowed to take his meals in the women's hostel and to spend the evening there, but come 11pm, a matron would give the signal to leave the place. He was, however, allowed to reappear there for breakfast.

One weekend, at the end of October, as he was appearing in the dining room for breakfast, Doris looked at him and said in a worried manner, "Are you unwell? You look as if you have had a sleepless night." "No," Rene said. "The first part of the night I slept very soundly, but suddenly I had an awful dream. I saw my parents and my sister in front of me, as I had seen them at the station the day I left France. They spoke to me and said I would never see them again. I now have a premonition that that is going to be so and thinking of them I could no longer sleep." Doris said, "Ridiculous. You have probably eaten too much and I bet your parents are all right and worrying as much about you."

They found out one year later that that this was the very weekend the Gestapo had arrested Rene's parents and sister and that they were on their way to the infamous extermination camp of Auschwitz. From that time on Rene had a serious belief in the existence of telepathy.

Both Doris and Rene were determined that they wanted to get married and reapplied to their respective COs, who once more tried to discourage them. However, in view of their determination they both gave them their approval.

They fixed the date for the 12th January 1944. Rene had chosen that date because it was the anniversary date of his parents' wedding in 1911 and not realizing then that he would never see them again, he wanted to show them he had been thinking of them. They had accumulated three leave passes to which they were entitled every three months, in order to be able to have a long honeymoon.

Drancy, Paris 1st November 1943

Drancy is a suburb to the north east of Paris city centre and the site of a large municipal housing complex built during the 1930s. The land for the site had been acquired in 1925 by the Seine Low Cost Housing Office (Les Habitations bon marche de la Seine). By 1935 the complex comprised five fourteen storey tower blocks and a series of four storey blocks constructed in a U shape, around a large open space, intended to be a public park. It was this latter, low rise part of the complex, which was destined to be used as an internment and transit camp for a variety of prisoners brought here from all over France. Amongst them were Franz, Irma and Georgette Falkenau who had arrived here on 1st November following their arrest in Grasse several days earlier.

The housing complex had not been made available to its intended tenants by the start of the war. It had been designed as a model community with a total of 925 flats, but by the start of the war none of them had been occupied, except by soldiers of the Gardes Mobile. It's design made its adaption for use as an internment camp very easy. By blocking in the ground floor windows and doors and by surrounding the entire complex with a seven foot barbed wire fence it was made a secured compound. Initially it had been used as a prison for the incarceration of French political prisoners opposed to Petain's Vichy regime – Communists, trades unionists, resistance fighters from a variety of political backgrounds and for a time it had also held British prisoners of war, before they were sent on to camps in Germany.

In August 1941 its role changed and it suddenly became the principal internment camp for Jews from all over France. The round ups started in Paris and soon spread to other areas of the country. Most of these were conducted by French gendarmes acting on the instructions of the German military authorities. The French police supervising the Drancy camp were noted for their brutality. Jewish children were immediately separated from their parents on arrival. Beatings and other forms of harsh treatment were commonplace, so much so that leaders of the Jewish community offered young men from their ranks to police the camp in the hope of reducing the ill treatment.

The wedding of Rene and Doris Falkenau, January 1944
For Renee Roost, far left of group, it is an occasion tinged with sadness.
She is concealing news of the arrest and deportation of Franz, Irma and
Georgette till after the honeymoon.
Left to right: Renee Roost, Peter Elliott, Peter Hancock, Rene, Doris, Judith
Elliott, Bertha Elliott, Alan Elliott, Elizabeth Hancock

The last photo taken of Rene with his family before his escape to England,
February 1942

Drancy, the internment camp to the east of Paris from which Franz, Irma
and Georgette are deported to Auschwitz October 1943

The death certificate of Pavel Jellinek, husband of Ellen Falkenau,
Theresienstadt November 1943

Conditions in the camp were primitive. Food supplies relied on gifts from various welfare organisations outside, administered by the General Union of Jews in France (UGIF). Water supplies were limited to a series of communal wash houses and latrines located in what became known as 'Chateau Rouge', one of the three blocks making up the housing complex. Inmates were only allowed to visit the latrines in groups of four, but it was one of the few places where they could talk freely and exchange news and information. Hence it became known as 'Radio Drancy'.

Overcrowding was chronic, with internees forced to sleep on mattresses on bare concrete floors. Even prior to Franz, Irma and Georgette's arrival numerous detainees had died, either as a result of starvation or from tuberculosis caused by the insanitary conditions. They were to spend nineteen days here and during that time must have spent many hours wondering about and discussing their fate with other prisoners. Knowledge of the convoys leaving at routine intervals from the nearby station of Bobigny was a commonplace, as was the process of selection and the issue of the 'purple invitation' informing detainees of their selection for deportation.

The Nazis astutely maintained the myth that the convoys of a thousand to twelve hundred people leaving at routine intervals, were heading for resettlement in the east. Where, was never specified, but the issue of a quantity of Zloty issued in exchange for any cash the detainees had kept, hinted at Poland. Eventually on 20 November, Franz, Georgette and Irma were taken to the station at Bobigny to board the cattle wagons of Convoy 62 which would convey them east. Their single suitcase containing their remaining possessions had been taken from them on their departure from Drancy. Each had been numbered and their ownership recorded to maintain the illusion that their belongings would be available for collection on their arrival.

Squeezed almost eighty people to a wagon, with only straw and the odd squalid mattress covering the wooden floor, but with almost no room in which to sit, at 11.50 a.m. they commenced their journey. Two pails were the only other items of comfort provided, apart from the small parcel of food to sustain them on the journey. One pail contained drinking water, the other was to permit them to relieve themselves on the journey lasting close to three days.

The other commodity which was in short supply was air. In the cramped and stifling conditions of the wagon it was necessary for those close to collapse to be manhandled and passed to either of the two sides of the wagon, where the narrow slits in the walls allowed them to briefly gasp the outside air.

Miraculously nineteen members of the convoy succeeded in escaping their captivity whilst the train was moving slowly through a tunnel near Lerouville, at around 8.30 p.m. on the first day of the journey. The convoy's final destination was Auschwitz. There, some 241 males and 45 females were selected for labour. The remaining 914 deportees were gassed on arrival, amongst them Franz, Irma and Georgette.

Almost a month later on 17 December 1943, Irma's 78 year old uncle, Auguste Roost, a former lawyer and uncle to Marcel and Renee Roost was also to make the fateful journey from Drancy to Auschwitz on Convoy 64.

Theresienstadt November and December 1943

As Rene and Doris were preparing to marry another part of the Falkenau family tragedy was unfolding many miles away in the centre of Europe. On the 10 November, Pavel Jellinek died. The reason given on the death certificate prepared by one of the camp doctors was pneumonia, but it is apparent that only the combination of the inhumane living conditions which he had been subjected to, could have caused the death of an otherwise healthy man at the age of 42. Only a month later, on the 15 December, Ellen, his 34 year widow was transported to Auschwitz concentration camp, where she was sent straight to the gas chamber on arrival.

Gateshead, England January 1944

Doris went up to her home town of Gateshead a few days before the date fixed for the wedding, in order to buy a dress. She did not want to get married in uniform. Rene only went up the day before the wedding. A last minute snag prevented the colleague who was going to be his best man from joining him.

When Rene got up to Gateshead, Doris told him that the only dress she liked was not her size, but was being altered and would be ready for the morning of their wedding. So that morning, they left her home early for Newcastle to fetch the dress. When they got there, they had to wait a while as the tailoress was still busy stitching it. By the time she brought them the carton containing the precious dress, they had run very short of time to get back to Gateshead and for Doris to get dressed and reach the church in time.

They tried to find a taxi, but there were none available. Just in time they jumped on a bus leaving for Gateshead. When they reached the High Level Bridge, the bus was halted in the middle of it by a traffic hold up. By now Doris and Rene were on hot coals. At her home everybody had started to get worried, wondering if they had eloped without waiting for the wedding ceremony. At long last they reached Low Fell with minutes to spare. Doris was helped by Bertha to put on her new dress whilst Rene rushed by car to fetch Renee Roost, his Belgian aunt, who had come specially from London the previous day and was waiting for him to fetch her at the Springfield Hotel where she had spent the night. She too was nervous when she had not seen Rene arrive at the agreed time and wondered if he had changed his mind at the last minute. In a few words Rene told her what had happened and they got to St Helen's Church just in time.

The few minutes that followed were probably amongst the most nerve wracking of Rene's life. He had been told that according to British tradition it was unlucky to see the bride before she came to the altar. He stood there in the deserted church, facing the altar with Peter Elliott, his future wife's 13 year old nephew standing next to him, acting as his best man, as a result of his army chum being refused leave to attend. Rene was much too worried to talk to him. His only thought was, "Will Doris make it in time?"

Suddenly there was a clatter of footsteps, a terrific noise of chairs being moved, which indicated that something was happening. But the organ which should have heralded Doris's arrival remained silent, although the organist's services had been paid for. Moments later Doris was standing next to him. It was the first time he had seen her out of uniform and in a civilian dress. She looked even prettier than usual in her pale green dress, with a sprig of white carnation pinned to her shoulder.

The ceremony was short and austere and they did not really mind that. After the vicar had uttered the usual words of the wedding service and Doris and Rene had said the important, "I do," the rings had been exchanged. They were then ushered into the sacristy where the vicar refunded them the money for the organist who, on account of war time duties, had been unable to get there on time. After all concerned had signed the register, they left the church for the short drive to Doris's home.

There for the first time, Rene met all of Doris's relatives and the friends of his new father-in-law, who had twice been mayor of the town and was now the longest serving alderman. He was well known in Gateshead mainly for his interest in public health and his achievements as chairman of the Hospital Management Committee. Thanks to his constant efforts, funds had been provided by the government, against many odds, for the construction of a new modern hospital on top of Sheriff Hill. It was known then as the Infectious Diseases Hospital, but in time it became the Queen Elizabeth Hospital, named after the wife of King George VI, who came to Gateshead immediately following the war to inaugurate it.

It fell to Rene's father-in-law, Alderman Peter Hancock, as chairman of the hospital board, to welcome the Queen and to introduce the local dignitaries and hospital staff to her. Alderman Hancock later mentioned to Rene how impressed he had been by the Queen's excellent memory. As he introduced each in turn to her, she had a friendly word for every one of them and it was quite surprising that she had read and memorised details concerning the long list of people she was to be introduced to. This list compiled by Alderman Hancock, at the request of the Queen's secretary and sent to Buckingham Palace by the Town Clerk, gave the order in which they were to be presented, the name of each person and their connection with the town or the hospital. It was remarkable for the Queen to have remembered all these details, but what was much more remarkable still, was that when, after the end of the official ceremony, she returned into the gardens walking between two lines of guests, watching her go to her car, she shook hands with many of them, remembering their titles and names.

Edinburgh January 1944

Following the reception at her parent's home, Doris left with Rene that same evening for their honeymoon. The first part of it was going to be spent in Edinburgh, where their friends, the MacLeods, had invited them to use their guest room. They had a very pleasant few days there, marred only by the fact that they ran out of cash. Rene's relatives had given him quite a substantial sum of money as a wedding present and knowing that he could withdraw it at the rate of three pounds a day, he had decided to put the whole amount in a Post Office savings account. On the second day of their stay in Edinburgh, Doris saw a nice dress in a shop. The dress cost nine pounds, so for three days Rene drew three pounds from the Post Office, but on the third day after paying him, the Post Office clerk confiscated his account book, saying that owing to recent frauds, they had instructions to send to London for inspection any books with three consecutive withdrawals. Rene explained that they were on their honeymoon, that all their money was in the Post Office. All to no avail. The book would have to go to London and would be forwarded within a week to their next address. He gave the address of the friends they were going to stay with in South Wales and left it at that. It was lucky that between them, by being careful, they had enough to last them a week.

Birmingham, England, January 1944

They left Edinburgh by train for Birmingham. The last time they had stayed in Birmingham had been at their respective hostels there. When the matron of the women's hostel had come to tell Rene it was time to leave, he had jokingly told her, "This is the last time that you will chase me out of here!"

"Yes, why? Are you getting posted?" she had asked.

"No, I am getting married to this young lady and next time we come we will stay in your married quarters on, the top floor," he had replied.

"You'd better let me know in good time when you intend to come, because the number of married quarters are limited and I usually keep them for our regulars."

They made a reservation there and then for the night they would transit through Birmingham on their honeymoon. When they reached the hostel a marvellous reception was waiting for them. The matron had remembered the occasion and they were offered a bottle of wine and a cake specially made for them, which they shared with the matron and the staff.

When they retired to their room, Doris got into bed first. Having finished undressing, Rene as he always did, sat on the end of the bed to remove his socks. Suddenly that end of the bed gave way under his weight and came crashing down with a loud bang. This had been heard outside and when he opened the door to go and report the accident, half a dozen worried faces had already gathered in front of the door. The matron seemed quite amused. They examined the bed together and found that there was a defect in the metal frame. As there was no other room available, the only solution that was available was to prop up that corner of the frame and rest it on a chair. Doris often wondered if this had been a practical joke, but Rene was convinced it was a pure accident.

Llanelli, South Wales, January 1944

In south Wales they stayed with the people in Llanelli Rene had befriended during the time he had been stationed there with the squadron of armoured cars. The Evans family made them welcome and Rene and Doris spent a week with them. Again the question of money came up. The Post Office book had not arrived. Luckily a British army unit was stationed in the vicinity and on production of Rene's pay book, he managed to get an advance.

London, January 1944

The last few days of their long honeymoon were spent in London. They stayed at the Averard Hotel in Lancaster Gate. Rene's first visit was to the Head Post Office in Kensington. After enquiries and a long wait, he was told that his Post Office savings book had gone to south Wales. He became very angry and demanded to get his money, book or no book. At first he was told that this was impossible, but at his insistence to see somebody more responsible, he was at last introduced to one of the more senior officials. Rene told him of the whole sequence of events and repeated his demand to have his money straightaway. Once more he was asked to wait whilst the official went to consult with his superiors. After a while he came back and said that subject to Rene signing a form guaranteeing that he would return the savings account book to the Post Office as soon as it came back into his possession, he would pay Rene the amount in full. Rene signed, took the money and promised himself never to put money in the Post Office Savings Bank anymore. A promise he kept to his dying day.

Droitwich, England, February 1944

After their honeymoon was over Doris and Rene went back to their respective units, she in Droitwich and he in Leamington Spa. As soon as she got back, Doris asked to be discharged from the army by virtue of the fact that she had become Belgian by her marriage to Rene. The commanding officer's answer was, "Sorry, that is not grounds for a discharge. We have many aliens enrolled in our forces. The only grounds for discharge would be under Paragraph 11." This paragraph referred to pregnancy.

From now on, Dons was very anxious to fulfil the conditions of Para. 11, because she had taken a real dislike to the army. She had never forgiven Rene's Colonel and her commanding officer for having spoiled their last Christmas Eve. Rene was, at the time, in charge of messing at Leamington. First the Colonel had instructed Rene to organise Christmas dinners in the Officers', NCOs' and a Troop Mess for all the members, plus a guest. On the strength of this, he had invited Doris to dinner in the NCO's mess.

But a few days before Christmas, probably because he had had a quarrel with his wife, the Colonel suddenly decided that no ladies would be admitted to the dinner. As presence at the dinner was not compulsory, Rene decided, as a protest, not to attend. Unfortunately it was too late to notify Doris not to travel to Leamington. When she arrived she found Rene in a shocking temper giving his last instructions to the sergeants responsible for the three messes. He had personally supervised the table arrangements and considered that his presence was no longer required.

Having told Doris what had happened, she suggested they should catch a train back to Droitwich where Rene could attend the dinner at her headquarters. When they eventually got there, they found they were too late for the dinner. Finally Rene decided to take her to the best hotel in town, where they had a very nice meal, "en tete a tete," at a small table for the two of them. They enjoyed the food, but it did not replace the party atmosphere they had hoped to find on such an occasion.

Theresienstadt, Czechoslovakia May 1944

During its existence as a concentration camp the Nazis had sought to maintain the fiction that Theresienstadt was for the resettlement of elderly and distinguished members of Jewish communities. Doubtless the presence of Paul Falkenau, as a retired and decorated officer of the Austrian army was a small contribution to maintaining this pretence. But mostly it was the Jewish community itself, which permitted the Germans to create this entirely misleading impression for the outside world, the culmination of which was the film made to depict the rich cultural life of the settlement. Production of the film by the Jewish director, actor and cabaret performer, Kurt Gerron commenced in February 1944. Gerron and most of those taking part in the film were subsequently deported to Auschwitz, where they were killed.

Apart from the efforts of the 'Jewish Cultural Council' to ensure that the education of Jewish children was maintained, a great deal of effort went into organising activities intended to sustain a cultural life for the older members of the settlement. A large number of artists, writers, musicians, scientists, scholars, diplomats and jurists were amongst those deported to Theresienstadt. Despite being prevented from bringing instruments into the camp in the early days following its creation, eventually four concert orchestras, as well as chamber ensembles and jazz groups were formed.

On 23 June 1944 the Nazis permitted a visit by representatives of the Danish Red Cross. It is clear that these visitors followed an official route which had been prepared by a red line on a map and do not appear to have sought to deviate from it. In preparation for the visit the camp commandant had organised 'Operation Embellishment' which had involved not only decorating and restyling some living quarters, but had also included the erecting of fake cafes and shops to create the impression that the Jewish inhabitants were living in relative comfort.

One problem, however, threatened to undermine this carefully constructed façade. Theresieinstadt remained seriously overcrowded. So it was that in the months leading up to the visit by the Red Cross deputation, that the Nazis sought to reduce the camp's population by the deportation of several thousand of the inmates to Auschwitz, where they were immediately gassed on arrival. All of the artisans who had contributed to 'Operation Embellishment were amongst the first to go. On 18 May 1944 time had also run out for Paul and Edita Falkenau. They were amongst a convoy of one thousand Theresienstadt inmates deported to Auschwitz and killed on arrival.

Singapore, May 1944

On the far side of the globe other members of the family had been facing similar hardships. The fall of Singapore to the Japanese in February 1942 had resulted not only in the capture of a very large number of allied prisoners of war, it had also resulted in the internment of several thousand enemy civilians. Some were employees of British, European and American companies on temporary deployment to the far east, but the largest number were British passport holders who were permanent residents of Singapore. Rupert Manasseh and his brother Ezekial were amongst those rounded up by the Japanese military authorities and marched the fifteen miles to Changi Gaol, on the edge of the city. Ezekial Manasseh had taken the precaution of placing the deeds to the many properties he owned in a safe. On top of these he had placed a joint of meat, knowing that it would soon putrify and become contaminated by maggots. He correctly anticipated that if the Japanese were able to open the safe, that they would be greeted by the foul smelling and fly blown remains of the meat and would consider it better to close the safe than examine its contents further. Sadly, whilst the deeds to his property survived the war, Ezekial did not.

The depredations suffered by inmates in Changi were no less barbaric or harsh than those faced by other members of the family confined in camps in Europe. If anything the conditions both physical and psychological could be even worse. Ezekial was to become a victim of what became known as the 'Double Tenth Atrocity'. On the 10th October 1943 all internees of Changi Prison were paraded in the main yard shortly after dawn. It was assumed that this was a routine roll call, but shortly after this military police and armed soldiers were placed on all doors. Various internees were called out by name and segregated from the others and labelled. The remainder were ordered back to their cell block yards where others were segregated and labelled. Whilst being made to stand out in the open yards in stifling heat, the Japanese systematically searched cells, often destroying or stealing internees property in the process. These searches lasted until dusk and only then were internees allowed to return inside the building. Many had not been fed since 6 p.m. the previous day and numbers collapsed due to exposure to the day long sun without food.

The purpose of these searches was to discover the whereabouts of a secret radio transmitter which the Japanese believed was broadcasting messages concerning espionage activities being conducted on behalf of the Allies. In point of fact, there was no radio transmitter, although a number of inmates had managed to conceal radio receivers which allowed them to obtain news and information about the current state of the war.

Despite the failed investigation, 57 internees, including Ezekial, were taken away by military police and moved to the internment camp at Sime Road. Here conditions were, if anything, even harsher than in Changi. They were confined in small cells or cages so small they could not lie down in comfort. No bedding was provided and bright lights were kept burning all night. From 8 am until 10 pm inmates were made to sit on the floor with their knees upright. They were not allowed to place their hands on the floor to steady themselves, or to move, or talk, except to ask to go to the lavatory. There was only one lavatory provided in each cell and the water flushing the pan had to be used for all purposes, including washing and drinking. Unsurprisingly almost all the inmates suffered bouts of enteritis and dysentery. No soap, towels or toiletries were permitted and the only clothes inmates were allowed were those they were wearing on arrival.

Food consisted of rice, occasional vegetable and weak tea with no milk or sugar. It is estimated that this provided the average inmate with little more than 600 to 800 calories a day, well below minimum nutritional requirements.Inmates had no access to medicines and medical care was almost totally absent. An inmate with a broken pelvis and possible ruptured kidney was told he was not ill enough to require treatment.

Three women inmates moved from Changi were detained in exactly the same conditions as their male counterparts, except that they additionally had to cope with insults and obscene gestures by Japanese prisoners, who subjected them to other forms of abuse.

All 57 were repeatedly subjected to various forms of torture and would frequently either stagger back to their cells or be carried back unconscious. Of the 57 internees moved to Sime Road, 12 died of sickness attributable to the conditions under which they were held. One of these was Ezekial Manasseh, who succumbed to the effects of disease on 17 May 1944. His brother Rupert was also to die as a result of the conditions in which he had been interned only four months later on 5 September 1944.

Leamington Spa, England June 1944

It took until June before Doris qualified for her release from the army. She and Rene got themselves two rooms in a house near the Masonic Hall in Leamington and lived there quite happily with their dog Micky, who had by then had half a dozen puppies.

Now the routine in camp changed and rumours spread that the new equipment and vehicles recently distributed to the various motorised units, were in preparation for a landing in Europe. Suddenly all the men, who up to then had been very depressed by what they saw as the lack of purpose in their drill and shooting practice, began to demonstrate zeal and determination in these activities.

Soon a contingent of Belgian forces, which included Rene, was sent to West Wratting near Newmarket. Whilst here, the men underwent training in the strictest secrecy to prepare them for a landing in Europe. Rene was instructed in field security activities by one of his colleagues, who had attended a special field security school in Matlock, in order to instruct others in the Belgian Brigade in turn.

The first duty of NCOs now was to warn the men of the danger of discussing any military matters in public places. The second was to observe the troops in the only two pubs in the place and listen and if needs be, send any offender overheard breaching orders back to barracks.

Meanwhile, at his course, Rene received training in how to protect his unit from enemy surprise patrols, by the placing and arming of booby traps and booby flares. He and the other participants were taught how, once on the other side, they had the dual task of watching that there was no infiltration of traitors amongst the new recruits who would join them and how field security should be organised in the towns and villages they were retaking from the Germans. It was also explained to them how they had to work in co-operation with the military police and a clear definition was given to them as to what this co-operation consisted of. In this way there would never be a clash in the performance of their respective duties.

Whilst in West Wratting there were several alerts in readiness for embarkation and both the military police and the new field security officers sealed off the camp. All men were confined to barracks. All telephone lines out of the camp were manned by trusted personnel and several times orders came: "Be ready to leave at five minutes notice." Every officer, NCO and man was expected to sit in his vehicle, ready to get and give the orders for departure. But on each occasion, after five minutes, the order came, "Action postponed. Resume camp activities as usual."

It reached a point where everyone wondered if these alerts were only staged to keep morale up and the men keyed up for action. Eventually some were even allowed to go back to Leamington on short leave and

Rene took the opportunity to do so. As soon as he got back to West Wratting another alert took place. This time they knew that it was serious when once more the men were confined to barracks and invasion money was issued to them. Rene was then told that he would not embark, but be assigned to supervise the embarkation at Newhaven. He was also told that he would be assigned to escort the first group of reinforcements, all legionaires, just completing their training in Leamington Spa.

Newhaven, England, July 1944

The next day the Brigade moved to Newhaven. There the men had to leave their vehicles in good order in a field. Whilst they were being embarked on MTBs, Rene with a few men and Military Police kept watch on the vehicle park. After a while a team of specially trained British army drivers drove the vehicles away, one by one, to embark them. A similar team in Arromanches, disembarked the vehicles and drove them into a field, where their Belgian drivers found them in the same order as when they had left them in Newhaven.

When the last vehicle was embarked in Newhaven, Rene's duties were finished and he went back to Leamington to await further instructions. A few weeks later, he was called into the Colonel's office and he was told to escort the legionnaires to Newhaven. He was instructed to take his kit bag with him, as he may have to go across. He was briefed not to tell anybody about it, not even his wife. Rene suggested to her that he might be away longer than usual and told her it would be best if she went to live with her parents in Gateshead, within the next few days.

Newhaven, England, August 1944

When he got to Newhaven, he was told by a Liaison Officer that he thought that the Warrant Officer in charge of the troop seemed too young and inexperienced to impose discipline on the tough legionaires and that he had received orders that Rene should act as second in command to the Warrant Officer, fresh from officers' training school. On reaching the Brigade, Rene should report to the Field Security Officer and receive further instructions.

Rene knew that if he had to embark he would not be allowed to take his dog Micky with him, so he instructed the driver who had brought him to Newhaven, to return Micky to his wife. She would no doubt understand from this, that he had embarked, a thing that he could not even tell the driver to convey to her. However, the driver later claimed to have lost the dog, and went to tell Doris about it. Nonetheless, she understood what this meant and left the next day for Gateshead. It was only years later that Rene discovered that the driver had not lost the dog, but had sold it to the pastry cook at the Officers' Mess, pretending that he was doing so on Rene's instructions. It was only after the war was over, that the true story of what had become of the animal came out.

One weekend Rene and Doris went on a sentimental journey to Leamington. They paid a visit to the lady at whose home they had stayed after returning from their honeymoon. Mrs. Smalford told them that some time after their departure, she found Micky sitting on her doorstep one morning. She had kept the bitch until the year prior to their visit, when she had to have her put to sleep, because of old age. Not knowing the true story and believing what the army driver had told Doris, they wondered how Micky had found her way from Newhaven to Leamington Spa, a distance of over 150 miles.

Another year elapsed and the mystery was solved. Whilst visiting his parents-in-law in Gateshead, they showed Rene a newspaper cutting with the photograph of a Chinese restaurant in Leamington Spa. Under it was a long write up about the place, which boasted about having acquired the services of a Belgian pastry chef. In an interview the chef described how he was using only the best butter and cream to make his Belgian pastries. Rene decided to investigate and went to the place and had coffee and pastries. He was satisfied that the pastries were of a familiar Belgian type and asked the Chinese owner of the restaurant if he could meet the pastry chef. He showed Rene the way to the workroom on the second floor and there, somewhat to his surprise, he found the pastry chef he had recruited whilst serving as Messing Officer.

In the course of the conversation, the chef said, "You remember your dog Micky? When you decided to get rid of it, I bought it from the driver who you had instructed to sell it. I had the dog for a while with me in the kitchen. Then one morning I found one of my kitchen helpers

Rene's Military Campaign 1944 - France,Belgium,Holland and Germany kicking the poor animal. I got into a violent temper and warned the fellow that next time I caught him ill treating the dog, I would box his ears. That same afternoon the dog disappeared and although he denied it, I always suspected the kitchen help of being responsible for the dog's disappearance."

Rene told the pastry cook the rest of the story and how, after either being kicked out,or having escaped of her own free will, Micky had remembered the place where Rene and Doris had lived and had tried to find them.

Arromanches, Normandy, August 1944

Following the embarkation at Newhaven, ninety troops were shipped on an MTB, which took fourteen hours to reach Arromanches. During that time Rene was kept busy, briefing his men, supervising the distribution of ammunition, iron rations and other equipment. Their instructions on landing were pretty vague, but they had been told that, they would get more definite instructions after landing.

They got to Arromanches early the next morning. After disembarking they followed the coast in a northerly direction. They had a very rough time, because although there was not very much fighting, the Germans before retreating had stuffed the area with mines, booby traps and other murderous devices. Despite all the precautions taken to clear mines from the road before advancing, including tapes marking the road to show the safe route, it was still the case that some, mainly tracked vehicles, hit some of the mines. One Bren gun carrier overturned and burst into flames killing its four occupants.

Booby traps were often placed in the most unexpected places. One man needing a toilet, went into an abandoned house. After he was finished, he pulled the chain and the cistern exploded above his head wounding him critically.

The Belgian Brigade was forced to advance with the maximum amount of caution. The bomb disposal unit was the busiest, together with field security, in their task of finding out how many sympathisers amongst the French, the enemy had left behind to inform on the strength of the allied army.

For Rene's French second cousin, Colonel Pierre Billotte, this was to be the climax of the battle he had waged against his country's aggressors since May 1940. He had been placed in command of a motorised brigade which formed part of General Philippe Leclerc's 2nd Army Division. This in turn was under the command of US Army General Leonard T. Gerow.

SHAEF, the Supreme Headquarters Allied European Forces, which included members of the American and British general staff, did not give a high priority to the retaking of Paris from the Germans. Their plan was to bypass Paris and push on to the German frontier. In this way German army units, in and around Paris, would be encircled and cut off from reinforcements and supplies. De Gaulle and the leadership of the Free French had other plans. For them the liberation of Paris had both symbolic importance, as well as the practical aim of boosting the morale of the French people and making them more willing to engage in resistance to the enemy. Following the Battle of Normandy Leclerc had pressed the American generals, Bradley and Patton, both superior to him in the chain of command, to turn their attention to Paris. Patton had initially roundly dismissed Leclerc's wishes.

However, it soon became apparent that events would compel a rethink of the issue. On 19th August the French Resistance Movement had instigated a rising in the city against the Germans. This was almost certainly encouraged by the French military leadership, which had close links to the leadership of the resistance. For a time Allied commanders wavered, uncertain how to respond to the situation. On 21st August De Gaulle urged Eisenhower to allow the French 2nd Division to press on to Paris. Later that same day, Leclerc knowing that the situation in the city was precarious, as lightly armed resistance groups engaged German units, ordered Lieutenant Colonel de Guillebon with ten tanks, ten armoured cars and 150 men to advance directly to Paris. General Gerow at first ordered Leclerc to recall de Guillebon, but at a meeting on 22nd August learned that Eisenhower had decided that Leclerc's entire 2nd Division should move on Paris.

At 6.30 a.m. on 23rd August they commenced their advance from positions outside the city. Leclerc intended that the city should be approached by two columns, one from the north via Versailles and the other from the south via Fresnes Croix de Berny. Pierre Billotte had command of the First French Army Brigade, assigned to make its approach from the south.Both battle groups were keen to achieve the honour of being the first to the city, but both encountered heavier resistance from the Germans than expected particularly from their 88mm artillery guns and the problem of mine fields. Eventually a small detachment of troops led by Captain Raymond Dronne entered Paris at 10.30 p.m. on the 24th August.

The next morning Dronne's detachment was reinforced by units from Pierre Billotte's brigade. By 10.30 a.m. Pierre Billotte was sufficiently confident of the ground his troops had secured to issue the following ultimatum to General Dietrich Von Choltitz, the Commandant of all German forces in the Paris region:

"During all yesterday my brigade has crushed all opposed strong points. It inflicted heavy losses and took numerous prisoners. This morning I entered Paris and my tanks occupy the Ile de Cite area. Large armoured units, French and Allied will join me soon. I estimate that from a strictly military point of view, the resistance of German troops in charge of defending Paris cannot be efficient any more. In order to prevent any useless bloodshed, it belongs to you to put an end to all resistance immediately. In the event that you estimate it would be good to carry on a struggle that no military matter could justify, I am determined to pursue it until total extermination.In the opposite case, you would be treated according to the laws of war. I am waiting for your answer for half an hour from the delivery of this ultimatum ."

The ultimatum was signed General Pierre Billotte. Pierre reasoned that for Von Choltitz to surrender to an officer of inferior rank to his own would be grossly humiliating, so he had styled himself general to spare his adversary's feelings. He need not have concerned himself. Following a rather longer than half hour delay, Von Choltitz signified his surrender of all forces under his command close to midday. For Pierre Billotte his reward was to be confirmed in the rank of general. Within a month he had been given command of the French 10th Infantry Division and became military governor of Rhineland Hesse Nassau following the occupation of Germany. From 1946 to 1950 he was France's military representative at the United Nations. He later went on to establish a political career as a left Gaullist deputy in the National Assembly and held two ministerial posts, first as Minister of Defence in the government of Edgar Faure and then as Minister of Overseas Territories from 1966 to 1968 in the government of Georges Pompidou. From 1965 to 1977 he also served as Mayor of the Paris suburb of Creteil, overseeing its development as a 'garden suburb'.

Soon units of the Belgian Brigade, including Rene's were provided with transport to Paris. From there, transport was supposed to be provided by the Americans, but something went wrong over liaison and they had to wait a whole day. Rene had quite a job keeping his men together in Paris, recently liberated and still celebrating.

Following the liberation of Paris the Belgian forces were again engaged in the task of clearing the enemy out of Normandy and northern France. Rene's company were sent into action approaching Le Havre, which had still to be liberated. One young officer named Lieutenant Freddy Verhaegen volunteered to be taken by the French Resistance, dressed in civilian clothes into Le Havre. They crossed the River Seine by boat. He then spent several hours in Le Havre, to assess the strength of the German garrison occupying that important port.

The Belgian forces had been earmarked to free Le Havre, but just as they were preparing to attack, information came that Brussels was likely to fall into Allied hands at any time. However, they were all anxious to move on, because they wanted to be in Brussels for the liberation. At last, some British transport was provided and they rushed to Brussels.

Brussels 4 September 1944

The high command wanted the Belgian Brigade to be the first to enter the capital. Orders came for the Brigade to be detached from the Second Canadian Army and to move at speed towards Brussels. In fact the Brigade reached the outskirts of Brussels just behind the Guards Regiment. The scene was indescribable. The population were overjoyed. A few hours earlier, people had been listening secretly and, at some danger to themselves, to the news and wondering if the announcement of an allied advance was reality or just propaganda. Then, like wild fire, the word spread ahead of the liberating forces, but it was only when the first tanks appeared at the end of a street, that the real jubilation started. On every flag pole, on every balcony, the Belgian flag suddenly appeared. These flags, hidden in the most amazing places, had been waiting for months to be displayed once more, without fear of reprisal.

As the Guards were approaching the city, the crowds in the street swelled to such an extent that the advance of the army columns was reduced to less than five miles an hour. People were ecstatic, shouting "Welcome" in English and throwing flowers in the path of the advancing troops. When the Belgian Brigade came on the scene, this enthusiasm increased in intensity, turning into a real frenzy. Taking no notice of the warnings of officers and NCOs, girls managed to climb onto the vehicles, flatly refusing to come down. They kissed the soldiers, often endangering the visibility of the driver. It was a miracle that nobody got hurt. It was a worrying time for the tank, Bren gun carrier and other commanders who were trying to stop the screaming girls from distracting the attention of their drivers.

The Brigade crossed Brussels from east to south, where its vehicles were taken to army barracks. With the exception of a few men placed on guard duty, all the men were allowed to go and celebrate in the city. Many came back drunk that evening, without having spent a penny. All the free drinks were offered either by the publicans, or by the guests. When Rene rejoined the Brigade the next day, the celebrations were still in full swing. He had gone to see numerous friends, many of whom had wondered what had become of him.

Antwerp, Belgium, 5 September 1944

The next day he got a pass to travel to Antwerp. There a nasty shock was waiting for him. He found the house in which he had spent so man happy years with his parents and sister, still standing. When he rang the bell, the door was opened by the family's old butler. Rene's presence seemed to give him a shock. He probably suspected, possibly hoped, Rene dead. Now, like a ghost, here Rene was, facing him, and he seemed uneasy. He showed Rene that the contents of the house had been emptied by the Germans. All that was left were a few crystal chandeliers, the kitchen furniture and the contents of the room occupied by Nicholas, the old butler. All the rest had, according to him, been removed six weeks earlier.

Further investigation revealed that the furniture had been taken with all its contents to a store only one street away There, the Germans had packed all the valuables and burnt all other things, like books, photographs or souvenirs. Whatever was worth taking, was then transported to barges marked ' Destination Germany.' On each crate was stuck a label reading ' Present to the German victims of British bombing from their Belgian friends.' Rene only had a few hours to spend in Antwerp and when he left, after making an inventory of the few remaining pieces, Nicholas, the old butler, seemed very relieved.

The Dutch Border, September 1944

Returning to his unit in Brussels, he was told to get ready for a move. He was posted to the 1st Battalion as second in command of a company of machine gunners on Bren gun carriers. The lieutenant in charge of the platoon drove in the first Bren gun carrier. Rene sat or stood next to the driver of the last vehicle. The order came to move in a north easterly direction towards the Belgian border. Intelligence reports informed them that the German forces had left the whole of the Belgian territory, but were digging in on the Dutch border. They made for a place called Ittervoort which is in Limburg and known as the 'three frontier area', because the Belgian, Dutch and German borders meet at this point. They had been warned to be very careful and to distrust the local population whose proximity to the German border and the similarity of language to German, had made them likely sympathisers with the enemy. The company were billeted in several farms. The people seemed to accept them with reluctance and they could feel a certain amount of hostility towards them. They only spent one night in Ittervoort and were glad to move on.

The next village on Dutch territory was called Thorn. When they reached it, they found the Germans waiting for them. A patrol was sent forward to test the strength of the enemy. It was commanded by Freddy Verhaegen, the young lieutenant who had taken the risk of spying out German positions in Le Havre. They progressed through Thorn without seeing any enemy, but as they came to the last house of the village, they were met by heavy machine gun fire. Treacherously, the machine gun was concealed in a haystack, just outside the village. Lieutenant Verhaegen was fatally wounded and so were two of his men. The others took cover and with the use of their Bren gun, showered the hay stack with bullets. Meanwhile a mortar attack had been ordered and minutes later the hay stack was ablaze. Those Germans who were still able to escape from the burning hay, met with a sudden death at the hands of the company's gunners. The death of Freddy Verhaegen was avenged.

The Germans, it was later found out, had retreated a good distance from Thorn and the men hidden in the haystack had been placed there as a rear guard defence. The company commanding officer, in his wisdom, decided to stop the advance in Thorn until further information was available on the true position and the strength of the German forces they were facing.

On the second day of their stay in Thorn, Rene took his turn on watch. The observation post was located inside the drying shed of a tile factory. Hidden by the tiles, he could see with his binoculars without being seen. During the night, Belgian mine clearance teams got busy, and they soon reported that the field was clear. The Germans, in their hasty retreat, had not had the time to mine the entire area. The Belgians, in turn, decided that the best way of preventing the Germans from coming back and surprising them in the village, was to place as many mines as were available in the fields surrounding it.

Such a mine field had been placed in the fields opposite the tile factory. It was not clear how the Germans found out about the mine field or whether it was just guess work on their part, but suddenly during the day, frightened horses, probably released by them, came galloping in the direction of the mine field. The Belgian forces managed to scare them away by organising a few salvos of mortar fire, near enough to them to make them turn back, but far enough away not to set off any of the mines.

On Rene's second watch, a few days later, as he was scrutinising the "no man's land" with his binoculars, he suddenly noticed a large bull and a cow approaching in the direction of the Belgian lines. Immediately he gave the alert. A smoke screen of mortar shells was dropped behind the animals and a patrol made a sortie to catch them and bring them back safely via the mine field corridor. Rene did not know whether their arrival was accidental or whether the Germans had sent them in the direction of the Belgian positions intending to sacrifice them, with the hope they would set off the mine field. If so, they did not succeed and Rene and his company were looking forward to having some fresh meat in place of the daily tins of corned beef.

An army butcher took possession of the two animals, slaughtered them and then sent quarters of the carcasses to the various units. The Colonel, having heard that Rene had been the first one to detect the animals and to take action, called him personally over the field telephone to congratulate him on his actions and to tell him that as a reward he could choose which part of the bounty he wanted for himself and his men. Rene told the Colonel he was very partial to ox tongue. "All right," he said. "The bull's tongue will be yours." Sure enough, a few hours later, a despatch rider brought Rene a parcel containing a large sized ox tongue. Rene handed it over to the man who acted as his driver and batman and told him to take good care of it until he came off guard duty, when he would personally supervise the preparation of the tongue.

Fifteen minutes before Rene's turn on watch was over, orders came from Brigade HQ to get ready to move. The sector was taken over by the Scots Guards and Rene's company was ordered to move to another sector near the Wessem Canal. As soon as one of the advance units of the Scots Guards came to relieve Rene of his post and when he had passed on to them all the company orders, he went back to his platoon to supervise the loading of the Bren carriers. Shortly after darkness fell his company were on the move.

They drove for about two hours and then the whole column came to a standstill. After a short wait, instructions came. "Dismount, take all your arms, ammunition and supplies out of the carriers. You will progress for about two miles on foot. The Bren carriers will move to the next village." The purpose of this exercise, was to take over positions left by another unit. This had to be done in silence so that the enemy would not realise that the Belgians had taken over their positions. Hence the disappearance of the noisy tracked vehicles and the progress on foot in the direction of the enemy.

However careful they had been to conceal their movement, the Germans must have had wind of it, because they were greeted with a salvo of 88mm fragmentation shells. Rene's platoon took shelter in a wood. This gave them some protection, but the noise of the shrapnel hitting the tops of the trees, the splitting and falling of the branches was terrifying. As soon as the shelling quietened down, they were ordered to move forward.

A reconnaissance party was sent in advance of Rene's company. It reported back that the enemy had crossed the canal and that the area south of the canal was safe. On the strength of this information, they were instructed to by-pass the trenches previously occupied by another unit and prepare new positions five hundred yards from the canal's edge. This meant digging a series of new trenches. They were specifically told that their new trenches had to be ready and camouflaged before dawn, which resulted in them digging feverishly the whole night. Rene's men achieved the impossible and they even managed to build him a shelter for use as a command post. Near an abandoned farm they found a heavy door. This was used as a roof for the shelter and two feet of earth on top of it protected it against possible falling shrapnel. Three sides of the shelter were dug vertically down into the earth and the fourth side faced onto the trench with two army blankets used as a doorway.

Thus, inside the shelter, Rene could read any messages coming from the company HQ and he could allow the men to come in turn to light a cigarette inside it, without risk of being seen by the enemy. Positioned in the trench, on each side of the shelter, were the two machine guns belonging to Rene's company. Well before dawn, he was able to report to the platoon commander that the work of digging in had been completed and that they were properly camouflaged against aerial observation.

Their Colonel had decided on a very unusual course of action. Normally machine guns are support weapons placed behind the infantry, shooting above and ahead of it, to compel the enemy to lie low whilst the infantry advances. In this particular case, gunners from motorised companies were placed in front of the infantry. The reason was that the High Command had given these Belgian units the task of covering a front normally held by a full brigade. This extends 16 miles and is usually protected by 2000 men. The Belgian Brigade only counted

3500 men all told, including the non combatant support services, which meant that it never had more than 435 men in the front line at one and the same time. It did not matter much by day, as visibility between posts was good in the flat terrain on which they were positioned and the cross fire of their machine guns could keep the enemy at bay. During the night however, they had to be organised for all round defence because their thinness on the ground meant the enemy could infiltrate their lines unnoticed and undetected.

To prevent any surprise incursion, Rene was instructed to place, well ahead of their lines, a protective system of booby traps. This consisted of metal rods placed vertically in the ground and rising approximately eighteen inches above it. The distance between these rods was approximately thirty yards. The top of each rod was shaped into a two pronged fork. In each of these an empty cigarette tin was placed, lying sideways. A Mills grenade was then lodged in the cigarette tin and a very fine metal trip wire was fastened to the next rod in line. Once all the grenades were in place, all Rene had to do was to go from one rod to the next and remove the safety pin from the grenade. The idea was simply that if an enemy patrol attempted to infiltrate the Belgian lines, they would hopefully, trip against the wire. A grenade would fall out of the cigarette tin, releasing the sprung lever, which in turn would set off the grenade.

It was well known that the Germans were good at detecting these trip wires by having one man move in front of the patrol, swinging a plumb line at the end of a rope. If the plumb line touched a trip wire, the man would feel it, but the weight of the plumb line string would not be strong enough to set off the grenade. He would then alert and stop the patrol, go down on his knees and search with a careful hand until he located the trip wire, which he would carefully cut. In order to avoid this risk Rene had placed a second line of booby traps nearer to their positions and in the immediate vicinity of the Belgian trenches, he had placed a line of booby flares. These were placed in the same way as the grenade booby traps, but would only set off a flare with a glowing red light which burned for about 30 seconds. They were bright enough to allow defenders to detect the outlines of the enemy, but didn't burn long enough for the enemy to detect their positions.

With the help of a half a dozen men, Rene started work on installing this layer of protection after dusk on the night of the company's arrival at their new positions and completed this work soon after darkness fell, so as not to be seen from the enemy lines. Whilst in these advanced positions, Rene knew they would not be disturbed by any oversight from higher authority and in defiance of customary orders, he wore his beret instead of his helmet which was hurting his head. Some of his legionnaires did the same, but their new recruits obediently wore their helmets as they had been trained to do at the training camp they had freshly come from.

During the third and last night of their stay in these positions, the Germans started again to plaster them with their 88mm fragmentation shells. Some shrapnel fragments were so big that they made the strangest noises whilst whizzing through the air. At one particular moment, Rene thought he heard the noise of an approaching motorbike and he was a bit puzzled why a despatch rider would drive through that hell fire. He soon discovered that what he had taken for the noise of a motorbike, was a fragment of shrapnel circling down and falling a few yards away from their trenches. A few minutes later there was another explosion right above their heads. The two young recruits standing on Rene's right side went down on their knees and at the same time, brought their heads down under the parapet of the trench. In doing so they exposed the back of their necks, and it was here that both were hit, practically simultaneously. Both boys were dead by the time members of the company reached them.

An hour later there was another burst of 88mm shell fire and soon after that Rene's field telephone rang. He was summoned from his post by the company commander, who informed him that a piece of shrapnel had fallen on a trip wire and had set off a booby flare which needed to be replaced. He asked Rene if he could come to his command post, where he would show him exactly where the flare was, which needed replacing.

To get from his outpost to the company HQ, Rene followed a row of fruit trees. At the end of the orchard and in line with the row of trees he was following, he came to the abandoned farm, where he found the captain in command of the company. He gave Rene a briefing and a man armed with a rifle, who was supposed to act as look out and protect him, whilst he worked on replacing the flare. All outposts had been warned by field telephone that Rene was moving to the south of their defences. He soon found the flare that had been fired and replaced it. All this had to be done in the dark. Whilst he was fixing the trip wire to the new flare there was a new burst of incoming 88mm shell fire. As soon as that had stopped Rene and his aide hurried back to report to the captain on the mission completed.

"Thank you very much," he said. "Will you find your way back to your trench?"

"Sure Sir, quite easily," replied Rene." All I have to do is to follow this row of trees and it leads me straight to it!"

"Good. Do you want a man for protection to go with you?"

"No Sir, that will to be unnecessary."

With these words Rene left. But he mistakenly followed the row of trees on the right of the one he had followed coming, which instead of leading him straight to his trench, brought him a bit to the right and in front of it.

By so doing he ran into his own row of booby traps and set off one of his flares. His first concern was not to be spotted by the enemy, so he threw himself flat on the ground, but the section nearest to his own had seen the flare go up and a figure go down on the ground. Thinking that it was a German patrol, they started to fire in Rene's direction with a Bren gun. The bullets fell so close to him that earth ricocheted in his face, but by pure luck not one of the projectiles hit him.

Whilst lying on the ground with the flare still alight, he had managed to see where his trench was. He was to the right of it and twenty yards in front. As soon as the flare went out, he made a dash for his trench. When he reached it he was met by one of his legionnaires on guard, who said to Rene, "Well Sarge, you are lucky that you got up just a fraction of a second before the flare went out and I recognised your balaclava. I thought it was a German and I was ready to shoot when he got up, but luckily I recognised you in time." He certainly would not have missed Rene had he not recognised him. Rene had tried to draw his attention whilst lying on the ground, but the noise of the hissing flare and the direction of the wind had carried his voice in the direction of the other section, who very suddenly and providentially, stopped firing.

The day after that happened, they finished their spell in the front line and as soon as dusk fell, they handed over their position to another battalion and they went to the rear for a well earned rest of four days. As soon as they returned to the village behind the lines, Rene met his driver and enquired about the ox tongue which in his hurry he had left in the Bren Carrier. The driver came out with a story which Rene never came to believe. According to him, when he found the tongue it was smelling and not fit for consumption and he had to throw it away. Rene was convinced that he had sold it to the villagers for a good price.

The four days were over very quickly and when they got back to their same trenches they found that there was less noise from the 88mm German guns, but that their own artillery, supported by the British and Americans, had become very active. The noise was as deafening, but they felt more secure than before. To Rene's surprise, one evening they got an unannounced visit from their Colonel and several of his officers. He seemed quite pleased with the way they had organised themselves. Before leaving he told Rene confidentially, that they would soon be moving, as a big action was imminent.

Action at last came on the 16th October. Luckily or unluckily, Rene's company's participation in it was pretty small. From 4 o'clock in the afternoon on that day, the combined artilleries started to shell the German positions. This went on non stop until 8p.m. They found themselves dazed by the continuous noise of the shells passing above their heads, so they could imagine the state of mind of the Germans who were at the end of the trajectory. At eight o'clock precisely the shelling stopped and was followed by a deadly silence.

At two minutes past eight, intense light provided by search light units which had advanced to the vicinity of the canal during the shelling, suddenly shone in the enemy's direction. This was intended to blind them and prevent them from seeing what the allied forces next had in store for them. The search lights had drawn some expected reaction from the Germans. Their machine guns and some automatic weapon fire tried to hit the search lights. This is what the Allied forces were waiting for, because they were now able to exactly locate the places where the firing was coming from. This was of particular importance to the flame thrower units mounted on Bren carriers which, before the end of the artillery barrage, had placed themselves very near the edge of the canal. At five minutes past eight, all hell was let loose. From the Allied side of the canal, Rene could see long sheets of flame cross the canal in regular bursts and land on enemy positions. Some sporadic machine gun fire still came from one or two bunkers on the other side, but one or two more bursts from the flame throwers neutralised this opposition within seconds. Rene saw later, the results of this use of the flame throwers on the protective doors and window shutters of the German bunkers. They had buckled like sheets of paper under the intense heat of the flames.

Whilst all this had been going on, some giant amphibious tracked vehicles supplied by the Americans and each containing a Bren carrier with a complete crew, had slowly advanced to the edge of the canal. They crossed the canal and reached the northerly side without meeting any opposition. As they climbed the other bank of the canal they advanced another hundred yards and turned in a half circle. The rear door was lowered, forming a ramp, and down it drove the Bren carriers.

For the next twelve miles until they reached the bank of a tributary of the Rhine called the River Waal, which flows into the Rhine near its mouth, they did not meet any opposition. As they advanced they found hundreds of German soldiers looking very haggard and dejected, only too keen on surrendering. The Allied troops did not even bother to round them up. They were simply told by gesture that they should march in a southerly direction with their rifles carried horizontally at the end of their upstretched arms. Once they reached the north side of the Wessem Canal, specially organised troops disarmed them, embarked them, packed by the dozens in the amphibious craft, which conveyed them to the south side of the canal to be marched to hastily organised POW camps.

Louvain, Belgium 17 October 1944

Rene only saw the beginning of this phase of the operation along the Rhine because as soon as the positions along the Waal were secured, the Belgian Brigade were informed that they were temporarily being withdrawn from the front line. The next day, being Rene's birthday, was easy to remember, because in addition, the Brigade moved back to Belgium. First they spent a few days in Louvain. Rene had remembered the kind gentleman he had met in 1940 during his trip from Toulouse to Lourdes and who had insisted on giving him and his cousin Roger Adler money, lived in Louvain. Rene had kept his address and went to his home with the intention of repaying him. He was met by the lady of the house who informed him that her husband had been arrested after the occupation of the south of France by the Germans and had died in a concentration camp. The son, for whom the poor man had had such worries and for whom he had been searching,was back home, but terribly emaciated after the years spent in compulsory labour in a German work camp.

Whilst in Louvain a rota was organised for the men to spend one week at home with their families. When Rene's turn came, he mentioned to his commanding officer that his parents were last heard of in the south of France. He told Rene that he had no authority to give him a leave pass to France, but after consultation with the Colonel and the Field Security Officer,it was decided to send Rene on a contrived mission to the American security HQ in Nice. In fact it only involved Rene taking documents to them, which could easily have gone by army mail.

This having been decided, Rene was issued with a document stating that he was going on a special mission and asking all military authorities to give him aid and assistance. One of the Brigade's jeeps took Rene to Paris. There he had to report to a British Transport Officer at Le Bourget Airport. He informed Rene that owing to fog the airport was closed. He gave Rene a letter of introduction to a hotel requisitioned by the British army and told him to report back at the airport the next day.

When Rene got to Le Bourget the next morning, the fog was nearly as thick as the day before, but when he reported to the Transport Officer he was told there might be a chance to get away. The sergeant told Rene that a US Air Force Dakota loaded with urgently needed equipment was going to attempt to take off, destination Marseilles. He told Rene that the pilot was only prepared to take two passengers. One was an American Colonel, the other would be Rene. He told him to make himself inconspicuous. "You may have noticed the three British officers, passing the hall. They too have a mission order for the south. I don't want them to see you, because one of them may want to take your place."

Rene sat quietly in a corner of the Operations Room and a few minutes later, a sergeant came to fetch him and took him straight onto the tarmac. Conditions were pretty bad, with hardly any visibility. When Rene got into the Dakota, he found there were no seats at all. The centre of the aircraft was full of large wooden crates stacked on top of one another and securely strapped to the floor. On one side there were some smaller, but longer crates, used by some of the men as seats. They made room for Rene and offered him three boxes of packed meals. The American Colonel came to sit next to Rene and whilst they started a conversation, a crewman placed straps around their waists and attached them to rails running along the inside of the aircraft's cabin.

Soon the engines revved up and they took off without being able to see anything through the cabin window other than the thick fog enveloping the plane. The pilot made a very steep ascent and within minutes they were cruising well above the clouds. This was the first time in a very long time that Rene had seen the sun and blue sky. The captain in charge of the aircraft came into the cabin and invited the Colonel and Rene to join him in the cockpit. He warned them that there were no seats and that they would have to stand behind his and his co-pilot's seat. The pair accepted the invitation and had a most enjoyable flight. The captain told them it was touch and go whether they had managed to take off from Le Bourget and if he had not had such an urgent consignment, he would not hake taken the risk of doing so.

The next problem came when they reached Marignane Control, where the pilot was informed that the airport was closed due to fog and he was instructed to land at Istres, 40 kilometers west of Marseilles. As they approached Istres, the captain spotted a small gap in the dense clouds. "Hold tight," he shouted to them and plunged into the gap like a fighter pilot. They descended below the clouds in a few seconds and were now making a direct approach to the grass covered airfield.

During this rapid descent, Rene suddenly felt a piercing pain in his left ear, as if a needle had pierced it. Next he had the impression of liquid running into it. He found out later that a vein had burst and resulted in a small haemorrhage which left him deaf in one ear for many days. As they were about to touch down, the captain reassuringly said, "Well friends, here comes the tricky moment. Last week one of my friends was blown up on a mine in this field." After these reassuring words he brought the aircraft down quite skilfully and Rene gave a sigh of relief when the wheels finally stopped turning. At Istres Airport their arrival had been anticipated and they were ushered to waiting jeeps.

Marseilles To Nice, October 1944

They were driven straight to the Canebiere in Marseilles. The offices of Thomas Cook had been requisitioned by the American forces and were used as billeting offices. Rene handed over his mission orders to a U.S. lieutenant who told him it was too late to proceed to Nice that same day. He would arrange for a room for him for that night and a jeep would take him to Nice the next morning. He got Rene a very nice room in a nearby hotel and suggested that he should come and have dinner with him at his Officers' Mess. He arranged to come and pick Rene up at his hotel around dinner time.

As Rene had two hours in front of him before their meeting, he took his limited luggage to his hotel room, had a wash and then decided to pay a visit to an old lady friend of his family who lived in Marseilles. He got to her flat, rang the bell and the old lady came to open the door and invited him in. He told her he was on his way to visit his parents, but the old lady had become deaf since the last time he had seen her two years earlier. She misunderstood what Rene had told her and said "Well, since you found out the sad news, I may just as well give you your mother's last message." She went to a writing cabinet, opened it and out of a drawer came an envelope containing a note which she handed over to Rene. He immediately recognised his mother's handwriting. The message read "They are taking us away without hope of return. We're very unhappy. If ever you see Rene don't tell him anything about it." He was stunned.

For a few moments he read and re-read the terrible message, then he tried to find out how the message had reached the old lady. All she could tell him was that one day the door bell had rung and when she opened the door, there was nobody there, but she had found in the letter box the envelope containing the short note. Since she could throw no further light on the subject, Rene left her and went back to his hotel room. As soon as he was on his own, he let go of his emotions and started to cry like a child.

When the U.S. lieutenant called for him from the porter's desk, Rene told him on the internal telephone that he had just had terribly bad news about his parents and sister and that he did not think that under the circumstances he would be good company for him. The lieutenant asked, "May I come up a moment to your room." "By all means do," Rene replied. A few seconds later he knocked at the door. Rene opened it and the lieutenant saw straight away what a state he was in. "Tell me all about it," he said. "Sometimes it can he a relief to talk about it to someone else."

Rene told him of his visit to the old lady and of his mother's message. He could see that the lieutenant was very moved, by his immediate reactions. "My friend," he said. "please accept my deepest sympathy. Locking yourself up to brood over your sorrow is no good. You must come with me to the Mess and take one or two stiff drinks and you will feel much better." He was so insistent that eventually Rene gave in. This was probably for the best.

When they got to the Mess, he introduced Rene to several of his colleagues. Before dinner he was given a large glass of Bourbon. During the dinner Rene shared a table with the Billeting Officer and two of his colleagues. He was a professional opera singer who had lived in New York until the start of the war and his two companions came from the opposite side of the USA. They talked very little about themselves and insisted on hearing more about how Rene had managed to get out of France and why his parents had not tried to follow him. Rene told them about his father's stubbornness and refusal to move away from Grasse, though Rene had insisted he should try to get to England.

By the time the evening was over, they had so filled Rene with drinks that two of them had to take him back to the hotel. He suspected they had even helped him to undress and find his bed. The next morning, before going to his office, the lieutenant came to wake Rene and to tell him that a jeep would first take him to a US military hospital to see to his deaf ear. Next he would be driven to Nice to the Ritz Hotel, headquarters of the US Security Services. Rene thanked his host for his kindness to him before he drove off east.

At the hospital, having found that the abrupt descent in the Dakota had burst the blood vessel and caused the haemorrhage obstructing Rene's ear, the doctor syringed it and told him that there was nothing else that could be done for him for the time being and that he would remain deaf in that ear for a week or so.

Before leaving the hospital Rene was offered a meal and for the first time discovered how wasteful the US troops could be. The Mess was organised on a self-service line, so that instead of helping yourself to the quantity of food you could reasonably consume, you instead queued up until you reached a hatch in front of the kitchen where your meal was simply handed to you on a metal tray. The tray was formed of several indented compartments to accommodate the courses of the soldier's meal. In one compartment was the soup, in another a slice of steak, big enough to feed two men, potatoes and vegetables were in another and a further one was reserved for the sweet.

With his shrunken stomach, Rene hardly ate half of the tray's contents. When he was finished, he followed other soldiers to the bins outside where they had to empty the remains of their meal from the tray. Before he could tip the contents of his tray into the bin, he was surrounded by French children asking him to tip the leftovers into containers brought by them. This he did, but was disgusted to see that many US soldiers refused and preferred to dump the leftovers in the dustbins.

His jeep driver had been waiting for him during his meal and they left immediately for Nice. They got to the Ritz Hotel in the late afternoon and Rene presented his mission orders at the check-in desk. A soldier was instructed to show him to the office of the captain in charge of security, but the captain was not there. The soldier invited Rene to take a seat and wait for his return. He was left alone in that office for quite a while and experienced for the first time how relaxed US army security seemed to be. All filing cabinets appeared to be unlocked. Stacks of documents were piled on the captain's desk and had he wanted to, he could have gone through the lot of them. When, eventually, the captain came, Rene showed him his mission orders. "Good. Can I see your security identity card now please?"

"Certainly Sir." But as Rene opened the left breast pocket of his uniform jacket, he suddenly discovered that his identity card was missing.

"This is very serious," said the captain. "You are here in a high security building. What has happened to your card?"

"Well Sir, I remember last using it at Le Bourget Airport. I can only have lost it either in the plane, the US army hotel, or the jeep that brought me here." Rene did remember opening that pocket to take out a handkerchief when he had felt the piercing pain in his ear during the flight in the Dakota. He therefore suggested that the most likely place would be the plane's cockpit.

"I shall organise a search for your identity card, but meanwhile I have to put you under close arrest until it is found." He telephoned and a few minutes later a young lieutenant appeared. The captain told him in a few words what had happened and told the lieutenant he was to guard Rene. He suggested that an extra bed should be installed for Rene in the lieutenant's room.

Once there, Rene explained to the lieutenant the sequence of events which had led to the losing of his ID card. "Now," said the lieutenant, somewhat taciturnly, "all this upsets my plans for tonight. I was going to go out with a nice French bird. I suppose I will have to cancel my date."

"Is she on the telephone?" asked Rene."

"Yes, she is."

"Why don't you ask her if she has a sister or a nice friend and then the four of us could go out together."

"That is a brilliant idea," the lieutenant said and immediately proceeded to ring his girlfriend. Sure, she had a friend willing to come and after Rene had given his word of honour that he would not try to escape, they went to meet the two girls and spent a very a nice 'close arrest' in one or two dancing and night clubs in Nice.

They returned to their room in the early hours of the morning. Rene had a very short sleep, because at ten o'clock he was called into the captain's office to be told, to his enormous relief, that his identity card had been found. As he had suspected, when he had pulled his handkerchief out of his pocket, the card had fallen on the floor of the cockpit immediately behind the captain's seat. Rene had to spend another night in Nice, but no longer under close arrest, to await the return of his ID card.

He took advantage of that day to complete the mission he had been sent on. After that he intended making his way to Grasse to find out what he could about his parent's arrest and deportation. When he reached Grasse, he went straightaway to the villa where his parents were living when he left them in 1942. The villa was called 'Villa des Anges,' – the Villa of the Angels. It was situated in a quiet road, immediately below and parallel to the main road from Grasse to Nice. The villa and the front garden were nearly at street level, but the rear garden formed a downward slope from which could be seen a valley and in clear weather, Cannes and the Mediterranean Sea.

The old lady owning the place told Rene how the Gestapo had come twice; first to investigate, next to arrest his parents. She could not throw much light on the reasons for their arrest, but she gave him one precious bit of information. His sister had apparently been working during the months preceding the arrest for a Doctor Colomban, who was also Mayor of Grasse at the time.

The doctor was away when Rene arrived to visit him, but his daughter gave him all the details of the first investigation and of his family's arrest. The Gestapo had arrived early one morning at the Villa des Anges saying that they had been informed that Rene had left for England and they wanted to know who had helped him. His parents had denied all knowledge of how he had got away, saying that he was not living with them and only visited them occasionally. Next they had said to Rene's father, "You are a Jew." Franz had denied it, but they had said "We will come back and prove it to you." Franz thought that he was safe, first because he did not belong to any religious community and secondly because he was an ex-officer who had served in the Austrian army in the 1914-18 war.

When Rene's sister, Georgette had given the details of this first investigation to Doctor Colomban, he had said, "They definitely will come back. Tell your father to pack your belongings and the three of you, each come with a suitcase and I shall hide you somewhere in the country." That same afternoon Georgette had come back in tears and said "My father thanks you for your kind offer, but he refuses. He says he has nothing to fear. As an ex-officer, they won't touch him."

The next day the Gestapo came back and took all three away by car to the Gestapo headquarters in Nice, the infamous Villa Mont Fleuri. Doctor Colomban's daughter told Rene that there was a rumour in town that his parents had been denounced by a painter decorator, who had been working in the Villa de Anges. This rumour was confirmed by several other people Rene met and at their suggestion he went to the police, to enter a formal complaint. He then went with a detective to the house of the suspected man. On their way they had agreed on tactics.

When they got to the fellow's home, his wife opened the door. The detective showed his warrant card and they were taken into the lounge, where her husband was to be found. The conversation started quietly enough with the police officer asking,"You remember the Falkenau family who lived at Villa des Anges, Avenue Riou Blanquet?"

"Certainly I do. I was there working when the Gestapo came to arrest them."

"Why were they arrested?"

"Well they were bloody Jews," said the man in an offhand manner.

"Did you have anything to do with their arrest?"

"No," he retorted, unconvincingly.

"By the way," said the police officer, "I forgot to introduce you, this is the son of the victims."

At this point the painter became very pale, then trying to compose himself, said, "Pleased to meet you sir. Your sister often talked to me about you."

Rene had ignored the hand he advanced to shake his and before Rene could say a word the detective said "In what way did Mademoiselle Falkenau talk about her brother?"

"She told me that he was in England and fighting for the good cause."

Now, the detective's line of questioning toughened and his tone hardened."To whom have you told what you knew about the son?"

"To nobody," replied the man.

A few more questions and the detective was as convinced as Rene that the fellow was lying. They left his house and once outside they compared impressions.

Rene had only a limited number of days available and wanted to see as many people he had known in the south between 1940 and 1942 as possible. At the detective's suggestion, he entered a formal complaint with the Republic's Prosecutor. This would allow the investigation to go on without his presence. It was suspected from things that Rene learned that the painter had sold the information about his parents to the Gestapo for 3000 Francs.

From Grasse he went back to Nice to see the civilian police there and to find out if they had any records of who had passed through the Villa Mont Fleuri. Here he discovered that before retreating, following the US landings in St Raphael, the Gestapo had had time to destroy all the records of their crimes. The only trace of their presence was a pile of bodies found in the cellar.

Rene was given a series of photographs of just the faces of these dead people. They were all of local people that the Gestapo had shot before evacuating the villa. Amongst them was a pretty 18 year old girl. Before killing her, the Germans must have tortured her, because Rene could still see on her face and body, traces of cigarette bums. The French police gave him these photos to keep as a reminder of what the Germans had done.

He was told that in Nice the best place to get the information he wanted was to contact the Ministry of War Victims and Refugees in Paris. It was likely that after a very short stay at the Gestapo headquarters in Nice, that his parents had been moved by train to the transit camp situated in Drancy near Paris.

His next journey was to St Raphael, where he met many of the people he had had business with during the two years he had stayed in the south of France. Many of these too, had disappeared, either deported or killed by the Gestapo, or as a result of having moved to another part of the country for their own safety.One of the first people he met was Madame Osee and her son, the owners of the Hotel Diana. She had heard rumours of his parent's arrest, but never any details. Not knowing that Rene was married now, she said, "Well Rene, now that you have lost your parents, consider me as your second mother. If, when you are released from the army you want to come and live with us, you will be very welcome." Rene thanked her for her kind offer and told her that he was married, that his wife expected a baby to be born in England in December and that when he was released from the army, he would have to choose between going to live in his parent's home in Antwerp or settling down in England.

He also met several other people, the Pastorellis, owners of the restaurant where he used to eat, Denis the customs officer, who had been so helpful, and many others. All told him that after his departure in 1942, they had been listening anxiously every day to the BBC, until one day they heard the agreed sentence, telling them that Rene had reached England safely. Apparently, those who had not heard the radio were told by those who had listened in and the news circulated around St Raphael amongst all his friends. Several told him they had been visited by his parents, but although they seemed to be apprehensive about their fate, nobody had managed to convince his father that it was time to go into hiding. They tried, vainly, to talk him into into it, but he wouldn't listen.

Having seen all those he wanted to see and found out more sad news than he was prepared for, Rene had to make his way to rejoin his company. Again, in a US Army Dakota, he was flown from Marseilles to Paris, there he was transferred to a small British Auster aircraft for the journey from Paris to Brussels.

On arrival in Brussels, he found out that his Brigade was in Brussels for the day, to attend a victory parade. It was not difficult to find out that they were all lined up on the main boulevard ready to parade in front of Prince Charles, brother of King Leopold, who was acting as a regent. He found his platoon, dumped his luggage inside his usual Bren carrier and found out where to rejoin his men after the parade for the journey back to Louvain.

Two days after his return they were notified that they were moving again, this time to St. Niklaas, near Antwerp, but on the opposite side of the River Schelde. They were told they were going there on 'rest and reorganisation'. They got there around four o'clock in the afternoon. The men were settled in the old barracks, but officers and NCOs were billeted in private houses near the barracks. Rene went to stay with an extremely nice family called Hermes. Later that afternoon, he went to the barracks to see how the men were settling in. He had his supper in the mess and then walked out of the barracks to the nearest bar at the corner of the street.

He had only been there a few minutes when a violent explosion shook the whole building. The ceiling plaster fell on top of customers, the lights went out, the windows were blown to bits. A few, including Rene rushed out into the street where shouts could be heard from one end to the other. Somebody shouted, "Go to Number 14, a woman is buried under the rubble." With three air force men and a young butcher's boy, Rene rushed into what was left of the building.

With their bare hands, they started to remove bricks and stone. After a while they uncovered the poor old woman, who was lying on her back. They had cleared down to her waist, when she asked them to be careful because she suspected that she had a broken leg. A large stone was lying on top of her legs. They took up positions at the four corners in an effort to lift it. Just as they were about to do so, what they first thought to be another explosion, covered the rescuers with a shower of bricks, beams and plaster.

Rene was the only one who was very lightly hurt. He had a cut on the forehead. It bled profusely for a few minutes but, miraculously, he soon found it was superficial. The three air force boys and the butcher were not so lucky. They were hit by a beam which must have missed Rene by a fraction. They were all taken to hospital and when Rene directed the ambulance men to the place where the old woman was lying, they found she was no longer alive.

It was only one hour later that the cause of the explosion was discovered. A V1 flying bomb meant for Antwerp had overshot the city.

Usually the fuel load was calculated to carry it to Antwerp. Once the fuel was used up, a gyroscope was activated, which made the bomb dive vertically. In this particular case, there was a defective gyroscope and although the engine must have cut out above Antwerp, the bomb went on gliding and came down on St Nikolaas, without the usual warning sound of its engine cutting out being detected.Fourteen houses were flattened. The bomb had fallen on the railway line separating these houses from the rear of the barracks. They found several railway sleepers that had landed in the middle of the exercise yard. The barrack buildings had not been damaged too much, except that all the windows had been blown in and many tiles on the rooves were missing. For the next few days, the men's main activity was to clear the rubble left by the blast.

Antwerp December 1944

On days of leave, they were allowed to go into Antwerp, Brussels or Ghent. Rene chose Antwerp mainly because he was looking out for some of his pre-war friends. Antwerp was not really the place to go to for a restful day. Every five minutes a V bomb was exploding in the city, causing indescribable damage. On one occasion, Rene saw two V bombs circling above the town. He was watching them from the opposite side of the Scheldt. Unaware of the danger to themselves, people were standing there, commenting to each other on the flight of the V bomb. All were probably hoping that their flight paths would cross and the two V bombs would collide and explode in the air.

This, however, did not happen and after a few minutes one engine was to heard stop. The V bomb nose dived and then the loud impact of the explosion was heard, followed by a column of black smoke coming from the direction where the V bomb had fallen. The second bomb fell a few minutes later. In town, nobody seemed to bother very much about the V bombs and life went on uninterrupted.

At the NCOs Mess, situated in the old Hotel Metropole, the shutters had been brought down to protect the large windows against the effects of the blast. A few weeks before the army's arrival, the Germans had started to bomb Antwerp with V2s.They were much more powerful than the V1s and their worst feature was that they were pure rockets.

This meant they came down without any prior warning and the blast of the explosion was ten times more devastating than one of the V1s.

One such rocket had landed and exploded on the stage of the Rese Cinema whilst a show was in progress. Nine hundred people, mostly soldiers, were killed in the cinema and several passers by were either killed or seriously wounded. Whilst Rene was out walking in the city, a V2 fell half a mile away from where he was. The detonation was so powerful that he shook involuntarily for a good two minutes after the explosion.

When he visited his parent's house in the Rue du Palais, he found that a British army postal unit was using the house as an NCO's Mess. Rene made the acquaintance of the sergeant major in charge, who invited him to come and spend the Christmas evening with him and his sergeants. He accepted the invitation and on Christmas Eve 1944, he was a guest in his own house. The turkey had just been placed in the centre of the long table, which extended from one end of the dining room to the other, when once again, a tremendous explosion shook the whole house. The ceiling came crashing down on the assembled company, the windows were blown out, doors were wrenched from their hinges, but no-one was hurt.

Whilst some of the sergeants got busy cleaning the pieces of glass away, the sergeant major recovered the turkey from under the plaster. Blowing on it to remove the powdered dust, he said with a smile and a chuckle, "Well, at least they didn't get our turkey."

A few pieces of cardboard were quickly nailed to the empty window frames and half an hour later, thanks to everyone's combined efforts, they were all seated once more around the big table to carry on their so rudely interrupted dinner. Looking around, the sergeant major said to Rene, "Sorry old chap, they made a bit of a mess of your nice house, but never mind, we will soon make them pay for it." Rene spent the night in the house and the next day he rejoined his unit in St Niklaas.

On New Year's day, he visited Ghent. He had just come back from visiting the people with whom he had stayed whilst stationed in Ghent at the outbreak of the war, when suddenly he heard the noise of machine gun fire. At the same time, he heard the too familiar sound of a German Messerschmidt. Before he had time to take cover, there was the plane at the end of the street, flying very low and shooting into the street in front of its path. As far as he could ascertain nobody in his vicinity got hurt and luckily this was the last time he ever saw a German plane again.

Holland January 1945

By mid-January the reorganised Belgian Brigade moved back into operations in Holland. Following the liberation of Belgium large numbers of new recruits had flocked to join the Brigade. This had always been anticipated by the Allied commanders and so provision had been made for the Brigade to be pulled out of the field to allow time for the training and preparation of these new recruits for operational duties. With its numbers substantially increased the Brigade had been reorganised along more conventional lines, with new infantry units operating independently of the three motorised companies which had formerly made up the major part of the Brigade's fighting strength. Rene had played a full part in the training of these new recruits, both on the parade ground and as a physical training instructor in ensuring their fitness for further military operations

The Brigade had just reached a place called Tiel near the mouth of the Rhine when the post brought Rene the news that Doris had given birth to a son on Boxing Day. He asked for compassionate leave to go and see her, but was told that as an offensive was imminent, all leave had been stopped until further notice. Meanwhile new positions had to be organised. Once more, on account of their proximity to the river, they were vulnerable to attacks from German patrols sent from the other side of the River Waal. The enemy came mainly by night, crossing in inflatable rubber dinghies. Rene and his comrades were kept continually on alert for such attacks. After a few rather harassing weeks, they were told that the Allied forces had moved deeply into Germany and soon they were on the move once more.

Oelde, Westphalia, January 1945

This time they crossed the German border and got to Oelde in Westphalia. All the houses previously owned by Nazis were found to be empty. Their owners had fled before the Allied advance. They were immediately requisitioned for the Brigade's use. Rene was assigned a very luxurious villa near the centre of the town. He lived there alone during the week, attended by two young German girls, who did the cleaning, prepared his breakfast and washed his underwear.

At the weekend, his villa was invaded by teams from the ENSA units sent to entertain the troops and invaded it felt, to the extent that after his first experience of an ENSA unit, he had a big notice nailed to his door and to the door of the adjoining bathroom. The notice read: "Strictly out of Bounds to all troops or MEMBERS OF ENSA." This did the trick, but it was not a remedy for the noise coming from the ground floor rooms. His usually peaceful lounge was turned into a rehearsal room. The carpets were rolled up and full use made of the parquet flooring for tap dance rehearsal. The piano was pretty good, but he wondered how long it would withstand the continuous thumping it received.

As often as his duties permitted, Rene got away for the weekend, but not without first locking his bedroom and bathroom doors. In the early days of the occupation of Germany, troops had been briefed on 'non fraternisation' except for those who like Rene had special duties and for whom speaking with the people was essential. The troops in general were not allowed to speak to the local population. Rene, on the other hand, had to find out as much as possible about local conditions. Who had been Nazis? Were there still some Nazis in the town? One such opportunity presented itself when a local locksmith had to come and repair a lock damaged by a visiting ENSA team. He started the conversation by asking Rene how it felt to live in this villa, which previously belonged to an important Nazi.

"I'd rather see you live in it, than those dirty so and sos," the locksmith said.

"Why do you call them that?" Rene asked. "I bet, not long ago, you were a very good Nazi yourself."

"Never," was the emphatic answer. "I am a Roman Catholic and as such always despised what the party stood for. I never joined the party and I suffered for it."

"Yes? How?" Rene enquired.

"Well, I was put on the same rations as foreign workers," the locksmith replied. "I had to work very often for people of the party who paid me with vouchers, which I am still waiting to be turned into money. Now that you are here, I am not much better off. I am still on small rations and I will also probably be paid with vouchers I can't cash. What I cannot understand is that some people like Dr Habig, the chief engineer of our local factory, who always was an important member of the Nazi Party, has been able to keep his post and does not suffer from any restrictions. This makes us wonder whether you people really want to give us justice."

This conversation made a deep impression on Rene and he immediately got in touch with the Special Branch to ask them whether they knew anything about Dr Habig and if they knew if he had special facilities permitting him to obtain unrationed supplies. The answer Rene received was that yes, they had a file on his past activities in the Nazi Party, but not enough evidence to prosecute him in any way. He had been left in his post because of his technical know how and because his employment in the factory was useful to the Allies.

The answer to the second question was, that as far as was known, he was on the same rations as the rest of the population of Oelde. This intrigued Rene. He sent for the locksmith and asked him to justify what he had previously said. The locksmith then revealed to Rene that he had quite often seen US army jeeps stop in front of Dr Habig's house, unload box after box of goods, which were taken into the house.

Suspecting the existence of an illicit black market, which to a certain extent could endanger field security for which he was responsible, Rene got in touch with the chief of the Military Police. They agreed to put the villa of Dr Habig under 24 hour surveillance and that Rene would be kept informed of the results and consulted on any further action to be taken. They did not have to wait long. On Sunday, around lunchtime, Rene's phone rang. The chief of the Military Police informed him that one of his undercover men had seen two American soldiers transfer a lot of boxes from a jeep into Habig's villa. They were still in the villa and he suggested sending six men and one sergeant to investigate. He offered to have Rene go with the raiding party and informed him that two jeeps were already on their way to meet up with him.

When they got to the villa the US army jeep was still parked at the front door They rang the bell and a maid opened the door. Rene and two military policemen pushed their way in whilst the others stood guard over the US jeep and the various entrances to the house. They found the Habig family having their Sunday lunch and entertaining the two American solders. They were asked to produce their identity cards and whilst one of the MPs questioned them, Rene started questioning Dr.Habig. He admitted that he had been receiving regular food supplies from the two soldiers who, prior to the arrival of Belgian forces, had been stationed in town.

He insisted that the supplies were for his own use and for the use of his family and that he did not sell any of it on the black market. Rene made him open his cellar, where we found all the supplies, including quantities of bottles of French wine, American and British spirits, probably stolen either by his countrymen, or the two American soldiers. On their radio the MPs ordered a three ton lorry with a fatigue to transfer all the goods to police headquarters. They arrested the two American soldiers and Doctor Habig and put them in cells at the local police station where the military police head quarters were situated.

Together with the military police sergeant, Rene started his report on the investigation. Since Rene's and the military policeman's reports went to two different authorities, they wanted to make sure that both were accurate in every detail. Rene did not manage to find his own chief until the late evening and whilst handing over his report to him, answered his various questions concerning the outcome of the investigation. After consultation with the chief of the Military Police, Rene's commanding officer decided that the case was too important to be dealt with at Brigade level and that the reports he and the military police sergeant had filed, were to be sent to the British Divisional Command for further action.

To their disgust, the decision which came back the next day, made them feel their efforts had been a total waste of time. The two American soldiers had to be released, because the British did not want to cause any unpleasant feelings on the part of their allies' forces. Doctor Habig had to be released, because he was indispensable to the running of the factory and all the confiscated goods had to be sent to Division Headquarters. Rene and his colleague were convinced that the Divisional Officers' Mess made good use of them.

From that day relations with Divisional Headquarters went from bad to worse, especially when officers of the Belgian Brigade heard that Divisional Military Police had been raiding cafes and public places, had ordered all the German civilians and British soldiers out of the place and then had started searching the Belgian soldiers on the premises. As soon as the commanders of the Belgian Brigade heard about this, they retaliated by sending their own police parties out to every establishment in their zone, including places reserved to officers. Adopting the same tactics as the British, they made the Germans and Belgians leave the place and submitted the British to a rigorous search. For this they received a protest from Division, but Colonel Piron, commander of the Belgian Brigade, told Divisional Command in no uncertain terms, that as long as they continued to interfere within his sector, he would retaliate. No further incidents took place after this.

Not very long after this, Rene was called into the Adjudant's office and informed that he had been instructed to find a few translators to attend to pre-trial investigations at the Belsen Concentration Camp and also a possible six weeks at the Luneburg trial which would follow. Since he knew of the situation concerning Rene's parents and of his anxiety to get further information about their fate, he had decided to put his name on the list. This would give him a chance to get first hand information from some of the 3000 Belgian Jewesses who had escaped the gas chambers of Auschwitz when the camp was about to be overrun by the Russians, but had been moved before their arrival to Belsen.

Bergen Belsen August 1945

A few days later, Rene arrived in Belsen, too late to see the open graves, often displayed in all their horror, in the Allied press. By then the huts for the inmates had been burnt to the ground and the 18,000 survivors of the camp rehoused in what used to be the barracks reserved for the army and the SS guarding the camp.

Rene was given a room in the NCOs' wing and taken to an office in the administration building. The biggest offices were occupied by the Polish investigators and translators, since the proportion of Polish inmates was much larger than any other contingent.

There were approximately 15,000 Polish women and children, compared with 3,000 Belgian, French, Dutch and other nationalities still in the camp. In the main exercise yard, on a notice board, were pinned the photographs of twenty four of the camp guards accused of war crimes. A notice translated in all languages invited the inmates to report to the investigators. A list of rooms was given, indicating the languages spoken in each room. A warning was given to the inmates to report only what they had seen with their own eyes and not to waste the investigators' time with hearsay, which was not admissible under British law.

As soon as these notices were placed, long queues formed in front of each office and the investigators started work. The inmates were brought into the offices one by one, invited to sit at a desk, where an investigator, assisted by an interpreter, would start their questioning. If the facts reported constituted a genuine case against one or more of the accused, a written statement would be prepared and typed by ATS girls. Then the statement, in the language of the witness, would be signed by him or her and the translation into English would be certified by the translators.

The prosecuting officer had decided to limit, to a reasonable number, the witnesses used for the actual trial. A selection had, therefore, to be made of those witnesses who knew the most information concerning the accused. They had also to be selected in order to ensure that they would be able to withstand the ordeal of cross-examination in open court. Every statement got a classification number, cross referenced, in order that when the trial proceeded, if a witness's statement was challenged and the prosecuting counsel needed corroboration, he knew which witness to call. This classification was done by all the investigators meeting in the evening around a long table. The officer presiding over that meeting would call out the name and serial number given to each of the accused and then each investigator in turn would hand over the statements referring to that accused and taken during that day. These would then be classified in respect of particular alleged events and compared with other statements, in order to find corroboration in several witness reports. Eventually a list of thirty five major witnesses was drawn up, with many others in reserve.

At the trial in Luneburg these witnesses were submitted to a real ordeal under the cross examination of the twenty four barristers defending the accused. One of the most searching and aggressive officers was Lieutenant Jedrzejowicz, the Polish tank corps officer defending Irma Grese, the 21 year old Chief Wardress of Bergen-Belsen. He submitted some of the Polish women to such an ordeal in his cross examination that one fainted and another started to cry hysterically and had to be released from further cross examination.

In response to this, a young Polish Jewess aged eighteen, gave him as good as she received. The questioning took time. The officer put the question to her in Polish. She gave her reply in the same language. Questions and answers were then translated into English for the benefit of the court, and in German for the accused. The cross examination of the young girl went as follows:

"You say that Irma Grese beat you with her stick?"

"Yes."

"What sort of a stick was it?"

"A normal walking stick."

"Can you describe this walking stick?"

"What do you mean?"

"Well, can you describe how long and how thick this walking stick was?"

"Well, I suppose the normal length and thickness of a walking stick."

"Can you say what sort of a handle this walking stick had? Was it in silver? Was it bone? What shape did it have?"

"I don't know."

"Since you cannot give any details about this walking stick, I suggest that this walking stick has only existed in your imagination."

No answer.

"You say in your statement that Irma Grese has also hit you with her fists. Another figment of your imagination?"

To this the girl angrily replied "If the honourable barrister had been beaten like us, by stick and fist, he would soon have found out that one is more concerned at avoiding the blows, than looking at the details of what hit you. The only difference we knew was when we were hit by the stick or the fist." When this was translated into English and German, those in the courtroom started to laugh loudly and the officer presiding had to call everybody to order. After this exchange the Polish officer said, "No further questions," and the Polish girl left the witness box with an air of triumph.

The trial lasted six weeks and at the end of it eleven out of forty four of the accused were condemned to death by hanging. They were Kramer, the tall and bulky chief of the camp, Klein, a small insignificant man, the doctor of the camp, who had used the inmates of the camp as guinea pigs. He had even tried artificial insemination, amongst the less dangerous of his experiments. Then there was Irma Grese, the 21 year old girl, rather pretty, but who kept her defiant look until the day the sentence was pronounced. She was full of bravado up to the day prior to her execution, believing until the last minute that as a woman, she would not be hanged. She was not so brave on the day prior to her execution, when her sister visited her in her cell and she fainted when Pierrepoint the hangman went to fetch her. Pierrepoint never spoke about his work, but in the Sergeants' Mess where he was taking his meals, he said that for the first time in his long career, he enjoyed ridding the world of these monsters.

Amongst the others convicted was a Polish woman, a Jewess, who had become the girlfriend of one of the German warders. She shared a hut with the other Polish girls, provoked them into speaking against the Germans, then told her boyfriend who arranged to send the too talkative girls to the gas chambers.

Whilst in Bergen Belsen and in Luneburg Rene spoke to many survivors. He was told by them that without a doubt his parents, if they had survived the three day journey in the cattle trains, packed eighty to a wagon, would on account of their age, have been taken by trucks straight to the gas chambers. His sister may have had a better chance of survival, but when he heard how the process of selection worked, he was convinced that she had died the same way as his parents.

One of the Belgian girls told him that she had been saved from the gas chamber by a German soldier. When the trains arrived in Auschwitz, the selection was made. The older people were sent to one side and told to board the lorries. The younger ones were told "Those of you who cannot walk four kilometres, stand to the right. You will be taken to the camp by lorries. The others stand to the left." The Belgian girl was nearly going to go to the right hand queue when the German soldier told her, "If you want to live, get into the left queue. Crawl the four kilometres if you must, even on your knees, but don't take the lorries." And so she did, although lorries were sent back, whilst the poor exhausted creatures were slowly marching on, to try to tempt them to board them and take them straight to the gas chambers. Knowing his sister, who was always a lazy walker, he was convinced she would have taken the fatal ride in the lorries at the same time as his parents.

Twenty eight years after he was at the Luneburg trial, Rene still remembered vividly all the grim revelations made during its course. Some times when a more comical detail was given, the tension in the austere cinema hall in which the tribunal was taking place, was broken by a loud outburst of laughter. The hilarity was shared by the accused, as if they did not realise the gravity of their situation.

Brussels, November 1945

When the trial was over, Rene returned to his battalion in Germany and resumed his security duties. Then one day information came through that new troops, freshly arrived from Belgium, were taking their place and they were returning to Belgium with a view to being demobilised. Up until then, they had been on the same pay as the British forces, but as soon as they got back to Brussels, they were returned to the pre-war soldiers' pay, which was next to nothing. Without hesitation, Rene applied for his demobilisation papers. He was given 3,500 Belgian francs, which at that time only just bought a pair of trousers. Had he been in the British army he would have received several hundred pounds as a gratuity and a set of clothes. These 3,500 francs or the equivalent of twenty five pounds, was all Rene and his fellow comrades got and it was all he possessed in the world apart from his parent's damaged house, which in fact legally, did not yet belong to him.

In accordance with the old Napoleonic laws, which still applied in Belgium, since there was no proof of the death of his parents, he would have to wait seven years before he got the accrued benefits of their estate and it would take thirty years from the date of their presumed deaths before he could claim full possession of their assets. In order to establish the presumed date of their deaths, he obtained a certificate from the French authorities, declaring that according to records found at the transit camp of Drancy, his parents and sister had been sent to Auschwitz on the 23 November 1943, and that this date was accepted by the Belgian authorities as the date of their presumed deaths.

Next, he had to contact the lawyer who had been appointed by a tribunal as trustee of his parent's estate. The man was so busy and had so many files to deal with that he had so far done nothing about the preservation of Rene's parent's estate. His first visit to the lawyer's office ended after a solid argument. Rene told him that since he had done nothing to repair the bomb damage to the house, he was going to deal with it himself. The lawyer then had the nerve to tell Rene that by law he was not allowed to do anything, as the property was not yet his. Rene told him that after what he had been through, he was not afraid of taking risks and if needs be, he would take the law into his own hands.

The lawyer was known to have been a Flemish nationalist before the war and as such pro-German. This encouraged Rene tell him that he was prepared to fight by all means, legal and otherwise, to dispossess him of his authority as trustee. He bluntly asked the lawyer what his activities had been during the war.

He replied very evasively to Rene's questions, who suddenly discovered less arrogance in the man's attitude. Eventually he agreed that Rene could take any steps he wanted, as long as he kept him informed. To safeguard himself against any vacillation on the part of the lawyer, Rene appointed a pre-war friend of his as his solicitor and all his further contacts with the trustee were now conducted through his friend, Emile Angenot, himself a barrister.

His first concern was to find the money to pay for the repair of the house. He was lucky enough to find a man who was interested in renting the house. He offered to give Rene quite a substantial amount as key money, subject to getting a three year lease. The Trustee agreed to the lease, but the rent had to go to him. Rene kept him in the dark about the key money and used it to have all the essential repairs done to the house. Having put all this in motion, he decided it was high time to go and see his wife and his new born son who, by now, was eleven months old and Rene had not yet seen him.

Gateshead, England, December 1945

He got himself to Gateshead and spent a week there at his parents-in-law's home. As a result of the fact that he had now let the house in Antwerp, his and Doris's original plan to go and live there, was squashed. Even if it had been possible, he would not have dreamed to live in that house where he had so vivid memories of the pre-war days and he could not have faced the idea of living in it with different furniture. He and Doris therefore agreed that the best thing would be to live in England.

However, when he applied for a resident's permit, he ran into difficulties. So many men of the Allied forces wanted to stay in England, that the British government was reluctant to grant residence permits, although many of them were married, like Rene, to British girls. He was only given a visitor's permit for one month. At the end of that period, and after consultation with the Belgian Embassy, he went back to Belgium. He re-enlisted in the forces and was posted to London to help with the liquidation of the Belgian Ministry of Defence.

Leamington Spa, January 1946

Amongst the tasks Rene found himself involved in was the preparation of the military vehicles used by the Belgian Brigade for transportation to dismantlers, who would reduce them to scrap metal. Many of the vehicles which had been used in the campaign in Europe had been returned to the Brigade's bases in Britain. As a result Rene found himself back in Leamington Spa where the Brigade's motorised companies had been stationed. Many of the Bren gun carriers used by the companies had been parked in a field attached to the camp, since the end of hostilities in May. Attempts at restarting the machines proved difiricult. The engine oil of these vehicles was particularly heavy and thick and had virtually solidified in the months they had been standing idle. Attempts at turning over the engines on the starter proved fruitless.

Eventually it was agreed that a possible solution was to strip down and clean up the engine of one of these vehicles. Once it was rebuilt and put in running order, it could then be used as a tow vehicle, allowing Rene's team to 'bump start' the remaining Bren carriers. Having got one Bren carrier in running order, they set to work to fire up the others. A single hawser was attached to the back of the working vehicle and the front of one of the remaining Bren carriers. With the second vehicle put in neutral, it was possible to tow it to a lane close to the field in which it had been parked.

The principle of a 'bump start' is simple and familiar to most drivers. In this instance the first Bren carrier set off down the lane towing the second vehicle, still in neutral. Once the two vehicles were travelling at sufficient speed the driver of the second vehicle rams it into gear and simultaneously turns the starter. Although this is often accompanied by a jolt on the part of the towed vehicle, it is often sufficient to turn the engine over and get it fired up and running under its own power.

Unfortunately on this occasion the engine on the second Bren carrier was so badly seized up that far from starting, the tracked vehicle simply behaved like a sledge. It swung at the end of its hawser in a wide arc and probably would have ended up in front of its tow vehicle, had it not made contact with a lamp post on the side of the lane, totally demolishing it.

It was quickly agreed that a second attempt might be successful in getting the engine to fire up, but that in order to counteract the tendency for the second vehicle to swing outwards on the end of its hawser, a second one should be attached on the other side of the two vehicles. Having attached it, the tow vehicle again set off down the lane with the second Bren carrier in tow. To add to previous misfortunes, when the second Bren carrier was rammed into gear, the jolt resulted in the original hawser breaking and once more the vehicle swung out in a wide arc, this time demolishing a lamp post on the opposite side of the lane.

Had these two separate 'accidents' occurred a day later they might have been even more costly for the Belgian military authorities than proved the case. The land on which the camp was located had been requisitioned at the start of the war from its private owners. The requisitioning order was due to run out on the following day and the land revert to its original owners. Although the work of decommissioning the military vehicles stored on the land would obviously continue, it meant that army engineers just had time to reinstate the lamp posts before the requisition order ran out. Any subsequent damage was likely to result in heavy claims from the private owners. Happily the work of moving the remaining vehicles to the dismantlers proceeded without any further mishaps.

During the following year, Rene managed to make many contacts who would prove useful to him and by the time the liquidation of the Ministry was completed, he had obtained his resident's permit in England.

London, October 1946.

He was again a civilian and he had no trouble in finding employment. He was appointed manager of the travel department of an important firm of shipping agents in the Victoria area The firm's main traffic was in freight, but it had only one employee dealing with passengers and then mainly booking them passage on steamships. Rene's job was to build up from scratch a proper travel agency. The firm was owned by an old man, a Mr Davies, a very autocratic gentleman, grandson of the founder of the firm, who expected everybody to jump at his command. He was assisted in the business by his son-in-law. This young man had many good ideas on developing new activities at the firm, but was kept in check by the old man. He was very enthusiastic about the idea of altering the ground floor premises and turning them into a proper travel agency, but once more, the old man objected to any alteration.

By October, 1947, when Rene had been exactly one year with that firm, the government decided to impose a complete ban on European holidays to conserve scarce currency reserves. Immediately Rene's director called him into his office and gave him notice that he was closing his department. He gave him the choice of either accepting a minor and poorly paid job in the freight department, or of resigning. Rene decided on the latter course.

For several months he had difficulties in finding the right job and accepted some stop gap employment. Then in March 1948, when the ban on tourism was lifted, he was offered a job at Thomas Cook and Sons.

In the same week a lady from the Belgian Embassy offered to advance Rene the money to start up his own business. He found very good corner premises in Buckingham Gate. These were shared with a car hire firm and within a few months, business started to come in quite well. Within less than a year, he had got an IATA license from the International Air Transport Association, permitting him to sell airline tickets and he was able to attract the custom of many firms of consulting engineers whose members were very frequently travelling to various parts of the world. Many asked to open a monthly account.

Whenever such a request was made, Rene explained to the principals that as his was a small firm working with limited capital, he could only extend the credit he was getting from his suppliers. This meant that he was quite prepared to let the bills run until the end of each month.On the first of the month he would send out a statement for all the tickets supplied during the month. He was pleased to get payment by the 10th of the month, so that he could meet his own payments to the airlines on the 15th.This went well for nearly five years, but in 1952, a credit restriction meant that all the normally prompt payers suddenly started to delay sending their cheques. As a result of this and in order not to get into trouble with IATA, he had to borrow money from the bank at an inflated rate of interest. This very much restricted possibilities for accepting further accounts. A few firms took offence when he insisted on being paid. Some even took their business elsewhere, to his relief.

Rene was very friendly at the time with the London manager of Sabena, the Belgian airline. He had been in the Belgian forces in the UK and when the war finished, he had been appointed to his post with the airline. The two men used to meet regularly at the travel agent's club. One day he told Rene that his company had bought two C54 aircraft, a military version of the DC4 aeroplane, from the US air force, for charter work. He informed Rene that if he ever got any charter business, he could do it quite cheaply.

It so happened that a month after that conversation, a man walked into the Buckingham Gate shop. He told Rene that he was a representative of the Pakistan Government and that he wanted to send sixty people by sea to Karachi. Various enquiries proved that there was not a hope of getting them away within the time limit required. Rene then remembered Sabena's offer. He rang his friend, Albert, who gave him a quotation for a one way trip to Karachi. It was no more expensive than the cost of a passage by sea. When the representative of the Pakistan embassy came back to the office to hear the result of Rene's research, he could not believe it was possible to fly as cheaply as use a sea voyage. Rene was asked to confirm the offer in writing, which he did after he had himself received written confirmation from Sabena. This resulted in getting a contract for fifteen charter flights to Karachi.

Karachi, Pakistan 1949

Rene went on eight of these flights. Some were quite amusing, others not so funny. The first departure from London was an event which caught the attention of the press. There were photographers at the airport, to take a picture of the party, because it had never been seen before, – sixty three passengers on one aircraft. The seats were most uncomfortable. They were in fact, bucket seats and Rene was very pleased when the captain invited him to travel in the cockpit, where there was ample room.

The cockpit was divided into two sections. Behind the captain's seat and also facing forward, sat the radio operator. His instrument panel formed a wall between him and the captain. Between the captain and the first officer, and set a little behind them, was the flight engineer's seat. Further back and facing the crew emergency door, was the folding table of the navigator. He sat facing the emergency exit and at a right angle to the rest of the flight deck. Next to him was the jump seat Rene occupied. A partition and a door separated the flight deck from the crew's rest room, which was fitted with two bunks.

Although flying took much longer in those days and the technical devices were less sophisticated than they are today, it seemed that the pilots had an easier life then. They had more take offs and landings to deal with than pilots have today, but between those two points, and apart from the responsibility of take off and landing, they had a very restful time during flights. The radio operator made contact with the ground every half hour. The navigator checked the plane's position every hour. This was mainly to check if any side wind had sent the plane off course.

Two out of the five flight deck crew took turns to sit in the captain's number one seat and the co-pilot's number two seat and that was only as a precaution in case the automatic pilot, commonly known in aviation circles as 'George' broke down. Rene was told the story of a cargo plane taking gold bullion from New York to Brussels. Four of the crew were sitting in the crew rest room playing cards, whilst the fifth one had just left the cockpit to go to the toilet at the tail end of the plane. Suddenly the automatic pilot broke. The plane nose dived and before the two pilots had managed to scramble into their seats and pull the joy stick with all their strength, the aircraft had dropped by 3,000 feet. Luckily they were at 10,000 when the problem occurred. Probably nobody would have heard of that incident if the member of the crew who had just been to the toilet had not been pitched forward and been hit by a few displaced bars of gold. He suffered a spinal injury and an investigation into the cause of this accident revealed all the details. From then on all pilots were instructed that number one and two seats should never be unoccupied.

Travelling at 10,000 ft in a non-pressurised aircraft had a very strange effect on Rene. He could not sleep and was hungry and thirsty all the time. On two occasions he travelled with a captain who, like him, could not sleep during a flight. As a result of this, the two of them sat at the controls the whole night, to the joy of the rest of the crew, who could have a restful night telling each other jokes. It took two return trips from London to Karachi before they ran out of jokes.

A trip to Karachi which now takes eight hours, then took twenty four hours. This included an hour stop for refuelling in Brussels, one hour in Rome, one in Athens and one in Bahrain. They usually arrived at Drigh

Road Airport at three o'clock in the morning, when the sun was coming up on the eastern horizon and when the tarmac had not yet had the chance to melt. As soon as the plane had touched down and taxied to its parking place on the apron, steps were brought to the aircraft. A doctor and a medical assistant came into the cabin and quickly shut the door behind them. Then, whilst the assistant fumigated the cabin to kill any possible stowaway flies, the doctor went into the cockpit to inspect the aircraft's log book. If the aircraft had been to Africa on a previous trip, the captain had to produce a disinfection certificate.

After a five minutes wait in tropical heat, the passengers were allowed onto the tarmac and escorted to the emigration and customs hall. There, every passenger had to fill in a form extending to four foolscap pages. The stupidest questions had to be answered such as: "Do you carry firearms? Do you carry drugs?" etc. etc. After a quick look at the form and having stamped it, the customs officer would proceed to a thorough search of each piece of luggage. These formalities took ten times as long as was needed in the slowest European airport at that time.

Once these formalities were finished, everyone walked through a swing door and found themselves in a very modern, marble floored, hall. There they observed the amazing contrast of a modern building being used in the most medieval ways by some of the local people. Walking into modern toilets, you would find a Pakistani in his white or light grey cotton shift like clothes, a fur lined cap on his head, only having his ablutions interrupted when he felt the need to spit on the floor. As a result of chewing bettel leaves, the spittle left a large red mark on the floor.

Walking out of the building, several taxi drivers simultaneously invited him to use their car. Accustomed to English ways, Rene went to the first taxi in the line and gave him the address of his local agent. He had been warned many taxi drivers were completely illiterate and had to be be directed to their destination with instructions on where to turn left or right. As a result he had learned the essential words for barking directions, 'daha' for right, 'baha' for left and 'bas' for stop. But on this occasion, he was pleasantly surprised to find that his driver knew his way and when he read out the address to him, he knew exactly where to take him.

A three mile journey on a dusty road and they entered the city separated from the airfield by rather barren land and a few fields. His first impressions of Karachi were ones of shocking contrasts. Some very luxurious buildings surrounded by well kept gardens, alternated with what once had been an open space and had now been turned into a shanty town for refugees.

Not many months earlier, partition of what had formerly been India, had taken place, with the result that thousands of Pakistani Moslems had had to leave the places in India where they had been born and had lived all their lives and find, if not security, at least the safety, of being amongst their own people, without risk of being massacred. The government had set in motion a rehousing programme, but this took time and meanwhile the refugees had to find a place to live. Huts were built with dried cow dung for walls and for rooves they used any other solid material to be found. All this gave the town a very untidy outlook. Passing these eyesores, they drove further into the centre of the city, with narrow and crowded streets. The car had to slow down and the driver had to continuously use his horn to open a passage for his vehicle, amongst the crowd of people walking, as if it was their right, in the middle of the road.

The driver stopped in front of Rene's agent's office and he asked him what he owed for the fare. "Thirty five Rupees Sir," he replied. Rene paid, but found this terribly expensive. It was the equivalent of three pounds and he had only travelled six miles. Rene met his local agent and discussed with him the possibility of return loads, as for the present, the Pakistan government only booked one way charters to Karachi. After their business was finished and he was about to take his leave of the agent, Rene mentioned that he found the Karachi taxis very expensive.

"How much were you charged?" asked the agent.

"Thirty five Rupees."

"What! That is what we pay for a whole day's hire! The driver must have noticed that you were a newcomer here."

Rene walked out of the building and saw the taxi he had arrived in waiting behind the other taxis in a rank. As Rene came level with where the taxi was parked, the driver opened his door and got out. Rene past him and was about to open the door of the first taxi in the line when the driver called to him. Opening the passenger door he said, "Here Sir, Here Sir." Thinking that he was going to fleece him again, Rene said, "No, not you. You have had me." Looking very puzzled, the driver said, "But why Sir? You have paid me for the whole day."

Only then did Rene understand that he must have been mistaken for a member of the aircraft's crew. They usually always took a taxi for the whole day. His driver took Rene back to his hotel and waited patiently until he decided to take another ride. When, after a few hours rest at the hotel, Rene emerged from the front entrance, the taxi driver jumped out of his seat to open the passenger door for him. By now he knew that it was Rene's first visit to Karachi. It was quite natural therefore, that he proposed to show him the sights around the town.

Their first stopping place was the Botanical Gardens. Next he took Rene to the area where the new housing scheme was coming into operation. Row after row of brick buildings were being hurriedly erected. Each house had only one room, which to Europeans would have looked like a shed, but for the refugees who would soon occupy them, it would be luxury after having lived in cow dung huts. Usually, when the rainy season came, the cow dung huts fell to pieces and the occupiers then took their sparse possesions to a drier place. Many had been squatting under the colonnades of public buildlings. In their new homes they would find solid rooves and walls, one tap with running water and two holes in the floor at the opposite ends of the room. One was under the tap, the other to be used as a toilet, at the other end of the room and behind a partition.

Aly, that was the name of the taxi driver, knew Karachi well. He took Rene to the beach at Clifton and waited for him whilst he had a walk to examine the expensive air terminal built by BOAC for their flying boats and which had never been used, because the flying boat service was withdrawn before the building was completed. One flying boat was still floating abandoned, near the pier.

After this interesting day, Aly took Rene back to the Grand Hotel for a meal and a rest. By then he found Aly had well deserved his 35 Rupees and he gave him a tip, expecting him to go home. When, around I a.m. Rene came out of the hotel to drive to the airport, Aly was still waiting for him. He took him to Drigh Road and when Rene asked him, "How much?" he said, "You not owe me nothing Sahib, you paid me for whole day at 3 o'clock, today. Finish at 3 o'clock. Only one thirty now." Rene gave him another tip for which Aly thanked Rene, as if he had given him a fortune and he insisted to know if and when he was coming back. Rene gave him the date of his next trip and sure enough, when he reached Drigh Road, Aly was waiting for him. He became an indispensable help and Rene used his taxi on his eight remaining trips to Karachi.

Generally trips involved leaving London on Friday night, reaching Karachi on Saturday and travelling back during the night from Sunday to Monday. On the one but last trip, Rene remained in Pakistan for three months. During the first week he employed Aly, who gave him a cheaper rate, but after that he found it less expensive to use a self-drive car. Even then, one day Aly came providentially to his rescue, on a day when he had engine trouble. He happened to pass by, saw Rene looking at the engine and stopped specially to help him to find the cause of the problem.

During the week Rene employed him, Aly took him to the race course. Rene had been invited to the grandstand by one of his clients. Aly came on several occasions and stood on the grass below the grandstand, waving his hand to draw Rene's attention, and making signs that he wanted to speak to him. Rene joined him on the lawn where he was given a tip for the next race. Rene did not know where Aly was getting his information from, but every time he received a tip, the horse won. Unfortunately, Rene did not invest enough faith in Aly's tips and only bet a small sum. Had he listened to him, he could have made a fortune.

Aly was useful too when Rene wanted to visit the shadier quarters of Karachi including its red ight district. He had been warned by British residents that it was pretty risky for a European to go on his own into that area. One evening when Rene was at a loose end, Aly proposed to take him to see the dancing girls in the native quarter.

Rene told him that he had been advised not to go there on his own. To this Aly replied "I park car, we walk together to native quarter. When you with Aly, you safe. When I say you friend of Aly, all men will respect you." And sure enough, Rene never felt safer. Everybody seemed to know him. He would shake both hands of people he met, as is customary in the east, then he would introduce Rene in English, "This my boss. He very nice. He not English, he from Belgium." Rene would then have to shake the hands extended in friendly greeting.

Aly took Rene into several places where the local people congregated to watch the dancing girls. They all sat on the floor or on cushions with crossed legs forming a circle around the performing girl or girls. They usually wore the tight silk trousers, rather revealing bra and had the naked midriff we associate with belly dancers. Strapped around their ankles they had either a chain, or a leather strap with a multitude of copper bells. These were used in certain dances to imitate the walk of the camels, because in Pakistan and India, camels pulling the carts through the streets were always fitted with these bells to warn pedestrians of their approach, because the pads of their feet are so soft that otherwise people would not hear them approach. As Rene was sitting watching the dance, Aly who was sitting behind him, suddenly pushed something on top of his ear. Instinctively Rene took it. It was a one rupee note rolled like a cigarette. Rene looked at Aly puzzled, who gestured that he should put it back where he had placed it. The dancing girl noticed it and came towards Rene. Whilst continuing to dance she removed the money, then with both hands caressed his face and placed an innocent kiss on his forehead. The whole gathering applauded loudly at that performance, which to Rene seemed very childish.

The music to which the girls were dancing was very monotonous and repetitive to European ears. It was played by a band which consisted of three men. One played a small organ with only three notes, played with the right hand, whilst he used his left hand to activate the bellows at the back of the instrument. The second one played a kind of rudimentary stringed instrument and the third one tapped with his fingers on two small drums.

On the first three flights to Karachi they mainly took Pakistan air force personnel, returning to their country after several months training in England. The fourth flight was of cargo. The aircraft was loaded with seven Tiger Moth aircraft, shipped in parts and packed in crates, together with several drop tanks. They had four seats for passengers in the front of the aircraft. Two of these seats were occupied by a British brigadier and his wife.

They loaded the freight at Bovingdon Airport in Hertfordshire. The runway on that airport is a mile long, but as the aircraft was loaded to its maximum permissible weight, the captain had to rev up the engines to maximum power, whilst holding the plane on its brakes, making the whole airframe of the aircraft shudder. Then, releasing the brakes, the aircraft immediately started down the runway at full speed and took off well before its end.

The flight was uneventful until they reached Karachi. Rene was sitting in the cabin in conversation with the brigadier, when the steward came to tell him that the captain wanted him. When Rene got to the cockpit the captain said, "You have been to Karachi before, where do you land?"

"On the runway," Rene replied sardonically.

"I know that silly, but which airport?"

"Drigh Road, the civil airport."

"Well there seems to be an argument down below. I have both the air traffic controls of Drigh Road and Mauripur on the radio and there seems to be an argument as to where I should come down."

They both listened in to the argument going on over the air between the two ground controllers. After a few minutes the captain cut in and said, "Look you boys, go on arguing between yourselves about where I should land. I am going to circle above Karachi. When you have made up your mind, let me know and I shall come down where you say."

It was soon dark and they were still circling above the town at about 3,000 ft. The sight of the thousands of street lights of various colours was quite breathtaking seen from that height. They were on their third circuit of the city. The captain said, "Never mind, the longer we fly, the more we get paid, and the less we will have to fly later to complete our month's flying hours." In accordance with flying regulations, aircrew could not fly more than 100 hours a month. Two Karachi return flights, plus two London-Brussels flights and they had reached their limit for the month.

As they were about to start the fourth circuit, they were instructed to land at the military airport in Mauripur. The captain asked Rene what he knew about landing facilities there. "Nothing," Rene said. "I have only landed at Drigh Road. I have visited Mauripur, but I have never been near the runway."

The captain was directed on his approach by the military air traffic controller at Mauripur. As they descended, they could see the runway, thanks to a long row of petrol cans lined up along both of its sides. From the mouth of each, a naked flame was burning, giving the pilot the outline of the runway. The captain put his landing lights on and made a perfect touch down. When they came to the end of the runway, they could not find any indication of the access road leading to the apron. They also seemed to have lost contact with ground control. So in the limited space available, the captain turned his aircraft in the direction from which they had come and waited.

After a few minutes wait, they saw two lights appear from the opposite side of the runway and move in their direction. Soon they saw in the beam of the aircraft's landing lights, a Pakistani air force NCO on a bicycle. He wasn't holding the handlebars. Instead he was holding, at arms length, two makeshift bats, rather like those used in table tennis. By a real feat of acrobatics he managed, still without touching the handlebars, to turn round in front of the aircraft and waving the bats, indicated to the pilot to follow him. He then directed the pilot safely to the apron.

After another few minutes wait in the dark, – the apron had no lighting at all except for a search light on top of the control tower, – they at last brought a long ladder which was placed against the aircraft exit door. The captain enquired about passenger steps and was told that there were none at this airport.

When the brigadier heard this he got into a terrible temper. "You don't expect my wife to go down that ladder. Tell your captain to take off again and land at Drigh Road." The message was conveyed to the captain. His answer came back, "If the brigadier is prepared to sign a paper saying that he will be responsible for the payment of extra landing charges, then the captain will be pleased to take off again, otherwise this is the end of this trip." The brigadier refused to sign the paper and 'Madam the Brigadier' had to descend by way of the ladder, in a very undignified manner, helped by the steward.

406

To Rene's huge surprise, when he left the airport office building, he found Aly waiting for him. Through some of his connections at Drigh Road, he had found out about the aircraft's diversion to Mauripur. This time they were staying in Karachi a bit longer than usual. The Pakistan air force had to unload the plane and there was freight to take back to Bovingdon. This allowed Rene to spend two nights at the Beach Luxury Hotel. This was then the most recently built hotel. It was situated near the harbour. The rooms at the back of the hotel faced a large garden, along a canal.

The soil of the garden was sandy, but hundreds of flowerpots with a magnificent variety of flowers, formed very decorative lines. Under Rene's window was a large terrace. Large round tables with still larger colourful umbrellas or sunshades, planted in the centre, were placed in a circle around a space specially provided for dancing. A four piece band led by a French violinist provided the music. During dinner the band played inside the dining room and then moved to the terrace as soon as the serving of dinner ended.

Rene had invited his local agent to come and have dinner with him. To Rene's surprise he had brought along two friends and four very attractive young ladies. Apparently it is a custom of the country to show your appreciation of an invitation, by extending it to some friends, mainly girlfriends. Rene had been prepared for a boring business dinner, but it turned out to be a very lively party and he saw the good sense of this oriental custom.

His next trip to Pakistan involved quite a different sort of incident. By then he had repatriated all the members of the Pakistan air force and the High Commissioner's Office in London had started recruiting Polish air force officers to act as instructors to the new Pakistan Air Force. They were enlisted for a trial period of six months, after which they were supposed to sign a contract for two years. They had been led to believe that they were going to get a very high rate of pay. What they had not been told, was that the cost of living was also very high. After having paid for their Mess bills, their laundry bill and any other essentials, they only had just enough money to spend an evening in town once a month.

Rene ferried three plane loads of these Polish boys to Karachi, some with their families. But after six months, he started to bring them back to England. Most of them would not sign the two year contract. A few, stayed, but mainly in civilian occupations.

The first lot of Polish pilots who flew out gave him a problem. As they were flying between Bahrain and Karachi, the captain noticed that they were flying tail heavy. He asked Rene to go and investigate how many passengers were standing near the tail end of the aircraft. He found a dozen of the Polish officers who had gathered around the galley and were using it as a bar. He asked them politely to return to their seats, but to no avail.

He reported back to the captain. Rene also told him what condition the Poles were in. The captain summoned the chief steward and instructed him to close the bar altogether. Luckily the two stewards were helped in their efforts by the captain simulating the effects of turbulence and putting the 'Fasten Seat Belts' sign on. Even then, the two stewards, both ex-paratroopers, had to combine their efforts to get some of the officers to their seats.

At the end of this same trip, another bad surprise was waiting for them. As usual, when they reached Karachi, the airport doctor and his assistant came on board to fumigate the aircraft and inspect the log book. When he saw that on the previous trip the aircraft had been to Africa, he demanded to see the aircraft disinfection certificate. The captain produced it, but this did not satisfy the doctor. According to him, a disinfection done in Brussels was not valid, it should have been done in London. The captain tried to explain that the Belgian certificates were accepted everywhere, including the most fastidious countries, like the USA, but the doctor was inflexible.

He got out of the aircraft and had the doors locked. After a long wait, the doors were reopened and under police escort, passengers and crew had to board coaches which took them to the Isolation Hospital at the other end of the airfield. It was three o'clock in the morning and nothing could be done until the opening time of the airport offices.

At nine o'clock Rene rang the Ministry of Civil Aviation and asked to talk to the Director, Wing Commander Awan, whom he knew personally, having met him on many occasions. Rene explained their plight to him and he promised to ring him back as soon as he had contacted his colleague at the public health department. An hour later he rang Rene back to tell him that there had been a terrible mistake. Belgium had joined the International Health Convention, two years after its creation. The instructions of the doctor at the airport had not been amended accordingly and therefore, he did not know that the Belgian certificate of disinfection was now accepted. He was very apologetic about the situation. He promised to come in person with his colleague from the Ministry of Health to release them and offer them a drink to make them forget their ordeal. They did not have to wait very long. Sure enough, the two officials came in a smart ministry car followed by a coach.

They were taken to the BOAC rest house and offered several rounds of drinks, at the expense of the Pakistan Government. The crazy thing was that at the Isolation Hospital, Rene's party had been in contact with other passengers suspected of being yellow fever carriers and the hospital never bothered to give them a preventative inoculation. They could have carried out the germ ten times over.

Rene's next meeting with Wing Commander Awan was two months later, when he had to deliver to him a protest concerning a very unpleasant happening. This was when he had started to ferry back some of the families of the Polish air force officers. On that occasion he had had a very rough journey out and had been very busy during the following day organising the return loads.

On the flight Rene had a very unpleasant captain, an Englishman by the name of Wood, one of the few English captains employed by Sabena. At the outset of the trip the steward had asked the captain if Rene could join the flight deck crew in the cockpit, but this the captain had refused. On all previous trips the captains had always asked Rene to join the crew table at the various stopovers, but this captain, although told that Rene was responsible for chartering the aircraft, refused to have anything to do with him.

On arrival in Karachi, Rene went to his hotel for breakfast and then to the various offices where he had to arrange the return loads. Usually he was at the airport two to three hours before takeoff and supervised the weighing in of passengers and luggage. In those days every passenger and every piece of luggage had to be weighed in order to establish a correct trim sheet. This determined where every item of luggage or cargo on the aircraft was to be placed in order to ensure the correct weight balance or trim of the plane. The margin of safety when loading was ridiculously small, compared with aircraft of today. Forty five kilos too much, or wrongly placed on the aircraft, could make all the difference between a smooth takeoff and a crash.

As the outward journey had not been too good, Rene decided to have a few hours sleep at the BOAC rest house. He had left instructions to be called three hours before the flight, but either somebody forgot to call him, or he fell asleep again after answering the knock at his door. The fact remains that he suddenly came to one hour before take off. He rushed to the airport, where the BOAC staff had already started checking in the passengers.

As soon as he got to the luggage room he noticed that the quantity of luggage seemed to be much larger than usual. He asked to see the load sheet and the first thing that attracted his suspicion, was that when he was shown the passenger manifest, every man was shown as weighing 75 kilos and every woman as 65 kilos, which was the average weight calculation for the trim sheet. Not being satisfied with the way the weighing in had been done, Rene instructed that every passenger and every piece of luggage be reweighed.

As a result he found they were 900 kilos over the safe weight limit. Finding that several passengers had more than the permitted weight, they were called and told that their excess luggage would have to follow on the next plane. Amongst them was a Wing Commander Malik, attached to the High Commissioner's Office in London. He had done several trips with Rene previously. Each time he had loaded three officer's metal trunks and a kit bag. On this occasion, Rene had to tell him that his three metal trunks had to be left behind, since the kit bag he was taking, was just the permitted weight. He did not protest and instructed the porters to take them away.

By then the captain had finished the documentation and organised the trim sheet. He then gave instructions as to how the luggage had to be loaded in the four compartments on the aircraft. Compartment B was on the side of the crew rest room. The loading was supervised by the

Flight Engineer. He suddenly approached Rene, knowing that he was supervising the control of the weighing in of luggage on each truck and said, "Rene, I think you have made a mistake for Compartment B2."

"No I did not," Rene replied. "The porters loaded exactly the weight prescribed by the captain."

"How can that be?" asked the disconcerted flight engineer. "The three metal trunks of Malik weigh more than that, I'm sure."

"What? The three trunks of Malik have been offloaded," Rene assured him.

"No, they are there under the aircraft."

Rene rushed to the apron and found that the three trunks he had refused to take had been smuggled through another door in the terminal to the aircraft. Immediately Rene called in the Airport Police to witness what had been done. Wing Commander Malik was interrogated and admitted having bribed porters to take the luggage to the aircraft.

For the first time the captain acknowledged Rene and came to speak to him about the incident. He now wanted to put on Rene the onus of responsibility for deciding whether the aircraft should take off as scheduled. Rene told him what he had just found out and that since Malik had managed to smuggle his trunks to the tarmac, there was no reason why the other excess baggage could not have followed the same way.

Rene told the captain that the final decision rested with him, but that he would feel happier if they delayed the flight, offloaded all the luggage and restarted weighing it all from scratch. The captain replied that they would never be able to offload and reload before the deadline for takeoff. This deadline was dictated by the fact that because of events in the middle east, they had to over fly Israel in daylight or otherwise run the risk of being shot at by the ground defences.

At last they both agreed that the safest thing would be to postpone the flight for twenty four hours. On the strength of what had happened and the police investigation that followed, Rene could hold the officer and thereby, his government, responsible for the twenty four hour demurrage charges incurred when a vessel, or in this case, a plane, is prevented from departing on time.

Once more Rene saw Wing Commander Awan at the Ministry of Civil Aviation. Having informed him of the events leading to the cancellation of the flight, Rene warned him that unless better security arrangements prevailed at the airport in the coming night, he might have to delay departure once more and charge the extra expenses to the Pakistan Government.

That evening, when Rene reached the airport, he found that every exit was guarded by two policemen and only one exit, also guarded, was reserved to the exit of luggage. Everything went to his satisfaction and they took off without further trouble. The journey back, however, was pretty bumpy. Crossing Saudi Arabia they were caught in a sandstorm. The meteorological office had told the pilot that they would be clear of it at 12,000 ft. Unfortunately, not being pressurised, the aircraft could not fly above 10,000 ft and they took the full impact of the storm.

There were thirty four women and fourteen children on board and although the captain had now invited Rene into the cockpit, he spent most of his time assisting the two stewards, who had their hands full looking after the air sick passengers. The going was so rough that Rene had to hold tight to the headrest of the bucket seat with one hand, whilst holding the paper bag over the mouth of a vomiting passenger with the other.

On another occasion there was a very unpleasant incident. London was fog bound and the forecast was that this might last for a few days. Sixty three passengers, most of them from Pakistan, had been brought from various parts of England to London. When it was found that they could not take off on the evening scheduled, Sabena arranged to accommodate the group in a hotel. The next morning the fog had cleared in Brussels, but London was still fog bound. By that time, Sabena in consultation with the Pakistan High Commissioner's Office in London, had agreed that the best thing would be to take the passengers to Brussels by rail and sea. When Rene got instructions to move them it was too late to catch the boat train to Ostend, but they could make it in time for the one to Calais. One more night in a London hotel and the twenty four hour delayed departure by boat train to Belgium had resulted in the Pakistan Government again having to pay the bill for their representative's negligence.

On his next trip Rene only had passengers travelling one way from London to Karachi. His agent in Karachi had been notified of this well in advance and had decided to organise a trip to England and the continent for businessmen. Travel Aids, Rene's company, was asked to book the hotels in Europe and the trip was arranged in order to visit four commercial fairs taking place practically in succession to each other in Milan, Paris, London and Geneva.

When the BOAC manager in Karachi heard that this trip was advertised there, he tried to stop it, using the cartel arrangements in place at the time to argue that this was contrary to existing airline licensing arrangements. But the trip had the blessing of the Pakistan Government and BOAC did not manage to prevent it. Looking back on it, their policy was foolish, because contrary to what they claimed, it did not take any business away from them, but created some at a later date. All the participants, with the exception of a few, were small businessmen who could not have afforded BOAC fares. Tempted by the cheap fare Rene's charter flight offered, they decided to take two months to visit the four fairs. In the London fair they found the goods their country needed. They placed their orders and went back to Karachi with samples of what they had bought. Later Rene was told by several of them that they had sold the whole of their orders on the strength of the samples and the goods were sold to retailers before they reached Karachi. They made such nice profits out of it, that a good number of them flew back to London to place new orders, but this time came by BOAC.

Amongst the members of the group was a wealthy Indian who decided he wanted to open a travel agency in Delhi. He had been so impressed by Rene's company's organisation that he wanted him to come to Delhi for one week at his expense, to act as a technical adviser for the opening of his travel agency. Rene told him that he was going back to Karachi with the party and he would spend a few weeks there on business. The Indian businessman insisted that Rene should come to Delhi for one week. Rene did not take the suggestion very seriously and made evasive promises.

Back in Karachi many members of the tour invited Rene to their homes. Amongst them was a Parsi doctor by the name of Mehta. Originally Rene had planned to stay only a few days in Karachi and had, therefore, the minimum amount of luggage with him. It was only on arrival in Brussels that Rene had been told that he was expected to stay in Karachi for some while. When Dr Mehta invited him to his party, he told Rene that everybody would be in evening dress, but that it did not matter if he did not have a dinner jacket and evening attire The thought of being, alone amongst the guests, the only person not in evening dress troubled Rene.

When he mentioned this to his local agent, he said, "Why don't you have one made here. The material is good and prices reasonable."

"How can I?" Rene replied, "The party is the day after tomorrow."

"Well, that is all the time you need. I shall take you to my tailor now, he will take your measurements. You can go for a fitting tomorrow and your suit should be ready by lunchtime the next day."

So, to the tailor they went and the next day Rene went for a fitting, during which the tailor practically tore the suit to pieces, but by lunchtime on the third day, he found it boxed and ready to wear on his bed in the hotel. It was the best fitting suit he had ever worn. The dinner jacket was white and the trousers black.

Doctor Mehta had told Rene he would send a car to pick him up at his hotel. At eight o'clock precisely, the agreed time, an elegant chauffeur driven car came to fetch him. As the car entered the large garden surrounding the doctor's villa the driver sounded his horn. This was the signal for the switching on of a fantastic display of fairy lights all around the garden. The car stopped in front of a wide marble staircase leading to an equally large marble terrace.

Doctor Mehta came to meet him at the foot of the staircase. Only then did he tell Rene that he was the guest of honour. He took him by the left arm and led him up the steps. As they reached the top of the staircase, eighty pairs of eyes were looking at them. Then, in a loud voice, Doctor Mehta said, "Ladies and gentlemen, I have the pleasure to introduce to you our guest of honour, Mr. Rene Falkenau, who has been responsible for the so perfect organisation of our European tour."

Still holding Rene by the left arm, he first took him to greet his wife, then he was introduced, one by one, to every one of the eighty guests. The sight was unforgettable, of all the ladies in their most colourful of saris. The men were in their dinner jackets, mostly of the oriental style, the jacket having a collar fitted at the neck like Victorian army dress uniforms and with trousers narrowing at the ankles.

After all the introductions were over, Rene was given a large glass of whisky and all the guests moved to the dining room. There, a fantastic buffet was laid out on a table twelve feet long and guests were invited to help themselves. Doctor Mehta filled Rene's plate with the most amazing variety of curries and he tried every type. The result of it was that the next day he was in bed with terrible indigestion. Doctor Mehta phoned later that morning to find out how Rene had enjoyed the evening. Rene told him that he had enjoyed every minute of it and thanked him for the surprise of being the guest of honour. When Dr. Mehta heard about Rene's indigestion, he offered to come and examine him.

When he arrived he made Rene put out his tongue, which was remarkably white. Out of his satchel he pulled a glass tube, open at both ends. Holding his finger over one end, he poured a white powder in the other. He told Rene to open his mouth and then holding the glass tube horizontally near his mouth, he blew the other end. In a sudden blast the powder entered Rene's throat and nearly choked him. However, it did the trick. A few hours later he was completely recovered.

This experience reminded Rene of the old joke about the farmer who had been advised by a vet to use a similar treatment for a sick cow. When the vet came the next day to see the result of the treatment, he found the farmer hoarse and having difficulty in speaking, "Well," he said, "did you do what I instructed you to do?" "Yes," said the farmer. "And how did it go?" enquired the vet. "Well, the cow blew first."

Another member of the European tour group invited Rene to his home a few days later. That man was a true Moslem and therefore, the ancient rules were observed. All the men ate together in one room whilst the women had their meal in an adjacent room. At the end of the meal his host decided to introduce Rene to his wife. He first entered the ladies' room to warn them of Rene's presence, then he took him inside. To mark his confidence in Rene, his wife was introduced unveiled, but all the other women in the room had covered their faces. Rene could only see their big eyes, looking at him from behind their yashmaks.

After the meal even the men separated into two different rooms, the older ones in one room and the younger ones in another. At first Rene was invited to join the older men. They all had long beards and wore typically traditional Pakistani clothes. Their bare feet were clad in slippers without heels or back. Very few of them spoke English and those who did, started to ask Rene questions about the last trip. They then translated the questions and Rene's answers for the others. Rene was very careful in his answers, especially when their questions were directed at finding out how their sons and daughters had behaved on their visit to Europe. They, being very religious and traditional in their beliefs, would probably have strongly disapproved of some of the places in Europe visited by their more emancipated sons and daughters.

After a while Rene's young host came to fetch him and the first thing he said was, "I hope that you have not told my father all the places we visited in Paris? I should have warned you of that." Rene's answer was "Have no fear, I have been very discrete about your evening activities in Paris." "Thank you so much," said his relieved host. "Now you had better come and join the younger generation."

He took Rene into the other room where some of the men were sitting, some standing in a circle. At the end of the room there was a screen. Rene's host took him behind the screen, which hid a row of whisky bottles and empty glasses on a table. He offered Rene a drink. As the young man poured it, Rene asked him, "Why the screen?" His answer was, "Although the elders may suspect that we infringe the rulings of the Koran, they may come to visit us in this room. They will possibly suspect what is happening behind the screen, but they will have the tact never to go behind it and we won't, by hiding the bottles behind the screen, compel them to tell us off." Rene found this solution quite clever, but terribly hypocritical.

On one other occasion, he was invited to a meal by semi religious Moslems. There ladies and men ate together at the same table, but there was a separation of the sexes in as much as the host sat on a seat in the middle of the table and Rene, as guest of honour, sat immediately opposite him. On Rene's right and on his host's left, sat all the men. On Rene's left and his host's right handside, sat all the ladies. The trouble was that although the host had seated his young wife next to Rene, he could not converse with her, as she only spoke Urdu. The man on Rene's right spoke a very basic English.

Rene learned to eat in the Moslem way. He picked up the food with his right hand, whilst his left hand, which should never touch food, was resting on his knee. The strict reason for this practice is to do with hygiene. The left hand must only he used for cleaning the lower parts of the body. He understood the good sense of this rule when, after dinner he had to visit the toilet. This consisted of a small room with just a hole half a foot wide in the centre. One had to be an expert to get rid of one's surpluses without soiling the ridge of the hole. No toilet paper was provided, but there was a pail of water in the corner with a metal jug, like a pint measure. This was used both for giving oneself a wash or to clean away any mess one may have made around the hole. Rene decided to make only a limited use of this uncomfortable toilet and to wait until he got back to his hotel to have a good 'sit down.'

The food in all these Moslem homes was plentiful, with lamb and rice the predominating dishes. It took him a while to get accustomed to the very hot and spicy curry.

Lahore, Pakistan July 1949

Whilst in Karachi, he got an invitation from one member of the tour group to spend a few days with him in Lahore, where he owned a well known restaurant named Lorang, after its owner. He was one of the few people of Indian origin who had not been chased out of Pakistan at the time of partition. Possibly the fact that he was married to a German woman had protected him. The restaurant, situated in the smart centre of Lahore, quite near the elegant Wellington Club and a regency colonnade, had a very good reputation in the city. One could eat either at tables for four situated in the centre of the large restaurant, or one could find little cubicles for four to six on the two sides of the restaurant. If diners wanted not to be seen, they could reserve a cubicle and be able to eat behind drawn curtains.

Mr. Lorang had a very nice villa situated near the main hotel, the Fallete. It was located in a large, elegant, tropical garden. Mr Lorang put at Rene's disposal the guest bedroom. This was a very large room. The floor was tiled with decorative stone. The walls and ceiling were white washed. A few picture frames containing exotic scenes contrasted with the whiteness of the decor. From the bedroom there was direct access to a large bathroom in which two baths were lined up one behind the other. Apparently something had gone wrong with the water supply and no water came out of the taps, but a servant scooped water from a well in the garden and filled the two baths pail by pail. The idea of two baths puzzled Rene, but he was soon to discover the logic of it. In Lahore the heat was so upsetting and unbearable, that immediately after lunch he would go and lie on his bed in his birthday suit, with the large fan on the ceiling turned on at full speed. Even so, perspiration would cover his body. After a siesta which would last until 4pm, he would plunge in one of the baths. The water was tepid, but by the time he had been in it five minutes, the water would become warm through the heat of his body. He would then get out and transfer himself to the second bath.

Whilst he was staying in Lahore, Rene was invited to the very exclusive Wellington Club. There, he was introduced to an Anglo-Indian judge. He invited Rene to attend his court the next day where a very important state official was on trial. The trial itself was conducted in a very European fashion. The judge, whilst wearing a white wig and the traditional red robe, the same as an English judge, conducted the trial in accordance with modern legal practice. Contrasting with this, Rene saw in the lower courts, scenes reminiscent of the middle ages. A poor devil who had stolen some food came in front of the judge, hands and feet manacled and secured by heavy chains. He had previously been made to walk through the streets of Lahore chained between two guards. It did not take long to condemn him to prison.

The next day Rene decided to go and visit another member of the tour party, a Mr. Khwafa, a sporting goods manufacturer from Sialkot. To travel to Sialkot, Rene had to take a rather old fashioned bus. He sat in a compartment for eight people, reserved for Europeans. This compartment, situated immediately behind the driver, had a wooden bench for four facing forwards and another for four people, sitting facing the back of the bus. Rene took one of the seats facing forward.

The rest of the bus behind this compartment had only two long benches running along the two sides. In the middle was an open space where some of the locals, who had not come early enough to find seats on the side benches, either sat on their parcels or bags, so filling a good part of the available space. Some others were just sitting cross-legged on the floor. Rene was one of only two Europeans in the front compartment, but the space reserved for other passengers was solidly packed. None of them would have thought of occupying the empty seats in the compartment reserved for Europeans. Apart from the windscreen, there were no windows at all on the sides or back of the bus. As soon as the bus left Lahore Rene found himself on a dusty country road and he could see that the bus left behind in its tracks a volume of dust, preventing him seeing the road immediately behind.

In Sialkot, Mr. Khwafa was expecting him and took, him on a visit of his factory. This was extremely interesting. He showed Rene the section where cricket bats and balls were made, then the section where footballs were sewn together and finally the section where tennis rackets were made. He gave Rene a tennis racket as a memento of his visit.

After an excellent lunch Rene returned that same evening to Lahore. The next day he received a telephone call from Delhi. The Indian businessman, Mr. Kohli had kept his word and as soon as he had got back to Delhi had registered a travel agency. He now insisted that Rene should come for one week at his expense and for a reasonably high fee, to select staff, organise the premises and discuss further cooperation with Rene's London office. As this was going to be his last week in the east before returning to England and because he had more business to attend to in Karachi before returning, Rene tried to find excuses not to accept the arrangement. Mr. Kohli insisted that if necessary Rene should come for a shorter stay. At last Rene promised he would go that same day to the Indian Consulate in Lahore to obtain a visa.

Rene called at the consulate that same morning and was told it would take fifteen days to obtain the visa as his application would have to be referred to Delhi. He rang Kohli, told him the situation and informed him that he would have to be back in England before that. "Never mind," he said. "I have influential friends here in government circles and I shall make sure that you get a visa immediately." The same afternoon the Indian Consulate rang Rene to say the visa had been granted by Delhi and would he come to the Consulate to have his passport stamped accordingly. That same evening Kohli rang him again from Delhi and told him he had booked a seat on Pakistan Airlines for him for the next morning. The ticket had been pre-paid and he only had to collect the ticket on departure at the airport. Rene had no more excuses not to go and he packed his case.

As this was going to be his last evening in Lahore, Mr Lorang decided to take him out for the evening with many of his friends. They visited several establishments and around 3 a.m. they landed in the best known night club in the town. They had a large table to themselves. Half an hour after they got there, Rene saw an American pilot by the name of Brown come in. He had met him on several occasions in Karachi and knew he was working for Pakistan Airlines, then known as Pak Air. He saw Rene, came to greet him and asked to be introduced to his friends. Without waiting for an answer he said, "I hope you don't mind me sitting with you boys, but I am here all on my own and that is no fun in this damned place." They accepted his company; they had no option to do otherwise, and he was rather entertaining.

Around five o'clock Captain Brown left them to go back to the hotel. As Rene had to report at 7 a.m. at the airport for his flight to Delhi, he and his friends agreed it was not worth going to bed and they went on drinking and talking until it was time for Rene to collect his luggage at the Lorang villa and drive from there straight to the airport. When they arrived they we went to the buffet for breakfast and who should they see there drinking one black coffee after another? None other than Captain Brown. It was with worried surprise that Rene heard that Captain Brown was going to pilot the aircraft taking him to Delhi.

A few minutes after take off, the first officer, whose acquaintance Rene had made at the buffet, came to tell him that Captain Brown was asking Rene to join him in the cockpit. There, he offered Rene the first officer's seat alongside himself. He told Rene he looked less tired than him, gave him the compass bearing and asked him to awake him if there was any problem. Meanwhile, 'George', the automatic pilot, would do the work, whilst he had a sleep in the command seat and the first officer was resting in the cabin.

They had been flying uneventfully for quite a while, when suddenly Rene saw in the distance, on the port side, what appeared to be a blanket of fog which seemed to be coming very quickly in their direction. He awoke Brown and pointing at the bank of dense cloud said, "What is this? Fog?" One look at it and Brown replied, "No, monsoon rain, and we'd better try to get away from it!"

Before he had time to pull the throttle the rain hit them. They were just on the edge of the cloud, but as the first burst of rain struck the wing,the aircraft shuddered to port. By then Brown had switched on the windscreen wipers on his side. Although the windscreen wipers were working at full speed, he couldn't see a thing. Rene, on the starboard side, still had a clear window except for a trickle coming over the edge, in the middle.

Brown pushed the throttles forward doubling the thrust of the engines. At the same time he made a movement to starboard taking the whole aircraft out of the cloud. Soon the rain cleared away and he switched off the screen wipers as they got away from the curtain of rain which prevented them from seeing anything on the port side. Now they could see a near vertical line of cloud extending down to the ground. When they were well clear of it, they again had blue sky and sunshine above them. Down below, on the starboard side, as far as they could see, the scenery was amazing. They could see rivers that had overflowed their banks flooding the whole countryside. Here and there a village was seen to be under water, the whiteness of the walls and the red or black of tiles on the rooves contrasting strangely with the brown mass of water surrounding them. From the height at which they were flying they could not see any sign of living creatures in all this desolation.

New Delhi, India, July 1949

Another half hour and they landed at Delhi airport. Kohli was waiting for Rene at the gate and drove him to the Imperial Hotel. On the short journey from the airport to the hotel, Rene had been surprised to see steam rising from the road and the neighbouring countryside. The heat of the sun was evaporating the moisture left on the ground by an early morning shower.

The rest of the day was sunny, but an unpleasant heat compelled him, after lunch, to take the siesta to which he had become accustomed in Lahore. In the late afternoon, he had his first business meeting with Kohli and his co-directors. They showed him the documents defining the formation of the company and describing its future activities. They had options on various sites for the premises and they all went together to have a look at them.

After a late evening session, Rene went back to the Imperial Hotel. The temperature during the day had been pretty high. The evening, although still warm, was much more pleasant and he spent some time on the terrace studying the documents given to him that afternoon. After a good night's sleep, he awoke in the morning as the sun was shining into his room. When he looked through the window he could not believe his eyes. The gardens under his window were completely flooded. He had the impression of being in Venice, with the water touching the walls below his window. He must have slept so soundly that he never heard the downpour of monsoon rain.

After breakfast a car came to fetch him at the main entrance. The car was in water up to its axles. To get in without getting wet he had to walk over beer crates turned upside down and forming a narrow bridge. Two hours later the heat of the sun had evaporated all the water, but it would fall down again a few hours later.

His morning was spent interviewing potential managers and staff and during the afternoon he drew up a list of all the information and accounts documents needed to run a travel agency properly. The next day was a Sunday and Kohli and his friends had arranged to take him on an excursion to the Taj Mahal. Unfortunately for Rene, on the Saturday night, as he was having supper at the hotel, he got a telephone call from London urging him to come back to his office there on a most important matter. He promised to return to Karachi and from there to take the first available plane to London. He cancelled all arrangements for the excursion to the Taj Mahal, gave his final advice in writing to Kohli and left next morning on his journey by air to Karachi.

There he found out that a, Convair aircraft of the Pakistani airline, Pak Air, was being flown to Amsterdam for a major modification. This was the only flight available that day, so he had no other alternative than to book a seat on it. The journey was uneventful until Athens. A few minutes after take off, Rene was looking from his window seat at the undercarriage slowly retracting under the wing. Suddenly, as it had gone half way through its elevation, the undercarriage fell back. He noticed several attempts to lift it, but each time it fell back.

At this point a buzzer summonsed the young Pakistani steward to the cockpit. A few minutes later he came back very excited and before the captain had had time to switch on the "Fasten Your Seat Belt" sign, the steward ran through the cabin shouting, "Fasten your belts, fasten your belts." Although he was coloured, Rene could see some pallor in his complexion. He went to his jump seat and strapped himself in. For two frantic hours they started to circle above Athens without getting one word of reassurance from the cockpit.

At the end of the two hours, the Flight Engineer came to where Rene was seated to have a look at the position of the undercarriage. He seemed satisfied that it was properly locked and told passengers that now that fuel had been used up, they would make an emergency landing. As they circled once more Rene could see fire engines and ambulances taking up positions along the runway. What an encouraging sight! Once more the plane circled over the sea, came down, practically to sea level and made a direct approach onto the runway from the south, coming in over the sea and heading in the direction of the mountains to the north of the airfield.

It touched down at the end of the runway, hurtled along it faster than usual, until the captain lowered the tail block onto the runway, instead of the nose wheel, to slow the aircraft. Only a few yards away from the end of the runway, the captain managed to reverse the pitch of his propellers and stop the plane right at the runway's end, facing the mountain. He taxied back a little way and stopped until a tractor took the aircraft in tow and brought it back to the apron.

Passengers were taken to a lounge in the airport building, where Rene met the captain. He told him that the cause of all the trouble was that a pipe carrying hydraulic fluid to various parts of the plane had burst somewhere along its length and a lot of the fluid had been lost. On account of this he could not retract his undercarriage, could not get his flaps down and he also knew that once on the ground, his brakes would not work. Whilst they were talking, the flight engineer came to show them the damaged pipe. It was only three feet long and one and a half inches in diameter. There were several layers of rubber in between metal gauze, but probably due to excessive heat, under tropical conditions, it had a split of about ten inches in length. This pipe, although tested at the factory to withstand a pressure of 6,000 Ibs, is normally only exposed to a maximum pressure of 3,000 lbs, in use in the aircraft. Luckily for the Pak Air pilot that a Scandinavian Airways System Convair had a spare pipe on board and its pilot was prepared lend it to him. This minimised the delay.

The captain of the Pak Air flight also explained to Rene why he landed on the tail block instead of the nose wheel. He knew he had no wheel brakes and that his only way of achieving full braking would be to reverse his propeller pitch, but there is a built in safety system which only allows the propellers to be reverse pitched when the speed of the aircraft is reduced. The only way of reducing his speed had been to trail the tail end of the aircraft on the ground This, at the time. had worried Rene a bit, because this was a Convair Mark 2, which like some later aircraft, had a staircase opening under the tail end used as a passenger entrance and exit. He feared this might prevent its use as an emergency exit.

Luckily the tail end was undamaged by the unusual impact. They left Athens two hours later and by then the captain had decided that he was not going to do any night flying and would spend the night in Rome. So passengers were taken, at the expense of the airline, to Hotel Opurinale for the night. As the crew were still out of permitted flying hours the next morning, it allowed passengers some more time in Rome and they only left in the early afternoon for Amsterdam.

It was only on arrival in Amsterdam that Rene found out that the aircraft had been flown there because there was suspected metal fatigue to the wings. On hearing this he was shocked that the airline dared load the aircraft with passengers.

Happily, the present Pakistan International Airlines is a reputable airline. Pak-Air which Rene flew on was then competing with another independent airline called Orient. Pak-Air was under the directorship of a brother-in-law of one of the ministers in the 1948-1949 government. On three occasions the airline had had a major crash. Following the first two, its aircraft were grounded for a while, but due to the influence of the minister, the airline was allowed to fly again and the inquiry findings shelved. On the third occasion a general and another high ranking individual were killed. There was such an outcry from the press and public opinion was inflamed to such extent, that this time the airline got grounded indefinitely and expelled from IATA, the International Air Transport Association. It was after these events that the Pakistan Government took over Orient Airline and formed a new national company under the name of Pakistan International Airline.

The only business Rene ever got from the newly opened Delhi Travel Agency was a party of ten wealthy coffee planters from Bangalore for whom he had to arrange a forty day trip around Europe. Their air tickets had been arranged in Delhi, but all ground travel arrangements and hotels had to be provided by Rene's firm. He had submitted an itinerary starting in Rome and finishing in London. This and his quotation for the tour were accepted without delay. The Delhi agency was less prompt when it to came to paying. Rene had to wait until the last minute before being paid and then only because he had sent messages that he would cancel the whole trip if he was not paid before the arrival of the party in Rome. When, at last, the cheque arrived and was cleared, the person who Rene had earmarked to take the party around was no longer available and he decided to be the tour leader himself.

When he met the party in Rome, he found that eight of the men were related and two of them had their wives with them. The first thing they told him when he met them was that in their own country they never handled money. Wherever they went they normally signed vouchers or IOUs which were then settled by their accountants. They asked if it would be in order for them to hand over all their travellers' cheques to Rene and they wanted him to arrange to give them daily the money they needed in the currency of the country they were visiting.

Each of them gave him eight hundred pounds worth of travellers' cheques. Six hundred were made out for what was then known as soft currency countries, France, Italy, Holland and England and two hundred for the hard currency countries, Switzerland and Belgium. Having worked out proportionately the number of days they were staying in each country, he found that they had as much as forty pounds per day available in the soft currency countries, but only ten pounds in the hard currency countries. This made them most unhappy because it was in those very two countries that the temptation to buy was the greatest.

In Lucerne for instance, they bought as many watches as their currency would allow. Contrary to what Rene thought, they were not for resale, but simply to give to their relatives and friends as a souvenir of their trip to Europe.

Generally speaking they were an extremely nice lot of people and Rene got on very well with them, but one incident in the early days of the trip broke the unity of the party. As they reached Paris, they discussed plans for the evening. Rene booked them good seats for the Casino de Paris and after that, it was decided to visit one or two night clubs. He warned them that in these clubs hostesses would rid them of their money in no time. He suggested that they should all pretend that they were not carrying any money and that each time a hostess asked them if they wanted another drink, they should refer them to him. In fact they decided not to carry any money and left it in Rene's care.

As soon as they got to the night club, they were given a large table. They had taken the ladies of their party back to the hotel after the show at the Casino de Paris. It was therefore, an all male party. Soon eight young ladies came to sit at their table. Rene ordered three bottles of champagne. As their job demands, the eight ladies drank very fast whilst the Indians, who were not accustomed to that drink, drank theirs very slowly, except for the only bachelor in the party called Sidanna who tried to compete with the girls.

Unfortunately the drink soon had a bad influence on him. Whilst Rene was trying to stop the girls from ordering more bottles of champagne, Sidanna gave in to the girl sitting with him, forgot the agreement and allowed the girl to order another bottle. Before it was opened, Rene warned the waiter that he was not going to pay for it. When Sidanna heard this, he became violent and told Rene he had no right to withhold money belonging to him.

Using the other members of the party as witnesses, Rene decided to hand over to him the whole amount he had been entrusted with on his behalf and got him to sign a receipt for it. When the majority of the party decided it was time to move to another place, Sidanna, still under the spell of the girl, decided he was not going with them. The girl asked Rene the name of the hotel he had to be returned to, as at that time, he was already showing signs of being incapable of giving any clear information.

They left and did not see Sidanna until next morning at breakfast. He was the last one to come down to the dining room and it was apparent that he was suffering from a terrible hangover. He hardly spoke to anyone. After breakfast Rene rushed out to the bank to get the amount of money needed for the day for each member of the party. As he was passing the head porter's desk, Rene was presented with a bill signed by Sidanna for the cost of a taxi and other expenses paid for by the night porter when Sidanna had been brought back to the hotel completely drunk. The bill represented half of the day's allocation. Rene promised to repay the Head Porter as soon as he had been to the bank, which he soon did.

A little later, in accordance with the daily routine, the members of the party came to sit around Rene in the lounge whilst he counted out and distributed their money. When Sidanna's turn came, Rene gave him his daily allowance minus the amount of the bill just paid to the porter. At this he got into a violent temper, accusing Rene of having conspired with everybody under the sun to rid him of his money. To this Rene replied, "Look here Mr Sidanna, the duties of a tour manager do not include the organising of your finances or to be responsible for you in the evening. As from today I shall limit my activities purely to those I am paid for. Here are all your travellers' cheques, spend the whole of your allowance in one day if you like, but don't come to ask for my help once you are broke. Further, after what you have said, from now on my duties will finish after dinner. You people can go where you want and I shall go on my own."

The rest of the party who had been witness to the whole scene, waited until Sidanna left, after having taken possession of the travellers' cheques Rene had returned to him. He was about to start to return the rest of the travellers' cheques to the others, when one of them acting as a spokesman for the group, firstly apologized for Sidanna's, rudeness. Next he told Rene that the rest of the party had full confidence in him and wanted him to carry on as their banker, evening entertainment advisor and even offered to pay him for his off duty time activities. In addition to that, he informed Rene that they had unanimously decided to send Sidanna to Coventry. He could be with them during the day time programme, but they had clearly told him that they no longer wanted him with them in the evening.

Night after night Sidanna instructed the hotel porter, in whichever city the party were staying, to order a taxi to take him to a nightclub. Night after night he was taken back drunk to the hotel. After the earlier experience Rene warned the porters that he would not be responsible for any debt Sidanna might incur. By the time they reached London, Sidanna owed money to all the other members of the group.

Rene was very surprised, a year later, to receive a large invitation card to attend Sidanna's wedding in Bangalore. Apart from the distance and the cost of the fare, one reason for not accepting the invitation was that Rene objected to a small note printed at the bottom left hand corner of the card. It simply read: "Guests are requested to bring their own ration of rice with them." That was really too much for Rene to accept!!

Of his eight flights to the east, Rene had mixed feelings, some good and some bad. Apart from his three month stay in Pakistan and India, on seven occasions they had been fast return trips leaving London on the Friday and back in London on the Tuesday. His neighbours could not believe their ears when he told them that he had been to Pakistan for the weekend.

Apart from his trip to Lahore and Delhi most of the time he stayed at Karachi's Beach Luxury Hotel and life there was quite pleasant. He had been given a room at the back of the hotel. His window overlooked the dance terrace, the artificial garden and at the end of it, the canal leading to the harbour. Below in the garden made up of row after row of flowerpots containing exotic plants and flowers and in which, every morning, just as the sun was coming up at the horizon, Rene could see the gardeners watering the flowers.

He was usually served in bed with a pot of tea and two biscuits. One biscuit was for him, the other for a regular visitor, a sparrow, which came onto the window sill, every morning, to collect the crumbs of the other biscuit. If, on occasions, after a late night, he did not get up straightaway after his tea had been brought into the room, the sparrow would sit on the window sill, chirping as hard as he could to tell him,

"Come on get up and get me that biscuit." Sparrows in that part of the world are quite cheeky.

When he went for his breakfast, either on the terrace or in the dining room, there would always be one or two sparrows perched on the seat opposite him and watching his every movement. If any of his food accidentally fell on the floor, they would swoop for it. If, after leaving the table he had left any food they would get on to the table and clear it, never would any of the waiters chase them away.

The shyer birds were watching from a recess in the ceiling of the dining room concealing the tubular lighting and from there would watch guest's every movement. Generally speaking these birds were reasonably quiet, except for some who found it necessary to accompany the four piece band playing at every meal. Day after day the French violinist and leader of the band would announce "By special request of the British High Commissioner" and he would start playing "La Mer" or "La Vie en Rose." This was repeated evening after evening, to the extent that after his return from Karachi, Rene could not face hearing these two tunes any more.

Whilst at the Beach Luxury Hotel, Rene witnessed the end of Ramadan and the Moslem feast marking the end of the fasting period. At the hotel, the end of Ramadan was celebrated by a feast for government officials, including the President of Pakistan.From his room window Rene was able to watch all the goings on, on the terrace below. All the officials gathered on the terrace a few minutes before dusk. As soon as the sun disappeared below the western horizon, the festivities started with a display by a military band. The musicians wore light khaki uniforms and their head dresses were turbans. They marched in formation in a manner probably taught them by the British army. After the display, all the guests rushed to a lavishly provided buffet and they made up in one evening for all the fasting during Ramadan.

Up to that time Rene had always had a room to himself, although it was a twin bedded room. One evening as he was coming back from his agent's office, he was stopped by the manager, who very delicately explained to him that in consideration of his lengthy stay, he had always been left alone in his room. Now, he said, they had reached the stage where, in view of the shortage of hotel rooms in Karachi, they had to place someone else in his room. Rene told him he would have no objection to sharing his room with one of the Pan American air hostesses who were stopping regularly at the Beach Luxury. The manager had a good laugh, but instead of an air hostess, he installed an engineer from GEC in the room. He was a very nice man and they soon became good friends.

The only rivalry they suffered was over the use of the bathroom. As Rene always awoke at 6 a.m. he usually won the race. The bathroom was so stupidly designed that the one who was second to use it, had to splash over the wet floor left by the previous user. The bedroom was a long and narrow room. As you entered from the corridor, the bathroom door was on the right hand side. Beyond it were the two beds, one behind the other. The width of the bathroom corresponded more or less to the width of the beds. In that narrow space was crammed the shower, a wash basin and the WC. Rene had to plan carefully what to do first. There was no plinth or curtain near the shower and the water outlet was a hole in the tiles behind the toilet. If he took his shower first, then he ran the risk of leaving a wet toilet seat and a wet floor for his room mate. In later years he saw many similarly designed showers in countries behind the Iron Curtain, but none as primitive as this one.

On his final trip to Karachi, he again only stayed twelve hours there. He had informed Aly of the date of his arrival and his faithful taxi driver was waiting for him at the airport. After a rather busy day and a late afternoon rest, Aly rushed him back to the airport. The speed at which he went reminded Rene of the occasion on his second trip to Karachi, when he was having a drink in the bar of the Grand Hotel. Suddenly a message was brought to him from the pilot flying the charter flight back to London, informing him that he had had to bring forward the takeoff time for the return trip.

A BOAC double decker bus was waiting outside to take Rene back to the airport. The driver had been instructed to take Rene back as fast as possible. He was the only passenger on board and sat in the seat behind the driver. In the headlight's beams he saw the countryside disappear at speed on both sides of the bus. Suddenly the bus driver put his brakes on sharply and stopped within yards of a camel cart travelling towards them in the middle of the road, the driver fast asleep. His driver had to get out of the coach and push the frightened camel onto the side of the road.

Another two miles further and a similar incident occurred. This time the driver decided to teach the camel cart owner a lesson. Again, he got out of his seat, conducted the camel past his coach and then made it turn around, so that when the cart driver awoke, he would find himself travelling back to where he came from. The driver had a good laugh whilst explaining to Rene what he had done.

Although Aly drove fast, he very cleverly managed to avoid the camel carts. When Rene got to the airport the captain was waiting for him. As usual Rene had paid Aly in advance. Before taking leave of him, Rene told him he was not quite sure when he would come back, but would let him know through his agent. On the aircraft he suddenly noticed that he had lost his wallet containing quite a bit of money, mainly in pound notes and Belgian francs. It had fallen out of the back pocket of his trousers.

A week later he got a phone call at his office in London from a gentleman who told him that he was an importer of exotic fruit who had just returned from Karachi. "When there," he said, "I always have Aly as my driver. Aly found your wallet behind the back seat of his car and by the Belgian francs in it, he knew it must be yours. So he has asked me to find you and return it to you. Sabena gave me your telephone number." When the wallet was returned to him there was not one penny missing. This shows how remarkably honest people can be, even in countries with extreme poverty. This was in fact Rene's last trip to the far east and he never got another chance to go further than Israel after that.

Hastings, England, 1950

In 1950 he attended the conference of British Travel Agents held in Hastings. Between the end of the Hastings conference and the beginning of an international conference in Athens, he had five days available. It gave him the idea of contacting the Yugoslavian airline to see if he could get a concessionary ticket to visit Belgrade. Just as he was busy talking to the representative of the Yugoslavian airline on the telephone, the representative of EL AL, the Israeli airline, suddenly arrived to see him. Rene indicated a chair to him and invited him to sit down whilst he was finishing his phone conversation. The EL AL representative overheard that the Yugoslavians could not give Rene an immediate answer and would have to submit his request to their head office in Belgrade.

As Rene put the receiver down the EL AL representative said "Why bother to go to Belgrade if there is so much fuss about it. Whilst you were talking I have consulted my timetable and I propose this to you. The Hastings conference, which I shall attend, finishes at lunch time. It will give me time after lunch to drive you to London Airport, to catch our late afternoon flight for Tel Aviv. There you will be our guest for four days and on the fifth day, we will fly you to Athens in time for the opening session of the International Conference." Rene accepted this kind offer and immediately rang the Yugoslavians to cancel his request, as he had had a better offer.

Tel Aviv 1950

As planned he attended the Institute of Travel Agents Conference in Hastings and then he was taken, accompanied by the EL AL representative, to London Airport for their flight to Tel Aviv. Service on the EL AL plane was extremely good. On arrival in Tel Aviv a very pretty girl was waiting on the tarmac, wishing them welcome to Israel and telling them the details of the formalities they would have to go through before being able to leave the airport.

Amongst other things, he had to fill in the same type of cumbersome, four page declaration, as he had previously had to fill in in Karachi. He also had to make a strict declaration of all monies imported.

He was taken by an EL AL representative to the hotel reserved for him. On the way to the city centre, they passed a shanty down very similar to the one he had seen on the outskirts of Karachi, with the difference that here, it was mostly uniform tents. It was explained to him that these were Jewish refugees from the Yemen. This reminded him of a story told to him by a Sabena steward, two years before. When the Arabs were starting to persecute the Yemenite Jews, a Sabena plane was chartered to ferry as many as possible to Israel. The company had been instructed to remove all the seats in order to allow as many refugees and belongings as weight permitted, to crouch on the floor of the plane. When the plane landed, all the Jews fell on their knees and prayed.

One of them who spoke English explained. "They are thanking God for having kept his promise, because in our bible it says that God will send big birds to fly us to the Holy Land."

The planes which they had never seen before, were to them, the big birds. The steward could not stand the smell in the cabin, so he sought refuge in the cockpit, but from time to time he opened the door of the cockpit to see if everybody was alright. It is lucky that he did so. As he was having another look he noticed that a space had been left open in the centre of the plane and some men had formed a circle around that empty space. On closer examination he found that pieces of wood and paper had been placed in the centre of the space and that one man was just about to light the paper when the steward intervened to stop him. From questioning it was found that they were about to light a camp fire to cook their meal and they were very surprised, when through their interpreter, they were told they had endangered the safety of the plane.

Rene's stay in Israel was going to last five days. The morning after his arrival was a Saturday, Sabbath day. All the shops were closed, no public transport except for 'Cheroots', big American limousines, eight seater taxis, driven by Arabs and on which you just paid for your seat and shared the vehicle with strangers going in the same direction. He enquired at the hotel desk on how to spend his day. It was suggested that he should take a boat trip on the River Yarcon. These boats were also operated by Arabs. The river flows through very picturesque countryside, with large trees on both sides spreading their heavily foliaged branches over the river banks and forming a shield against the blazing sun. From time to time they passed under fishermen's nets. These were large square nets held up by ropes at the four corners. Each rope went through a pulley attached to a tree. This seemed a very primitive way of fishing, but was apparently very effective. It needed four men to pull the ropes, plus one man in a rowing boat to collect the fish once the net was lifted out of the water by the four men.

After an hour's journey, the boat stopped at the foot of an impressive waterfall and Rene followed the other passengers along stone steps leading to the upper reaches of a pier. Close by was another pier, along which several boats were moored. Rene was ushered to one of these boats and sat down, whilst other passengers were still descending the steps to get aboard. Almost at the same moment, a man accompanied by his wife, and a pretty young lady came to sit opposite him. With them were two young children. Rene noticed that the man was looking at him rather intensely. Suddenly he said, "Excuse me, do you live in Israel?"

"No, I am on a five day visit here."

"I thought so. Where do you come from?"

"I come from England."

"Are you British?"

"No, I am Belgian, but I have lived in England since the war."

"How strange, I used to live in Belgium before the war and your face is very familiar," the man said.

"Where did you live?" Rene asked.

"In Antwerp, I was in the diamond business."

"Small world," replied Rene. "I was born in Antwerp and lived there until 1934. My father was one of the directors of the Diamond Club."

"Yes, what was his name?"

"Franz Falkenau."

"Oh, I knew him very well, he was a very important man. Where does he live now?"

"Unfortunately he died in Auschwitz."

A sad look came over the face of the man. "I have also lost several relatives in the same circumstances. I am very sorry to hear about your father, he was such a nice man."

Rene smiled, appreciating the man's comments about his father, but for the rest of that day images and thoughts flooded his mind. The man and his family had found safety in Israel, but why had his own father resisted his efforts to get him, his mother and sister to safety? Did he really believe that his service in the Austrian army would render him safe from the anti-Jewish laws, which he knew had already made the lives of his brother Paul and sister Melanie's families in Prague so miserable? After all, Franz's own part in the Czech national liberation struggle would hardly have left an army record which marked him out as a loyal Austrian citizen. Besides which, as Irma had discovered during her stay in Vienna during World War 1, Germans thought no better of their Austrian allies, than they did of those they fought against. Did he imagine that the Vichy government would indefinitely stand as a bulwark against German racial laws? There had already been sufficient signs of its complicity in the drafting of anti-Jewish regulations. Was it simply fatigue or false courage that led his father to refuse offers of sanctuary?

As Rene was driven back to his hotel in Tel Aviv it was the faces of the members of his family who had been lost which suddenly came into view through the window of his taxi. Was that his cousin Ellen Jellinek and her husband Pavel? Had they they magically and miraculously survived and found their way here to Israel?

The mind can play funny tricks on you when in a heightened state of emotion. A second glance dispelled that illusion. More faces of family members and snatches of conversation filled his head. Old uncle Auguste Roost, the wise old Antwerp lawyer, who had followed his parents and sister to Auschwitz and Aunt Mela, sent from the comfort of her home in Prague to the ghetto in Lodz. Then there was his grandfather's sister, great aunt Sal Adler, with whom he had spent time in London as a child in 1919. She had been the first of the family to be sent from Mechlen to Auschwitz in 1942. So many of the family lost to irrational hatred. A sense of sadness seemed to crush his chest, almost stifling his breathing.

As he fought against it, he began to think about the good fortune he now enjoyed. Not just the many near brushes with death he had encountered in those terrible years of war and his own survival, but also the luck of finding Doris and the way her family had treated him as a truly adopted son. He had become much more than a son in law to her parents and brother in law to her sister. They understood what he had gone through and his emotional needs and they satisfied them in a quiet and entirely undemonstrative way. Rene would always refer to Doris's father as if he were his own – "How is father? Is father coming with us?"

And now there were his two children and a third on the way. In the three years since his business had been established with a little help from his Czech cousin, George Falkenau, now settled in England with Marjorie, his English bride, Travel Aids had prospered and become one of London's leading retail travel agencies. In his mother's three surviving sisters, Emmy, Helene, and Renee, he still retained some links with his past in Belgium and Renee in particular, made it her responsibility to attempt to partially fill the void left by his mother's death.

As the sun began to set on the terrace of his hotel, he reflected that despite all of the suffering he had seen and the pain he had endured as the news of the loss of one family member had followed another, he still had much to be grateful for.

For other members of his family, it was Rene Paul's indomitable spirit, his unerring cheerfulness and unflappability in the face of adversity which singled him out. He bore what he had suffered during those recent years with stoicism and without rancour. And even today that is the hallmark of a real man.